Writing
as Thinking

A GUIDED PROCESS APPROACH

MARCELLA FRANK

American Language Institute, New York University

PRENTICE HALL REGENTS, *Englewood Cliffs, New Jersey 07632*

Library of Congress Cataloging-in-Publication Data

Frank, Marcella.
    Writing as thinking : a guided process approach/Marcella Frank.
       p.   cm.
    ISBN 0-13-969619-9
    1. English language—Textbooks for foreign speakers.   2. English
   language—Rhetoric.   I. Title.
PE1128.F674   1989
428.2'4—dc20   89-16228
                                                    CIP

Cover design: Lundgren Graphics
Manufacturing buyer: Mike Woerner

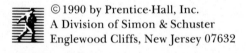 © 1990 by Prentice-Hall, Inc.
A Division of Simon & Schuster
Englewood Cliffs, New Jersey 07632

Printed in the United States of America
10 9 8 7 6 5 4 3 2

ISBN 0-13-969619-9

Prentice-Hall International (UK) Limited, *London*
Prentice-Hall of Australia Pty. Limited, *Sydney*
Prentice-Hall Canada Inc., *Toronto*
Prentice-Hall Hispanoamericana, S.A., *Mexico*
Prentice-Hall of India Private Limited, *New Delhi*
Prentice-Hall of Japan, Inc., *Tokyo*
Simon & Schuster Asia Pte. Ltd., *Singapore*
Editora Prentice-Hall do Brasil, Ltda. *Rio de Janeiro*

Contents

3 Education   51

4 The Family   95

7 Newspapers   194

8 Capital Punishment   232

9 **The Research Paper**   **275**

Appendix A: Grammar and Usage   **307**

Appendix B: Punctuation and Spelling Rules   **361**

Appendix C: Checklists for Composition   **373**

Preface

Writing as Thinking: A Guided Process Approach is a writing workbook for advanced ESL/EFL students in freshman English writing classes. It may also be
used, with some modification, in pre-freshman English classes or in remedial
classes for native speakers.

This text is on a higher level than my earlier *Writing from Experience*. The
composition subjects require more thought on the part of the students and
more attention to the composing process, especially the revision stage. Also,
in this text, reading selections related to the subject of the composition play
an important role in helping to enhance the students' thinking and writing
skills as well as to encourage good reading habits.

Special Features

1. The text has a unity of content and structure that is unique. Most of
the units are on one general subject, and all the discussion, writing, and reading deal with that subject. This kind of intensive focus enables students to
consider the subject in some breadth and depth.

2. The text uses a *guided process approach* for the compositions. It provides for the three stages of writing that are associated with a process approach—prewriting, writing, and revision. For each unit, the text gives procedures for the prewriting stage as well as suggestions for the next two stages.

3. The text places special emphasis on critical thinking. At every step along the way, students are given the opportunity to explore and expand their thinking on a particular subject and to present their thoughts in compositions that are clear, logical, and convincing.

The experience of critical thinking begins with a brainstorming procedure that permits students to look at the subject of a composition from a broad point of view and continues with a gradual focusing on a narrower aspect of the subject that provides the unity required for a carefully thought out composition.

In the process of clarifying their own thinking, students are given practice in searching for higher levels of generalization under which they can put minor points. By putting seemingly isolated facts into larger patterns, students can develop greater maturity in thinking.

4. Discussion and readings on the subject of the composition are integrated within the writing process. While the preliminary discussion of the subject encourages students to consider the subject from the broadest perspective, the reading selections enable students to expand their thinking about and knowledge of the subject.

5. The extensive practice in summary writing trains students to read carefully for ideas, to observe the rhetorical techniques that professional writers use, and in general to improve their own writing.

6. An awareness of audience and purpose is built into the writing and reading activities. While the main composition of each unit has an informative purpose—the clear and logical presentation of opinion, exposition, and argument, of the kind expected in writing papers for college classes—many of the writing assignments in the Extra Discussion and Writing sections have a persuasive purpose that allows students to express their own feelings or reactions.

7. The workbook format of *Writing as Thinking* in the composition section allows for guidance in the rhetorical development of compositions without the need for long explanations. Rhetorical requirements are built into Chapters 2 through 8 and are most apparent in the guides provided for each composition.

The workbook format also allows for the inclusion of teacher-guided procedures for the preliminary discussion of each composition.

8. The subjects of the compositions in *Writing as Thinking* range across the curriculum, especially the liberal arts curriculum; they deal with social, political, and educational issues.

The practice work in *Writing as Thinking* begins with a unit on summary writing. This is done in preparation for the summary work included in each of the units that follow. The practice work ends with a research paper, which is the culmination of the work students have been doing up to this point in incorporating the information from their reading into their writing.

Format

Chapters 2 through 8 each consist of five sections. The contents in all these sections are related to the general subject of the composition.

> Composition (procedures for discussing, writing, and revising)
> Vocabulary and Usage
> Reading for Summary Writing
> Reading for Further Ideas
> Extra Discussion and Writing

Composition

This is the central part of each chapter. The composition has been placed first in the chapter because, after students have the opportunity to think about a subject through discussion and writing, the readings on the subject will be more meaningful to them as they revise their papers.

The compositions that are called for are typical of papers required in freshman writing classes. In addition, some of the compositions are to be written as answers to essay questions. Working with such questions gives students practice in finding the key expressions in the questions that indicate what is being asked.

The composition section consists of three stages: prewriting, writing, and revision.

Prewriting stage. This is a discussion stage that encourages students to consider a subject from a broad point of view. The text suggests procedures for the discussion in order for the teacher to elicit information about the subject from the students. These procedures may also be the basis for group discussions of the subject of the composition.

Writing stage. At this stage the text provides help in two ways:

1. It gives suggestions for narrowing down the thesis and finding classifications that help with the organization.
2. It provides a guide for outlining and organizing each composition. The repetition of this guide in each chapter reinforces an understanding of the rhetorical requirements for writing compositions.

Revision stage. In this stage, the text encourages students to incorporate ideas or support from the readings. Students are urged to check each of their succeeding drafts against the checklist in Appendix C for revising and editing compositions. This checklist requires that students first study the content and organization of their composition, then the paragraphing and sentences, and finally the grammar and usage. Students are also asked to make a final check from the Symbol Chart for Correction of Compositions, which gives more explanations about problems in grammar and usage.

For each composition, suggestions are made on how to use the Revision and Editing Checklist for peer evaluation.

Vocabulary and Usage

Words that ESL/EFL students might need in order to talk or write about the subject of a composition are listed and defined. Brief usage notes that can help students avoid mistakes are also given here. In addition, because even advanced students continue to have trouble with part of speech endings of words, word form exercises are included in this section.

Reading for Summary Writing

This kind of writing represents the closest connection between reading and writing. In each chapter, three selections are given for outlining and summarizing. Such practice gives students training in the kind of summarizing they need to do for academic purposes. It also helps them improve their own reading and writing skills.

Reading for Further Ideas

This section includes several additional reading selections that students can use for more information about the subject of the composition. In order for students to gain practice answering the kinds of questions used in essay exams, they are asked to write questions based on these selections and to give answers to their questions.

Many of the readings in these sections are from current periodicals or textbooks and are on the level college students are expected to handle. The selections have not been simplified, but some of them have been shortened.

The readings are intended to stimulate student thinking on the subject of the composition, to provide more vocabulary, and to make available authoritative support for the points students make in their compositions. The discussion questions on the readings encourage students to read critically—to distinguish fact from opinion, to be aware of unsound reasoning, to observe attitude and tone. The questions also ask students to examine the rhetorical techniques used by the authors. Questions leading to cross-cultural exchange are also included.

Extra Discussion and Writing

While there are still some writing assignments in this section that have an informative purpose, many require students to write for other purposes and audiences. The emphasis in this section is on persuasive or expressive writing. Students are asked to express honest feelings, often by writing journal entries and letters, and by giving their reactions to articles, speeches, and cartoons.

Procedures for the Teacher

Since the procedures followed by the teacher play an important role in the approach to writing used in *Writing as Thinking*, I am suggesting some procedures that I have found successful in guiding the stages of composition writing.

Procedures to Guide the Discussion of the Composition

Before the discussion of the composition, assign one or two of the readings in order to stimulate student thinking on the subject of the composition. A free-writing practice on the subject of the composition might also precede the discussion in order for students to get down their first thoughts on the subject.

For the discussion, student books should be closed. Put on the board the outline or the column headings suggested in the discussion section of the text. Then ask students to supply the information, and list these student ideas on the board in phrases in random order, regardless of whether they are specific or general points, or whether they cut across each other. For a composition of argument, try to place opposing points of view side by side in the columns. It is advisable to pursue one point in some depth before asking for another.

Write on the board separately whatever vocabulary a student is searching for (some of this vocabulary can also be found later in the vocabulary section of the text).

At the end of the class discussion, ask students to examine the random points listed on the board in order to organize the smaller points under the larger ones. Ask students if they can subsume all or most of the points under one larger heading that can serve as the controlling idea. This part of the discussion is very important, since it involves the kind of classifying that is characteristic of mature thought.

Procedures to Guide the Writing of the Composition

Draw attention to the instructions about writing the composition that are given in the text. After the composition has been assigned and before it is due, assign the readings in order to discuss them in class.

Procedures for the Evaluation of the Composition

Have students consult the Revision and Editing Checklist and the Symbol Chart for Correction of Compositions in Appendix C before they hand in what they consider a final draft for grading. Ask them to rewrite their papers as many times as necessary to produce papers that represent the best they can do. On the papers that are handed in, mark the mistakes with the correction symbols, write down your comments, and return the papers for correction or further revision.

Students who are having problems on the sentence level should be referred to my *Writer's Companion,* which explains in detail and in the same alphabetical order the usages included in the Symbol Chart for Correction.

For the final draft, or actually even for earlier drafts, you might have students bring to class enough copies of their papers for peer evaluation. Peer evaluation works best when students have the kind of special guidance contained in the Revision and Editing Checklist, especially the first part, which deals with the organization and development of ideas. Have the student evaluator make comments on the student paper. Encourage students to make comments about the good points of the paper before they mention the points that need improvement.

An alternative to peer evaluation is for the teacher to reproduce one student's paper for the entire class to evaluate according to the criteria in the Revision and Editing Checklist. For this purpose, it is best to avoid using a very poor or a very good paper. Choose one that has possibility for real improvement. However, it is useful sometimes to reproduce an excellent paper to give students an idea of what an A paper is like and to point out how it satisfies many of the criteria on the Revision and Editing Checklist.

More specific procedures for each chapter, as well as more details about the subject of the composition, will be found in the teacher's manual. In addition, the manual contains models of some of the summaries; these models are set up so that they can be reproduced and distributed to students for comparison with their own work.

A final note about classroom procedures: Because some of the information in the readings, especially the statistics, will need to be brought up to date, it is advisable for you to bring to class current articles related to the subject of the composition and to encourage interested students to share articles they have found with the class.

To the Student

This is a different kind of writing book from those you have used before. It is a workbook that has built into it a process for you to develop your thinking and writing skills, while at the same time improving your reading skills. It will also make you aware that there are many types of writing, depending on the purpose of the writer and the intended reader.

Four sections in the book provide practice in writing for different purposes.

Composition. The writing in this section has an informative purpose. You will be encouraged to express your ideas in a clear, logical, and convincing way. This is the kind of writing that is expected in your college classes.

Vocabulary and Usage. This section contains vocabulary and definitions that can help you as you write about the subject of the composition.

Reading for Summary Writing. The kind of writing in this section will help you understand the main ideas in your readings and express these ideas in your own words. It will develop your ability to pick up and remember the important points in the large amounts of reading you need to do for your college classes and will be useful preparation for the research paper.

Reading for Further Ideas. In this section you will be given the opportunity to ask and answer questions based on the reading selections.

The reading selections in both the Reading for Summary Writing and the Reading for Further Ideas sections require you to read actively rather than passively in order to do the required writing practice. This practice also helps establish good study habits that will be useful to you as you prepare for examinations. In addition, because these readings are on the same general subject of the composition, they make available more information and vocabulary that can be used for the composition in the first section.

Extra Discussion and Writing. In this section you will be writing to persuade others, as well as to express your thoughts freely. This is the kind of writing that you might be doing outside of class in your everyday life. It includes journal entries, letters, reactions to articles, speeches, cartoons.

The text places the greatest emphasis on the first two kinds of writing, the compositions and the summaries, since they are most important for your college career and for your future professional career. The process of writing that is set up in the composition section for the informative purpose should help you clarify and expand your own thinking. It gives you an opportunity to discover for yourself what you really think and to write down your thoughts in the most effective way.

Some of the compositions are to be written at home, some in class. For all these compositions, the text provides help through teacher-guided discussion of the general subject and then through suggestions on finding a thesis to narrow down the broad topic. For the composition written in class, you will be given an essay question and encouraged to find the key expressions that indicate what the question is really asking for. (This is the kind of writing that will help you when you take essay examinations.)

Here is some advice for writing the home compositions assigned in the composition section.

When you begin the composition, write the first draft in the way that is best for you—quickly from brief notes, letting the ideas flow freely, or more slowly from the suggested outline in the text. (Do not be too concerned about correct grammar and usage at this stage.) Then write stronger outlines in the form given in the composition section. Successive outlines are needed as you sharpen your ideas and attempt to present the thesis more clearly and strongly. Wait several days between drafts so that you can look at your composition with fresh eyes.

Do as much of the reading as possible before you write your first draft, but do not look at the readings while you are writing, in order to avoid being unduly influenced by them. You might want to reread some of the articles as you rewrite your paper. Use the readings to add authoritative support to the points you make, but do not overuse them. The ideas you express should be your own. Do not be afraid to draw on your own beliefs and experience for support. If you write honestly, you will have less trouble writing the paper. Also, you will produce a stronger composition that will be interesting to the reader. Always put yourself in the position of the reader who is trying to follow your ideas.

In the process of revision, you will have to make many decisions as you clarify your thoughts. You will need to determine what to omit, what to add, what to strengthen for a unified paper. It is this process that helps develop your critical thinking skills.

As you revise your composition, check first for the ideas and then for their organization and development. The Revision and Editing Checklist will be of help for this purpose. As a final check, look over your paper for possible errors in grammar and usage. Consult the Symbol Chart for Correction of Compositions for problems at this level.

At some stage in the drafting of your composition, the teacher may have you make multiple copies of your paper for comments from your classmates. Objective comments by other students as well as by the teacher will give you a better insight into what works well in your paper and what could be improved.

One final but very important piece of advice about writing in general: You might do what many professional writers do, and that is keep a journal in which you freely enter your thoughts, feelings, reactions. You might copy down, or cut and paste in your journal, anything that interests or excites you—articles, poems, cartoons, even advertisements—and you might make comments about them. In this way you will be building up a verbal stock that you can draw on in later writing. By keeping such a journal, you will also begin to understand more about yourself—your interests, your tastes, who you are.

Acknowledgments

I would like to give special thanks to Anne Riddick and Peggy Gordon for seeing the book through the various stages of production. Additional thanks are due to Arisa Yoshida, who wrote the student research paper. Finally, I wish to thank the many students at New York University, who, by using parts of the book in pre-publication form for many years, helped me sharpen the focus of the book.

CHAPTER 1

Summary Writing

A *summary* is a restatement, in shortened form and in your own words, of the main ideas contained in a reading selection. It is best to prepare the summary from an outline.

Outlining and summary writing will help you to read actively instead of passively. They will help you distinguish between generalizations and their supporting details. They are useful aids in preparing for tests, especially essay exams, because they make it easier for you to memorize main points in readings and to state them more easily.

Preparation for the Summary

Reading

Skim through the whole selection first to get the central idea. Go right to the end, scanning quickly, to get a sense of what the author intends.

Reread the selection. Study the beginning and the end carefully for clues to the central idea. Underline the important phrases in the main points that support the central idea. These are usually stated in the opening sentences of paragraphs, but they are sometimes embedded in the middle or end, or they may not be stated at all—just implied. Circle the signals that indicate the author is moving from one main point or subpoint to another. *Do not underline too much.*

Mark in some other way the statements that sum up the central idea of the reading selection, or that tell you the end of a main point has been reached, as well as any significant statements you might want to quote in your summary.

Outlining

Prepare an outline of the main points and their subpoints. Write the important phrases (those you underlined) in the margin of the book before you write the outline on a separate sheet of paper. In both cases, number the points and subpoints according to the conventional system of outlining, as illustrated below.

I. First main point (Use Roman numerals for main points.)
   A. First subpoint (Use capital letters for subpoints of main points.)
      1. Further subdivision (Use Arabic numerals for further subdivision.)
         a. Further subdivision (Use small letters for further subdivision.)
         b.
      2.
   B.
II.

Capitalize the first word of each of the main points and all further divisions. Do not use periods at the end of phrases. All the points in an outline may be written as full sentences or as phrases. The phrases should be long enough so that a reader can see clearly how they relate to the central idea of the reading selection.

You may copy phrases from the reading, but try to use your own words as much as possible. Omit description adjectives and most examples.

The length of the outline is determined by the required length of the summary. A more detailed outline makes it easier for you to write the summary. A shorter outline enables you to see more clearly what the main points and subpoints are.

Writing the Summary

In writing the summary, follow the same order as the reading. It's a good idea, however, to begin with a reference to one or more of the following: the author and his or her qualifications; the publication and the date; the central idea and its importance; the author's attitude and purpose in writing the selection. Be sure to use your outline as a guide; whatever points you have included in the outline should be accounted for in your summary. Keep a sense of proportion; write more about main points than about minor ones.

Be sure that the entire summary has a form of its own, with full sentences and with transitions (connections) between each point. (Writing transitional expressions in the margin of the outline makes it easier for you to incorporate them in the summary.) Usually you do not need to include examples given in the selection unless they are important to the point being made. The assigned length of a summary will determine how many examples or subpoints you include.

Avoid quoting too much; use your own words as much as possible. You may repeat a few words or short phrases from the reading selection, especially those you have marked as important. Use quotation marks around longer quoted sentences and phrases. Phrases should fit into the structure of the sentences which contain them.

Don't overload your sentences in order to pack in as much information as possible. Be sure you are clear in presenting opinions. Distinguish between the author's point of view and that of any other person to whom he or she refers. For the author's development of ideas, you might use words like *begins, continues, goes on to, concludes.* If you refer to the author's actual statements, you might use verbs like *says, states, discusses, mentions, believes, argues.* The verbs, however, should be in the same tense, either all present or all past. (The present tense is more usual.)

Do *not* introduce your ideas or your attitudes or interpretation, into a summary. Your ideas will be added later only if you are asked to comment on, or to react to, what the author has said.

Caution: Do not spend so much time writing the first part of the summary that you have little space left for the summary of the rest of the reading selection.

A Sample Outline and Summary

The following reading selection from *The Pocket History of the United States* shows how the selection may be marked in preparation for an outline and a summary. Phrases giving the main points and their subpoints have been underlined. Phrases that signal connections from one main point or subpoint to another have been circled. Sentences that indicate the end of one point have been put within parentheses.

The Colonial Heritage

Allan Nevins and Henry Steele Commager

I. Part of the heritage
A. common language

Part of the heritage that the colonies were to bequeath the young nation is evident at a glance. The fact of a common language, the English tongue, was of immeasurable value. It was one of the great binding elements which made a true nation possible. The long and steadily broadening experience with representative forms of government was another priceless part of the heritage. We may take

B. representative government

it rather for granted until we remember that the French and Spanish colonies had nothing to show in representative self-government; the British alone permitted their colonists to erect popular assemblies and to create governments in which both electors and representatives had real political responsibility. The result was that British colonists were politically minded and politically experienced. The respect paid to essential civil rights was

C. civil rights

another important element in the heritage, for the colonists had as firm a belief in freedom of speech, of the press, and of assembly as did Britons at home. These rights were not completely secure, but they were cherished. The general spirit of religious toleration in the

D. religious tolerance

colonies, and the recognition that different sects could and should get on with entire amity, must be included in the roster. Every faith was protected under the British flag; despite the traditional fear of Catholicism in England, Parliament was even charged by some colonials after 1763 with showing excessive favor to that religion.

E. racial tolerance

Equally valuable was the spirit of racial toleration, for people of different blood—English, Irish, German, Huguenot, Dutch,

Swedish—mingled and intermarried with little thought of any difference.

(And we should certainly mention) the strong spirit of individual enterprise which manifested itself in the colonies, an individualism always noteworthy in Britain herself, but which was now heightened under the pressure of life in a rich but wild and difficult land. The British never permitted such monopolies within the colonies as had crushed individual effort in the French and Spanish dominions. Enterprise irrepressibly responded to opportunity. (Taken together, these parts of the colonial heritage were a treasure worth far more than shiploads of gold or acres of diamonds.)

F. individual enterprise

Two basically American ideas had (also taken root) during the colonial period. (One) was the idea of democracy, in the sense that all men are entitled to a rough equality of opportunity. It was to gain opportunity for themselves and still more for their children that a host of settlers had come to the New World. They hoped to establish a society in which every man should not only have a chance, but a good chance; in which he might rise from the bottom to the very top of the ladder. This demand for equality of opportunity was to bring about increasing changes in the social structure of America, breaking down all sorts of special privileges. It was to effect marked changes in education and intellectual life, making America the "most common-schooled" nation in the world. It was to produce great political changes, giving the ordinary man a more direct control of government. (Altogether, it was to be a mighty engine for the betterment of the masses.)

II. Two basically american ideas
A. democracy (or equality of opportunity)

1. social changes
2. educational changes
3. political changes

(The other basic idea) was the sense that a special destiny awaited the American people and that they had before them a career such as no other nation was likely to achieve. This general

B. special destiny

wealth, the energy of the people, and the atmosphere of freedom
which enveloped both imparted to Americans a fresh and buoyant
optimism and an aggressive self-confidence. The idea of a peculiarly
fortunate destiny was to be one of the main forces in the swift
expansion of the American people across the continent. It was
sometimes to have <u>evil effects</u>; that is, it was to lead Americans to   *1. evil effects*
rely all too easily on Providence when they should have been taking
painful thought to meet their difficulties—it was to make them
complacent when they should have been self-critical. But, along with
the idea of democracy, it was on the whole to give American life a
<u>freshness, breadth, and cheerfulness,</u> that were matched nowhere   *2. good effects*
else. The new land was a <u>land of promise, of hope, of steadily</u>
<u>widening horizons.</u>

The Outline

From this marked reading selection, the following outline may be made.

The Colonial Heritage

I. Parts of the heritage
    A. A common language
    B. Representative government
    C. Respect for civil rights
    D. Religious toleration
    E. Racial toleration
    F. The spirit of individual enterprise
II. Two basically American ideas
    A. Idea of democracy—equal opportunity
        1. Social changes
        2. Educational changes
        3. Political changes
    B. Sense of special destiny
        1. Evil effects
        2. Good effects

The Summary

Now we are ready for the summary. The following summary has been reduced to half the original length. Parentheses have been placed around supporting details for main points, many of which can be omitted if a shorter summary is desired.

> The heritage that the colonies left to the new nation can be quickly seen. Very valuable was the fact of a common language, English (which acted as a unifying element). Another priceless part of the heritage was the experience with representative forms of government. (The British colonies, unlike the French and Spanish colonies, were permitted to have governments that gave political experience to both the representatives and the people who elected them.)
>
> Another important element in the heritage was the respect paid to civil rights. (The colonists believed strongly in freedom of speech, of the press, and of assembly.) In addition the colonists believed in religious toleration. (Every faith was protected in the British colonies.) Racial toleration also was part of the heritage. (People of all races mixed and intermarried.)
>
> We must also include in the heritage the spirit of individual enterprise which developed in the rich but wild land. (The monopolies that had discouraged individual effort in the French and Spanish colonies were not permitted in the British colonies, and so the British colonists could take great advantage of the opportunities that were open to them.)
>
> During the colonial period, two basic American ideas also began to develop. The first (or One) was the idea of democracy, which granted to everyone the same opportunity to get ahead. The demand for equality brought about many social, educational and political changes. (Or, more fully: The demand for equality brought about many social changes by breaking down special privileges. It also produced educational changes by offering the most education provided by any country in the world. In addition, it produced political changes by giving its citizens more responsibility in government.)
>
> The other (or The second) basic idea was the sense of special destiny. (The wealth of the country, the energy of the people, the atmosphere of freedom gave them a feeling of optimism and strong self-confidence.) This feeling of special destiny sometimes had bad effects. (There were times when the American people trusted in fate when they should have tried harder to face their difficulties.) On the whole, however, those two basic ideas gave the Americans a sense of freshness, cheerfulness and hope that could be found nowhere else.

Summary Practice

For the next three reading selections, you will be writing outlines and summaries. Keep the outline short so that the main points can be clearly seen. Depending on the length of the selection, you will be asked to write a summary of approximately 150, 200, 250, or 300 words. In doing these practice exercises, follow the guidelines below. They are a summary of the points made so far.

1. For the outline, use the alternate number-letter system for the main points and their subpoints. The underlined phrases in the opening sentences of paragraphs usually become the main points on the outline.

2. For both the summary and the outline, follow the same order as the reading selection. If you wish, you may begin the summary with a reference to the source of the selection (author, publication) and to its central idea.

3. Keep a sense of proportion. Write more about the points the author devotes more attention to.

4. Concentrate more on the main points than on examples or other supporting details.

5. Use proper transitions between the main points and the subpoints of your summary; your summary must have an organization of its own.

6. Use your own words as much as possible, except for key phrases. You may quote important phrases or sentences.

7. Be careful not to overload any sentence with so much information that the sentence is hard to read.

8. Be consistent in your use of verb tenses. Use all present tense (the author states, feels) or all past tense (the author stated, felt). The present tense is more common in a summary.

9. Do not include your own ideas or your own attitude or interpretation. The summary should be an objective restatement of what the author has said.

Reading 1

The Japanese Yen for Work

Bernard Krisher

This article was written when the author was Newsweek's *Tokyo bureau chief. The word* yen *in the heading is a play on words. The yen is the Japanese unit of currency, but it is used here in its other (informal) meaning of* strong desire. *Because the article was written in 1973, it is quite likely that the statistics given in the last paragraph are out of date and that the situation regarding employment in Japan may have changed. In 1981, William Ouichi discussed the Japanese labor-*

management harmony that is the subject of this article in his much publicized book
Theory Z: How American Business Can Meet the Japanese Challenge.

Length of summary: Approximately 150 words

Why do Japanese work very hard?

Japanese workers aren't motivated primarily by money or the prospect
of climbing to the top. Basically, they work for the team. Their attitude is a
throwback to feudal days when *daimyo* (feudal lords) protected and provided
for their followers and demanded loyalty and obedience in return. Today, the
daimyo are gone, replaced by corporations—but the tradition of obedience
remains. Company presidents often take a paternalistic interest in their employees. For example, Takeshi Hirano, president of one of Japan's leading
fishing and canning firms, attends ten or more employee weddings a month,
and members of his board go to "many, many more."

As a result, the Japanese worker usually feels a deep loyalty to his firm,
which almost always employs him until he retires or dies. Working for the
advancement of the company is elevated into a life goal for the worker. Japanese society encourages this by identifying a man not by his profession, but
by the company he works for. "If you ask a man what he does," says one
Japanese businessman, "he will say he is with Mitsubishi regardless of
whether he is a driver or vice president." Often a Japanese employee's life
revolves more around his company than his family. A 1971 government poll
revealed that almost one-third of Japanese employees felt that work was the
most meaningful part of their lives.

Company officials work hard at maintaining a team spirit among employees. In many firms, the work day starts with group exercise, the chanting
of a company song or a slogan-packed speech by the president. Sometimes
whole plants are shut so that workers and employers can go off together for
company-paid overnight trips. Along with teamwork comes harmony. Most
firms have management-labor councils that hold year-round discussions with
employees—not just on wages and vacation issues, but also on production
rates, new machinery and how to improve working conditions. As a result of
this team effort, strikes are infrequent, and when they occur, they are usually
symbolic and end after a day; workers just care too much that other companies will get ahead of their own. Niroshi Naruse, a 29-year-old checker in
Kinokuniya, a Tokyo supermarket, puts it this way: "We all have pride working here, knowing it is the most reputable supermarket in Japan."

There is also a philosophic basis for the Japanese work ethic of which
Westerners are often not aware. It is based on Confucianism, which promul-
gates the doctrine that work is a virtue.

And, of course, there are practical reasons Japanese work so hard. One
is to save for retirement. While U.S. social-security payments now average
$270 a month for a retired couple, Japanese at present receive only $75—
hardly enough even in a country with a lower standard of living. Many com-
pany-financed pension programs in the U.S. are six times bigger than those

in Japan, and the Japanese employee must work hard when younger to provide for his retirement, which starts at the age of 55. In recent years, young Japanese workers have been muttering about this and about other aspects of their work life. A few even reject the traditional hard-work ethic that created the Japanese economic boom. But Japan still has a long way to go before it has to worry about a slackening of the national passion to work.

Reading 2

The Problem of Generations

Bruno Bettelheim

This essay first appeared in 1961 in a volume of essays called Youth: Change and Challenge. *Bettelheim is a well-known psychologist who has written many works on psychology, especially on the problems of young people. The essay was written at a time when people had begun to speak of the "generation gap." Although this term is not used much today, the problem it refers to still exists.*

Note Bettelheim's use of a long quotation at the beginning of the article to support his main point. Watch for the author's use of figurative language—from accounting (assets and liabilities) and cooking (frosting on the cake)—and be sure to interpret these terms correctly.

Note: *The selection may seem sexist because the author takes up only the problems of male youth. In another part of his essay, however, the author writes about the problems of female youth.*

Length of summary: Approximately 200 words

Most serious writers on the problem of youth have recognized that youth's present difficulties in Western society are closely related to changed social and economic conditions and to the ensuing difficulty for youth in finding self-realization in work. As Goodman observes: "It's hard to grow up when there isn't enough man's work," and he continues, "To produce necessary food and shelter is man's work. During most of economic history most men have done this drudging work, secure that it was justified and worthy of a man to do it, though often feeling that the social conditions under which they did it were not worthy of a man, thinking, "It's better to die than to live so hard"—but they worked on.... Security is always first; but in normal conditions, a large part of security comes from knowing your contribution is useful, and the rest from knowing it's uniquely yours: they need you."

Just as in this country an earlier generation needed youth because the economic security of the family depended on its contribution, so in Russia today youth is needed because only it can carry on the task of creating the new and better society; and in Africa because only it can move society from tribal confusion toward modern democracy. If the generations thus need each other, they can live together successfully, and the problem of their succession, though not negligible, can be mastered successfully. Under such conditions youth and age need each other not only for their economic but even more for their moral survival. This makes youth secure—if not in its position, at least in its self-respect. But how does the parent in modern society need the next generation? Certainly not for economic reasons any more, and what little expectation a parent may have had that his children would support him in old age becomes superfluous with greater social security. More crucially, the status-quo mood of the older generation suggests no need for youth to create a much different or radically better world.

In many respects youth has suddenly turned from being the older generation's greatest economic asset into its greatest economic liability. Witness the expense of rearing and educating youth for some twenty or more years, with no economic return to be expected. Youth still poses emotional problems to the preceding generation, as of old. But in past generations these emotional problems were, so to speak, incidental or subservient to economic necessity. What at best was once the frosting on the cake must now serve as both solid food and trimmings—and this will never work.

Thus the economic roles, obligations, and rewards are no longer clearly defined between the generations, if not turned upside down. Therefore, another aspect of the relation between the generations looms even larger; in a balance sheet of interaction that is no longer economic but largely emotional. Modern man, insecure because he no longer feels needed for his work contribution or for self-preservation (the automatic machines do things so much better and faster), is also insecure as a parent. He wonders how well he has discharged that other great function of man, the continuation of the species.

At this point modern youth becomes the dreaded avenging angel of his parents, since he holds the power to prove his parents' success or failure as parents; and this counts so much more now, since his parents' economic success is no longer so important in a society of abundance. Youth itself, feeling insecure because of its marginal position in a society that no longer depends on it for economic security, is tempted to use the one power this reversal between the generations has conferred on it: to be accuser and judge of the parents' success or failure as parents.

Reading 3

The Peter Principle Is Alive and Well...

Albert Shanker

This article appeared in the New York Times *on January 23, 1974, in a column called "Where We Stand: A Weekly Column of Comment on Public Education" (an advertisement). At that time Albert Shanker was president of the American Federation of Teachers.*

The authors of the Peter Principle, Laurence J. Peter and Raymond Hull, wrote about the so-called principle in 1969. It states that "in a hierarchy, every employee tends to rise to his level of incompetence." Many people, in agreement with Shanker, feel that this principle still applies today. The article explains why work gets accomplished in spite of the incompetence at the top. Note the way Shanker introduces and concludes his article to make the article relevant to the hierarchy in his own field, education.

Length of summary: Approximately 250 words

Over the years many books have been written on the authoritarian nature of the relationship between teachers and students. There has also been discussion, although much less, of the authoritarian and hierarchical relationship among teachers, assistant principals, principals and school superintendents. A number of teachers have argued that the supervisor-subordinate relationship is more appropriate to a factory or the military than to a school, where professionalism is the overriding factor.

Those who espouse the latter view were both amused and comforted when Laurence J. Peter and Raymond Hull brought forth their now classic work, *The Peter Principle: Why Things Always Go Wrong*. The Peter Principle, "In a hierarchy, every employee tends to rise to the level of his incompetence," seemed to explain much of what was wrong: There is great upward mobility in our society, and employees keep getting promoted to the next higher position because they do well in their present one. When the employee reaches a job he cannot do well (the level of his incompetence) promotion ceases, and he remains on a job which he cannot perform.

cynade.

The Peter Principle continues to this day to intrigue the inquiring mind. In the July–August 1972 issue of the Harvard Business Review, Lane Tracy, Associate Professor of Management at Ohio University, in an article *Postscript to the Peter Principle,* subjects its content to further examination. Knowing how painful it is for most people to face unpleasant truths about themselves, Tracy wisely employs the satirical approach.

Tracy goes along with the Peter Principle, observing that since "men are usually promoted on the basis of faith that training and experience will develop their 'potential,' rather than on any hard evidence of their ability to handle the new job, it only requires a slight weakening of our faith in the powers of education to realize that sooner or later, and probably sooner, most men will come to rest in a job that is too much for them. Moreover, our eyes and ears, if not our very souls, confirm that many men have already reached that position."

His problem with the Principle is that, in spite of the strong arguments for it, "our organizations seem to function well. Workable decisions *are* made, orders *are* transmitted and carried out, and as often as not the product *is* delivered on time . . . Therefore we are faced with the question: If the Peter Principle is basically valid, why do not more things go wrong?"

Tracy concludes that there must be large groups of people "to whom the Peter Principle does not apply. These people cannot be part of the organizational hierarchy, for there the Peter Principle operates at full force. And yet, to be in a position to carry out the necessary functions of planning, directing, and controlling the enterprise, such people must reside at all levels of the administrative hierarchy. What class of people fits this description? The obvious answer is *secretaries* . . . Whenever an executive falters, either because he has reached the level of his incompetence or because he is moving up so fast that he does not have time to learn his job, his secretary is ready and waiting to take over."

Secretaries, unlike their executive counterparts, are competent because no matter how efficiently they perform, women are not expected to aspire beyond certain "women's" positions and "there is no cultural expectation of a regular or rapid advancement for women. Women are generally assumed to be flighty, irrational, and interested only in marriage and producing babies; they are not promoted till they have proven otherwise."

Tracy discovered structures in medicine and education similar to what secretaries have to put up with. "Nurses are in a position to monitor and correct some of the physicians' worst abuses," is his tongue-in-cheek comment. "Primary and secondary school teachers implant the study skills with which many college students manage to learn in spite of the tutorial incompetence of their professors." Farms and industry, he contends, can survive managerial incompetency because of the experience and skills of the cheap labor provided by various racial and ethic minorities.

He points out that every great civilization, including ours, has been built on the "bedrock of a subordinate class," but now we are faced with a grave threat because the subordinate classes are demanding "that they be admitted to the Peter progression, and our own professed belief in equality seems to have trapped us into permitting this catastrophe to occur. We are even abetting the process of our demise with mass college education, civil rights legislation, equal employment opportunity pledges, and recruitment of executives from minority groups. The problem is not that members of the subordinate groups do not belong in the executive hierarchy, but simply that there will be no one left to do the productive work. Black Power and Women's Lib may be proper expressions of rights, but they are bad economics."

Upward mobility has already robbed our nation of good boxers, chefs, waiters, shoe rebuilders, police officers and others. "Now," says Tracy, "if Women's Lib has its way, we will lose our supply of good secretaries." It is just this sort of structural weakening of society "which eventually brought ancient Rome to her knees."

Tracy urges that we must abandon our traditional vertical hierarchies and look for new forms of organization—forms which are not subject to the Peter Principle. "If continued suppression of minority groups and women is unacceptable to us—that is, if we lack the stomach for it—we must find some efficient way to reorganize ourselves . . . The choice is ours, but we had better make it soon, or our organizations may peter out."

If Tracy is right, the relationship between teachers, principals and superintendents may soon be radically transformed. The transformation will be a byproduct, not of the conflicts between differing groups within the schools, but rather of the larger struggle for greater equality throughout our society.

CHAPTER 2

Language

Composition

Requirements for a Home Composition

---

1. Use white $8\frac{1}{2}'' \times 11''$ paper; write on one side only.
2. Type your composition double spaced on unlined paper (if hand-written, the paper should be clearly written on every other line). A typewritten page, double-spaced, is about 250 words.
3. Indent each paragraph, use wide margins ($1''$ to $1\frac{1}{4}''$), and number each page in the upper right-hand corner.
4. Include a separate page with the title, the thesis sentence, and the outline.

Procedures for Discussion

The teacher puts this heading on the board:

A Comparison Between English and (Your Language)

and adds the following rough outline:

I. Comparison of the writing systems
   Symbols used
   Direction of the writing
   Spelling
   Punctuation
II. Comparison of the grammatical systems
   Word forms (inflections)
   Word order
   Structure words

    The teacher then calls on students of different language backgrounds to come up to the board to write a sentence like "Where did you learn English?" in their own language and to explain the symbols used in the sentence and other aspects of the writing system. Other students can then ask questions.
    For the grammatical systems, the teacher asks individual students to discuss each point in the outline and to put examples on the board.

Writing the Composition

Write a 500 to 600 word composition comparing the writing and grammatical systems of English and your language.

Suggestions for the Content and Organization

You may use the two main points (the writing and the grammatical systems) and as many of the subpoints from the discussion outline as you wish. Or you may focus on only one of the main points if you have a lot to say about it. Point out important similarities and differences, not trivial ones. Use examples, but keep a good balance between general statements and examples. If there are too many examples, the reader loses track of the general point and may find your paper dull.
    You may organize the composition by first pointing out the similarities and differences in the writing system and then in the grammatical system. Or you may point out only the differences first, and then similarities in both the writing and the grammatical systems. You could also mention the similarities, but concentrate on the differences, since these are what cause you trouble in

learning English. As you write, use transitions between the points that remind the reader you are making a comparison.

Guide for the Outline and the Composition

The following guide will help you in preparing to write your composition. On the left side of the guide is the outline with suggestions for handling the introduction, transitions, and the conclusion of this composition. On the right side are general comments about how introductions, transitions, and conclusions may be written. (If you are accustomed to writing a first draft from rough notes, use this guide for your second and succeeding drafts.)

Outline	*General Comments*
Title	Use initial capital letters for all words except articles, short prepositions, and short conjunctions. Try to use an interesting title that reflects your thesis.

Introduction
This can be personal—from your own experience.
Or it can be general—for anyone learning a new language.
Or it can be even more general—about the need for language as a means of communication.
	Purpose of the introduction:
	  to catch the reader's interest
	  to give a general idea of the subject
	An introduction may include:
	  a quotation
	  a story, perhaps personal
	  a rhetorical question (which you
	    will answer)
	  a definition
	  a statement of a belief you will
	    argue against
	  a surprising or shocking fact
	  a statement of a serious problem

Transitional lead-in This states that you are comparing the two languages and gives the basis for comparison.	Usually at the end of the introduction. Gives an indication of the central idea and the way it will be developed (may be in the form of a question).

I. First main point
This gives the first point of comparison.
  A. First supporting detail
 	
  B. Second supporting detail
       etc.
	New paragraph. The first sentence: (1) mentions the general idea of the paragraph (from the important word[s] in the outline); (2) relates this sentence to what was said before.
	
	Should be related to the preceding subpoint.

Continue with your other main points and their supporting details.)

For each main point, remind the reader which point of comparison you are discussing.

Note: Long subpoints may begin new paragraphs.

(Follow the suggestions given for the first main point.)

Conclusion

You can go back to your personal experience, or you can be more general.

The conclusion should round out the composition in a strong and satisfying way, perhaps by referring again to whatever you used to introduce the composition.

Notes: (1) The conclusion should not add any new ideas that need further development. (2) If your last point ends on a strong note that points up your thesis, you may not need to add a conclusion.

Support for the points you make can come from your own beliefs and experience or from the readings in this chapter and elsewhere. (Be sure to identify your sources and to use quotation marks around the exact words of an author.) The support can be in the form of examples, current facts and figures, or authoritative opinion. Use enough support to make your point convincing to the reader.

Finally, keep in mind that this composition represents your own opinions. By stating them honestly and strongly, you will have a composition that the reader will find interesting enough to continue reading.

Revising the Composition

In succeeding drafts, try to sharpen your thesis and show more clearly how each main point contributes to the development of the thesis. Try writing down the opening sentences of your paragraphs on a separate sheet of paper to see if they make a clear sentence outline. Go over the reading selections again for further ideas or additional support.

Consult the Revision and Editing Checklist for guidance on organization, paragraphing, and sentences. You can get needed vocabulary help in the vocabulary section that follows on pp. 19–22. Make a final check with the Symbol Chart for Correction of Compositions for the grammatical structures and usage in your composition.

Evaluation

If there is an exchange of student compositions, the Revision and Editing Checklist can serve as a guide in the evaluation of another student's composition. Use the following procedure in checking for the writer's organization and development of ideas.

1. Without looking at the other student's outline page, make an outline and a one-sentence summary of the central idea (or thesis) of the whole paper. Can you find a clear line of development? Do your summary sentence and your outline agree with those of the writer?
2. Find the support for each point made in the writer's paper. Is the support adequate and convincing?
3. Write on the student's paper what you consider the good points of the composition and what needs to be improved.

Vocabulary and Usage

    Vocabulary
    Usage Notes
    Word Forms

Vocabulary

The following lists of expressions may be useful to you in talking and writing about your comparison of languages. The first list gives expressions needed for making comparisons. The second list gives vocabulary for discussing writing and grammatical systems.

Expressions of Comparison

compared with
in comparison with
Compared with (or *In comparison with*) English, Russian has many more word endings.

Similarities	*Differences*
as . . . as	comparative:
Greek is *as* difficult *as* Russian [is].	_____ **-er than**
	more _____ **than**
	German is more highly inflected *than* Russian [is].

the same as
similar to
like

The word order of English is almost *the same as* (that of) Spanish.

similarity (*between*, for two)

One *similarity between* French and Spanish is in the position of adjectives [give examples]. Another [or a second] similarity is . . .

both

Both English and German are derived from the same branch of languages.

differ from
be different from

English *differs from* Spanish in several ways.

difference (*between*, for two)

One *difference between* English and Spanish is in the punctuation of questions [give examples]. Another [or a second] difference is . . .

unlike

Arabic, *unlike* English, is written from right to left.

, but (used only before the second unit of comparison)

English uses articles, *but* Russian does not.

, while, whereas (used before the first or the second unit of comparison)

English uses articles, *whereas* Russian does not.

Whereas English uses articles, Russian does not.

; however   , on the other hand (used only before the second unit of comparison)

English uses articles; *however,* Russian does not.

English uses articles; Russian, *however,* does not.

English uses articles. Russian, *however,* does not.

Writing Systems

alphabet   Each symbol (a letter) usually represents one sound. An alphabet consists of symbols for vowel sounds and symbols for consonants.

characters   (used especially in Oriental languages) Each symbol represents one idea.

script   handwriting (as opposed to print).

capital letter   A larger letter that begins the first word in a sentence or that begins a proper noun, as opposed to a small letter.

direction of the writing   (alphabet or characters)

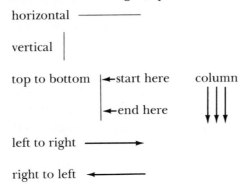

horizontal

vertical

top to bottom   start here   column

end here

left to right

right to left

punctuation marks

.	period
,	comma
:	colon
;	semicolon
?	question mark
!	exclamation point (or, mark)
—	dash
( )	parentheses
" "	quotation marks

spelling   In phonetic systems, each symbol represents only one sound. English is only partially phonetic. It has many irregularities. For example, it uses the five vowel letters *a, e, i, o, u* to represent more than seventeen vowel sounds.

Grammatical Systems

Word Forms:

inflections   These are special forms, especially endings, that indicate different grammatical purposes. English has very few inflections:

for nouns: *-s* for plural; *'s* for possessive

for adjectives: *-er, -est* for comparison

for verbs: *-s* for third person singular; *-ing* for progressive; *-ed* for past

for adverbs: *-ly* to change from adjectives

declension   These are classes of nouns and pronouns (also adjectives and articles) that have different forms (inflections) for different grammatical purposes.

person   In English, we use person with nouns, pronouns, and verbs: first person (with *I, we*), second person (with *you*), third person (with *he, she, it, they*). Some European languages have a special familiar pronoun.

number   Nouns, pronouns, and verbs are either singular (for one) or plural (for more than one).

case   Case refers to different forms used for nouns or pronouns. In English, personal pronouns have separate forms for subject *(I)*, object *(me)*, possessive *(my)*. The English noun changes only for the possessive *('s)*.

gender   Some languages have different forms for nouns, pronouns, and adjectives according to whether they are considered feminine, masculine, or neuter. English has gender only for the pronouns *he, she, it*.

conjugation   Classes of verbs that have different forms (inflections) for different grammatical purposes.

tense   Roughly, the time indicated by the verb. Grammar books usually list six tenses for English.

voice   The distinction between an active verb (Columbus *discovered* America) and a passive verb (America *was discovered* by Columbus).

Word Order:

The normal order of English is subject—verb—object (or whatever else completes the verb).

subject   What is being talked about: *Columbus* discovered America.

predicate   What is said about the subject: Columbus *discovered America*.

Structure Words:

articles   In English, only *the* and *a(n)*.

prepositions   Examples are *on, in, with, by*.

conjunctions   Examples are *and, or, but*.

Usage Notes

Use *the* if the word *language* follows the name of the language.

> *Example:*   She is studying *English*.
>
> but
>
> She is studying *the English language*.

The word *alphabet* is generally noncountable. Do not use the plural. Use *the* with *alphabet*.

> *The English alphabet* consists of twenty-six letters.

Use *letters* to refer to individual symbols in the alphabet. The plural is used only to refer to different systems of alphabets.

> The English and the Korean alphabets are quite different.

The words *slang, vocabulary, pronunciation*, and *grammar* are not countable. Do not add *-s* to these words.

Use capital letters for every word of nationality or language, whether the word is a noun (He speaks *French*) or an adjective (He speaks the *French* language).

Use *the* with certain grammatical terms:

> *the singular, the plural*
> *the present, the past, the future*

Grammatical terms used in general statements can be:

singular with *the*

> *The subject* comes before *the verb*.

or plural without *the*:

> *Subjects* come before *verbs*.

Use a hyphen for numbers twenty-one through ninety-nine.

> The English alphabet has *twenty-six* letters.

Word Forms

Use the correct forms for the words in parentheses.

The answers are on p. 354. If you need help with this exercise, refer to the explanations under Word Forms in Appendix A.

1. One unabridged dictionary gives the (define) _____ of more than 500,000 words.

2. (Phonetic) _____ is the study of speech sounds.

3. The English language has strict rules about the (punctuate) _____ of sentences.

4. Extra information in a sentence may be placed within (parenthetic) _____.

5. The written symbols of a language are arranged (alphabet) _____. Children memorize this (alphabet) _____ order. (*Note:* Some adjectives may end in *-ic* or *-ical*; for example, history, geography.)

6. Some expressions may be (grammar) _____ correct but inappropriate in certain situations.

7. An (exclaim) _____ sentence in Spanish often has an (exclaim) _____ mark (or, point) at both the (begin) _____ and the end of the sentence.

8. A class of *nouns, pronouns,* or *adjectives* which has different forms for case, number, gender is called a (decline) _____.

9. A class of *verbs* which has different forms for tense, number, person, etc., is called a (conjugate) _____.

10. English has very few word endings; it is not a highly (inflect) _____ language.

11. Informal English permits the (omit) _____ of some structure words.

12. A (compare) _____ between languages (emphasis) _____ both (differ) _____ and (similar) _____.

13. English grammar is (basic) _____ simple; English (pronounce) _____, however, is difficult because of spelling (irregular) _____ (use the plural).

14. Some foreign students have (difficult) _____ in (hear) _____ and (distinct) _____ between English sounds.

15. (Compare) _____ with Russian or Greek, English grammar is (relative) _____ easy to learn because it has very few (inflect) _____.

16. Anyone (compare) _____ English with French will find that these languages are not (total) _____ different.

Reading for Summary Writing

For the following three reading selections, prepare a brief outline for class discussion before you write the summary. After the class discussion of each selection, you will write:

1. A longer, revised outline of the reading selection, using an alternation of numbers and letters.
2. A one-sentence summary of the reading selection. The sentence should include the central idea and the main points used to develop this idea (from the outline).
3. A summary of the reading selection. The length assigned in the text will determine the amount of detail you can include in the outline and summary.

Guidelines for Writing (Review)

1. For the outline, use the alternate number-letter system for the main points and their subpoints. The phrases you underline in the opening sentences of paragraphs usually become the main points or subpoints on the outline.
2. For both summary and outline, follow the same order as the reading selection. If you wish, you may begin the summary with a reference to the source of the selection (author, publication, etc.) and to its central idea.
3. Keep a sense of proportion. Write more about points the author devotes more attention to.
4. Concentrate more on the main points than on examples or other supporting details.
5. Use proper transitions between the main points and the subpoints of your summary; your summary must have an organization of its own.
6. Use your own words as much as possible, except for key phrases. You may quote important phrases or sentences.
7. Be careful not to overload any sentence with so much information that the sentence is hard to read.
8. Be consistent in your use of verb tenses. Use all present tense (the author states, feels) or all past tense (the author stated, felt). The present tense is more common in a summary.
9. Do not include your own ideas or your own attitude or interpretation. The summary should be an objective restatement of what the author has said.

Reading 1

The Language of the In-Crowd

Glenn Leggett, C. David Mead, and Melinda Kramer

The term in-crowd *used in this selection is an informal expression for those who follow the latest trends. Some slang is being used more frequently now in formal speech and writing. This is in line with many other recent trends toward greater informality in social customs.*

Slang should not be confused with colloquial language. Colloquial *means acceptable in informal speech and writing (for example,* kid, cop*). Definitions for such words are labeled* informal *(or* colloq.*) in dictionaries.*

Length of summary: Approximately 150 words

Slang consists of the rapidly changing words and phrases in popular speech that people invent to give language novelty and vigor. Slang words, in fact, are fun—unless you don't happen to know what they mean. Then they can seem like the strange tongue of a secret sect.

Slang often is created by the same process we use to create most new words: by combining two words *(ferretface, blockhead)*; by shortening words *(pro, prof, vet, max)*; by borrowing from other languages *(kaput, spiel)*; and by generalizing a proper name *(the real McCoy)*. Often slang simply extends the meaning of phrases borrowed from other activities *(lower the boom* from sailing; *tune in, tune out* from radio; *cash in your chips* from poker). A great deal of slang gives a new range of meaning to existing words *(tough, heavy, high, joint, turned on, bombed out)*.

Slang is—and has always been—part of the current language, adding spontaneity, directness, color, and liveliness. Over three hundred years ago, Pilgrim youngsters were inventing slang terms, turning the traditional fare-well—"God be with you"—into the flippant "good-by." Thus slang often contributes directly to the growth of the language as slang terms move gradually into general use. Words like *rascal* and *sham* were originally slang terms; short-ened forms such as *A-bomb, ad, gym,* and *phone* are now appropriate to most informal writing. Reports on education routinely refer to high school *drop-outs*. To see soft drinks and potato chips called *junk food* in the pages of a magazine surprises no one. When slang is clear, precise, vivid, and descriptive in ways that more standard words are not, it tends to enter general usage. In informal writing, well-chosen slang terms can be very effective:

> Has Harold Wilson *Lost His Cool?*
>
> Headline, *New York Times*

> Heaven knows there are large areas where a shrewd eye for the *quick buck* is dominant.
>
> FREDERICK LEWIS ALLEN, *The Big Change*

But slang has serious limitations. It is often imprecise, understandable only to a narrow social or age group, and usually changes very rapidly. You may be familiar with the latest slang, but who remembers *lollapalooza, balloon juice,* or *spooning?* The fact that *hep* became *hip* within a few years suggests how short-lived slang can be.

Enjoy slang for the life it can sometimes give to speech. But even in conversation, remember that it may not be understood and that a little goes a long way. If you rely on *nifty, lousy, tough,* and *gross* to describe all objects, events, and ideas, you don't communicate much. In writing, use slang primarily when it serves some legitimate purpose, such as capturing the flavor of conversation.

> The bouncer told the drunk he had better back off or he was likely to get his lights punched out. Then he firmly steered the drunk through the door and out of the bar.

Except in carefully controlled contexts, slang and standard language usually make an inappropriate mixture:

> The very notion of venture capital is so alien in Communist China that no government official was willing to risk giving the two [young Chinese entrepreneurs] permission to set up shop. The decision was bucked up all the way to Premier Zhao Ziyang. He flashed the go-ahead last year, and the company began operation in January.
>
> *Business Week*

While we are not likely to resist such usages as *set up shop* in a magazine aimed at a fairly broad, general business audience, the slang expressions *bucked up* and *flashed the go-ahead* here seem out of place in a news story concerning the head of the Chinese government. The best rule of thumb is to assess your audience and purpose carefully in deciding whether a slang term is appropriate.

Discussion

1. The *Random House Dictionary* defines slang as "very informal vocabulary that is characteristically more metaphorical and ephemeral than ordinary language." Relate this definition to the one given in the reading selection.

2. According to the authors, how are slang words created?
3. What do slang words add to the language? Some slang words have a humorous effect—for example, *flatfoot,* an older slang word for policeman. Many slang words are intended as insults, expressing dislike or hate—for example, *pig* for policeman.
4. What advice is the reader given about the use of slang?
5. Some slang words that are still used have come into the language from jazz (*cat* for man; *green* or *bread* for money). Others have come from drug users (*turn on* for excite; *turn off* for bore). Still other slang words have been coined by the news media in connection with a current event (*Irangate* for the Iran-Contra hearings in the United States, as a parallel to the earlier Watergate hearings). What are some slang words that you have heard used by Americans? Give some examples of slang words used in your language and tell what they express.

Reading 2

English, the Language, Reconquering Polyglot India

William K. Stevens

The following article about the English language in India appeared in The New York Times. *The headline (given above) reflects one of the main concerns of the article.*

> *Since this journalistic article is the result of some research, notice how the author identifies his sources of facts and opinions, and notice which sources he quotes. As you reread the article, underline all references to sources to see where the author identifies them specifically and where he refers to them more generally (some authorities, some experts, etc.).*

Length of summary: Approximately 200 words

After three decades of often bitter squabbling over what the national language of this country of many languages should be, it appears that English is winning.

Despite longstanding official attempts to make Hindi the country's chief language at all levels, the language of the British colonizers has become the voluntary, preferred choice of urban Indians and India's educated, rapidly burgeoning middle class.

English is also the language of commerce, finance, science, technology and the social sciences. And, as even a casual look suggests, it is the main language of advertising, the most influential newspapers, the rapidly growing magazines and the budding national television network.

No longer a language strictly for the British-educated elite of pre-independence years, authorities say, English is now permeating areas it never reached before.

Working-class urban fathers who speak it a little are sending their children to school to learn to speak it fluently in the hope that better jobs will lift them into the middle class.

Schools in which English is the medium of instruction are springing up everywhere and cannot seem to keep ahead of demand. In the relatively affluent Punjab, there are said to be 5,000 such schools, although many are of uncertain quality, catering to that state's substantial middle class.

"Even the poorest person would like to send his child to a school where the medium is English," said Dr. S. P. Bakhshi, the head of such an institution. Dr. Bakhshi, principal of New Delhi's Modern School, which has 1,100 applicants a year for 200 places, added, "They say, 'I'll cut back to only one meal a day to pay for it if you'll let my child in.'"

Fluency in English greatly enhances the marriageability of middle-class daughters. And a sort of English chic has developed. "It is the fashion to learn English in the same way it is to have stereos and radios and electronic gadgets," Dr. Akhileshwar Jha, a linguist at Delhi University and a recognized authority on the subject, said recently.

English commands respect, as Rama Jha, a university English teacher and the wife of Dr. Jha, finds when she rides on city buses. "The conductor is very polite when you use English," she said, "but unpleasant and uncooperative otherwise."

Many authorities cite more substantial and possibly more durable causes for the resurgence of English. One is that to the extent that English is becoming the language of the world and, particularly, of world commerce, science and technology, it is to the advantage of Indians to speak it.

Some authorities say further that the structure, vocabulary and flexibility of English give it an innate advantage over Hindi, which, according to Dr. Jha, "is not able to cope with the experiences of the modern world."

Finally, English is widely and increasingly viewed as a vital key to good jobs, financial success and personal advancement.

"Some of the people believe now that if you don't study English you're going to be a nobody, an ordinary person," Dr. Bakhshi said. For urban jobs in the private sector, Dr. Jha said flatly, "English is a must."

Whatever the reasons, English is spoken the length and breadth of the land by many in India's modern sectors. "Infinitely more than Hindi," Dr. Jha wrote recently, English "has quietly established itself in India as its de facto national language."

Not all experts agree with that conclusion. Some point out that even though English may be the premier language of emerging India, it is still spoken by only 15 million to 20 million of the country's 700 million people.

Furthermore, linguists say, Hindi has spread rapidly in the traditional, largely rural world in which most Indians live.

As many as 150 million Indians may now speak Hindi, far more than those who speak any other language. It is being more widely accepted in non-Hindi regions, authorities say, not least because it dominates the movies.

"Only 10 to 20 percent of the people in all of India cannot understand Hindi at all," B. N. Tiwari, another Delhi University linguist, maintained.

He and others believe that Hindi therefore has a better claim to be the "link language" in a country with at least 50 major regional languages, 14 of which are officially recognized.

Some analysts see the strong emergence of English in India's modern sectors, and the parallel establishment and spread of Hindi, as one expression of a deeper conflict between modern India and traditional India. Unless and until this conflict is resolved, they speculate, India will probably never have a truly national language—and it may not have one in any case.

Some who favor English as the single national language argue that democracy demands it. Since the decisions that affect the lives of the most Indians are now primarily made in English, they argue, and the most trenchant discussions about what is going on in the country are carried on in the English news media, most Indians are increasingly cut off from public life.

Hindi and English are both established as official national languages for governmental use. Originally, Hindi was to stand alone. But opposition over the years from states where Hindi is not spoken, particularly in the south, has enabled English to hold its own in central Government use.

Analysts on both sides of the argument concur that, for all the new vigor and popularity of English, it faces a quality problem: although the use of English is increasing, authorities say, it is frequently spoken badly, and is even more frequently read and written with poor fluency.

Indian English has adopted many local words and expressions, as is the case in many other countries where the use of English has expanded.

Conversely, in a kind of cross-fertilization that may be producing a sort of "Hindish," Hindi has incorporated many English words. Some authorities place the proportion of English in Hindi as high as 30 percent.

Discussion

1. What is the irony of the headline of this article? How is this headline related to the central idea of the article?
2. According to the article, what are the practical advantages that a *knowledge* of English gives to the Indian middle class?
3. What social benefits does the use of English bring to its speakers?
4. What are some other reasons that authorities give for the resurgence of English?
5. While some experts agree that English has become the *de facto* (actual, as opposed to legal) national language, others disagree. What reasons do they give for their disagreement?
6. How many major languages does India have? Which are the two official languages for government use? Which language is the Indian government attempting to make the national language?
7. Why do some analysts view the emergence of English and the spread of Hindi as "one expression of a deeper conflict between modern India and traditional India"?
8. What are the language problems caused by the increasing use of English in India?
9. The article explains why English has re-emerged in India for practical purposes. What is the situation in your country regarding the study of English? Is the study of English increasing, and if so, what are the reasons?

Reading 3

Italian Groups Fight to Preserve Dialects

Ernest Sakler

The following article takes up a subject that has been causing a number of political problems throughout the world—the struggle of ethnic minorities to preserve their own dialects. In some cases, such ethnic groups have even asked for their independence—for example, the Basques in Spain.

The International Herald Tribune, March 26, 1979, p. 14. Reprinted with permission of United Press International, Copyright 1979.

The word dialect, *which frequently appears in this article, refers to a variety of the same language, according to linguists. However, the word is also used loosely to cover what linguists actually consider different languages.*

Note the use of metaphor at the beginning to introduce the central idea and the use of a quotation at the end to round out this idea.

Length of summary: Approximately 150 words

Italy's trampled regional subcultures are raising their heads again.

Sicilians want the Sicilian dialect taught in their schools. Piedmontese want courses in Piedmontese. Sardinians have been fighting to use their language in airport announcements and university papers.

For centuries intellectuals and bureaucrats imposed literary Italian as the only language worth mentioning. So the renaissance of Italy's myriad dialects is a potential revolution.

Unlike English dialects, which differ only in shades, Italian dialects are so different that a Milanese will not understand a Neapolitan speaking Neapolitan, let alone a Calabrian speaking Calabrian.

The dialects developed separately from the corruption of Latin in the Dark Ages, when illiteracy was rampant and communications among regions and even between neighboring cities was almost nonexistent.

When civilization blossomed again after the year 1000 and travel resumed, the dialect of Florentine merchants became a sort of lingua franca. Helped by the prestige of such writers as Dante, Petrarch and Boccaccio, it evolved into the national language of Italy's upper class.

Local dialects lived on among the people, in most cases looked down upon as the language of the ignorant and underprivileged or at best used for fun in folksy poems and plays.

* * *

Writers, teachers and bureaucrats gradually imposed "Italian"—the language evolved from Florentine—as the only written language and the only one worth speaking among cultured persons. They laid down firm grammatical rules and made sure no dialect words crept into the dictionary. Dialects were barred from classrooms, courts, public speeches and official correspondence.

In recent years, the revival of "micro-nationalisms" among European minorities such as the Welsh in Britain, the Bretons and Corsicans in France, and the Catalans and Basques in Spain encouraged Italy's dialect-speakers to seek rights of their own.

Sardinians, whose archaic tongue is classified by most linguists as a language in its own right, were among the first to seek the same rights won by German-speaking Italian citizens in the Aldo Adige (South Tirol) and French-speakers in the Aosta valley. But so far they have met with no success.

A university student who wrote his graduation paper in Sardinian had it turned down. An airline employee who announced flights over the airport loudspeaker in Sardinian and locally spoken Catalan was reprimanded. He did it again shortly afterward to applause from a planeload of Catalan tourists from Spain.

*   *   *

In Sicily, where local dialects had a brilliant if short-lived literary tradition in the 13th century, the town of Milazzo has decided to start teaching dialect in schools in the coming year. There has been a revival of Sicilian-language puppet shows, and a publishing house has just reprinted an 1857 dictionary of the Sicilian dialect and is working on an updated one.

Similar movements have sprung up in other parts of the country.

In Piedmont, the regional government has been fighting an unsuccessful battle against the central government in Rome in an attempt to have the Piedmontese dialect taught in schools. Regional legislation to that effect was vetoed by Rome three times in 19 months on constitutional and legal technicalities.

"This is a typical case of restrictive bureaucrats wearing blinders when making a decision," said the sponsor of the law, Socialist councilman Giuseppe Calsolaro. "The truth is that Rome does not want the teaching of local dialects and cultures. And then they complain if autonomist movements spring up."

Discussion

1. What is the origin of most of the dialects in Italy, and why did they become so different?
2. Why did the Florentine dialect become the official language?
3. What does the writer mean by "micro-nationalism"? What is meant by a "lingua franca"?
4. What examples are given of Italian dialect speakers attempting to get rights of their own?
5. Do you have an "official" language in your country? Are there groups of people who speak dialects or languages other than the official language? Does this situation cause political problems for the central government? Is there any feeling that one dialect or language is "superior" to another?

Reading for Further Ideas

The reading selections in this section are intended not only to give you additional information about the subject of the composition but to continue to sharpen your reading skills and, in addition, to give you practice in preparing for essay examinations.

After you have skimmed through each selection and underlined the main points, make an outline from memory. Then check the reading selection again and make a more exact outline. This time, make a one-sentence summary of the main idea.

With this preparation, write a question for each selection that you think might be given on an essay examination. Without concentrating on details, make the question as comprehensive as possible. (You may also ask a question comparing the selection with others on the same subject.) Then write the answers and check them against the reading selection.

In writing your question, keep in mind the date and source of the selection (newspaper or magazine, textbook, other kind of book). Such sources often have different purposes and may therefore affect the way your questions might be asked.

Reading 1

Educated or Standard English

W. Nelson Francis

The following selection is from a college text whose author has written many works on the English language and on linguistics. Note his definition of standard English in terms of who uses it and how it is acquired. Note also his use of many examples to make his meaning clear.

As you read, watch for the author's distinction between what is considered standard English in the United States and in Great Britain.

In this selection, the author refers to several speech areas in the United States. Linguists divide the United States speech areas into three main groups— Northern (including New York City); Midland, or General American (which consists of all of middle America, from the East Coast to the West Coast); and Southern (especially the Southeast). Generally, a speaker from one area can understand the speech from another area. Some speech differences are beginning to disappear because of the influence of television.

Reprinted from *The English Language: An Introduction*, by W. Nelson Francis, by permission of W. W. Norton & Company, Inc. Copyright © 1963, 1965 by W. W. Norton & Company, Inc.

Educated or Standard English is that naturally used by most college-educated people who fill positions of social, financial, and professional influence in the community. Some people learn it as their native speech, if they come from families that already belong to this social class. Others acquire it in the course of their schooling and later by conscious or unconscious imitation of their associates. Control of standard English does not, of course, guarantee professional, social, or financial success. But it is an almost indispensable attribute of those who attain such success.

In addition to its social importance, educated English is on the whole a more flexible and versatile instrument than the other social varieties. As the language of the professions and the learned disciplines, it is called on to express more complex ideas, for which it has developed an extensive vocabulary. Its grammar, too, is more complex, and it uses longer sentences with more levels of subordination. This does not mean that it presents greater difficulties to the listener or reader, provided he is familiar with its vocabulary and grammar. But the fact that it is often used to express complicated and difficult material means that, unskillfully used, it can be vague or obscure. When its resources of vocabulary and grammar are overexploited in the expression of simple ideas, it may become the inflated jargon sometimes called "gobbledygook."

> With regard to personnel utilizing the premises after normal working hours, it is requested that precautions be observed to insure that all windows and doors are firmly secured and all illumination extinguished before vacating the building.

This is obviously only a much elaborated expression of the request that can be more simply and effectively stated:

> If you work late, be sure to lock the doors and windows and turn off the lights when you leave.

In the first sense of the phrase "good English," this translation is good and the gobbledygook which it translates, though it contains no errors of grammar or usage, is incredibly bad.

The British version of standard English, RP, is the same for all speakers regardless of their place of origin. In America, however, there is no such thing as a single standard form of American English, especially in pronunciation. The nearest thing to it is the speech of anonymous radio and television announcers, which one linguist has aptly called "network English."[1] In contrast to the well known individual commentators, who are allowed to use their native regional pronunciation, the network announcers all use a common version of English which is in most features that of the Inland Northern area....

---

[1] William A. Stewart, in a discussion of the problem of teaching standard English to nonstandard speakers, Bloomington, Indiana, August 1964.

Because of its nationwide use, network English is an acceptable standard form everywhere. But it is not a prestige dialect. Educated speakers in Boston, New York, Philadelphia, Richmond, Charleston, Atlanta, or New Orleans use the dialects of their own regions in educated form. The last five Presidents of the United States are a good example of the diversity of pronunciation to be found in standard English. President Johnson speaks the educated South Midland speech of Texas. President Kennedy's Boston speech, with its lack of postvocalic /r/ and its intrusive /r/ at the end of words like *Cuba*, was very distinctive. President Eisenhower's speech was a good illustration of the Middle Western variety sometimes called General American. It betrayed his Kansas origin in spite of a military career that took him to many parts of the English-speaking world. President Truman retained many of the South Midland features of his native Missouri, and President Roosevelt spoke the educated version of New York City speech, somewhat modified by his Harvard education and New England connections. Although most of these men had long careers in politics and frequently addressed nationwide audiences, each of them used the educated version of his native regional dialect.

Reading 2

Five Styles of Language

W. Nelson Francis

The following selection comes from The English Language: An Introduction. *Francis is summing up the five styles of language that are described by a well-known linguist, Martin Joos, in* The Five Clocks. *Note that these styles are differentiated according to the receiver of a communication (the listener or the reader) and the purpose of the communication. The term* consultative *is Joos' own and is not generally used as a classification of language usage by other language experts.*

For educated adult speakers, Martin Joos has identified and named five styles, each suited to a particular kind of occasion and characterized by certain features which identify it to the listener. The central and, in a sense, unmarked style Joos calls **consultative**. In this style we open a conversation with a stranger; it is safe for that purpose because it will neither offend him by unsolicited intimacy nor throw him off by undue formality. It is also the appropriate style for a discussion of more or less serious matters by a relatively small group; it pays listeners the compliment of assuming that they are interested and serious and hence do not need to have their interest aroused by either the elaborate figurative language of the formal style or the slang and occasional profanity of the casual style.... It is obviously a style whose major purpose is communication, with a minimum of the social, esthetic, and emotional overtones that characterize other styles.

The **casual style** is that appropriate to easy conversation among acquaintances and friends, except when the seriousness of the occasion or the subject calls for the consultative. In pronunciation it makes much use of elided and slurred forms like /gɔ́nə/ for *going to* and /wáčə dú:in/ for *what are you doing*. Its sentences are often elliptical, even telegraphic, dropping redundant grammatical and semantic features in the interest of directness and brevity, as in *Coming tonight?* for *Are you coming tonight?* and *Joe here?* for *Is Joe here?* Depending on the speaker, it may include slang and occasional profanity. In America, at least, it makes use of first names more often than titles and surnames. Since it is not used to convey very serious or complex information (even close friends shift to consultative for that), it makes considerable use of general-purpose, semantically nearly empty words and phrases like *gimmick, thingumajig,* and *nice.* Its deficiencies in communicative power are often acknowledged by frequent interpolation of phrases like *you know, I mean, as a matter of fact,* and *actually.* When written, as in informal friendly letters, it uses contractions like *won't* and *can't,* abbreviations and clippings like *Dr.* or *doc* for *doctor* and the dash as a general-purpose punctuation mark. It is the style most commonly used by high school and college students except in class, where they usually shift to consultative.

People who habitually use casual style where the situation normally calls for consultative are considered "refreshing" or "fresh" depending on the attitude of the person making the appraisal. On the other hand an occasional shift to casual style, either in writing or in speech, may produce a desirable effect. A teacher who habitually uses it in class usually loses the respect of his students, who feel they are being patronized. But if in a particular emergency he can switch from the consultative *I'd like you students to be quiet* to the casual *Shut up, you guys,* he may get the quiet he wants....

The **intimate style** is used by people who know each other so well and whose relationship is so close that each can predict the other's reactions to a given situation with accuracy a large part of the time. It thus serves chiefly to maintain contact and corroborate the accuracy of each speaker's judgment of the other's reactions. Much of this communication is carried on by other than linguistic means—between intimates a raised eyebrow, a shrug of the shoulder, or a groan can serve as well as or better than verbal expression. Grammar is reduced to a minimum; utterances are typically very short; there may be long periods of silence that in any of the other styles would be interpreted either as rudeness or as a desire to end the conversation. Vocabulary, too, is

much reduced, and the words that are used often have special meanings deriving from some shared experience which the world outside the intimate
group (usually but not always a pair) does not know about. Pronunciation,
too, may be altered; an intimate pair may use a broad form of regional dialec-
tal pronunciation, even though one or both of them are not native speakers
of that dialect. Words are slurred and clipped, accidental mispronunciations
may be purposely preserved....

When intimates wish to communicate information about something
outside the very restricted range to which intimate style is appropriate, they
shift to casual or even consultative style. For this reason, intimate style does
not often get written down. The act of writing, relatively laborious as it is,
usually is the result of the desire to convey some kind of new information to
whoever is going to read the product....

The three styles so far discussed have in common the fact that they are
primarily conversational; they imply the presence and participation of another beside the speaker. The participation, especially in consultative style,
may be no more than signaling at brief intervals that one is paying attention,
which may be done by brief oral attention-signals (*yes, unh-hunh*) or, when the
two parties can see each other, by unobtrusive gestures. But the listener is
usually expected to become a speaker in his turn, and he knows the signals
that mark the places where he can begin speaking without causing a rude
interruption. When written, the consultative, casual, and intimate styles suppose a specific reader or small group of readers who would respond in this
way if present, and are more or less expected to answer letters addressed to
them.

In contrast, the other two styles, the **formal** of expository discourse and
the **frozen** of literature, are not conversational but informative and discur-
sive. The hearer or reader is not given the opportunity to intervene, to ask
questions, to make comments, or to indicate his lack of comprehension. Instead of the give and take of the conversational situation, the user of formal
style—the lecturer, preacher, newscaster, commencement speaker, judge, or
legislator speaking on the floor (not in committee)—is alone before an audience. Without benefit of the "feedback" that is available to the conversation-
alist, he is obliged to hold his audience's attention on the one hand by making
sure that he is understood and on the other by avoiding boresome explicit-
ness or repetition.

The grammar of formal style is more closely organized and less tolerant
of loose or mixed constructions. The vocabulary is more ample than that of
the conversational styles, with a wider range of nearly synonymous words and
phrases, though large areas of vocabulary—slang, for exmple—are ruled out
except for special effects which actually constitute lapses into the conversational mode. Pronunciation is meticulous; slurring and contractions are
avoided, and tactical features like disjuncture, stress, and intonation are carefully observed. The general pattern of organization avoids backtracking, sec-
ond-thought interpolation, and repetition in varied terms, all of which are

characteristic of conversation. The result is to place a much heavier burden of thought and planning upon the formal speaker or writer....

The formal style is thus the typical style of responsible public writing. By native speakers it is learned relatively late, if at all—usually not until the beginning of schooling and in most cases not until long after that. It has for many, perhaps most, people the qualities of a mode of language that has been learned consciously, as one learns a foreign language, rather than largely unconsciously, as one learns one's mother tongue. The range of competence of its users is greater than that of users of the conversational styles, from the virtuosity of a Churchill to the inept and platitudinous fumblings of a poor after-dinner speaker. Most of the effort in a typical college composition class is concerned with increasing the students' skill in formal style. And rightly so: the central mode of written language for the educated man in our society is formal educated standard English. Ninety-nine people out of a hundred must learn this in school.

What Joos calls **frozen** style is primarily the style of literature, at least in the broad sense of the word. In this sense, literature can be defined as those samples of language which the whole community or a segment of it values to the point of wishing to preserve their exact expression as well as their content. Once the words have been arranged, they are set or frozen into an unchangeable pattern (though the author himself may exercise the privilege of changing them). This definition would not satisfy the literary critic, who usually would like to include an esthetic criterion in his definition. Nor is it a value judgment. Not all literature is good, by any standard of measurement including its use of language. But all literature does have the quality of rigidity of language.

Reading 3

English: Its Origin

Henry Alexander

The following selection explains how English is related to other languages. The passage first gives correlations between common words used in the Germanic family of languages, and then gives even more correlations between these common

From *The Story of Our Language*. Reprinted by permission of the author and publisher. Copyright 1940. Published by Thomas Nelson & Sons, Inc.

words in English and those in the Indo-European family of languages. In your
question, consider the significance of these correlationships. You might also ask and
answer a question about the meaning of the terms cognate *and* Aryan.

One of the far-reaching discoveries of the 19th century was that many languages show important resemblances in their structure, and that these features are to be explained, not by a process of borrowing but by descent from a common ancestor. Languages are like plants or animals, which may differ considerably today but may still exhibit certain characteristics pointing to a common origin or parent stock. By grouping together those which show these similarities we are able to draw up various genera, families and classes. Languages, too, may be divided into families. To indicate a common descent for a group of languages or a group of words we use the term *cognate*. Some idea of the evidence on which these relationships are based may be obtained from the following facts.

Let us make a list of some common terms in several European languages and compare their appearance. We may take the first four numbers and the closest family relationships; many striking resemblances will emerge, which cannot be accidental.

English	*German*	*Dutch*	*Swedish*	*Danish*
one	ein	een	en	een
two	zwei	twee	två	to
	(German *z* = *ts*)			
three	drei	drie	tre	tre
four	vier	vier	fyra	fire
	(German *v* = *f*)			
father ·	vater (*v* = *f*)	vader	fader	fader
mother	mutter	moeder	moder	moder
brother	bruder	broeder	broder	broder
sister	schwester	zuster	syster	soster

... These and other similarities of an equally fundamental nature point to a common ancestry for this group of languages. They are called the Teutonic or Germanic group and are usually divided into three sub-groups, North Teutonic, East Teutonic and West Teutonic. All these are descended from one parent language, which is called Primitive Teutonic. The relationship can best be shown by the following table, which includes only the more important languages.

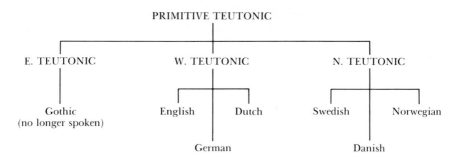

This, however, is not the whole story. If we go a stage further and compare this Teutonic group with non-Teutonic languages, we discover equally remarkable resemblances. Taking some of the words used before, let us compare their forms in English, representing a Teutonic language, with those found in Latin or Greek, which belong to two different branches, the Italic and the Hellenic respectively. We might also include French, which is a modern development from Latin, just as Modern English is from Old English.

English	Latin	French	Greek
one	unus	un	cf. oinos
			one (on dice)
two	duo	deux	duo
three	tres	trois	treis
father	pater	père	pater
mother	mater	mère	meter
brother	frater	frère	phrater

The resemblances are not so close as before, but they are too great to be merely accidental. A similar comparison with other languages, such as the Celtic group, would reveal more features in common. As a result of this evidence we can now draw up a more complete table to show the relationship between these larger linguistic units, the Teutonic, Italic, Hellenic, Celtic and other groups. There are altogether nine of these, and they include most of the European and some of the Indian languages. For this reason they are often called the Indo-European family of languages. Another term is the Aryan family. Aryan is thus not a racial but a linguistic label. The people who speak the Aryan or Indo-European languages are not a racial unit; they include, and no doubt always included, many varied stocks. It is difficult to say when or where the parent language from which these groups are descended—primitive Aryan or Indo-European—was originally spoken, except that it was some time before 2000 B.C., possibly 3000 or 4000 B.C. Scholars formerly thought that the original home of this ancestral tongue was somewhere in Asia, but the modern view is that it was more probably in Northern or Central Europe.

The accompanying diagram shows the relationship of English to the Indo-European family. Again, only the more important languages and groups have been included—the table is considerably reduced and simplified; only six of the nine (or eleven) branches are shown.

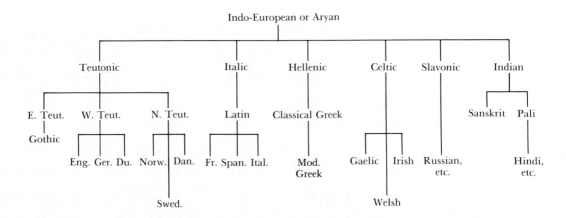

A glance at this genealogical table will show that the nearest relatives of English are German and Dutch; the Scandinavian languages are also very close, in some respects actually closer. Rather more distant are Greek and Latin (with its modern descendants French, Spanish and Italian) and the Celtic languages, including the language of the ancient Britons, and modern Celtic forms of speech, such as the Gaelic still spoken in the Highlands of Scotland and in parts of Canada, especially Nova Scotia, the recently revived Irish language of Eire, and the Cymric of Wales.

Extra Discussion and Writing

Letters

1. Write a letter to a member of your family who is still in your native country about the kinds of problems you are having with English pronunciation because of the differences between English and your language. Consider the sounds and the way they are put together to form the "music" of the language. Tell how English sounds to you.
2. Write a letter to one of your teachers in your native country. Tell about the difficulties you are having writing college compositions in English.

Among others, consider such differences between your language and English as: the length and structure of sentences; the required style for organizing and developing ideas.

Note: The kind of informative writing stressed in college English classes requires clarity and conciseness. In other words, what is required is plain English that goes straight to the point, without sentimental adornment or poetic expressions. For the same kind of informative writing, other languages may place greater value on eloquence or a well-turned phrase. They may allow more use of digressions (getting off the point) or indirectness (going around the point). They may not require as many transitional expressions as English does to make the connections between points.

Report to the Class

In every language there are some differences between the informal and the formal styles of the language. Here is a list of such differences in English. Some of the characteristics of these styles have already been given in the article on pp. 36–39 that deals with five styles of language.

Write a report for your classmates discussing the difference between the informal style and the formal style *in your language.* Include vocabulary, grammar, and writing. Give examples.

Informal Style	*Formal Style*
Purpose: A conversational exchange (including friendly letters)	*Purpose:* The serious communication of information (lectures, articles and books, newscasting)
Vocabulary	*Vocabulary*
May include some slang and vulgar language	Avoids slang or vulgar language
Uses informal word equivalents.	Uses more "book" words, especially of Latin origin
Words not always carefully used	Wider range of vocabulary— words carefully chosen for their exact meaning
Grammar	*Grammar*
May omit some structure words.	Keeps most of the structure words
Sentences may be strung together loosely, often with *and, so.*	Uses longer sentences
	Uses complex sentence structure.

Writing (for informal letters)
Uses contractions
Uses the dash as an all-purpose
   punctuation mark
Ideas are presented freely, as in
   the flow of speech

Writing
Avoids contractions
Careful punctuation
Careful organization and
   control of ideas

Reactions

Reading 1

France Gets Tough with "Le Hot Dog"

Increasing numbers of English words are creeping into many other languages as the influence of American culture spreads. The following article discusses the strong efforts of the French government to keep the French language "pure" by prohibiting the use of Franglais. Do you think it's possible for a government to stop the spread of foreign words?

Are English words appearing in your language, and if so, in what areas of life—food, entertainment, technology, business, transportation? Give some examples. Is your government trying to stop the importation of such words?

Hopeful French actors may be dismayed to learn that they will no longer be able to turn up at "le casting" in search of a job.

That word and 126 other popular English expressions used in cinema, television and advertising were banned last week by Georges Fillioud, Communications Minister, in the latest stage of France's perennial war on "Franglais."

Within six months of official publication of a list of 127 French replacement terms, public establishments, but not newspapers and magazines, will face legal action if they use such words as "drive-in cinema" instead of "ciné-parc" or "casting" instead of "distribution artistique."

An official of France's High Committee for the French Language, a Government body, said such legal action could include fines of up to 50 francs ($7) for each banned word, multiplied by the number of times it is used, or such sanctions as state intervention to keep a product off the market if its user instructions include forbidden terms.

Other words on the list of Franglais undesirables include "le flashback," "pay TV" (now "télévision à péage"), "mailing" ("publipostage") and "jingle" ("sonal").

Protecting the French language has been a Government priority since former President Valery Giscard d'Estaing began a crusade against foreign intruders several years ago. But some commentators have questioned the wisdom of trying to legislate language in a country where "le hot dog" is a standard menu item and "le jogging" is fast becoming a national sport.

The use of "Franglais" first became punishable by law in 1977, when the Government decided to make pure French compulsory in advertising guarantees and in instructions for the use of machines, bills and receipts.

The following year, British Airways became the first big company to fall afoul of the law. The airline was fined 80 francs, a symbolic gesture, for selling tickets for international flights printed only in English.

Perhaps the most bizarre case, however, was in 1980, when the Government sued France's state-owned Seita tobacco company for marketing a new brand of cigarettes called "News."

Even the military has seen fit to join the war on words, banning such common terms in French as "le jet" (now "l'avion à réaction") and "le blackout" ("le silence radio").

While the Government has insisted that the language law aimed to protect the consumer from possible confusion, it has caused many a befuddled French shopper looking vainly for "le discount" to wonder whether this was really "le fair play."

Reading 2

The Fumblerules of Grammar

The following humorous piece by William Safire appeared in The New York Times *Magazine section on November 4, 1979, in the column "On Language." Each rule commits the exact fault it tells the reader to avoid; this is the reason for the use of the invented word "fumblerule," fumble being an attempt to grab hold of something but missing it.*

Do you know many of these rules? Most are observed by serious writers, but a few, although they may be taught to schoolchildren, are unrealistic and are often not observed even by educated speakers.

Get together in groups to see how many of these "fumblerules" you can correct. What strict rules about the use of your language have you been taught?

Not long ago, I advertised for perverse rules of grammar, along the lines of "Remember to never split an infinitive" and "The passive voice should never be used." The notion of making a mistake while laying down rules ("Thimk," "We Never Make Misteaks") is highly unoriginal, and it turns out that English teachers have been circulating lists of fumblerules for years.

As owner of the world's largest collection, and with thanks to scores of readers, let me pass along a bunch of these never-say-neverisms:

- Avoid run-on sentences they are hard to read.
- Don't use no double negatives.
- Use the semicolon properly, always use it where it is appropriate; and never where it isn't.
- Reserve the apostrophe for it's proper use and omit it when its not needed.
- Do not put statements in the negative form.
- Verbs has to agree with their subjects.
- No sentence fragments.
- Proofread carefully to see if you any words out.
- Avoid commas, that are not necessary.
- If you reread your work, you will find on rereading that a great deal of repetition can be avoided by rereading and editing.
- A writer must not shift your point of view.
- Eschew dialect, irregardless.
- And don't start a sentence with a conjunction.
- Don't overuse exclamation marks!!!
- Place pronouns as close as possible, especially in long sentences, as of 10 or more words, to their antecedents.
- Hyphenate between syllables and avoid un-necessary hyphens.
- Write all adverbial forms correct.
- Don't use contractions in formal writing.
- Writing carefully, dangling participles must be avoided.
- It is incumbent on us to avoid archaisms.
- If any word is improper at the end of a sentence, a linking verb is.
- Steer clear of incorrect forms of verbs that have snuck in the language.
- Take the bull by the hand and avoid mixed metaphors.
- Avoid trendy locutions that sound flaky.
- Never, ever use repetitive redundancies.
- Everyone should be careful to use a singular pronoun with singular nouns in their writing.

- If I've told you once, I've told you a thousand times, resist hyperbole.
- Also, avoid awkward or affected alliteration.
- Don't string too many prepositional phrases together unless you are walking through the valley of the shadow of death.
- Always pick on the correct idiom.
- "Avoid overuse of 'quotation "marks."'"
- The adverb always follows the verb.
- Last but not least, avoid clichés like the plague; seek viable alternatives.

Reading 3

Table of Alphabets

The table on pages 48–49 from the American Heritage Dictionary *gives the Hebrew, Arabic, Greek, and Russian alphabets. All of these alphabets have been derived from the same source and therefore show some similarities.*

Alphabetic writing is the most recently developed writing system. In the oldest writing systems that are known, one symbol stands for a whole word; *each symbol, or character, represents a picture or an idea (as it still does in Chinese). In another stage of writing, called syllabary writing, each symbol represents a syllable consisting of a* consonant plus a vowel sound *(as it still does in Japanese). In a final development, each symbol, or letter in an alphabet, represents a* single sound.

It is believed that our Western alphabets originated from a syllabary used by Semitic traders from ancient Phoenicia (now Lebanon). These traders took their language with them throughout the Mediterranean. The Greeks adopted the Phoenicians' syllabary system but added separate symbols for vowel sounds. The Russians derived their alphabet directly from the Greek alphabet. Most other European languages based their alphabets on the Roman alphabet, which was also modified from the Greek alphabet.

Get together in groups to discuss the alphabets in the table. Discuss especially the similarities and differences between the Greek and the Russian alphabets. Make a comparison also of the Hebrew and Arabic languages, both of which are in the Semitic family.

Next, if your language does not have an alphabet, explain to the group how words are arranged in your dictionary.

TABLE OF ALPHABETS

The transliterations shown are those used in the etymologies of this Dictionary.

Arabic

The different forms in the four numbered columns are used when the letters are (1) in isolation; (2) in juncture with a previous letter; (3) in juncture with the letters on both sides; (4) in juncture with a following letter.

Long vowels are represented by the consonant signs 'alif (for ā), wāw (for ū), and yā (for ī). Short vowels are not usually written.

Transliterations with subscript dots represent "emphatic" or pharyngeal consonants, which are pronounced in the usual way except that the pharynx is tightly narrowed during articulation.

Hebrew

Vowels are not represented in normal Hebrew writing, but for educational purposes they are indicated by a system of subscript and superscript dots.

The transliterations shown in parentheses apply when the letter falls at the end of a word. The transliterations with subscript dots are pharyngeal consonants, as in Arabic.

The second forms shown are used when the letter falls at the end of a word.

Greek

The superscript ' on an initial vowel or rhō, called the "rough breathing," represents an aspirate. Lack of aspiration on an initial vowel is indicated by the superscript ', called the "smooth breathing."

When gamma precedes kappa, xi, khi, or another gamma, it has the value n and is so transliterated. The second lower-case form of sigma is used only in final position.

Russian

[1] This letter, called tvordiĭ znak, "hard sign," is very rare in modern Russian. It indicates that the previous consonant remains hard even though followed by a front vowel.

[2] This letter, called myakiĭ znak, "soft sign," indicates that the previous consonant is palatalized even when a front vowel does not follow.

Forms 1	2	3	4	Name	Sound
ا	ا			'alif	'
ب	ب	ـبـ	بـ	bā	b
ت	ت	ـتـ	تـ	tā	t
ث	ث	ـثـ	ثـ	thā	th
ج	ج	ـجـ	جـ	jim	j
ح	ح	ـحـ	حـ	ḥā	ḥ
خ	خ	ـخـ	خـ	khā	kh
د	د			dāl	d
ذ	ذ			dhāl	dh
ر	ر			rā	r
ز	ز			zāy	z
س	س	ـسـ	سـ	sin	s
ش	ش	ـشـ	شـ	shin	sh
ص	ص	ـصـ	صـ	ṣād	ṣ
ض	ض	ـضـ	ضـ	ḍād	ḍ
ط	ط	ـطـ	طـ	ṭā	ṭ
ظ	ظ	ـظـ	ظـ	ẓā	ẓ
ع	ع	ـعـ	عـ	'ayn	'
غ	غ	ـغـ	غـ	ghayn	gh
ف	ف	ـفـ	فـ	fā	f
ق	ق	ـقـ	قـ	qāf	q
ك	ك	ـكـ	كـ	kāf	k
ل	ل	ـلـ	لـ	lām	l
م	م	ـمـ	مـ	mim	m
ن	ن	ـنـ	نـ	nūn	n
ه	ه	ـهـ	هـ	hā	h
و	و			wāw	w
ى	ى	ـيـ	يـ	yā	y

HEBREW			GREEK			RUSSIAN	
Forms	**Name**	**Sound**	**Forms**	**Name**	**Sound**	**Forms**	**Sound**
א	'aleph		Α α	alpha	a.	А а	a
ב	bēth	b (bh)	Β β	beta	b	Б б	b
ג	gimel	g (gh)	Γ γ	gamma	g (n)	В в	v
ד	dāleth	d (dh)	Δ δ	delta	d	Г г	g
ה	hē	h	Ε ε	epsilon	e	Д д	d
ו	waw	w	Ζ ζ	zēta	z	Е е	e
ז	zayin	z	Η η	ēta	ē	Ж ж	zh
ח	ḥeth	ḥ	Θ θ	thēta	th	З з	z
ט	ṭeth	ṭ	Ι ι	iota	i	И и Й й	i, ĭ
י	yodh	y	Κ κ	kappa	k	К к	k
כ ך	kāph	k (kh)	Λ λ	lambda	l	Л л	l
ל	lāmedh	l	Μ μ	mu	m	М м	m
מ ם	mēm	m	Ν ν	nu	n	Н н	n
נ ן	nūn	n	Ξ ξ	xi	x	О о	o
ס	samekh	s	Ο ο	omicron	o	П п	p
ע	'ayin		Π π	pi	p	Р р	r
פ ף	pē	p (ph)	Ρ ρ	rhō	r (rh)	С с	s
צ ץ	ṣadhe	ṣ	Σ σ ς	sigma	s	Т т	t
ק	qōph	q	Τ τ	tau	t	У у	u
ר	rēsh	r	Υ υ	upsilon	u	Ф ф	f
שׂ	sin	s	Φ φ	phi	ph	Х х	kh
שׁ	shin	sh	Χ χ	chi / khi	kh	Ц ц	ts
ת	tāw	t (th)	Ψ ψ	psi	ps	Ч ч	ch
			Ω ω	ōmega	ō	Ш ш	sh
						Щ щ	shch
						Ъ ъ	''1
						Ы ы	y
						Ь ь	'2
						Э э	e
						Ю ю	yu
						Я я	ya

Reading 4

Doonesbury

Garry Trudeau

The "Doonesbury" cartoons appear in hundreds of newspapers throughout the country. By satirizing American politics and culture, they make a strong appeal to politicians in Washington and to students on college campuses.

> *The following "Doonesbury" cartoon, published in 1974, makes a satiric comment on the language used by American youth of the 1960s and early 1970s. Discuss with your classmates the language used in the cartoon—the amount of verbal communication that is taking place, the slang and hesitation expressions. What is the cartoonist implying about the quality of verbal communication?*
>
> *Discuss the kinds of hesitation expressions you have in your language.*

DOONESBURY   **by Garry Trudeau**

DOONESBURY. Copyright 1974 G. B. Trudeau. Reprinted with permission of Universal Press Syndicate. All rights reserved.

CHAPTER 3

Education

Composition

Requirements for a Home Composition

---

1. Use white $8\frac{1}{2}'' \times 11''$ paper; write on one side only.
2. Type your composition double spaced on unlined paper (if hand-written, the paper should be clearly written on every other line). A typewritten page, double-spaced, is about 250 words.
3. Indent each paragraph, use wide margins ($1''$ to $1\frac{1}{4}''$), and number each page in the upper right-hand corner.
4. Include a separate page with the title, the thesis sentence, and the outline.

Procedures for Discussion

The teacher puts this heading on the board:

What I Expect to Get from My College Education

The teacher then asks students to give their expectations. These are listed on the board in phrases, in the random order that students give them.

At the end of the discussion, the teacher asks how the points on the board may be organized under broader headings.

Writing the Composition

Answer the following essay question. (The composition may be assigned to be written at home or at the next class meeting.) Read the question carefully and underline the important parts that indicate what the question is actually looking for. Notice how many parts need to be answered.

> *Question:* Some reasons given for why students want to go to college are: preparation for a professional career, cultural stimulation, service to others, self-improvement. What do *you* hope to get from your college education? State your reasons clearly and give examples of kinds of courses that would help you realize your objectives.

Suggestions for the Content and Organization

Whether you write your answer to this essay question at home or in class, consider the following advice:

Decide how you will organize your points under the larger classifications. Can you find an even broader classification under which all your points can go?

Discuss only what is most important for *you* (this composition is about *your* expectations). Your broadest classification can provide your thesis or point of view.

If you write the composition in class, you may not have time to write a formal outline. Your composition should be of a reasonable length, determined by the amount of time of your class meeting rather than by the number of words. Write from notes that have some kind of organizational structure, and that indicate how you will handle the introduction and the conclusion.

Write carefully, since you may not be able to rewrite the paper. Time yourself so that you can write about each point listed in your notes and still have time at the end to look over your paper.

Guide for the Outline and the Composition

If you write the composition at home, or if you rewrite the class composition, the following guide should help you.

On the left side of the guide is the outline with suggestions for handling the introduction, transitions, and the conclusion of this composition. On the right side are general comments about how introductions, transitions, and conclusions may be written. (If you are accustomed to writing a first draft from rough notes, use this guide for your second and succeeding drafts.)

Outline

Title

General Comments

Use initial capital letters for all words except articles, short prepositions, and short conjunctions. Try to use an interesting title that reflects your thesis.

Introduction

This can be personal—earlier expectations of your own or your family's.

Or it can be general—expectations of anyone going to college.

Or it can be even more general—the value of a college education or the natural desire to learn.

Purpose of the introduction:
to catch the reader's interest
to give a general idea of the subject
An introduction may include:
a quotation
a story, perhaps personal
a rhetorical question (which you will answer)
a definition
a statement of a belief you will argue against
a surprising or shocking fact
a statement of a serious problem

Transitional lead-in

This gives the broad expectations of college education that you will discuss.

Usually at the end of the introduction. Gives an indication of the central idea and the way it will be developed (may be in the form of a question).

I. First main point

This gives the first specific expectation from your college education.

  A. First supporting detail

  B. Second supporting detail
      etc.

New paragraph. The first sentence:
(1) mentions the general idea of the paragraph (from the important word[s] in the outline; (2) relates this sentence to what was said before.

Should be related to the preceding subpoint.

(Continue with your other main points and their supporting details.)

For each main point, remind the reader that you are giving another argument about whether a married woman with preschool children should go to work.

(Follow the suggestions given for the first main point.)

Note: Long subpoints may begin new paragraphs.

Conclusion

You can go back to individual experiences or you can be more general.

You may suggest a compromise.

The conclusion should round out the composition in a strong and satisfying way, perhaps by referring again to whatever you used to introduce the composition.

Notes: (1) The conclusion should not add any new ideas that need further development. (2) If your last point ends on a strong note that points up your thesis, you may not need to add a conclusion.

Support for the points you make can come from your own beliefs and experience or from the readings in this chapter and elsewhere. (Be sure to identify your sources and to use quotation marks around the exact words of an author.) The support can be in the form of examples, current facts and figures, or authoritative opinion. Use enough support to make your point convincing to the reader.

Finally, keep in mind that this composition represents your own opinions. By stating them honestly and strongly, you will have a composition that the reader will find interesting enough to continue reading.

Revising the Composition

In succeeding drafts, try to sharpen your thesis and show more clearly how each main point contributes to the development of the thesis. Try writing down the opening sentence of your paragraphs on a separate sheet of paper to see if they make a clear sentence outline. Go over the reading selections again for further ideas or additional support.

Consult the Revision and Editing Checklist for guidance on organization, paragraphing, and sentences. You can get needed vocabulary help in the vocabulary section that follows on pp. 55–56. Make a final check with the Symbol Chart for Correction of Compositions for the grammatical structures and usage in your composition.

Evaluation

If there is an exchange of student compositions, the Revision and Editing Checklist can serve as a guide in the evaluation of another student's composition. Use the following procedure in checking for the writer's organization and development of ideas.

1. Without looking at the other student's outline page, make an outline and a one-sentence summary of the central idea (or thesis) of the whole paper. Can you find a clear line of development? Do your summary sentence and your outline agree with those of the writer?
2. Find the support for each point made in the writer's paper. Is the support adequate and convincing?
3. Write on the student's paper what you consider the good points of the composition and what needs to be improved.

Vocabulary and Usage

Vocabulary
Usage Notes
Word Forms

Vocabulary

The following words may be useful to you in talking and writing about the composition on college education.

School Offerings

college   Usually, a four-year undergraduate liberal arts school. It is often part of a university, which consists of many schools, mostly graduate, that prepare students for professions such as law, medicine, or business. Sometimes the word *college* is also used for such professional graduate schools within a university (Teachers College, College of Dentistry).

course   A subject in a school that offers a certain number of credits. In most colleges, a course carries from 2 to 4 credits. Usually, 120 to 128 credits are required for an undergraduate degree.

general education   The program of courses that are not specialized and that prepare a student for general personal growth, rather than for a specific career. The program includes the liberal arts.

liberal arts   Includes such general education courses as literature, history, languages, mathematics, the fine arts, social sciences, and the natural sciences.

humanities   Includes all the liberal arts courses except the sciences.

curriculum   The total number of courses of study.

extracurricular   Referring to school activities that are not part of the regular course of study (the curriculum).

prescribed courses   Courses that are required in order to satisfy the requirements for graduation from a school.

electives   Courses that may be chosen freely.

prerequisite   A course of study that is required before a student can take another course of study.

matriculate   To satisfy all the requirements needed to enter a college or university.

Educational Goals

objectives   Goals.

objective (adjective)   Judging fairly, without prejudice; tolerant; open-minded. Opposed to *subjective*—allowing one's personal feelings to influence one's judgment.

critical thinking   Ability to solve problems, to make wise decisions, to distinguish fact from opinion, to examine objectively and clearly.

socialization   Adjusting to the rules of one's society.

potential (noun)   An inborn ability that may or may not be realized.

self-realization, self-fulfillment   The state of realizing one's potential.

morality   An inner sense of what is right or wrong.

ethics   Standards of right or wrong behavior. Certain fields may have their own code of ethics—for example, business or medicine.

insight   Intuitive understanding.

awareness   Understanding of oneself or one's surroundings.

information   Facts learned from reading or observation.

knowledge   Understanding that comes from an examination of facts.

wisdom   Good judgment that is based on one's knowledge.

Other Vocabulary

fraternity   An organization for men students in college. Members often live together in the same house.

sorority   An organization for women students in college. Members often live together in the same house.

parochial school   A school run by a religious institution.

Usage Notes

Do not add the plural ending *-s* to noncountable words. Use a singular verb.

> society (as an abstract idea)
> information
> knowledge
> vocabulary
> homework (but assignments)

Such words are used without *the* unless there is following modification.

> *the* society *we live in*
> *the* information *I need*

Do not use *the* after *go to* (a school)

> go to ⎧ school
> ⎨ elementary school
> ⎬ high school
> ⎩ college
>
> *but*
>
> go to *the university*

Use *the* with the name of a university only if the name is in an *of* phrase.

> *the* University *of Pennsylvania*
> *but*
> New York University

Use a small letter for names of subjects

> physics, sociology, chemistry

But use a capital letter if the word is the name of an actual course: Physics I, Chemistry II.

Word Forms

Use the correct word forms for the words in parentheses.

The Answers are on p. 354. If you need help with this exercise, refer to the explanations under Word Forms in Appendix A.

1. The goal of education is to eliminate (illiterate) _illiteracy_ : and to transmit our cultural (inherit) _inheritance_ .

2. In the United States, education is not (central) _centralized_ . Public schools are (regulate) _regulated_ by the state government, but the schools are (operate) _operated_ by the local governments.

3. General (culture) _cultural_ subjects are often (call) _called_ (human) _humanities_ .

4. (Universe) _Universal_ (compel) _compulsory_ education means that all children must attend school up to a certain age.

5. To (doctrine) _____ students means to teach them to accept certain beliefs without (question) _questioning_ these beliefs.

6. (Element) _elementary_ school is also called (prime) _primary_ . school; high school is also called (secondary) _secondary_ school.

7. In (vocation) _vocational_ schools, students prepare themselves to work in various trades or (occupy) _occupation_ .

8. In (progress) _progress_ education, children are (suppose) _suppose_ to learn by (do) _doing_ , not only by (read) _reading_ .

9. In college, students must take the (require) _required_ subjects before they can take the (elective) _elective_ . ones; that is, those that are (option) _optional_ .

10. Students have a (choose) _choice_ of fields they may (special) _specialized_ in.

11. College provides a very (stimulate) _stimulating_ experience. It allows us to study a field we are (interest) _interested_ in, both in (deep) _depth_ and (broad) _breath_ .

12. Critical thinking helps us to find (solve) _solution_ to problems, to make wise (decide) _decisions_ , and to think (object) _objectively_ .

13. (Adjust) _Adjustment_ to one's society is one of the (object) _objective_ of education.

14. Cultural (stimulate) _stimulation_ and intellectual (grow) _grows_ are other goals of education.

15. A student (prepare) _____ to enter a good college must work

hard in (second) _Secondary_ school.

Reading for Summary Writing

For the following three reading selections, prepare a brief outline for class discussion before you write the summary. After the class discussion of each reading selection, you will write:

1. A longer, revised outline of the reading selection, using an alternation of numbers and letters.
2. A one-sentence summary of the reading selection. The sentence should include the central idea and the main points used to develop this idea (from the outline).
3. A summary of the reading selection. The length of the summary will be indicated in the text. This assigned length will determine and amount of detail that can be included in your outline and summary.

Guidelines for Writing (Review)

1. For the outline, use the alternative number-letter system for the main points and their subpoints. The underlined phrases in the opening sentences of paragraphs usually become the main points on the outline.
2. For both summary and outline, follow the same order as the reading selection. If you wish, you may begin the summary with a reference to the source of the selection (author, publication, etc.) and to its central idea.
3. Keep a sense of proportion. Write more about points the author devotes more attention to.
4. Concentrate more on the main points than on examples or other supporting details.
5. Use proper transitions between the main points and the subpoints of your summary; your summary must have an organization of its own.
6. Use your own words as much as possible, except for key phrases. You may quote important phrases or sentences.
7. Be careful not to overload any of the sentences with so much information that the sentence is hard to read.
8. Be consistent in your use of verb tenses. Use all present tense (the author states, feels) or all past tense (the author stated, felt). The present tense is more common in a summary.
9. Do not include your own ideas or your own attitude or interpretation. The summary should be an objective restatement of what the author has said.

Reading 1

Schooling and the New Illiteracy

Christopher Lasch

The author of the following selection, a professor of history at the University of Rochester, has written many books on American history, culture, and politics. In this selection, he deplores the decline of academic standards in higher education in the United States.

Length of summary: Approximately 300 words

Recent developments in higher education have progressively diluted its content and reproduced, at a higher level, the conditions that prevail in the public schools. The collapse of general education; the abolition of any serious effort to instruct students in foreign languages; the introduction of many programs in black studies, women's studies, and other forms of consciousness raising for no other purpose than to head off political discontent; the ubiquitous inflation of grades—all have lowered the value of a university education at the same time that rising tuitions place it beyond reach of all but the affluent....

What precipitated the crisis of the sixties was not simply the pressure of unprecedented numbers of students (many of whom would gladly have spent their youth elsewhere) but a fatal conjuncture of historical changes: the emergence of a new social conscience among students activated by the moral rhetoric of the New Frontier and by the civil rights movement, and the simultaneous collapse of the university's claims to moral and intellectual legitimacy. Instead of offering a rounded program of humane learning, the university now frankly served as a cafeteria from which students had to select so many "credits." Instead of diffusing peace and enlightenment, it allied itself with the war machine. Eventually, even its claim to provide better jobs became suspect....

At the same time, the student movement embodied a militant anti-intellectualism of its own, which corrupted and eventually absorbed it. Demand for the abolition of grades, although defended on grounds of high pedagogical principle, turned out in practice—as revealed by experiments with ungraded courses and pass-fail options—to reflect a desire for less work and a wish to avoid judgment on its quality. The demand for more "relevant" courses often boiled down to a desire for an intellectually undemanding curriculum, in which students could win academic credits for political activism, self-expression, transcendental meditation, encounter therapy, and the study and practice of witchcraft. Even when seriously advanced in opposition to sterile academic pedantry, the slogan of relevance embodied an underlying antagonism to education itself—an inability to take an interest in anything beyond immediate experience....

In the seventies, the most common criticism of higher education revolves around the charge of cultural elitism.... Two contributors to a Carnegie Commission report on education condemn the idea that "there are certain works that should be familiar to all educated men" as inherently an "elitist notion."... The Carnegie Commission contributors argue that since the United States is a pluralist society, "adherence exclusively to the doctrines of any one school...would cause higher education to be in great dissonance with society."

Given the prevalence of these attitudes among teachers and educators, it is not surprising that students at all levels of the educational system have so little knowledge of the classics of world literature.... At a high school "without walls" in New Orleans, students can receive English credits for working as a disc jockey at a radio station and reading *How to Become a Radio Disc Jockey* and *Radio Programming in Action*. In San Marino, California, the high school English department increased its enrollments by offering electives in "Great American Love Stories," "Myths and Folklore," "Science Fiction," and "The Human Condition."

Those who teach college today see at first hand the effect of these practices, not merely in the students' reduced ability to read and write but in the diminished store of their knowledge about the cultural traditions they are supposed to inherit. With the collapse of religion, biblical references, which formerly penetrated deep into everyday awareness, have become incomprehensible, and the same thing is now happening to the literature and mythology of antiquity—indeed, to the entire literary tradition of the West, which has always drawn so heavily on biblical and classical sources. In the space of two or three generations, enormous stretches of the "Judaeo-Christian tradition," so often invoked by educators but so seldom taught in any form, have passed into oblivion. The effective loss of cultural traditions on such a scale makes talk of a new Dark Age far from frivolous. Yet this loss coincides with an information glut, with the recovery of the past by specialists, and with an unprecedented explosion of knowledge—none of which, however, impinges on everyday experience or shapes popular culture.

The resulting split between general knowledge and the specialized knowledge of the experts, embedded in obscure journals and written in language or mathematical symbols unintelligible to the layman, has given rise to a growing body of criticism and exhortation. The ideal of general education in the university, however, has suffered the same fate as basic education in the lower schools. Even those college teachers who praise general education in theory find that its practice drains energy from their specialized research and thus interferes with academic advancement. Administrators have little use for general education, since it does not attract foundation grants and large-scale government support. Students object to the reintroduction of requirements in general education because the work demands too much of them and seldom leads to lucrative employment.

Under these conditions, the university remains a diffuse, shapeless, and permissive institution that has absorbed the major currents of cultural modernism and reduced them to a watery blend, a mind-emptying ideology of cultural revolution, personal fulfillment, and creative alienation. Donald Barthelme's parody of higher learning in *Snow White*—like all parody in an age of absurdities—so closely resembles reality as to become unrecognizable as parody.

Beaver College is where she got her education. She studied *Modern Woman, Her Privileges and Responsibilities:* the nature and nurture of women and what they stand for, in evolution and in history, including householding, upbringing, peacekeeping, healing and devotion, and how these contribute to the rehumanizing of today's world. Then she studied *Classical Guitar I*, utilizing the methods and techniques of Sor, Tarrega, Segovia, etc. Then she studied *English Romantic Poets II:* Shelley, Byron, Keats. Then she studied *Theoretical Foundations of Psychology:* mind, consciousness, unconscious mind, personality, the self, interpersonal relations, psychosexual norms, social games, groups, adjustment, conflict, authority, individuation, integration and mental health. Then she studied *Oil Painting I* bringing to the first class as instructed Cadmium Yellow Light, Cadmium Yellow Medium, Cadmium Red Light, Alizarin Crimson, Ultramarine Blue, Cobalt Blue, Viridian, Ivory Black, Raw Umber, Yellow Ochre, Burnt Sienna, White. Then she studied *Personal Resources I and II:* self-evaluation, developing the courage to respond to the environment, opening and using the mind, individual experience, training, the use of time, mature redefinition of goals, action projects. Then she studied *Realism and Idealism in the Contemporary Italian Novel:* Palazzeschi, Brancati, Bilenchi, Pratolini, Moravia, Pavese, Levi, Silone, Berto, Cassola, Ginzburg, Malaparte, Calvino, Gadda, Bassani, Landolfi. Then she studied—

...A latter-day Madame Bovary, Snow White is a typical victim of mass culture, the culture of commodities and consumerism with its suggestive message that experiences formerly reserved for those of high birth, deep understanding, or much practical acquaintance of life can be enjoyed by all without effort, on purchase of the appropriate commodity. Snow White's education is itself a commodity, the consumption of which promises to "fulfill her creative potential," in the jargon of pseudo-emancipation....

Snow White's instructors assume that higher learning ideally includes everything, assimilates all of life. And it is true that no aspect of contemporary thought has proved immune to educationalization. The university has boiled all experience down into "courses" of study—a culinary image appropriate to the underlying ideal of enlightened consumption.

Discussion

1. What are some developments in higher education that the author believes have lowered the quality of education today?
2. The author claims that, beginning in the 1960s, the university changed. "Instead of offering a rounded program of humane learning, the university now frankly served as a cafeteria from which students had to select so many 'credits'." How does the author again pick up the idea of the university as a "cafeteria" in which students pick and choose courses without any guidance?
3. According to the author, what demands did the students make of the university in the sixties because of their anti-intellectualism? What does the author say was actually behind these demands?
4. What are the fields of study that the author feels should be taught in the university as part of general education? Do you agree?
5. Why is the author pessimistic about the re-establishment of general education programs in the university?
6. Comment on the author's tone and attitude in this selection. What do you think of the way the selection ends?

Reading 2

Campus Mood: The Focus Is on Grades

Edward B. Fiske

The purpose of the following article was to point out the change in student attitudes from the period of the late 1960s and early 1970s to just a few years later, in the late 1970s. Note the technique used in the introduction to catch the attention of the reader.

Length of summary: Approximately 250 words

Shortly before noon one day recently, 18 members of the Spartacus Youth League gathered near the sundial at Columbia University and, chanting slogans and carrying placards, began marching in a circle to protest a visit to the campus by recruiters from the National Security Agency.

About 100 yards away a larger group of students, apparently oblivious to the demonstration, gathered quietly in a line to await the noon opening of the new student-run cooperative grocery store.

The relative size of the two groups suggested much about the interests and priorities of the current generation of students of campuses throughout the metropolitan area.

In contrast to the 1960's—when student activities such as Mark Rudd at Columbia were drawing large numbers of students to antiwar demonstrations and leading takeovers of campus buildings—students now show little outward interest in social and political issues.

Libraries and study areas are populated into the early hours of the morning, and the main priority on most students' minds would seem to be what the Columbia College dean of students, Henry S. Coleman, termed "the almighty grade point average."

The 'Silent Generation'

The common wisdom is that the pendulum of campus life has swung back to where it was in the 1950's, when writers spoke of the pervasive apathy of the "silent generation." In fact, interviews by The New York Times at a dozen local colleges and universities suggest that the situation is not quite that simple. If there is a new "silent generation" today, it is one whose character has been profoundly shaped by the turbulence of the intervening decade.

Though outwardly inactive, students who grew up watching a war on their living-room television sets seem to be far better informed about current issues and injustices in the world than their predecessors of two decades ago.

"It's just that we're much more cynical about our ability to change things," said Gary Cohen, a senior at Columbia. "With all of the political protest of the 1960's, very little happened."

The economic situation means that even relatively affluent students must now help support themselves, and the intense competition for jobs and places in graduate schools has put pressures on present-day students that were unknown in the 1950's.

"Most of them are so weighted down by the academic challenges they face that they don't seem to enjoy college," said Howard Crosty, dean of students at Rutgers. "I don't think today's students have enough fun."

Generalizations about the mood of an entire campus—much less that of an entire college generation—are always dangerous, but the themes of declining political activism and increased academic seriousness run through interviews on all of the campuses surveyed.

The Kent State Issue

At Rutgers, for example, only 200 students showed up for a recent appearance, sponsored by the student government, of one of the students wounded by National Guardsmen at Kent State in 1970, and a group of students at Barnard College recently abandoned plans for a rally in favor of elective abortion. "We were afraid that no one would show up," said Joan Storey, one of those involved.

Polls indicate that students are informed about issues such as the racial situation in South Africa, but many did not know who Mark Rudd was when he recently surrendered to the police after years of hiding. And efforts to encourage divestiture by the colleges of stocks in companies doing business in South Africa will often draw considerable support.

By and large, though, the issues that inspire student action are local. Students at Queens College, for example, have organized lobbying efforts in behalf of low tuition and increased legislative support for the City University, and a one-day boycott of the food service at Columbia last spring to protest its quality was 95 percent effective. "People are more concerned with what affects them directly," said Howard Leib, a sophomore.

At Cornell a student recently started a campaign of "civil disobedience" urging people to violate parking violations to protest inadequate parking space on the campus. The dome of Sibley Hall now bears the painted inscription "Protest Student Activism."

A search for security seems to dominate much of student life. "There's a trend toward nice safe curriculums," said David Alexander, a law student at the State University Center at Buffalo.

Placement offices have extended their hours, and last spring at New York University more than 500 juniors signed up for workshops on topics such as résumé-writing and interviewing skills. At Rutgers, lines begin forming the night before when such major companies as Bell Telephone announced job interviews.

'A Lesson in Frugality'

"There's a sense of scarcity around," said the Rev. William Starr, Episcopal chaplain at Columbia. "The idea of dropping out and dropping in—taking a year off to do tenant organizing or something—is really gone. At Columbia the children of the middle class are getting a lesson in frugality."

Such attitudes affect social activism. "We circulated a petition on [stock] divestiture, and some students told us they wouldn't sign because they didn't want trouble from the C.I.A.," said Mr. Starr. "Maybe they're right."

Students suggested other factors in the social attitudes of the mid-1970's, including the absence of leaders and the lack of a single overriding issue like the war in Vietnam. "There's so much ambiguity today," said Mari-anne Goldstein, a junior at Barnard. "Everyone was against the war, but on an issue like abortion you can find right and wrong on both sides."

Students on local campuses are clearly part of the turning inward that seems to be evident in society as a whole. The best-seller lists at campus stores invariably include the popular self-help works such as "Your Erroneous Zones."

"The key is finding a place for yourself—answering the question: Where do I go in a huge world?" said Sari Sweden, an 18-year-old student at the State University of New York at Buffalo.

Some see the developing pragmatism as unfortunate. "In turning inward there is a danger people may be becoming more selfish," said Richard Cheshire, vice president for public affairs at Colgate University. Others take a somewhat longer view and suggest that today's students are no different from those of the 1960's.

Kenneth Goodsell, a Columbia sophomore, argued that the antiwar youth of the last decade had a life and death stake in the war's being ended. "The sellout came not in the 70's but in the 60's, when the civil-rights movement gave way to antiwar protests and students began to overlook what was still happening on the domestic front."

Extracurricular activities such as glee clubs and campus radio stations seem to be doing relatively well, though here again some significant changes have taken place.

"College students are more interested in smaller, more specialized groups than in large national movements," said Brian Guillorn, president of the Student Union Polity, which coordinates student activities at Columbia. "I imagine it's because in a smaller group they have more control."

The gymnasium at Columbia, which was the focus of bitter controversy when it was built a decade ago, draws large numbers of students for jogging and intramural sports, and spectator sports are making a big comeback on some campuses.

Escape From Pressure

"People here go nuts over sports," said Rob Gleaner, a student-government official of Rutgers. "The reason is simple—escape from the growing pressures associated with high academic standards and the demands of a tightening job market."

"Escapism" is a word that tends to pop up frequently in discussions with students and faculty members. Science-fiction clubs are thriving at several local colleges. Asked why his own group seems to be doing so well, Richard Lappin, a junior who heads the one at Columbia, replied: "It's entertainment. It fits in with the times."

The consumption of alcohol is clearly on the increase, and it now ranks alongside marijuana and cocaine at the top of student preference. "In private, students use dope, but at public events alcohol is taking over," said Miss Storey at Barnard. The use of hard drugs is said to be rare, and marijuana has taken on a different function than in the past.

"Ten years ago pot smoking was a radical political act," sais Tim Weiner, a Columbia senior. "Now everyone does it, and it's become personalized and depoliticized. If it can be said that there is a cogent reason for smoking pot, it's inward-directedness."

Students at some colleges reported that it was customary now to serve wine at campus gatherings, and that its presence or absence would sometimes determine the attendance level. "Drinking is an occupational hazard of being a student activist," said Ellen Doherty, a student member of the Barnard board of trustees. "I could easily get drunk three or four times a week just going to meetings."

Some universities have become concerned about the level of student drinking. Colgate, for example, recently set up a committee of students, faculty members and administrators to study the question of alcohol abuse on the campus.

College students have always been known for their penchant for beer, and many faculty members believe that, despite some problems, the trends of the last few years have essentially consisted of what some called a healthy "return to normalcy."

Others, though, are disturbed by what they see happening, especially in relation to academic work. For example, Charles R. Decarlo, president of Sarah Lawrence College, expressed fear that education had become a process for earning credentials to the exclusion of any sense of joy in learning for its own sake.

"There's a curious paradox" he said. "Students work hard, but there is a decline in serious intense intellectual focusing. They don't know how to concentrate. They are full of anxiety about getting a job; but there is no motivation that proceeds from within, and when that happens there is a decline is quality. The only goal seems to be to get enough work together—to put some sort of mental act together to go out and get a job."

Discussion

1. How do the two contrasting scenes at the beginning of this article serve to bring out the theme of the article?

2. Where does the writer of this article get much of the information that supports the points he is making about the student attitudes of the late 1970s?

3. Why are the students no longer interested in social and political activism? What are their concerns at the time this article was written? How concerned are you about getting good grades?

4. The author says that students in 1977 do not have enough fun because of their "increased academic seriousness." Have you observed whether this is true about college students today? Are you enjoying college life? Or is your concern for good grades spoiling some of the pleasure you might get from school life?

5. The author mentions the lack of interest in the appearance at Rutgers University of one of the students wounded by National Guardsmen at Kent State University in 1970. After only seven years, this indifference about an event that shook the whole fabric of U.S. campuses seems surprising to the author. (What had happened at Kent State was that, for the first time in U.S. history, students were fired on by a government militia. This event, plus the U.S. bombing of Cambodia during the Vietnam war, caused such a spontaneous outburst of student protest throughout the country that many colleges and universities had to close their doors for the balance of the school year in order to prevent student violence.)

   Is there political activism among the students in your country? What form does this activism take?

6. There is a tendency to put labels on different generations that reflect the essential attitudes of each generation. This article refers to the "silent generation" of the 1950s, when campuses were free of student activism for different causes. Because of a similar lack of student interest in fighting for larger issues and because of a concern only for personal affairs, the period beginning with the late 1970s has been characterized as the "me" generation by a well-known writer. What evidence does the author present that would justify the use of this term? Cite examples given by the author of the only kinds of issues students actively demonstrate for.

7. From what you have seen of the students on your campus, what social or political issues concern them? Are they active in fighting for these issues?

8. How does the author say the students in the late 1970s are escaping from the pressure of "high academic standards and the demands of a tightening job market"? How do the students in your school relax? sports? clubs? drinking? drugs? How concerned are you about getting a good job after graduation?

9. Although the time of writing of this article and that of "The New Illiteracy" is almost the same, 1977 and 1979, there seems to be an important difference of opinion about the academic atmosphere on college campuses. What is this difference?

Reading 3

3-Year Survey Finds College Curriculums in the U.S. in 'Disarray'

Edward B. Fiske

The following article discusses the results of a three-year study made by the Association of American Colleges. The report, called "Integrity in the College Curriculum," criticizes the present state of college programs and offers a list of desirable "experiences" that should be provided by colleges.

The headline (above) and the opening paragraph of this article draw attention to the existence of a serious and troubling problem. By doing so, the author uses one of the techniques intended to catch the attention of the reader. The article also fulfills the requirement of a newspaper story by giving a summary of the main points at the beginning and then developing each point at greater length later on.

Length of summary: Approximately 250 words

American colleges and universities have allowed their curriculums to slip into a state of "disarray" and "incoherence," putting in question the quality of what the country's college students learn, a major higher education organization charged yesterday.

In a 47-page report called "Integrity in the College Curriculum," the Association of American Colleges said that while the institutions seemed confident that a college education should take four years, they were less sure about "its content and purpose."

The association's report reflects mounting national concern about the quality of undergraduate education. It faulted faculty members more interested in scholarly research than in teaching and college administrators who have adopted what it called a "misguided marketplace philosophy" to compete for able students.

'Fads and Fashions Enter'

"It is a supermarket where students are shoppers and professors are merchants of learning," the association said. "Fads and fashions, the demands of popularity and success, enter where wisdom and experience should prevail."

The document, prepared by a panel of 18 educators, called on colleges and universities to change doctoral courses to offer training in teaching as well as in academic content. It also described a nine-point "minimum required curriculum" that it said would prepare both liberal arts and professional students to "live responsibly and joyfully, fulfilling their promise as individual humans and their obligations as democratic citizens."

The model curriculum would require written and spoken literacy, a sense of history, an understanding of numerical data and a "study in depth" of a particular academic field.

The Association of American Colleges, which opened its four-day annual meeting in Washington yesterday, represents 560 public and private research universities, liberal arts colleges and other institutions with an interest in curriculum issues. The new chairman is Bernard Harleston, the president of the City College of New York.

The report was based on a three-year analysis of college curriculums around the country. It is the latest in a series of national reports raising questions about undergraduate education in the country's 3,000 colleges and universities.

In October, T. H. Bell, then Secretary of Education, made public a study sponsored by the National Institute of Education, the research arm of the Federal Department of Education, citing "warning signals" about the quality of higher education.

Another Report a Month Later

A month later the National Endowment for the Humanities released a report charging that American colleges were failing to give students "an adequate education in the culture and civilization of which they are members." The author, William J. Bennett, the chairman of the endowment, last week succeeded Mr. Bell as Secretary of Education.

The wave of reports on undergraduate education comes at a time of national concern over the quality of elementary and secondary schools. In two to three years, most state legislatures have enacted bills ranging from stiffer requirements for high school graduation to merit pay plans for teachers.

"Integrity in the College Curriculum" said that improvement of education at the elementary and high school level was linked to higher standards at the college level. The report declared, "In the end, the quality of American life is at stake, the wisdom and humanity of our leaders, our ability as citizens to make informed choices, and the dedication with which we exhibit humane and democratic values as we go about our daily lives."

'Serious Weaknesses' Seen

Three years ago, the report said, leaders of the association became concerned about "mounting evidence that undergraduate programs in American colleges and universities were afflicted by serious weaknesses." The evidence included declining enrollments in foreign languages and other areas of the humanities, a lack of science education for nonscientists, fuzzy curriculum requirements and lack of a coherent rationale for degree requirements.

The Project on Redefining the Meaning and Purpose of Baccalaureate Degrees was organized under a committee of 18 prominent educators. Among them were Ernest L. Boyer, president of the Carnegie Foundation; Richard Kuhns, professor of philosophy at Columbia University; and Frederick Rudolph, professor emeritus of history at Williams College, who became the principal author of the report. The project was supported by the Pew Memorial Trust and four other foundations.

The panel analyzed the academic programs of 11 institutions, ranging from a community college to several research universities, and held several conferences.

The 11 schools were Brooklyn College of the City University of New York; Carnegie-Mellon University, Pittsburgh; the Empire State College of the State University of New York; Grinnell College in Iowa; Hampshire College in Amherst, Mass.; Maricopa County Community College District in Phoenix; Rhode Island College in Providence; St. Mary's College in South Bend, Ind.; the University of Tennessee in Knoxville; Tuskegee Institute in Alabama and Washington University in St. Louis.

'Evidence of Decline' Noted

The investigators reported: "Evidence of decline and devaluation in college curriculums is everywhere."

"The business community complains of difficulty in recruiting literate college graduates," it said. "Remedial programs, designed to compensate for lack of skill in using the English language, abound in the colleges and in the corporate world. Writing as an undergraduate experience, as an exploration of both communication and style, is widely neglected."

"Foreign language incompetence is now not only a national embarrassment," the report said, "but in a rapidly changing world it threatens to be an enfeebling disadvantage in the conduct of business and diplomacy."

The failure of college curriculums to keep pace with scientific and technological change, it continued, means that "we have become a people unable to comprehend the technology that we invent."

While many colleges require students to take a "general education" program for broad knowledge and thinking skills, it said, these programs are often little more than "distribution requirements," for example, two courses each in the humanities, social sciences and sciences, that reflect political divisions in the faculty.

Similarly, in most colleges the "major" or "concentration" program was described as "little more than a gathering of courses taken in one department." Today's majors, it said, are not so much "experiences in depth" as they are "bureaucratic conveniences."

The association cited numerous causes of "unhappy disarray" in undergraduate curriculums, including an unwillingness of faculty members to uphold academic standards in the face of student demands.

"Today's student populations are less well-prepared, more vocationally oriented and apparently more materialistic than their immediate predecessors," the study declared. "A survival ethic encourages a hunkering down, a diminished vision" in colleges.

'Research Not Teaching'

Another factor, it continued, is the academic "value system" that "puts little emphasis on good teaching, counseling of students, and working with secondary schools." The report noted that most young faculty members entered the classroom having had no formal instruction in how to teach, and they soon learned that "research, not teaching, pays off."

The panel said that "the enemy of good teaching is not research, but rather the spirit that says that this is the only worthy or legitimate task for faculty members."

The report spelled out a "minimum required curriculum" it said was designed to cover the "intellectual, aesthetic and philosophic experiences" necessary to educate a person.

The report listed nine "experiences" that it said "should inform all study." They were:

1. Inquiry, abstract logical thinking, critical analysis.
2. Literacy: writing; reading, speaking, listening.
3. Understanding numerical data.
4. Historical consciousness.
5. Science.
6. Values.
7. Art.
8. International and multicultural experiences.
9. Study in depth of a discipline or group of disciplines.

The association emphasized that most of these "experiences" should not be confined to specific academic departments. The use of numerical data, for example, runs across the academic spectrum. "By the same token," it declared, "there is no defensible reason why English departments should alone bear the responsibility for literacy in the American college and university."

Copies of "Integrity in the College Curriculum" are available for $3 from the Association of American Colleges, 1818 R Street NW, Washington, D.C. 20009.

Discussion

1. What kinds of institutions were surveyed in the preparation of the report, "Integrity in the College Curriculum"?
2. What are the three reasons given in the report for the concern about the quality of undergraduate education? Are there some courses offered by your school that you would consider merely fads?
3. What two suggestions does the report make for improving the quality of college education?
4. There has long been a controversy about how much general education (also called liberal education) should be offered to all students to achieve the kind of goals mentioned in the report. What criticism does the report make of existing "general education" programs in many colleges? According to the report, which kinds of courses should be required for general education?

   What general education courses are required in your school? Which courses would you add or drop?
5. The article mentions another study by the National Endowment for the Humanities in which warnings are given about the need to improve the quality of college education. How does this study see our schools as failing to give an adequate education?
6. What kinds of skills and competencies does the report suggest are not being developed in today's college graduates?
7. What does the report say about the majors offered in most colleges? Are you satisfied with the kinds of courses required for your major?
8. What factors, according to the report, are causing the decline in standards in American colleges?
9. In the article that follows, the list of ten desirable skills for college graduates was prepared by the dean of a business school. In "Integrity in the College Curriculum," the list of nine experiences a college should offer was prepared by a committee of eighteen prominent educators. In what ways do these lists differ, and in what ways are they similar? Check your school catalog for the statement of the goals of its educational program.
10. This article and "The New Illiteracy" are both critical of higher education today. How would you compare these articles in terms of style and presentation of ideas?

Reading for Further Ideas

The reading selections in this section are intended not only to give you additional information about the subject of the composition, but to continue to sharpen your reading skills, and in addition, to give you practice in preparing for essay examinations.

After you have skimmed through each selection and underlined the main points, make an outline from memory. Then check the reading selection again and make a more exact outline. This time, make a one-sentence summary of the main idea.

With this preparation, write a question for each selection that you think might be given on an essay examination. Without concentrating on details, make the question as comprehensive as possible. (You may also ask a question comparing the selection with others on the same subject.) Then write the answers and check them against the reading selection.

In writing your question, keep in mind the date and source of the selection (newspaper or magazine, textbook, other kind of book). Such sources often have different purposes and may therefore affect the way your questions might be asked.

Reading 1

Business School Dean Offers Some Advice

Edward M. Mazze

*comparison
&
contrast
about
college.*

In the following article, the Dean of the School of Business Administration at Temple University gives some advice on the educational preparation needed to take one's place successfully in the work force. Study his advice and note how many of his suggested goals you will have reached by the time you graduate.

As you read, you will note that the author seems to use the words knowledge *and* skills *interchangeably. See whether you think there is a difference in the meanings of these two words.*

Learning the culture of the work force is a process that begins in high school, if not earlier. Yet most college graduates enter the work force lacking skills necessary for long-term survival and success. They are too fact-oriented, accumulating solutions to yesterday's problems, and employers must invest time and effort in training them for their first position.

As an educator preparing people for positions in business and government, I have found that there are 10 areas in which graduates must have knowledge if they are to reach their goals:

1. Knowledge of written and oral communications, so they can get their messages across concisely and clearly. They should know how to listen, question and observe behavior. Communication is essential in selling ideas, influencing others, giving feedback, and for working effectively as a member of a team. It is important for gaining the support needed to get a job done despite resistance. Effective communicators know how to motivate and control a large and diverse group of people, and develop cooperative relationships with and among peers and individuals outside the organization.

2. An awareness of the laws of economics. This knowledge is essential in understanding inflation, market control and monetary, fiscal, tax, employment and international trade policies. Although economics may seem strange to nonbusiness graduates, it is the language of work.

3. An understanding of the computer. The computer is more than a machine and a language. It is a way of dealing with information to solve complex problems. An overemphasis on programming languages makes the graduate unaware of how to design management-information systems. In college, students spend too much time behind the machine rather than thinking how the computer can be used to solve an organization's two basic problems: to increase productivity and to survive in competitive markets.

4. An ability to look at and define problems objectively. A college education is often a collection of courses without any connecting fiber. Yet decision-making is a function of being able to integrate what seem like unrelated variables, and understanding the balance between analytical and intuitive skills. Without knowing these variables, it is impossible to determine what information is needed, know how and where to get the information and select the information that is pertinent.

5. A strong background in specific disciplines—whether it be accounting, marketing, chemical engineering, mathematics, political science or biology—and the new technologies of these disciplines. This includes understanding their foundation, history and philosophy.

6. An appreciation of lifelong learning, which may require returning to college for an advanced degree or taking continuing-education courses for licensing purposes such as in accounting and real estate. Familiarity with the literature of the field and the industry are minimums.

7. The intellectual integrity to know what is right and how business should be conducted. Values and ethics are learned in the early stages of life. Yet they need to be reinforced during the college years.

8. Skills that prepare individuals to set realistic goals for their careers, goals that can withstand sudden changes as well as unexpected opportunities. As part of this process, graduates must know how to manage their time. If one can set measurable goals, he or she can then develop basic goals, policies and strategies for an organization despite uncertainties traceable to technological change, economic and political events and government regulations.

9. An appreciation of the global aspects of the work environment. Most domestic decisions have international implications. With many colleges no longer requiring foreign languages for graduation, we have lost an edge in understanding different cultures. Some critics say this is a major reason for falling behind in the world marketplace.

10. A knowledge of public management. People live, work and vote in communities, even though they often do not understand how local government operates.

These 10 skills are not taught in any organized way in colleges. They are picked up in small pieces in some courses, extracurricular activities, cooperative-education programs, part-time jobs, by reading, and, sometimes, on the first job through company training programs.

Reading 2

Five Ways to Wisdom

In the following article, note what is said about the goals of a college education, and compare these goals with those given in preceding articles. Look for criticisms of education that are similar to ones made in other articles.

Note also the concrete style that a mass magazine like Time *uses to make the article more readable. This style is reflected in the subtitle, "As U.S. colleges open their doors, how can they also open minds?," and in the opening paragraphs of the article.*

Opening day! In front of the brick dormitory, the dust-streaked family car lurches to a halt with its load of indispensable college supplies: one Sony stereo with headphones, two gooseneck lamps, five pairs of blue jeans, two down parkas (one old, one new), one pair of Rossignol skis... and one nervous freshmen wondering whether anybody will like him. The older students have an easier time of it, needing only to unpack what they left in storage over the summer: more lamps, more blue jeans, boots, bicycles, one unused thesaurus donated by an out-of-date uncle... And now, from any reopening dormitory window on any campus from Chapel Hill to Santa Cruz, can be heard the thrumming, insistent sound of the contemporary campus: *Tattoo You... Vacation... Hold Me...*

These are the rites of initiation. Orientation meetings on subjects like time management. Tryouts for the glee club or the football team. Beer bashes. Join the struggle to save Lebanon; join the struggle to save Israel. At Princeton the freshmen and sophomores meet each other in a traditional series of games and rope pulls known as Cane Spree, which custom decrees that the freshmen lose. At Gettysburg College, the rituals of getting acquainted are even more folksy: a "shoe scramble" determines who will dance with whom. At Carleton, there is a fried-chicken picnic and square dancing on the grassy area known as the Bald Spot.

Along with the social games, though, a lot of intellectual choices have to be made, courses picked, books bought. Will it be the class known as "Slums and Bums" (Urban Government) or "Nuts and Sluts" (Abnormal Psychology)? The students joke about these things because they know the choices are serious; their future lives depend on them, and so does much else besides. It has been said that every nation has only a few years in which to civilize an onrushing horde of barbarians, its own children.

The barbarian hordes beginning their classes this month may be the largest in U.S. history, a tribute to both parental prodigality and the ideal of universal education. Though the crest of the 1950s baby boom has passed the college years, a larger percentage of high school graduates now goes to college (61%, *vs.* 40% a generation ago), and the number of older and part-time students keeps increasing (34% of students are over 25). All in all, the number of Americans who are signing up for some form of higher education this fall total a mind-boggling 12.5 million. Mind-boggling not only because of the quantity, but because there is very little agreement on what they are learning or should be learning.

Under the dappling elms of Harvard, which likes to think that it sets the national tone in such matters, President Derek Bok traditionally welcomes each graduating class into "the company of educated men and women." The phrase goes trippingly on the tongue, but what does it mean? Does any such community exist? Are the millions of people now engaged in earning diplomas really being educated?

The statistics of growth, unfortunately, are also the statistics of glut. When the 2.4 million college students of 1949 swelled into today's 12.5 million, the educational system was all but overwhelmed. The most prestigious institutions took easy pride in the numbers they turned away, but the states, somewhat idealistically committed to a policy of open admissions, had to double the number of public colleges, from some 600 to more than 1,250. Most of the new schools were two-year community colleges that featured remedial and vocational classes.

The overall quality of education almost inevitably sank. "Every generation since Roman days has decried the weakening of educational standards," sighs one Midwestern university dean, but the statistics provide sad evidence that there has been a genuine decline. Average scores in reading on the Scholastic Aptitude Tests (SATs) have dropped from 466 out of a possible 800 in 1968 to 424 in 1981, when the decline leveled out; mathematics scores over the same period sank from 492 to 466. A study conducted at the University of Wisconsin reported that at least 20% of last year's entering freshmen "lack the skill to write [acceptably] and 50% are not ready to succeed in college algebra."

"They don't know how to write, they don't read, they have little contact with culture," says Professor Norman Land, who teaches art history at the University of Missouri, in a typical complaint. "Every so often I give them a list of names, and they can identify Timothy Leary or the Who but not Dante or Vivaldi. They haven't received an education; they've just had baby sitting." Nor are the criticisms entirely about intellectual shortcomings. "I think students are becoming less reflective, less concerned about fellow human beings, more greedy, more materialistic," says Alexander Astin, professor of higher education at U.C.L.A. "They're interested in making money and in finding a job that gives them a lot of power and a lot of status."

College officials tend to blame student shortcomings on the high schools, which undeniably need reform and renewal, but the high schools can blame the elementary schools, the elementary schools the family at home, and everybody blames TV. Wisconsin's President Robert O'Neil, however, argues that the colleges are "in part to blame." Says he: "Having diluted the requirements and expectations, they indicated that students could succeed in college with less rigorous preparation." Mark H. Curtis, president of the Association of American Colleges, is more caustic: "We might begin to define the educated person as one who can overcome the deficiencies in our educational system."

The traditional curriculum, such as it was, virtually disintegrated during the campus upheavals of the 1960s, when millions of students demanded and won the right to get academic credit for studying whatever they pleased. There were courses in soap opera and witchcraft. Even more fundamental, and even more damaging, was the spread of the "egalitarian" notion that everybody was entitled to a college degree, and that it was undemocratic to base that degree on any differentiations of intellect or learning. "The idea that cosmetology is just as important as physics is still with us but is being challenged," says Curtis.

"Quality," argues Chester E. Finn Jr., professor of education and public policy at Vanderbilt, "is almost certainly going to turn out to be the foremost national education concern of the 1980s, much as equity was the premier issue of the 1960s and 1970s." The counterrevolution has actually been well under way for some time. In 1978 Harvard announced with great fanfare a controversial new core curriculum, and in 1980 Stanford inaugurated an elaborate system of seven tracks that would carry every student through the basics of Western civilization. "A miracle has happened among Stanford undergraduates," Charles Lyons, director of the Western-culture program, proudly told the faculty senate last spring. "They do talk about Plato at dinner and about Shakespeare on the lawns."

Other colleges followed suit. Amherst now requires all freshmen to take an interdisciplinary program called Introduction to Liberal Studies. At Washington University in St. Louis, the science and math requirements, which were cut in half during the heady days of student power, have been restored to the old levels (four semester-long courses). "The students were evading the real purpose of their education," says Associate Dean Harold Levin, adding, in the language of deans everywhere, "The product we were turning out was not what we wanted." All told, according to a survey of 272 universities and colleges last spring, 88% are engaged in revising their curriculums, and 59% of these are increasing their programs of required courses in general education. That, presumably, will improve the "product."

While the educators reorganize their methods, the fundamental goals of the process—truth, knowledge, the understanding of the world—remain somewhere just beyond the horizon. It was said of Goethe, after his death in 1832, that he was the last man to know everything worth knowing. Today's cliché is that 90% of all scientists in the history of the world are alive now. Yet their knowledge has become hopelessly fragmented; the specialist in recombinant DNA feels no more obligation to understand laser surgery than to hear the latest composition by Pierre Boulez.

As scientific specialties spawn subspecialties, the rapidly growing mass of information has confused the arts and humanities as well. Historical research now presupposes a mastery of old tax records and population movements, and anyone who ventures into such popular fields as American literature or impressionist art must wade into a rising tide of studies, analyses, psychographic portraits and sheer verbiage. In addition, all the political trends of the past two decades have tended to multiply the demands for studies in fields once ignored: Chinese history, the languages of Africa, the traffic in slaves, the thwarted ambitions of women.

Not everyone is overawed by the so-called knowledge explosion. "What happens," says Computer Scientist Joseph Weizenbaum of M.I.T., "is that educators, all of us, are deluged by a flood of messages disguised as valuable information, most of which is trivial and irrelevant to any substantive concern. This is the elite's equivalent of junk mail, but many educators can't see through it because they are not sufficiently educated to deal with such random complexity." To many experts, the computer seems a symbol of both the problem and its solution. "What the computer has done," according to Stephen White of the Alfred P. Sloan Foundation, "is to provide scope for analytical skills that never before existed, and in so doing it has altered the world in which the student will live as well as the manner in which he will think about the world...No adult is truly civilized unless he is acquainted with the civilization of which he is a member, and the liberal arts curriculum of 50 years ago no longer provides that acquaintance."

Acquaintance seems a bare minimum, and even that is difficult enough to attain in a world where millions cannot read and millions more read mainly falsehoods or formulas. Yet the basic questions of education still reach deep into every aspect of life: What is it essential to learn—to know—and why? Everyone seems to have his own answer, but there are interesting patterns among those answers. They can be organized into five main ideas:

I. Education Means Careers

Today's most popular answer is the practical one, on which students are most likely to agree with parents virtually impoverished by tuition bills: an education should enable a student to get a better job than he would otherwise be able to find or fill. In a Carnegie Council poll, 67% of students cited this as an "essential" purpose of their education. A 9.8% unemployment rate makes this purpose seem all the more essential. Michael Adelson, 23, who studied psychology at U.C.L.A., has been unable to find a job in his field for a year and a half, and he now wishes he had chosen engineering. He calls his bachelor of arts degree "completely useless."

The idea that education has a basically social purpose derives more or less from Plato. In his *Republic*, the philosopher portrayed a utopia governed by an intellectual elite specially trained for that purpose. This form of education was both stern and profoundly conservative. Children who attempt innovations, warned Socrates, acting as Plato's narrator, will desire a different sort of life when they grow up to be men, with other institutions and laws. And this "is full of danger to the whole state." To prevent any innovations, Socrates forthrightly demanded censorship so that students could not "hear any casual tales which may be devised by casual persons." When asked whose works he would ban, Socrates specifically named Homer. The poet's crime, he said, was to provide "an erroneous representation of the nature of gods and heroes."

Political pressure of this kind has never been far from the campus, but the overwhelming influence on U.S. education has been not politics but economics: the need for a technologically trained managerial caste. The very first Land Grant Act, in 1862, handed out 30,000 acres per Congressman for the building of state colleges which "the leading object shall be...to teach such branches of learning as are related to agriculture and the mechanic arts." These needs keep changing, of course, and over the decades the U.S. economy demanded of its universities not only chemists and engineers but lawyers and accountants and personnel analysts, and then, after Sputnik's shocking revelation of the Soviet lead in space, yet more engineers.

Students naturally respond to the economy's needs. The Rev. Theodore Hesburgh, president of Notre Dame, complained last year that "the most popular course on the American college campus is not literature or history but accounting." This criticism reflects the fact that less than half the nation's swarm of college students go to liberal arts colleges; the rest are seeking not just jobs but entry into the middle class.

There are now thousands of Ph.D.s unable to find anyone willing to pay them for their hard-earned knowledge of Renaissance painting or the history of French monasticism, but any Sunday newspaper overflows with ads appealing for experts in electromagnetic capability, integrated logistics support or laser electro-optics. Says George W. Valsa, supervisor of the college-recruiting section at Ford: "We are not ready to sign a petition to burn down liberal arts colleges, but don't expect us to go out and hire many liberal arts graduates." Ford does hire nearly 1,000 graduates a year, and most of them are engineers or M.B.A.s.

This is not the old argument between the "two cultures" of science and the humanities, for science too is often forced to defer to technical and vocational training. In 1979, according to one Carnegie study, 58% of all undergraduates pursued "professional" majors (up from 38% a decade earlier), in contrast to 11% in social sciences, 7% in biological sciences, 6% in the arts and 4% in physical sciences. Rich and prestigious private universities can resist this rush toward vocational training, but public and small private colleges are more vulnerable. "The bulk of the institutions will have to give in to a form of consumerism," says U.C.L.A.'s Astin, "in that they need applicants and will therefore have to offer students what they want."

Says Paul Ginsberg, dean of students at Wisconsin: "It's becoming increasingly difficult to persuade a student to take courses that will contribute to his intellectual development in addition to those that will make him a good accountant." Quite apart from the pros and cons of professional training, the idea of educating oneself in order to rise in the world is a perfectly legitimate goal. But Ginsberg has been receiving letters from high school freshmen asking about the prospects for professional schools and job opportunities when they graduate from college seven years hence. Says he: "I don't know at what point foresight ends and panic sets it."

II. *Education Transmits Civilization*

Jill Ker Conway, president of Smith, echoes the prevailing view of contemporary technology when she says that "anyone in today's world who doesn't understand data processing is not educated." But she insists that the increasing emphasis on these matters leaves certain gaps. Says she: "The very strongly utilitarian emphasis in education, which is an effect of Sputnik and the cold war, has really removed from this culture something that was very profound in its 18th and 19th century roots, which was a sense that literacy and learning were ends in themselves for a democratic republic."

In contract to Plato's claim for the social value of education, a quite different idea of intellectual purposes was propounded by the Renaissance humanists. Intoxicated with their rediscovery of the classical learning that was thought to have disappeared during the Dark Ages, they argued that the imparting of knowledge needs no justification—religious, social, economic or political. Its purpose, to the extent that it has one, is to pass on from generation to generation the corpus of knowledge that constitutes civilization. "What could man acquire, by virtuous striving, that is more valuable than knowledge?" asked Erasmus, perhaps the greatest scholar of the early 16th century. That idea has acquired a tradition of its own. "The educational process has no end beyond itself," Says John Dewey. "It is its own end."

But what exactly is the corpus of knowledge to be passed on? In simpler times, it was all included in the medieval universities' *quadrivium* (arithmetic, geometry, astronomy, music) and *trivium* (grammar, rhetoric, logic). As recently as the last century, when less than 5% of Americans went to college at all, students in New England establishments were compelled mainly to memorize and recite various Latin texts, and crusty professors angrily opposed the introduction of any new scientific discoveries or modern European languages. "They felt," said Charles Francis Adams Jr., the Union Pacific Railroad president who devoted his later years to writing history, "that a classical education was the important distinction between a man who had been to college and a man who had not been to college, and that anything that diminished the importance of this distinction was essentially revolutionary and tended to anarchy."

Such a view was eventually overcome by the practical demands of both students and society, yet it does not die. In academia, where every professor is accustomed to drawing up lists of required reading, it can even be played as a game. Must an educated man have read Dostoyevsky, Rimbaud, Tacitus, Kafka? (Yes.) Must he know both Bach's *Goldberg Variations* and Schoenberg's *Gurrelieder?* (Perhaps.) Must he know the Carnot Cycle and Boole's Inequality? (Well...) And then languages—can someone who reads only Constance Garnett's rather wooden version of *Anna Karenina* really know Tolstoy's masterpiece any better than some Frenchman can know Shakespeare by reading André Gide's translation of *Hamlet?* Every scholar likes to defend his own specialty as a cornerstone of Western civilization, and any restraints can seem philistine. George Steiner approvingly quotes, in *Language and Silence*, a suggestion that "an acquaintance with a Chinese novel or a Persian lyric is almost indispensable to contemporary literacy." On a slightly more practical level, intellectual codifiers like to draw up lists of masterworks that will educate any reader who is strong enough to survive them—thus Charles Eliot's famous five-foot shelf of Harvard Classics and all its weighty sequels.

It was the immensely influential Eliot, deeply impressed with the specialized scholarly and scientific research performed at German universities, who proclaimed in 1869, upon becoming president of Harvard, the abolition of its rigid traditional curriculum. Basic education should be performed by the high schools, Eliot declared; anyone who went on to college should be free to make his own choice among myriad elective courses. The students chose the practical. "In the end, it was the sciences that triumphed, guided by the hidden hand of capitalism and legitimized by the binding ideology of positivism," Ernest Boyer and Martin Kaplan observe in *Educating for Survival*. Before long, however, the inevitable counterrevolution against the elective system began; there was a "core" of certain things that every student must learn. Columbia established required courses in contemporary civilization; the University of Chicago and St. John's College duly followed with programs solidly based on required readings of classic texts.

St. John's, which is based in Annapolis, Md., and has a smaller campus in Sante Fe, N. Mex., is a remarkable example of an institution resolutely taking this approach. Ever since 1937, all of St. John's students (683 this fall on both campuses) have been required to read and discuss a list of 130 great books, drawn heavily from the classics and philosophy but also from the ranks of modern novelists like Faulkner and Conrad. The students must take four years of math, three of a laboratory science, two of music and two years each of Greek and French. That is just about it. This modern liberal arts version of *trivium* and *quadrivium* includes no such novelties as psychology (except what can be learned in the works of Freud and William James) and no sociology (except perhaps Jane Austen.)

St. John's is aware of the obvious criticism that its approach is "elitist" and even "irrelevant" to the real world. But President Edwin DeLattre's mild voice turns a bit sharp when he retorts, "If knowing the foundations of one's country—the foundations of one's civilization—if understanding and learning how to gain access to the engines of political and economic power in the world—if knowing how to learn in mathematics and the sciences, the languages, the humanities—if having access to the methods that have advanced civilizations since the dawn of human intelligence . . . if all those things are irrelevant, then boy, are we irrelevant!" DeLattre is a philosopher by training, and he offers one definition that has an ominous but compelling reverberation in the thermonuclear age: "Don't forget the notion of an educated person as someone who would understand how to refound his or her own civilization."

III. *Education Teaches How to Think*

Aristotle was one of those who could found a civilization, and while he thought of education as both a social value and an end in itself, he ascribed its chief importance to what might be considered a third basic concept of education: to train the mind to think, regardless of what it is thinking about. The key is not what it knows but how it evaluates any new fact or argument. "An educated man," Aristotle wrote in *On the Parts of Animals*, "should be able to form a fair offhand judgment as to the goodness or badness of the method used by a professor in his exposition. To be educated is in fact to be able to do this."

The Aristotelian view of education as a process has become the conventionally worthy answer today whenever college presidents and other academic leaders are asked what an education should be. An educated man, says Harvard President Bok, taking a deep breath, must have a "curiosity in exploring the unfamiliar and unexpected, an open-mindedness in entertaining opposing points of view, tolerance for the ambiguity that surrounds so many important issues, and a willingness to make the best decisions he can in the face of uncertainty and doubt..."

"The educated person," says University of Chicago President Hanna Holborn Gray, taking an equally deep breath, "is a person who has a respect for rationality, and who understands some of the limits of rationality as well, who has acquired independent critical intelligence, and a sense not only for the complexity of the world and different points of view but of the standards he or she would thoughtfully want to be pursuing in making judgments."

This is an approach that appears to attach more importance to the process of learning than to the substance of what is learned, but it does provide a way of coping with the vast increase of knowledge. "The old notion of the generalist who could comprehend all subjects is an impossibility, and it was even in past ages," says Chicago's Gray. "Renaissance humanism concentrated on social living and aesthetic engagement but left out most of science. To know all about today's physics, biology and mathematics, or even the general principles of all these fields, would be impossible." To make matters still more difficult, the fields of knowledge keep changing. Says Harvard's Henry Rosovsky, dean of the faculty of arts and sciences: "We can't prepare students for an explosion of knowledge because we don't know what is going to explode next. The best we can do is to make students capable of gaining new knowledge."

The old Aristotelian idea, combined with a contemporary sense of desperation about coping with the knowledge explosion, helped inspire a complete reorganization—yet again—of Harvard's curriculum. At the end of World War II, Harvard had curtailed Eliot's electives and launched a series of general education courses that were supposed to teach everyone the rudiments of science and the humanities. But by the 1960s, when rebellious students seized an administration building, that whole system had broken down. "At the moment," a saddened Dean Rosovsky later wrote to his colleagues, "to be an educated man or woman doesn't mean anything...The world has become a Tower of Babel."

Out of Rosovsky's unhappiness came what Harvard somewhat misleadingly calls its core curriculum. Inaugurated in 1979, after much faculty debate and amid considerable press attention, this core turned out to be a rather sprawling collection of 122 different courses, ranging from Abstraction in Modern Art to Microbial and Molecular Biology. Students are required to select eight of their 32 courses from five general areas of knowledge (science, history, the arts, ethics and foreign cultures).

Harvard's eminence exerts a wide influence, but other first-rate institutions, like Columbia, Chicago and Princeton, point out that they have taught a more concentrated core and steadfastly continued doing so throughout the 1960s. "It makes me unhappy when people think that Harvard has done some innovative curriculum work," says Columbia College Associate Dean Michael Rosenthal (a Harvard graduate). "They have millions of courses, none of which, you could argue, represents any fundamental effort to introduce people to a kind of thinking or to a discipline."

But that is exactly what Harvard does claim to be doing. "The student should have an understanding of the major ways mankind organizes knowledge," says Rosovsky. "That is done in identifiable ways: in sciences by experiment, conducted essentially in mathematics; in social science through quantitative and historical analysis; in the humanities by studying the great traditions. We are not ignoring content but simply recognizing that because of the knowledge explosion, it makes sense to emphasize the gaining of knowledge."

If anyone objects that it is still perfectly possible to graduate from Harvard without having read a word of Shakespeare, Rosovsky is totally unfazed. Says he: "That's not necessary."

IV. Education Liberates the Individual

The current trend toward required subjects—a kind of intellectual law-and-order—reflects contemporary political conservatism. It implies not only that there is a basic body of knowledge to be learned but also that there is a right way to think. It implies that a certain amount of uniformity is both socially and intellectually desirable.

Perhaps, but the excesses of the 1960s should not be used to besmirch reforms that were valuable. They too derived from a distinguished intellectual tradition. Its founding father was Jean-Jacques Rousseau, who argued in his novel *Emile* that children are not miniature adults and should not be drilled into becoming full-grown robots. "Everything is good as it comes from the hand of the Creator," said Rousseau; "everything degenerates in the hands of man."

Isolated from the corrupting world. Rousseau's young Emile was given no books but was encouraged to educate himself by observing the workings of nature. Not until the age of twelve, the age of reason, was he provided with explanations in the form of astronomy or chemistry, and not until the social age of 15 was he introduced to aesthetics, religion and, eventually, female company. That was how Emile met Sophie and lived happily ever after. It is a silly tale, and yet there is considerable power to the idea that a student should be primarily educated not to hold a job or to memorize literary monuments or even to think like Aristotle, but simply to develop the potentialities of his own self—and that everyone's self is different.

While there is probably not a single university that has not retreated somewhat from the experimentation of the 1960s, and while the rhetoric of that decade is now wildly out of fashion, a few small institutions have tried to keep the faith. For them, education is, in a sense, liberation, personal liberation. At Evergreen State College in Washington, which has no course requirements of any kind and no letter grades, a college spokesman describes a class on democracy and tyranny by saying, "We will try to find out who we are, and what kind of human beings we should become." At Hampshire College, founded in Massachusetts in 1970 as a resolutely experimental school, students still design their own curriculums, take no exams and talk of changing the world. "I don't see myself as giving a body of knowledge or even 'a way of learning,' " says Physics Professor Herbert Bernstein, "but as involved in something beyond that—to help people find their own path and the fullness of who they are."

The times have not been easy for such colleges. Not only do costs keep rising, but many students now prefer conventional courses and grades that will look impressive on job applications. Antioch, which expanded into an unmanageable national network of 32 experimental institutions, stumbled to the verge of bankruptcy in the 1970s, and is drastically cutting costs to survive. But the spirit of Rousseau flickers on. Rollins, which has sometimes been dismissed as a Florida tennis school, is trying to organize a conference for such like-minded colleges as Bard, Bennington, Sarah Lawrence and Scripps on how best to pursue the goal of "making higher education more personal and developmental rather than formalistic."

Even when these enthusiasts do bend to the current pressures for law-and-order, they tend to do it in their own dreamy way. At Bard, where President Leon Botstein decided last year that all students should attend an intensive three-week workshop on how to think and write, the students pondered such questions as the nature of justice. What color is justice? What shape is it? What sound does it make? What does it eat? "I can't think of anything," one student protested at the first such writing class. "Don't worry about it," the teacher soothingly answered. Among the students' offerings: "Justice is navy blue, it's square. It weaves in and out and backs up...Justice is black and white, round...It has the sound of the cracked Liberty Bell ringing." Workshop Director Peter Elbow's conclusion: "We're trying an experiment here, and we're not pretending that we have it under control or that we know how it works."

V. *Education Teaches Morals*

The U.S. Supreme Court has forbidden prayers in public schools, but many Americans cling to the idea that their educational system has a moral purpose. It is an idea common to both the Greeks and the medieval church ("O Lord my King," St. Augustine wrote in his *Confessions*, "whatsoever I speak or write, or read, or number, let all serve Thee"). In a secular age, the moral purpose of education takes secular forms: racial integration, sex education, good citizenship. At the college level, the ambiguities become more complex. Should a morally objectionable person be allowed to teach? (Not Timothy Leary, said Harvard). Should a morally objectionable doctrine be permitted? (Not Arthur Jensen's claims of racial differences in intelligence, said student protesters at Berkeley.)

Many people are understandably dismayed by such censorship. But would they prefer ethical neutrality? Should engineers be trained to build highways without being taught any concern for the homes they displace? Should prospective corporate managers learn how to increase profits regardless of pollution or unemployment? Just the opposite, according to *Beyond the Ivory Tower*, a new book by Harvard's Bok, which calls for increased emphasis on "applied ethics." (Writes Bok: "A university that refuses to take ethical dilemmas seriously violates its basic obligations to society.")

Religious colleges have always practiced a similar preaching. But some 500 schools now offer courses in the field. The Government supports such studies with a program known as EVIST, which stands for Ethics and Values in Science and Technology (and which sounds as though a computer had already taken charge of the matter). "The modern university is rooted in the scientific method, having essentially turned its back on religion," says Steven Muller, president of Johns Hopkins. "The scientific method is a marvelous means of inquiry, but it really doesn't provide a value system. The biggest failing in higher education today is that we fall short in exposing students to values."

Charles Muscatine, a professor of English at Berkeley and member of a committee that is analyzing liberal arts curriculums for the Association of American Colleges, is even harsher. He calls today's educational programs "a marvelous convenience for a mediocre society." The key goal of education, says Muscatine, should be "informed decision making that recognizes there is a moral and ethical component to life." Instead, he says, most universities are "propagating the dangerous myth that technical skills are more important than ethical reasoning."

Psychiatrist Robert Coles, who teaches at both Harvard and Duke, is still more emphatic in summing up the need: "Reading, writing and arithmetic. That's what we've got to start with, and all that implies, at every level. If people can't use good, strong language, they can't think clearly, and if they haven't been trained to use good, strong language, they become vulnerable to all the junk that comes their way. They should be taught philosophy, moral philosophy and theology. They ought to be asked to think about moral issues, especially about what use is going to be made of knowledge, and why—a kind of moral reflection that I think has been supplanted by a more technological education. Replacing moral philosophy with psychology has been a disaster, an absolute disaster!"

Each of these five ways to wisdom has its strengths and weaknesses, of course. The idea that education provides better jobs promises practical rewards for both the student and the society that trains him, but it can leave him undernourished in the possibilities of life away from work. The idea that education means the acquisition of a cultural heritage does give the student some grasp of that heritage, but it can also turn into glib superficialities or sterile erudition. The idea that education consists mainly of training the mind does provide a method for further education, but it can also make method seem more important than knowledge. So can the idea that education is a form of self-development. And the teaching of ethics can unfortunately become a teaching of conventional pieties.

To define is to limit, as we all learned in school, and to categorize is to oversimplify. To some extent, the five ways to wisdom all overlap and blend, and though every educator has his own sense of priorities, none would admit that he does not aspire to all five goals. Thus the student who has mastered the riches of Western civilization has probably also learned to think for himself and to see the moral purposes of life. And surely such a paragon can find a good job even in the recession of 1982.

Are there specific ways to come nearer to achieving these goals? The most obvious is money. Good teachers cost money; libraries cost money; so do remedial classes for those who were short-changed in earlier years. Only mediocrity comes cheap. Those who groan at the rising price of college tuition (up as much as $7,000 since 1972) may not realize that overall, taking enrollment growth into account, college budgets have just barely kept up with inflation. Indeed, adjusted for inflation, four years of college today costs less than a decade ago, and faculty salaries in real dollars declined about 20% during the 1970s. Crocodile tears over the cost of higher education come in waves from the Federal Government, which has so far held spending to roughly 1981 levels, and proposes deep cuts (*e.g.*, nearly 40% in basic grants) by 1985. This is an economy comparable to skimping on the maintenance of an expensive machine.

But money alone will not solve all problems, as is often said, and this is particularly true in the field of education. If improving the quality of American education is a matter of urgent national concern—and it should be— then what is required besides more dollars is more sense: a widespread rededication to a number of obvious but somewhat neglected principles. That probing research and hard thinking be demanded of students (and of teachers too). That academic results be tested and measured. That intellectual excellence be not just acknowledged but rewarded.

These principles admittedly did serve the system that educated primarily those few who were born into the governing classes, but the fact that elitist education once supported elitist politics does not mean that egalitarian politics requires egalitarian education. Neither minds nor ideas are all the same.

All that the schools can be asked to promise is that everyone will be educated to the limit of his capacities. At the community college minimum, it may have to mean teaching basic skills, at least until the weakened high schools begin doing their job properly, as Philosopher Mortimer Adler urges in his new *Paideia Proposal*. This calls for a standardized high school curriculum, in three categories: fundamental knowledge such as history, science and arts; basic skills such as reading and mathematical computation; and critical understanding of ideas and values. These essentials must really be taught, not just certified with a passing grade. Beyond such practical benefits, though, and beyond the benefits that come from exercising the muscles of the mind, higher education must ultimately serve the higher purpose of perpetuating whatever it is in civilization that is worth perpetuating. Or as Ezra Pound once said of the craft that he later betrayed, "The function of literature is precisely that it does incite humanity to continue living."

This is the core of the core idea, and surely it is by now indisputable that every college student improves by learning the fundamentals of science, literature, art, history. Harvard's Rosovsky may be right in suggesting that it is "not necessary" to have read Shakespeare as part of the process of learning how to think, but he is probably wrong. Not because anyone really *needs* to have shared in Lear's howling rage or because anyone can earn a better salary from having heard Macbeth declaim "Tomorrow and tomorrow and tomorrow..." But he is enriched by knowing these things, impoverished by not knowing them. And *The Marriage of Figaro* enriches. *The Cherry Orchard* enriches. *The City of God* enriches. So does a mastery of Greek, or of subnuclear particles, or of Gödel's theorem.

In a sense, there really is no core, except as a series of arbitrary choices, for there is no limit to the possibilities of learning. There are times when these possibilities seem overwhelming, and one hears echoes of Socrates' confession, "All I know is that I know nothing." Yet that too is a challenge. "We shall not cease from exploration," as T. S. Elliot put it, "and the end of all our exploring/ Will be to arrive where we started/ And know the place for the first time." The seemingly momentous years of schooling, then, are only the beginning.

Henry Adams, who said in *The Education of Henry Adams* that Harvard "taught little, and that little ill," was 37 when he took up the study of Saxon legal codes and 42 when he first turned to writing the history of the Jefferson and Madison Administrations, and 49 when he laboriously began on Chinese. In his 50s, a tiny, wiry figure with a graying beard, the future master of Gothic architecture solemnly learned to ride a bicycle.

Reading 3

U.S. Universities

Henry Steele Commager

* comparison & Contract about Colleges. (handwritten annotation)

*The following selection by a well-known historian is from a book intended to ac-
quaint foreign students in the United States with American customs and
institutions.*

*Note the three patterns of universities that Commager says have emerged in
the United States, particularly the "multiversity." Not also the functions that the
American "multiversity" are expected to perform in our society.*

*In your questions, you might compare this selection with one or more of the
other articles dealing with American education. This selection differs from the
others in that it is more concerned with the structure and goals of American
universities than with academic standards. Note especially what the author says
should be the goals of all education. Since the purpose of the book is to inform and
its author is an academician, a formal and objective style is used.*

Universities everywhere reflect something of their society, but nowhere
so elaborately or so faithfully as in the United States.

Out of this special situation Americans created, quite unconsciously, a
new and distinctive kind of university—what Clark Kerr, former president of
the University of California, has called the "multiversity." Over a period of six
or seven centuries the university has taken three characteristic forms—over-
lapping, to be sure, but distinct. The original university which emerged in
Italy and France in the twelfth and thirteenth centuries, was what we would
now call a professional school, designed to train theologians, doctors, lawyers, and philosophers who were usually teachers. This was the university that
spread so swiftly throughout Europe from the thirteenth to the nineteenth
centuries and to the new world as well. At Oxford and Cambridge there developed within this original pattern, a second pattern. These universities
were rural rather than urban, and therefore residential; they took a collegiate
form. Their function was not only to train the young for the professions, but
to preserve the heritage of the past and transmit it to succeeding generations
and to prepare them morally as well as intellectually for the larger duties of
government and society. With the opening of Göttingen University in 1737
there emerged a third—and since then dominant—pattern of the university:
an institution designed chiefly for carrying on research in order to expand
the boundaries of knowledge.

To these three familiar kinds of university Americans have added the multiversity—an institution expected to perform not only all the old familiar functions but, in addition, to cater to all the interests and needs of society and to train in all the skills which society thinks it needs. This very American concept of the federal university was launched by the Act of 1862 creating so-called "land-grant colleges" in every state, designed to stress agriculture and the industrial arts. Where the traditional university had only four faculties, the American university might have (and often does have) a score or more. It was expected to teach all subjects, to prepare for all professions and all careers. It was required to instruct undergraduates in everything from remedial reading to classical archeology, and to train graduate and research students who could in turn go out and staff other universities. It was expected to prepare not only doctors, lawyers, and theologians, but engineers, architects, librarians, nurses, foresters, farmers, bankers, businessmen, school teachers, football coaches, and—for those who had no clear aim—"to prepare for life." It was also expected to carry on research in all conceivable and some inconceivable fields, scholarly and practical, and to serve government and society at every level—the local community, the state, and the nation. And for good measure it was assumed that it would provide moral and social guidance to the young, act as a matrimonial agency and a psychiatric clinic, and supply culture and entertainment to the public....

It is the effort to respond to these myriad pressures and demands that explains much of the miscellaneous and incoherent character of higher education in the United States—miscellaneous in external variety, incoherent in internal organization. Here two thousand institutions of "higher learning" reveal almost as many and diverse characteristics as would any two thousand business or governmental enterprises. Some are, by any standards, affluent and distinguished centers of learning; some are liberal arts colleges (an American invention, this, for the liberal arts college as such is unknown in European education) all of whose students are preparing for professional careers or for research. Hundreds are "junior" colleges and community colleges which provide an education equivalent to that of the French lycée, the German gymnasium, or the Swedish high school, though with less rigorous standards than these. Hundreds of vocational schools train farmers and teachers and accountants and nurses for their chosen careers—institutions which, abroad, are rarely attached to a university. The variety is both qualitative and quantitative. There are institutions, like Harvard, with a library of eight million volumes, or California with a glittering galaxy of Nobel Prize winners on its faculty, or the Institute for Advanced Study at Princeton devoted exclusively to research. There are struggling colleges with pitiful libraries of ten or twenty thousand volumes, laboratories inferior to those of a good high school, and students admitted without reference to academic qualifications. There are public universities, and private, and a mixture of the two; while the majority are secular, there are Protestant, Catholic, and Jewish universities. There are great urban universities like Columbia, Chicago, or the University of California at Los Angeles, and small colleges that retain some of their pastoral character, like Amherst, Carleton, or Grinnell.

All this is entirely natural, perhaps inevitable, and it is interesting to note that it is this American type of university that is spreading in the newly emerging nations of Asia and Africa. After all, a nation with two hundred million people needs the most miscellaneous institutions to provide it with the myriad services that it requires, and if it wishes to call these institutions universities, high schools, technical colleges, or normal schools, that is merely one reflection of a classless society. More, there is something to be said for the American practice of mixing various functions in the same institutional container. Europeans will argue that nursing or library training or business are not "university" subjects, and should therefore be banished from the precincts of Minerva to the workaday world. Americans respond, somewhat inconsistently, with three arguments. First, they cheerfully challenge the traditional hierarchy of subjects, arguing that anything is a proper area of study if properly studied. Second, they submit that if you have to train nurses and librarians and businessmen anyway, how much better to train them at a university, where they will be exposed to the atmosphere of learning, where they will have a chance to pick up at least a smattering of "culture," and where they might catch a glimpse of the scientific potentialities of the subjects they are studying. And third, they ask the very hard-headed question why society should not use the institutions that it already has—the campus, the buildings, the libraries and laboratories and playing fields—for whatever it wants done, instead of going to the trouble and expense of building separate institutions for every separate discipline or professional career. . . .

Needless to say, the intimate relationship of the American university to the community, and to government, is fraught with danger, as is the principle that the university exists to serve the community. One manifestation of that danger is the pressure from government during wartime to force universities to devote their resources to what is always euphemistically called "defense" work. Another is the demand from students that the university be "relevant" to their own interests, to the concerns of their society. For the university is not a servant of its own immediate society; it is the servant of the larger community of learning—the community of the past and the community of the future; it is not a servant merely of its own city or state or nation, but of mankind.

Extra Discussion and Writing

Journal Entry

Compare the American system of education with the one in your country. Write freely, since you are the only one who will see this entry.

Letters

1. Write a letter to one of your teachers in your country making the same comparison of American education and the education in your country as you did in your journal entry. However, this time, revise the journal entry for the letter so it is more carefully controlled and correct—but keep it friendly, since you know the teacher.
2. Write a letter to a member of your family who is still in your native country telling about your school experiences in the United States. You might include references to the campus, classes, teachers, friends, your living quarters. Since you are writing home, express your opinions honestly.
3. Write a letter to a younger teenage brother or sister about something you are studying in one of your classes. Make the explanation as informative as possible, but state it simply and clearly. Try to include general principles.

Group Report

Form small groups to prepare a report on the ideal college. Include goals (in terms of general and specialized education), kinds of courses (curriculum), teachers, school environment. Consider whether your ideal college should be open to all high school graduates or only to those of superior intellectual achievement. Consider also what standards should be maintained.

Then prepare to give a panel report in which each member of the group discusses one of these aspects of the ideal college.

Reaction

The following cartoon comes from The New Yorker *magazine. What is it trying to tell us about American education?*

"*. . . and give me good abstract-reasoning ability, interpersonal skills, cultural perspective, linguistic comprehension, and a high sociodynamic potential.*"

Drawing by Ed Fisher; ©1981 The New Yorker Magazine, Inc.

CHAPTER 4

The Family

Composition
Vocabulary and Usage
Reading for Summary Writing
Reading for Further Ideas
Extra Discussion and Writing

Composition

Procedures for Discussion
Writing the Composition
Revising the Composition

Requirements for a Home Composition

1. Use white 8½″ × 11″ paper; write on one side only.
2. Type your composition double spaced on unlined paper (if hand-written, the paper should be clearly written on every other line). A typewritten page, double-spaced, is about 250 words.
3. Indent each paragraph, use wide margins (1″ to 1¼″), and number each page in the upper right-hand corner.
4. Include a separate page with the title, the thesis sentence, and the outline.

Procedures for Discussion

The teacher puts this question on the board:

Should a Married Woman with Preschool Children Go to Work?

Under the question, the teacher heads up two columns:

Yes   No

Then the teacher asks for arguments for either side and lists the arguments in phrases under the appropriate column in the random order they are given. Whenever possible, when an argument for one side is listed, the argument for the other side (the rebuttal) should be solicited from students and listed in the opposite column.

At the end of the discussion, the teacher ask students to try to organize the listed arguments under broader headings.

Writing the Composition

Write a 500 to 600 word composition of argument on the question of working mothers.

Suggestions for the Content and Organization

Consider putting minor points under broader ones. You might think in terms of the three traditional roles of a married woman: mother, homemaker, wife. Then narrow down your subject—find a thesis or a point of view. You might consider these:

Children's needs as opposed to mothers' needs
Breakdown of family life—are working mothers to blame?
The effect of changing times on traditional roles in the family
The working mother's double burden

Restrict yourself to one position. You may admit that there is some justification for the other side, but your position has greater weight. In a composition of argument or opinion, there is often no one "right" answer. The decision is made according to your viewpoint. But your arguments or opinions must be presented logically, clearly, and convincingly. As part of the introduction, you might want to include conditions for your position (for example, there is no argument if a woman has to go to work because of economic necessity). Also, you might want to limit your argument to the situation in your country.

Guide for the Outline and the Composition

The following guide will help you in preparing to write your composition. On the left side of the guide is the outline with suggestions for handling the introduction, transitions, and the conclusion of this composition. On the right side are general comments about how introductions, transitions, and conclusions may be written. (If you are accustomed to writing a first draft from rough notes, use this guide for your second and succeeding drafts.)

Outline

Title

General Comments

Use initial capital letters for all words except articles, short prepositions, and short conjunctions. Try to use an interesting title that reflects your thesis.

Introduction

This can be based on individual experience—your own or that of others. Or it can be more general—for example, changing views about marriage and the family.

Purpose of the introduction:
  to catch the reader's interest
  to give a general idea of the subject

An introduction may include:
  a quotation
  a story, perhaps personal
  a rhetorical question (which you will answer)
  a definition
  a statement of a belief you will argue against
  a surprising or shocking fact
  a statement of a serious problem

Transitional lead-in

This states the position you will take and the basis for this position. It may also give conditions that will restrict your argument.

Usually at the end of the introduction. Gives an indication of the central idea and the way it will be developed (may be in the form of a question).

I. First main point

This is the first argument about whether a married woman with preschool children should go to work.
  A. First supporting detail
  B. Second supporting detail
       etc.

New paragraph. The first sentence: (1) mentions the general idea of the paragraph (from the important word[s] in the outline); (2) relates this sentence to what was said before.

Should be related to the preceding subpoint.

Note: Long subpoints may begin new paragraphs.

(Continue with your other main points and their supporting details.) For each main point, remind the reader that you are giving another argument about whether a married woman with preschool children should go to work.

(Follow the suggestions given for the first main point.)

Conclusion

You can go back to individual experiences or you can be more general.
You may suggest a compromise.

The conclusion should round out the composition in a strong and satisfying way, perhaps by referring again to whatever you used to introduce the composition.

Notes: (1) The conclusion should not add any new ideas that need further development. (2) If your last point ends on a strong note that points up your thesis, you may not need to add a conclusion.

Support for the points you make can come from your own beliefs and experience or from the readings in this chapter and elsewhere. (Be sure to identify your sources and to use quotation marks around the exact words of an author.) The support can be in the form of examples, current facts and figures, or authoritative opinion. Use enough support to make your point convincing to the reader.

Finally, keep in mind that this composition represents your own opinions. By stating them honestly and strongly, you will have a composition that the reader will find interesting enough to continue reading.

Revising the Composition

In succeeding drafts, try to sharpen your thesis and show more clearly how each main point contributes to the development of the thesis. Try writing down the opening sentences of your paragraphs on a separate sheet of paper to see if they make a clear sentence outline. Go over the reading selections again for further ideas or additional support.

Consult the Revision and Editing Checklist for guidance on organization, paragraphing, and sentences. You can get needed vocabulary help in the vocabulary section that follows on pp. 99–100. Make a final check with the Symbol Chart for Correction of Compositions for the grammatical structures and usage in your composition.

Evaluation

If there is an exchange of student compositions, the Revision and Editing Checklist can serve as a guide in the evaluation of another student's composition. Use the following procedure in checking for the writer's organization and development of ideas.

1. Without looking at the other student's outline page, make an outline and a one-sentence summary of the central idea (or thesis) of the whole paper. Can you find a clear line of development? Do your summary sentence and your outline agree with those of the writer?
2. Find the support for each point made in the writer's paper. Is the support adequate and convincing?
3. Write on the student's paper what you consider the good points of the composition and what needs to be improved.

Vocabulary and Usage

Vocabulary
Usage Notes
Word Forms

Vocabulary

The following words may be useful to you in talking and writing about the subject of working mothers.

the home (as a symbol)   A loving home environment. The place where one finds shelter and affection in the midst of the family.

women's liberation   A movement that was revived in the 1960s to get more social, economic, and political rights for women.

nurturing   Providing physical and emotional nourishment; providing careful training and education.

self-realization, self-fulfillment   Realization of one's potential.

household chore   A small, uninteresting job around the house.

modern conveniences

> **home appliances**   Electrical conveniences in the home that make housework easier—refrigerators, stoves, dishwashers, washers, dryers, vacuum cleaners, etc.

> **convenience foods**   Foods already prepared—frozen foods (including TV dinners), packaged food.

homemaker   A person who takes care of a home, usually a housewife.

housekeeper   A person hired to take care of a home.

standard of living   A person's way of life as determined by the amount of purchasing power the person has.

emotional bonding   The emotional attachment of a child to the adult who provides nurturing care.

"latchkey kids"   A term used by sociologists to refer to children, usually young adolescents, who must let themselves into an empty home with a key after school because both parents are at work. The term is associated with the lack of adult supervision, protection, and affection which children used to get when their mother was at home.

juvenile delinquency   Antisocial or criminal behavior of young people, usually age 18 or younger.

breadwinner   A person who works to support dependents; traditionally this has been the husband.

dilemma   A situation requiring a choice between alternatives, neither of which is satisfactory.

controversy   argument, dispute.

day care center   A place that takes care of infants and preschool children while their mothers are at work. Also called **day nursery**.

socialization   The process of acquiring the physical, mental and social skills that a person needs to survive and to become both an individual and a member of a society." From *Sociology*, 2nd ed., Donald Light, Jr., and Suzanne Keller, 1979, p. 109.

sexist   Referring to the economic exploitation and social domination of women by men.

feminist   A person, usually a woman, who strongly advocates equal rights for women.

Usage Notes

Use the correct adjective form.

> econom*ic* need (financial need)
> a country's econom*ic* problems (refers to the economy)
>
> *but*
>
> econom*ical* purchase (money-saving, thrifty purchase)

Do not add the *-s* plural endings to the following noncountable words:

work (in general), but *jobs* (specific kinds of work)
works are countable accomplishments, such as works of art
housework (but household chores)
homework (but assignments)

Do not use *the* with words that refer to abstract ideas:

society
human nature
happiness
equality
inequality
independence

But use *the* with the words above (except human nature) if they are followed by modifiers:

the happiness *of all the people*
the society *in which we live*

Avoid the use of the informal word *kid* in your composition. Use *child* instead.

Do not confuse:

grow up: become mature. Children grow up fast. (*Grow up* is an intransitive verb. It does not take an object.)

bring up: raise. Parents bring up their children. (*Bring up* is a transitive verb. It takes an object.)

In general statements, avoid the awkward *he/she* pronoun by using a plural class noun.

Children need the love of *their* parents.

versus

A child needs the love of *his or her* parents.

Use a singular verb with *the number*.

The number of working mothers *has* increased.

versus

A greater *number* of mothers *are* entering the work force. (*a number* = some, many)

Word Forms

Use the correct forms for the words in parentheses.

The answers are on p. 354. If you need help with this exercise, refer to the explanations under Word Forms in Appendix A.

1.1 In earlier times, some of the women's (responsible) _____ in the home were to provide a sense of (tranquil) _____ and (stable) _____.

2. Children need a feeling of (secure) _____ and (protect) . in the home.

3. Is it possible for a woman who works full time to fulfill all the traditional (expect) _____ of a mother (satisfactory) _____?

4. There are many (convenient) _____ today that (light) _____ the household chores.

5. Today's woman wants to work not only to achieve (finance) _____ (independent) _____ but to avoid (bore) _____ chores and to (broad) _____ her outlook on life.

6. Lack of parental (supervise) _____ may lead to juvenile (delinquent) _____.

7. In many families, two incomes are an (economy) _____ (necessary) _____.

8. Many teenage suicides have been attributed to (emotion) _____ (insecure) _____ because both parents are out of the house during the day.

9. The question of working mothers is a (controversy) _____ and (emotion) _____ subject.

10. A sense of (moral) _____ comes from early (train) _____ in the home.

11. Many women (profession) _____ are reluctant to give up their careers for full-time care of their children.

12. The (avail) _____ of contraceptives and (abort) _____ has made it possible for a women to have the (choose) _____ of whether she wants to continue to work or not.

13. The (social) _____ of children was once the (response) _____ of the family, the school and the church.

14. A woman (leave) _____ her job to take care of a new baby may (jeopardy) _____ her career.

15. Because she is now more (educate) _____, a woman wants to achieve (finance) _____ success and (equal) _____ with men.

16. After World War II, women entered the work force in (increase) _____ numbers.

17. Today's women are (face) _____ with a dilemma. They realize that not all of them can be "supermoms," with the double burden of (have) _____ a full-time career and (take) _____ care of their home and family.

Reading for Summary Writing

For the following three reading selections, prepare a brief outline first for class discussion before you write the summary. After the class discussion of each selection, you will write:

1. A longer, revised outline of the reading selection, using an alternation of numbers and letters.
2. A one-sentence summary of the reading selection. The sentence should include the central idea and the main points used to develop this idea (from the outline).
3. A summary of the reading selection. The length assigned in the text will determine the amount of detail you can include in the outline and summary.

Guidelines for Writing (Review)

1. For the outline, use the alternate number-letter system for the main points and their subpoints. The phrases you underline in the opening sentences of paragraphs usually become the main points or subpoints on the outline.
2. For both summary and outline, follow the same order as the reading selection. However, you may begin the summary with a reference to the source of the selection (author, publication, etc.) and to its central idea.

3. Keep a sense of proportion. Write more about points the author devotes more attention to.
4. Concentrate more on the main points than on examples or other supporting details.
5. Use proper transitions between the main points and the subpoints of
   your summary; your summary must have an organization of its own.
6. Use your own words as much as possible, except for key phrases. You
   may quote important phrases or sentences.
7. Be careful not to overload any of the sentences with so much information that the sentence is hard to read.
8. Be consistent in your use of verb tenses. Use all present tense (the author states, feels) or all past tense (the author stated, felt). The present
   tense is more common in a summary.
9. Do not include your own ideas or your own attitude or interpretation.
   The summary should be an objective restatement of what the author has
   said.

Reading 1

College Women and Careers

Mirra Komarovsky

*The following article was written by a former professor of sociology. As you read,
note the results of the study the author made. Note also what the author has to say
about equality for women in and out of the home.*

*Note: The colleges mentioned in this article, the women's Seven Sisters Col-
leges and the better known Ivy League schools, are prestigious schools in the north-
eastern part of the United States. The Ivy League schools are Yale, Harvard,
Princeton, Brown, Columbia, the University of Pennsylvania, Cornell, and Dart-
mouth.*

Length of summary: Approximately 200 words

Many young women now say they'd pick family over careers, according
to a recent newspaper article. Are we, then, witnessing a conservative back-
lash on the college campuses?

On the contrary, all available evidence points to the opposite direction in the college woman's ideals of a good life.

Consider, by way of illustration, views of a random sampling of undergraduates at one of the so-called Seven Sisters colleges whom I studied at three different points: in 1943, 1971, and 1980.

The question that I put to the students read: "Assume that you will marry and that your husband will make enough money so that you will not have to work unless you want to. Under these circumstances, what would you prefer?"

One option was "not to work at all or to stop after childbirth and decide later whether to go back." The proportions giving this response declined from 50 percent in 1943 to 18 percent in 1971 and, finally, to only 6 percent in 1980.

At the other extreme were women who "wanted to work full time with a minimum of interruption for childbearing (or to work part-time with pre-school children only)." In 1943 and 1971, 20 percent chose this response, but last year 53 percent chose it.

The conflicts that women express today do not signify a conservative trend.

Quite the contrary, women are making a radical discovery that their society, for all the rhetoric of equality, says to them, in effect, what a male senior at an Ivy League college recently told me:

"I would not want to marry a woman whose only goal is to become a housewife. This type of woman would not have enough bounce and zest in her. Moreover, I want an independent girl, one who has her own interests and diversion. However, when we both agree to have children, my wife must be the one to raise them."

He continued, with obvious pride in his egalitarianism:

"I believe that no woman should be barred solely on grounds of sex from the highest offices, that women should have absolutely equal opportunities in business and the professions, but I still insist that a woman who is a mother should devote herself to her children."

Young women are becoming aware that the call to equal opportunities for women outside the home is an empty slogan as long as the society insists on traditional role segregation within the family.

Some women react to this discovery with equanimity, others with frustration, resignation, or indignation—making in their personal lives whatever makeshift arrangements they can.

But the real touchstone of their aspirations is the longing for a society in which the rhetoric of equality will be realized in fact. There is no denying that this would require major institutional changes.

We have much to learn, for example, from Sweden: modified work patterns for both sexes, housing patterns permitting more cooperative ties among child-rearing families, parental leaves from work, accessible childcare centers of high quality for all economic classes. In my interviews with blue-collar homemakers, many young mothers felt trapped by around-the-clock child care, isolation from adults, and were bewildered about many problems of child-rearing. Moreover, community child-care centers could have great educational values for young children.

Other changes in public opinion are long overdue.

Dr. Benjamin Spock urged women to realize that it is "much more creative to rear and shape the personality of a fine lively child than it is to work in an office or even to carve a statue."

It is quite true that building bridges, writing books, and splitting the atom are no more essential to society than child-rearing. But, in my opinion, it will be increasingly difficult to make women believe it unless men believe it, too.

And when they do believe it, they will wonder at the bizarre values of their predecessors.

A newspaper article that I read a couple of years ago described several men who taught kindergarten. When asked what they did, they found it expedient to reply that they were elementary-school teachers. This is the symbol of the suspicion and the scorn that men today may encounter if they are involved in that "most creative and essential" task of shaping the personalities of young children.

Discussion

1. Note the use of a question in the introduction that will lead to the main concern of the article. Does the author give an affirmative or a negative answer to the question?
2. What sources of information does the author use to support the point she is making in this article?
3. What kind of study did the author use to arrive at the percentages she gives in the article?
4. According to the author's research, what percentage of women said they would quit work after childbirth in 1943? in 1971? in 1980? What percentage said they wanted very little time off for childbearing in 1943? in 1971? in 1980?
5. What contradictory statements by a male student does the author quote to support her conclusion that equality between women and men does not exist?
6. Why does the author feel that Sweden provides greater opportunity for equality between the sexes?
7. What does Dr. Spock, a prominent American authority on children, say about raising children? Does the author feel that men believe this too?
8. What is the author trying to prove by ending the article with the experience of some male kindergarten teachers?

Reading 2

Money Need, Social Change Combine to Cut Apron Strings

Philip Shabecoff

The following article was written by a reporter for The New York Times. *The headline points to the two main reasons why women are working out of the house. The words "Cut Apron Strings" in the title express figuratively the main idea of the article, that women are no longer confined to their traditional role as homemaker.*

Some of the statistics in this article are now somewhat out of date. Even more recent figures, as given in the selections that follow, show that the percentage of married women, including those with young children, who are entering the work force is continuing to rise.

Length of summary: Approximately 250 words

Sometime this year, probably within the next month or so, the percentage of American women who hold or are looking for work is expected to reach 50. According to figures released last week, in April, 49.7 percent of all women—a new high—were in the labor force, an increase from March's 49.3 percent and a signal of a continuing upward swing.

In the last decade, the Labor Department says, 14 million new jobs have been filled in this country and women have filled 10 million of them. Last year, in large part because of the rapid entry of women into the labor market, the number of jobseekers grew just about as rapidly as the number of jobs. That is one reason why the unemployment rate stayed so high last year—the average, 7 percent, give or take a tenth of a point—despite the fact that employment rose at a record rate, by 4.1 million jobs.

Some economists and politicians discuss the phenomenon in a faintly accusatory manner. Though the suggestion is never directly put, it is there: If only women would stay in their traditional homemaker's role, instead of seeking liberation through a different lifestyle, the nation's unemployment troubles would be solved. Or, such commentators recommend, unemployment should be redefined, so that "nontraditional" workers such as women be properly weighted. But such scapegoat thinking, other experts contend, only obscures fundamental economic reasons for the trend.

Undoubtedly, social factors play a role in the growing flood of women into the work force. "But the fact is more and more women are working out of necessity," says Alexis M. Herman, director of the Women's Bureau of the Labor Department. "Women don't have the option of working inside the home or outside the home any more," she adds. "Economic needs require that they go out and find a job."

Miss Herman has estimated that 60 to 65 percent of women who hold jobs do so for purely economic reasons. Many of them must work because they are the only source of economic support for themselves and their families. A Women's Bureau study published in mid-1976 showed that over 23 percent of working women have never been married. Another 19 percent of women workers were widowed, divorced or separated from their husbands, and because of social and cultural trends, the number of women living without husbands is increasing. In 1960, for example, 28 percent of women aged 22 to 24 were single; by 1976 the number had risen to 46 percent. For most of them, there is little alternative to work other than welfare or unemployment compensation. As Geraldine Coleman, a 27-year-old mother of three who works as an auto mechanic for Sears Roebuck and Co., puts it, a job is not simply a matter of lifestyle: "I work because it is a matter of survival. A single parent like me needs a job and needs one at a male salary."

More than half of all working women, however, are married, some of them to men who are unable to work, and still more have husbands who are unemployed for one reason or another. These women, too, must work as the sole support of their families and themselves. Of working women with working husbands, close to half had husbands who earned $10,000 a year or less when the data for the 1976 women bureau study was collected. "Often," Miss Herman explains, "a second income means the difference between poverty and an adequate standard of living."

But it is not just the wives of low-wage earners who are taking jobs to supplement their husband's income, and help keep the family budget solvent in the face of inflation. Women in middle-income families are taking jobs in response to the economic squeeze. In part, such women are going to work to maintain the standard of living to which they have become accustomed. But increasingly, a second income is being sought to achieve traditional goals, such as college education for their children or for a one-family home.

Sandra Hall, whose husband is a Secret Service agent, recently went to work as a computer repair specialist. "I work first of all for the money," she said. "One income wasn't sufficient. We want to maintain a middle-class lifestyle—meaning for us a townhouse in Reston [VA] and braces on the boy's teeth. Also they are continually raising utility rates and other things are going up all the time. Of course I've always wanted to work anyway. I've been working all my adult life."

"I'm working at this job for one reason—to make enough money to put my kids through college," said a woman with a civil service job in Washington whose $26,000 a year salary is only marginally below her husband's. When both children are in college at the same time all of her after-tax salary, working costs deducted, would go for tuition and school expenses.

The cost of that other American dream, the suburban home, is also rising so fast that it is fading beyond the reach of many one-income families that could, in past generations, have afforded one. In fact, the cherished notion of the American family, in which the father goes out to earn daily bread and the mother stays at home in a cottage, with or without a rose garden, to take care of the children, is now more myth than reality.

Two years ago, the Urban Institute extrapolated from Bureau of Labor Statistics data that only 19 percent of all Americans were members of families in which the father worked and the mother stayed at home, with one or more children. Ralph Smith, an economist with the institute, said that the number of these supposedly archetypical family groups will continue to shrink.

Changes in the structure of the economy have also contributed to the rapid growth of the percentage of women in the labor force, says Julius Shiskin, director the Bureau of Labor Statistics. While employment has been declining or stagnant in manufacturing and construction industry, which are dominated by men, it has been rising fairly rapidly in clerical and service industries. Few working women now have jobs such as Mrs. Coleman's: Being an auto mechanic is generally considered man's work. Women are concentrated chiefly into 20 of the 480 categories listed by the Labor Department, most of them clerical, such as secretarial or bookkeeping, or service, such as sales clerks, nurses aides and waitresses. But with women pouring into the workplace at an accelerated rate, most economists predict that more of them will be moving away from such traditional women's work.

Discussion

1. What sources does the author draw on for the information in this article?
2. What was the unemployment rate in the United States in 1978? The article says that according to some experts, this rate of unemployment is so high because of the entrance of women into the job market. Do you hear this kind of argument these days? What is the unemployment rate in the United States today?
3. According to this article, what percent of the labor force is made up of women? What percent of women are working for economic reasons? What percent of all working women are married?
4. What are the two main reasons given in the article for why married women work?
5. The traditional view of the home in the United States (and probably still in many countries) was one in which the father went out to earn the

money (the breadwinner) and the mother stayed home to take care of the home and the children (the ideal home being a suburban cottage with a rose garden). According to the Urban Institute, what percentage of all American families actually fit this pattern? In your country, is the traditional family where the father goes out to work and the mother stays home still the most common? Is this family arrangement beginning to change?

6. According to the Bureau of Labor Statistics, what kinds of work are most women doing?

Reading 3

The Second Stage

Betty Friedan

The following selection is from Betty Friedan's The Second Stage. *Her first book,* The Feminine Mystique, *written in 1963, initiated the women's movement. According to Friedan, the feminine mystique was the traditional and supposedly sacred view of the woman as the happy suburban housewife "completely fulfilled in her role as husband's wife, children's mother, server of physical needs of husband, children, home."*

The first stage of the women's movement, says Friedan, was fought against the "old structure of the unequal polarized male and female sex roles." In their struggle for equality, however, some militant feminists went too far and also rejected the family itself. In the second stage, Freidan believes that women should fight for a restructuring of our institutions so that women can be truly free to choose their roles—including the important choice of having children.

Length of summary: Approximately 150 words.

The women's movement is being blamed, above all, for the destruction of the family. Churchmen and sociologists proclaim that the American family, as it has always been defined, is becoming an "endangered species," with the rising divorce rate and the enormous increase in single-parent families and people—especially women—living alone. Women's abdication of their age-old responsibility for the family is also being blamed for the apathy and moral delinquency of the "me generation."

Can we keep on shrugging all this off as enemy propaganda—"their problem, not ours"? I think we must at least admit and begin openly to discuss feminist denial of the importance of family, of women's own needs to give and get love and nurture, tender loving care.

What worries me today is the agonizing conflicts young and not-so-young women are facing—or denying—as they come up against the biological clock, at thirty-five, thirty-six, thirty-nine, forty, and cannot "choose" to have a child. I fought for the right to choose, and will continue to defend that right, against reactionary forces who have already taken it away for poor women now denied Medicaid for abortion, and would take it away for all women with a constitutional amendment. But I think we must begin to discuss, in new terms, the choice to *have* children.

What worries me today is "choices" women have supposedly won, which are not real. How can a woman freely "choose" to have a child when her paycheck is needed for the rent or mortgage, when her job isn't geared to taking care of a child, when there is no national policy for parental leave, and no assurance that her job will be waiting for her if she takes off to have a child?

What worries me today is that despite the fact that more than 45 percent of the mothers of children under six are now working because of economic necessity due to inflation, compared with only 10 percent in 1960 (and, according to a Ford Foundation study, it is estimated that by 1990 only one out of four mothers will be at home full time), no major national effort is being made for child-care services by government, business, labor, Democratic or Republican parties—or by the women's movement itself.

Discussion

1. According to the author, what serious social problems have been blamed on the women's movement?
2. What is meant by the "biological clock"?
3. What are some of the conditions mentioned by the author that prevent women from freely choosing to have children?
4. According to the author, what percentage of mothers with children under 6 are now working? What was the percentage for working mothers in 1960? What is the estimated percentage of working mothers for 1990?

    (In "The Parental-Leave Debate," a selection on pp. 116–117, a chart accompanying the article indicates that as of 1986, 50 percent of married women with children under 2 were in the work force, up from 25 percent in 1970. As with all statistics, however, the reader must consider the variables that affect the interpretation—in this case, for example, whether the women are married or not (Friedan doesn't tell us this), whether the statistics include women with part-time jobs, and the age of the children.)

More recent statistics from the Bureau of Labor Statistics cited in *The New York Times* of October 4, 1987 (page 4E) are that nearly two-thirds of all mothers are in the work force at least part time, and that among mothers whose youngest child is between 6 and 13 years old, nearly three-quarters work.

Note: The Medicaid program mentioned in the article is a federal program to help poor people pay their medical bills.

Reading for Further Ideas

The selections in this section are intended not only to give you additional information about the subject of the composition but to continue to sharpen your reading skills, and in addition, to give you practice in preparing for essay examinations.

After you have skimmed through each selection and underlined the main points, make an outline from memory. Then check the reading selection again and make a more exact outline. This time, make a one-sentence summary of the main idea.

With this preparation, write a question for each selection that you think might appear on an essay examination. Without concentrating on the details, make the question as comprehensive as possible. You may also ask a question comparing the selection with others on the same subject. Then write the answers and check them against the reading selection.

In writing your question, keep in mind the date and source of the selection (newspaper or magazine, textbook, other kind of book). Such sources often have different purposes and may therefore affect the way your questions might be asked.

Reading 1

Repeated Marriage: A Growing Trend?

Andree Brooks

The following article discusses a troubling social problem—the breakdown of the American family through divorce and remarriage. As you read the article, note the high rate of divorce and the reasons for it. Note also the difficulties that multiple marriages cause for both children and parents.

The New York Times, February 7, 1985, p. C1. Copyright © 1985 by The New York Times Company. Reprinted by permission.

The earliest pattern of the American family was the extended family, when several generations lived together. A more recent one is the nuclear family, when only the parents and their children live together. Now sociologists are beginning to use the term extended family again. This time they mean the stepfamilies that include half brothers and sisters, and stepmothers and stepfathers.

Observe the use of an introductory quotation that leads into the subject of the article and a concluding quotation that suggests a solution to the problem being discussed.

"Instead of wedding 'until death do us part,' couples will enter matrimony knowing from the start that the relationship is short-lived. And when the opportunity presents itself, they will marry again...and again...and again."

This prophecy, made by Alvin Toffler 15 years ago in his classic work, "Future Shock," is coming true, according to therapists and divorce lawyers who see a growing number of people who have been married three and even four times. "A generation or two ago you entered a marriage and you stayed with it for better or worse," said Dr. Clifford Sager, director of family psychiatry at the Jewish Board of Family and Children's Services in New York City. "Today we are seeing much more short-term bonding, with an increasing number of men and women going through serial marriages."

The professionals and those who have been through serial marriages cite many reasons. Among them: the comparative ease of divorce, and the greatly lessened social stigma that it now carries; a romanticization of marriage that cannot live up to the long-term reality; a "flip the dial" attitude that fosters moving on as soon as problems or ennui set in; the economic independence of women; a level of affluence that makes multiple families possible for some; an attitude among the so-called me generation that places fulfillment of personal needs ahead of compromise or sharing, and medical advances that have prolonged vigorous life.

The stages at which people change marriage partners also seems to follow Mr. Toffler's predictions. Jeroll R. Silverberg, national vice president of the American Academy of Matrimonial Lawyers, said that the first marriage generally occurs during the college years and is normally brief, lasting no more than two or three years. The second is longer-term, entered for the purpose of childbearing. The third is a midlife protest against aging; it usually is short and involves the marriage of a man to a much younger woman. Finally, there is the later, "mature relationship"—a marriage of age peers in which companionship is the key.

Why not simply live together? "People are still very traditional," said Dr. Harold Lief, a professor of psychiatry at the University of Pennsylvania, who studies contemporary marriage. "It's also more efficient," he said. "Society is still geared to married couples, whether it's the I.R.S., Blue Cross coverage or getting a credit card. You also feel your relationship will have a better chance that way."

There are no firm statistics on how widespread the phenomenon has become. However, there are clear indications and some early interpretations that can be based on current data, according to Suzanne Prescod, editor of Marriage and Divorce Today, a newsletter for family therapists.

Census figures generally show that 50 percent of American marriages now end in divorce, she said. Eighty-five percent of these divorced people remarry, usually within five years, with 60 percent of those marriages ending in divorce. Assuming that about a quarter of these twice-divorced people "get disillusioned or drop out," she continued, about three-quarters will go on to marry again.

Figures from the National Center for Health Statistics support what Mrs. Prescod says. Although they do not chart the number of prior marriages, they show, for example, that 647,000 divorced men remarried in 1981, compared with 334,000 in 1971. Similarly, 616,000 women who married in 1981 had also been married at least once before, compared with 423,000 in 1971. More serial marriages are now possible, Mrs. Prescod said, because more people are divorced: the increase in divorces that began in the 1970's has created a larger pool of people available to remarry.

Divorce lawyers and mental-health practitioners say that the cumulative effect of these remarriages is starting to be seen. For example, Raoul Lionel Felder, a Manhattan divorce lawyer, says he now has his "regulars."

"We are representing the same people through three divorces," he said. At least 60 percent of his clients, he added, are on their second divorce.

Experts and participants differ on how serial marriages affect personality, well-being, child development and inheritance.

"The age of serial marriages gives me a chance to have more chances," said Richard, a 46-year-old New York City entrepeneur who recently was divorced from his third wife (and who asked that his full name not be used). The acceptability of divorce, he conceded, was a motivating force once he decided the relationships were not going well. Nevertheless, he says the divorces have given him a feeling of personal failure. But he also blames society for the pressure that suggests that being married—to anyone—is better than being single.

Others who have remarried welcome the opportunities for growth. Kay Marie Porterfield, a writer in Denver who is on her third marriage, says she has become more realistic and tolerant of a partner. "I don't expect a husband to 'save' me, or 'take care' of me or carry my weight," she said. Three marriages, she insists, have made her a stronger, more compassionate person.

Others are less sure. "I've changed my name so many times I don't know who I am anymore," said Barbara Freedman, a Manhattan social worker who has been married three times, having been widowed as well as divorced. She went on: "It's disruptive. It's hard to maintain a stable core of friends or pattern of life. So much of your structure is built around your marriage."

Experts see more disturbing patterns. "It definitely diminishes self-esteem," said Stanley Rosner, a psychologist in New Canaan, Conn., and co-author of "The Marriage Gap," a study of the breakdown of contemporary marriages. "These people end up feeling like losers even though they may only be responding to external cues." Repeated emotional upheaval, he said, is driving some of them to heavy drinking and drug use.

Children of parents who marry several times are another concern. "The youngsters are the saddest part," said Dr. Robert Garfield, an assistant professor of psychiatry at Hahnemann University in Philadelphia who specializes in stepfamily issues.

"I see children not being able to concentrate, a sense that nothing lasts and a loss of faith in relationships," Dr. Garfield said. "They never develop trust or long-term values. They become self-centered and cynical." Other experts, including Dr. Rosner, maintain that such children will continue the pattern because it is so familiar.

Multiple marriages also aggravate sibling conflicts. "We are entering a period of interfamily feuds the likes of which you have never seen," said William Selsberg, a lawyer in Stamford, Conn., "Who is entitled to get college money if there isn't enough to go around? How do you equitably settle the claims of the children from the different marriages when the parent dies? What if the children from a former marriage are left out of the will? Estate planning is becoming impossible."

The adults also suffer financially, gradually getting poorer. "You see their life style getting progressively worse each time they marry again," said Mr. Felder, the Manhattan divorce lawyer. "Equitable distribution depletes the assets. They're stuck with regular commitments to a spouse or children from a previous marriage. It's a finite cup. Only so many people can take from that cup before it's empty."

Mrs. Prescod foresees that the practical and psychological problems resulting from multiple marriages may become so severe that they will inspire reappraisals, with premarital and marital counseling becoming routine and divorce more difficult. "I already hear some of the therapists say that we should be putting more energy into learning how to make and save a good first marriage," she said.

Reading 2

The Parental-Leave Debate

Barbara Kantrowitz

This article takes up the issue of a national policy on maternal leave. Read to see where the United States stands in relation to other developed countries in making it possible for a mother with a new baby to return to her job. This issue is particularly important now because so many women are in the work force. A chart that accompanies this article shows that 50 percent of married women with children under 2 are in the work force, up from 25 percent in 1970.

Compare the lack of a national policy regarding a parental leave in the United States with the national policy in Sweden that is mentioned in the article "College Women and Careers."

Lillian Garland wanted to take two months off from her job as a bank receptionist after she gave birth to her daughter, Kekere, 1982. But when she told the California Federal Savings and Loan Association that she was ready to return to work, she learned that her job had been filled—despite a California law that guarantees mothers their jobs after "maternity disability" leaves of up to four months. Garland took her case to the state's Department of Fair Employment and Housing, setting in motion a series of legal actions that have ended up before the U.S. Supreme Court—and have made Garland a new symbol of the growing national debate over parental leave.

Although Garland did eventually return to work for California Federal, the bank challenged the California law on the ground that it conflicts with the federal Pregnancy Discrimination Act of 1978. That law requires companies with employee-disability policies to provide pregnant women with the same benefits as other disabled workers. The bank claims that the California law gives women benefits that men don't get.

When the Supreme Court hears the case—probably later this year—it will hardly be the only forum for discussion of the parental-leave issue. In the House of Representatives, Colorado Democrat Patricia Schroeder has introduced a bill that would provide a minimum of 18 weeks of unpaid leave for any employee who wants to stay home with a newborn, newly adopted or seriously ill child; hearings are scheduled to be held early next month. Unions have become active in seeking parental-leave clauses in their contracts. And in the last few months two distinguished panels of business, labor and child-care experts at Yale and the Economic Policy Council have recommended that job-protected leaves of up to six months be made available—with partial pay—to new parents....

The Schroeder bill, which is supported by NOW and does treat men and women equally, has drawn fire from the U.S. Chamber of Commerce. Employers should be allowed to decide if they are going to offer parental leave, argues James A. Klein, the chamber's manager of pension and employee benefits. He also contends that a mandatory national policy would hit small businesses the hardest because they often lack the resources to find and train temporary help to replace workers on leave.

Those who support a national policy say that the United States is lagging behind much of the world on the issue. Sheila B. Kamerman, professor of social policy and planning at Columbia University School of Social Work, has studied parental-leave policies for more than a decade. She says that the United States "is unique among more than 100 other countries—including almost all the advanced industrialized countries and many less-developed ones"—in having no national legislation that guarantees a woman her job while she is on leave. The federal Pregnancy Discrimination Act, she points out, applies only to women who work for companies with employee-disability policies; it does not help the majority of women who, Kamerman says, work for smaller companies that are less likely to offer such benefits.

But a federal policy on parental leave is not likely to be enacted without considerable debate, if only because there is still no agreement on how much time new parents want or need. Many child-development experts say that four months is the minimum required for mothers to "bond" with their babies. Obstetricians generally say it takes a woman six to eight weeks to recover physically from a normal childbirth.

Yet many women are returning to work even sooner, either out of economic necessity or, Kamerman says, because they are being pressured by employers into coming back. Since the passage of the federal pregnancy law, some companies have instituted parental-leave policies in order to avoid charges of sex discrimination, but studies show that even given that chance, fathers are likely to take only a few days off after the birth of a child. Even if they can afford the loss of income, the time off, they often feel, would hurt their competitive position in the business world.

Although she is not directly involved in the Supreme Court case brought by the bank, Lillian Garland still has a considerable interest in the outcome. A decision in favor of the California law could mean back pay for the time she was out of work after her leave ended. But whatever the outcome, the case has already focused national attention on an issue that Schroeder calls "an idea whose time has come."

Reading 3

Women of Europe Prove Differences

Robbie B. Snow

In the following article, the author discusses a book about European women that had recently been published. The book points out some differences between the way European and American women see themselves. To catch the attention of the reader, the article begins with a statement of what these differences are.

If you come from a Western European country, see if you agree with Shari Steiner's conclusions about the way European women view their roles and purposes.

To the women of France, being a wife is the most important role. To the women of Italy, it is being a mother. The women of Germany are battling to find a compromise between being a "lady" or being a "warrior." English women talk more about their plight and the women of Sweden have taken the Viking tradition into the marketplace and won.

These are only a few observations Shari Steiner makes in her new book, "The Female Factor: A Report on Women in Western Europe," published by G. P. Putnam Sons.

Ms. Steiner's knowledge of how the women's movement is affecting Europe comes first hand. She has spent the last 14 years living in Europe with her family.

"I started as a correspondent for the 'International Herald Tribune' stationed in Rome. I was writing stories mainly on how the changing laws and ideas about women were affecting them in various countries. Pretty soon, it got to the point where I decided to put all of the information into a report. I was lucky. I sold the idea to the first publisher I visited," she said, before a recent lecture at Stanford University. The lecture was sponsored by the Center for Research on Women (CROW) at Stanford.

Gives Closer Look

Although Ms. Steiner admits to the sin of generalization in her book, she has still managed to give a closer look at what makes the European woman so different from her American counterpart.

The Salt Lake Tribune, March 1, 1977. Reprinted by permission.

"The French woman probably has the best idea of who she is and what she wants to become," she explained. "The process of learning who she is begins when the child is small. She is taught at an early age that attractiveness to the opposite sex is important and how best to achieve it.

"France has a much lower divorce rate than the U.S., mainly because they view marriage differently. To the French, marriage is something on which to build. You start with the marriage and then you go from there to build a private life. Parental togetherness is also stressed. School is held on Saturday mornings so parents can have time alone.

A Mother First

"The Italian woman, on the other hand, is a mother first. Mothers have great responsibility and status in Italy. I liken them to the American businessman, because society has awarded them the same status. Most women control the family money. The Italian woman's greatest fears are of being alone, not having a child or having a child that is deformed. It is interesting to note that before abortion became legalized in Italy there was an even number of births to illegal abortions. If an Italian woman didn't think she was ready for the responsibility she found a way to terminate it.

"English women are more like we. Their roles and purposes are less defined. I also predict that England will continue in its tradition of strong female leaders and elect Margaret Thatcher prime minister within the next five years. Her successor may also be a woman.

Under More Stress

"German women are under more stress than any other European female. They are torn between the idea of being a 'lady' and living in a world away from men with its own set of rules and goals, or being a 'warrior' and competing for success on male terms.

"There is more violence among German women than any other European country and they also have the highest suicide rate of any female population. I think this is because they keep coming up against a society which is too rigid to change. They have given up talking about problems and are now confronting the issues in a physical sense.

"There is zero population growth in Sweden and being a mother and a worker are of equal importance. Sweden recently enacted a law granting seven months maternity leave. There is one month before the baby is born and six months afterward.

"The interesting thing is that the six months of leave after the baby is born also includes the father. Parents can work a swing shift worked out between their respective employers who are required by law to help arrange the schedules. It will no longer be a penalty to hire women, or a burden for the woman to work, since employers will have the equal chance of losing a man as well as a woman for the same reason—pregnancy."

Women, an International Class

Ms. Steiner sees women as an international class—as much, if not more so, than the working class.

"Women are a large group of people with the same problems and the same things which are important to them. The Pill is probably the one thing that has created a woman's class, because it has opened up a whole new way of thinking. Biology is no longer destiny. Society is beginning to see that it is no longer a good thing to have a lot of children. All it boils down to is that half of the world's population has to rethink what else they can do."

She points out that Europe hasn't had the major surges of public opinion for and against the women's movement. But in Europe most women are already considered responsible and contributing members of society.

Extra Discussion and Writing

Journal entry

Write about your impressions of children in the United States. Discuss their behavior, and their attitudes toward their elders and toward others in authority. Discuss your feeling about whether there is a lack of parental supervision in the home perhaps because so many mothers are working out of the home. Compare the training American children seem to get in their homes with the training you received at home. Since you are writing only for yourself, state your feelings freely.

Letters

1. Write a letter to one of your teachers in your country about the same subject as the journal entry above. This time, revise the journal entry for the letter so it is more carefully controlled and correct. But keep the letter friendly, since you know the teacher.
2. *For women students only:* You have seen statistics indicating that many women in the United States are marrying later than they used to because of the time needed to prepare for a career. You have seen other

statistics indicating that the choices of marriage for a woman over thirty are greatly reduced. Write a letter to a family member in your country discussing this matter and saying what you expect your future plans for marriage and a career to be.

3. Write a letter to a close American friend describing the kind of man or woman you would like to marry. Use a friendly but serious tone.

Sayings

1. *Woman's place is in the home.* This saying has often been tied in with discussion of human nature—especially the "natural" roles of men and women with regard to the family. Give your opinion about whether taking care of the home and the children is a "natural" function only of women and whether men are incapable of performing these functions.

2. *Education begins at home.* Discuss the role of each parent in educating young children. What kind of early training can children get if both parents work full time?

3. *A woman is weak; however, a mother is strong.* This is a Chinese saying. How do you interpret it?

4. *Home is where the heart is.* What does this saying mean to you?

Reactions

Reading 1

Study of American Couples

A 1983 book called American Couples *made a study of the private lives of 6,000 ordinary American couples all over the country. Among the findings listed in an advertisement for the book were the following:*

1. Both men and women feel it is the husband's responsibility to provide for his wife. If the man is not a good provider, the relationship may be in jeopardy.

From an advertisement in *The New York Times* on October 23, 1983, for *American Couples* by Philip Blumstein and Pepper Schwartz, 1983, William Morrow, 105 Madison Ave., New York, N.Y. 10016.

2. *Women do most of the housework, even if both partners have full-time jobs. The more household chores a man has to perform, the less happy he is likely to be with the relationship.*

3. *The money that a working woman brings home earns her power in the household and respect from her partner—unless she makes enough to threaten his dominant role.*

What is your reaction to these findings? In a marriage, do you expect the husband to be the main breadwinner in the family? Why or why not?

Reading 2

"She's Leaving Home"

The Beatles

In the late sixties and early seventies (the period generally called the sixties), many young people were feeling alienated from their parents, as well as from all of society, whose authority-figures were called "the Establishment." The home, which once provided a loving environment, mostly because mothers were at home, was now an empty shell. Family ties and structures were weakened. Many young people turned away from their parents and to their peers (people their own age) for support and direction. It was the time of runaway youngsters living freely as "hippies" in the streets or in communes.

"She's Leaving Home" was very popular during this period. What feelings of both the girl and the parents are reflected in the song? What is your reaction to the lyrics? What do you consider ironic in this song?

Wednesday morning at five o'clock as the day begins,
Silently closing her bedroom door,
Leaving the note that she hoped would say more,
She goes downstairs to the kitchen, clutching her handkerchief.
Quietly turning the back door key,
Stepping outside she is free.

(*She*)   We gave her most of our lives,
(*Is leaving*)   Sacrificed most of our lives,
(*Home*)   We gave her everything money could buy.
She's leaving home after living alone for so many years (Bye-bye).

Father snores as his wife gets into her dressing-gown,
Picks up the letter that's lying there.
Standing alone at the top of the stairs she breaks down
And cries to her husband, "Daddy, our baby's gone!
Why would she treat us so thoughtlessly?
How could she do this to me?"

(*She*)   We never thought of ourselves,
(*Is leaving*)   Never a thought for ourselves,
(*Home*)   We struggled hard all our lives to get by,
She's leaving home after living alone for so many years (Bye-bye).

Friday morning at nine o'clock she is far away,
Waiting to keep the appointment she made,
Meeting a man from the motor-trade.

(*She*)   What did we do that was wrong?
(*Is having*)   We didn't know it was wrong.
(*Fun*)   Fun is the one thing that money can't buy.
Something inside that was always denied for so many years (Bye-bye).
She's leaving home (Bye-bye).

CHAPTER 5

Television

Composition

Requirements for a Home Composition

1. Use white $8\frac{1}{2}'' \times 11''$ paper; write on one side only.
2. Type your composition double spaced on unlined paper (if hand-written, the paper should be clearly written on every other line). A typewritten page, double-spaced, is about 250 words.
3. Indent each paragraph, use wide margins (1" to $1\frac{1}{4}''$), and number each page in the upper righthand corner.
4. Include a separate page with the title, the thesis sentence, and the outline.

Procedures for Discussion

The teacher puts on the board headings for two columns:

Advantages of TV   *Disadvantages of TV*

Then the teacher asks for student opinions. These are listed on the board in phrases under the appropriate column in the random order each student gives them. (It is desirable to place opposing points of view side by side.)

Writing the Composition

Answer the following essay question. (The composition may be assigned to be written at home or at the next class meeting.)

Question: It has been said that American television is the one common bond that unites all classes of people. Some people feel that this unifying bond is producing good results—for example, it is forming a more aware and a better-informed citizenry. Others feel that television is merely providing an escape; it is taking people away from more worthwhile pursuits. It has even been accused of encouraging young people to perform the same kinds of violence they see on television. From what you have seen of American television, do you think it is beneficial or harmful to its viewers? Support your opinions by specific examples.

Read the question carefully and underline the words that indicate what the question is actually asking for. (If you are not living in the United States, refer to the kind of television you see in the country where you are living at the time you are writing this composition.)

Suggestions for the Content and Organization

Whether you write your answer to this essay question at home or in class, consider the following points.

Think in terms of different classes of television programs. Such classifications can help you think more comprehensively about the subject of television.

Narrow down your answer to one position. You may admit that there is some justification for the other side, but that your position has greater weight. In a composition of argument or opinion, there is often no one "right" answer. The decision is made according to your viewpoint. But your arguments or opinions must be presented logically, clearly, and convincingly.

You may answer the question in terms of:

the effects of television on its viewers, both children and adults;
the value of the information we get from TV;

the kinds and quality of television offerings;
what you think should be the purpose of television.

You may discuss television programs in general, or you may concentrate on one or more types of TV offerings.

If you write the composition in class, you may not have time to write a formal outline. Your composition should be a reasonable length determined by the amount of time of your class meeting, rather than by the number of words. Write from notes that have some kind of organizational structure, and that indicate how you will handle the introduction and conclusion. Write carefully, since you may not be able to rewrite. Time yourself so that you can write about each point listed in your notes and still have time at the end to look over your paper.

Guide for the Outline and the Composition

If you write the composition at home, or if you rewrite the class composition, the following guide should help you.

On the left side of the guide is the outline with suggestions for handling the introduction, transitions, and the conclusion of this composition. On the right side are general comments about how introductions, transitions, and conclusions may be written. (If you are accustomed to writing a first draft from rough notes, use this guide for your second and succeeding drafts.)

Outline	*General Comments*
Title	Use initial capital letters for all words except articles, short prepositions, and short conjunctions. Try to use an interesting title that reflects your thesis.
Introduction This can be personal—about yourself, your family, or others you know.	Purpose of the introduction: to catch the reader's interest to give a general idea of the subject
Or it can be more general—about the widespread influence of TV or TV's effect on the family or on society.	An introduction may include: a quotation a story, perhaps personal a rhetorical question (which you will answer) a definition a statement of a belief you will argue against a surprising or shocking fact a statement of a serious problem

Transitional lead-in

This suggests the position you will take regarding the beneficial or harmful effects of TV.

Usually at the end of the introduction. Gives an indication of the central idea and the way it will be developed (may be in the form of a question).

I. First main point

This gives the first beneficial or harmful effect of TV.

New paragraph. The first sentence: (1) mentions the general idea of the paragraph (from the important word[s] in the outline; (2) relates this sentence to what was said before.

A. First supporting detail

B. Second supporting detail
     etc.

Should be related to the preceding subpoint.

(Continue with your other main points and their supporting details.) For each main point, remind the reader that you are giving another beneficial or harmful effect of TV.

(Follow the suggestions given for the first main point.)

Note: Long subpoints may begin new paragraphs.

Conclusion

This can go back to your personal experience, or it can be more general. You may suggest how to use TV to best advantage.

The conclusion should round out the composition in a strong and satisfying way, perhaps by referring again to whatever you used to introduce the composition.

Notes: (1) The conclusion should not add any new ideas that need further development. (2) If your last point ends on a strong note that points up your thesis, you may not need to add a conclusion.

Support for the points you make can come from your own beliefs and experience or from the readings in this chapter and elsewhere. (Be sure to identify your sources and to use quotation marks around the exact words of an author.) The support can be in the form of examples, current facts and figures, or authoritative opinion. Use enough support to make your point convincing to the reader.

Finally, keep in mind that this composition represents your own opinions. By stating them honestly and strongly, you will have a composition that the reader will find interesting enough to continue reading.

Revising the Composition

In succeeding drafts, try to sharpen your thesis and show more clearly how each main point contributes to the development of the thesis. Try writing down the opening sentences of your paragraphs on a separate sheet of paper to see if they make a clear sentence outline. Go over the reading selections again for further ideas or additional support.

Consult the Revision and Editing Checklist for guidance on organization, paragraphing, and sentences. You can also get needed vocabulary help in the vocabulary section that follows on pp. 128–129. Make a final check with the Symbol Chart for Correction of Compositions for the grammatical structures and usage in your composition.

Evaluation

If there is an exchange of student compositions, the Revision and Editing Checklist can serve as a guide in the evaluation of another student's composition. Use the following procedure in checking for the writer's organization and development of ideas.

1. Without looking at the other student's outline page, make an outline and a one-sentence summary of the central idea (or thesis) of the whole paper. Can you find a clear line of development? Do your summary sentence and your outline agree with those of the writer?
2. Find the support for each point made in the writer's paper. Is the support adequate and convincing?
3. Write on the student's paper what you consider the good points of the composition and what needs to be improved.

Vocabulary and Usage

Vocabulary
Usage Notes
Word Forms

Vocabulary

The following words may be useful to you in talking and writing about the composition on television.

anchorman, anchorwoman   A TV newscaster who coordinates reports from various correspondents.

cable TV   A commerical TV system offering subscribers many programs on special channels by means of a cable.

cartoon   (Reduced from animated cartoon) "A motion picture consisting of a sequence of drawings, each slightly different from the preceding one so that, when filmed and run through a projector, the figures seem to move." (*Random House Dictionary*). Cartoons are usually shown on TV for children. Many are full of violence.

commercial   An advertisement of their product by the sponsor of a TV program.

documentary   A program based on true facts. Often contains film clips of real events.

game show   A program in which prizes are offered to selected viewers for getting the right answers, the lucky numbers, the most points, etc. The prizes are donated by companies to get publicity for their products.

network   A group of stations linked together so that the same program can be broadcast or telecast to all.

prime time   The time in the evening when the largest number of people are viewing TV. Although officially given as 8 p.m. to 11 p.m., many believe it starts one hour earlier.

producer   A person responsible for getting a show ready for presentation.

screen   The surface on which pictures are projected, as in motion pictures or TV.

serial   One program in a series dealing with the same characters.

sit-com   For situation-comedy; a serialized comedy using the same characters. Each program revolves around one troublesome situation which is resolved by the end of the program.

soap opera   A daytime melodrama presented serially (the name is based on the household products that sponsor the programs.) Some are now appearing at night. Soap operas are more informally called "soaps."

sponsor   The company that is paying to produce a particular television program so that it can advertise its product.

trivia (plural, often with a singular verb)   Unimportant matters or details. Some TV game shows deal with trivia (**trivial**, adjective).

variety show   A program containing different forms of entertainment, such as comedy, songs, dances.

VCR   For video cassette recorder; an instrument for recording the picture and the sound of a TV program so that it can be played back later on a TV set.

vicarious   Participating in the experience of others secondhand.

viewer   A person who watches TV.

Usage Notes

the mass media	*Media* is the plural (from Latin) of *medium*. It requires a plural verb. *The* is used before *mass media*.
information	*Information* is a singular, noncountable noun; it is not used with an *-s* ending. *An* is not used before it.
television (also TV)	*Television* may be used in two senses: As an abstract concept, the word is noncountable and is used without an article.
	Television may be harmful to some children.
	She watched *television* all day.
	As the set itself, the word is countable and requires an article if singular.
	She sat before the *TV* all day.
the news	*News* is noncountable and requires a singular verb. It also requires *the*.
society	*Society* may be used in two senses. As an abstract concept, it is noncountable and used without an article.
	Society makes certain demands on us.
	When it refers to a particular group, the word is countable and requires an article if singular.
	The *society* in which we live
advertising, advertisement	*advertising* is noncountable. An article is not used.
	There is too much *advertising* on TV.
	advertisement is countable and adds *-s* for the plural. (The

	singular requires an article.)
	There are too many *advertisements* on TV.
an effect, to affect	*effect* is a noun; *affect* is a verb (= have an effect on)
	Violence on TV has a bad *effect* on some children.
	Violence on TV often *affects* children who are already aggressive.

Word Forms

Use the correct forms for the words in parentheses.

The answers are on p. 355. If you need help with this section, refer to the explanations under Word Forms in Appendix A.

1. Researchers are studying the (effect) _____ of TV viewing on children's reading habits. They are even studying the way TV viewing (effect) _____ children's eating habits.

2. TV can be (benefit) _____ to its viewers if the programs are carefully (choice) _____.

3. There may be some (distort) _____ of the news on TV in order to present an (occur) _____ in an (entertain) _____ way rather than in a purely (inform) _____ way.

4. Some experts claim that the (violent) _____ in the TV cartoons are merely an outlet for children's (hostile) _____ and (aggressive) _____ and are not (harm) _____.

5. Lately more and more long TV stories are being (serial) _____ so that parts can be presented on (succeed) _____ days or weeks.

6. The soap opera *Dallas* permits its viewers to (fantasy) _____ about life among the (wealth) _____, the (power) _____, and the (beauty) _____.

7. Elderly or sick people turn to TV for (relax) _____ and (recreate) _____.

8. TV is the most (influence) _____ medium of communication in American life.

9. Most of the (finance) _____ support for TV programs come from the sponsors.

10. Too much TV (view) _____ may lead to (passive) _____ and a lack of (create) _____.

11. TV has made some (comedy) _____ very (success) _____ and (wealth) _____.

12. One (critic) _____ of TV news is that it often does not present an event in (deep) _____.

13. The (document) _____ is intended to give (fact) _____ information to the TV (view) _____.

14. Game shows provide (excite) _____ to the TV audience and are more (economy) _____ to produce than other types of programs.

15. Many TV programs have been (critic) _____ for placing too much (emphasis) _____ on sex and (violent) _____.

16. Children (watch) _____ too much TV and (eat) _____ a lot of junk food while they watch are (get) _____ fatter.

Reading for Summary Writing

For the following three reading selections, prepare a brief outline for class discussion before you write the summary. After the class discussion of each reading selection, you will write:

1. A longer, revised outline of the reading selection, using an alternation of numbers and letters.
2. A one-sentence summary of the reading selection. The sentence should include the central idea and the main points used to develop this idea (from the outline).
3. A summary of the reading selection. The length assigned in the text will determine the amount of detail you can include in the outline and summary.

Guidelines for Writing (Review)

1. For the outline, use the alternate number-letter system for the main points and their subpoints. (The phrases you underline in the opening sentences of paragraphs usually become the main points or subpoints on the outline.)
2. For both the summary and the outline, follow the same order as the reading selection. However, you may begin the summary with a reference to the source of the selection (author, publication, etc.) and to its central idea.
3. Keep a sense of proportion. Write more about points the author devotes more attention to.
4. Concentrate more on the main points than on examples or other supporting details.
5. Use proper transitions between the main points and the subpoints of your summary; your summary must have an organization of its own.
6. Use your own words as much as possible, except for key phrases. You may quote important phrases or sentences.
7. Be careful not to overload any of the sentences with so much information that the sentence is hard to read.
8. Be consistent in your use of verb tenses. Use all present tense (the author states, feels) or all past tense (the author stated, felt). The present tense is more common in a summary.
9. Do not include your own ideas or your own attitude or interpretation. The summary should be an objective restatement of what the author has said.

Reading 1

The Flickering Blue Parent: Children and Television

Mary J. Gander and Harry W. Gardiner

This selection appeared in a college text. Although the selection is part of a chapter, it has a form of its own, with an introduction and a conclusion. Note what the authors say about the negative effects of television and the advice given to parents about how to handle the situation.

From Mary J. Gander and Harry W. Gardiner, *Child and Adolescent Behavior*, pp. 363–364. Copyright © 1981 by Mary J. Gander and Harry W. Gardiner. Reprinted by permission of Scott, Foresman/Little, Brown College Division.

The word flickering *in the title symbolizes television; it indicates the way the light from the television screen appears in the room.*

Length of summary: Approximately 150 words.

Ninety-six percent of American homes have at least one television set which is turned on for an average of six hours each day. During the last three decades television has become a major agent of socialization, often competing with parents, siblings, peers, and teachers.

Kenneth Keniston, chairman of the Carnegie Council on Children, has referred to television as the "flickering blue parent occupying more of the waking hours of American children than any other single influence—including *both* parents and schools." Singer and Singer have characterized it as "a member of the family."

How much television and what kinds of programs do children watch? The answer depends on many factors, including children's age and season of the year. According to Winick and Winick, school-age children watch television between seventeen and thirty hours a week. For preschool children it is often as high as fifty-four hours a week. Nancy Larrick, a reading specialist and children's author, has pointed out that "by the time the child goes to kindergarten, he or she will have devoted more hours to watching television than a college student spends in four years of classes.... And by the time the youngster graduates from high school, he or she will have spent roughly 11,000 hours in school compared to more than 22,000 hours in front of television."

Children are not just watching so-called children's programs. On the contrary, according to figures released by the A. C. Nielsen Company, only 13 percent of television viewing among six- to eleven-year-olds occurs on Saturday between eight A.M. and one P.M. The largest portion of their viewing, 33 percent, takes place between eight and eleven P.M. Monday through Saturday and between seven and eleven P.M. on Sunday.

Who selects the programs that children watch? According to Bower, when mothers and children watch together, the mother makes selections in 37 percent of the cases; joint decisions occur 27 percent of the time; 33 percent of the time children decide by themselves. In a study by Lyle and Hoffman, over 60 percent of mothers of first-graders reported that they placed no restrictions on the amount of time they permitted their children to watch television.

Teachers, schools, and parent associations have become increasingly concerned about the effects of television on school performance. Based on their classroom experiences, many teachers have reported mounting incidences of fatigue, tension, and aggressive behavior, as well as lessened spontaneity and imagination.

So what have schools been doing? At Kimberton Farms School in Phoenixville, Pennsylvania, parents and teachers have been following written guidelines for five years which include no television *at all* for children through the first grade. Children in second grade through high school are encouraged to watch no television on school nights and to restrict viewing to a total of three to four hours on weekends. According to Harry Blanchard, head of the faculty, "You can observe the effects with some youngsters almost immediately....Three days after they turn off the set you see a marked improvement in their behavior. They concentrate better, and are more able to follow directions and get along with their neighbors. If they go back to the set you notice it right away."

As Fiske has pointed out, "In the final analysis, the success of schools in minimizing the negative effects of television on their (children's) academic progress depends almost entirely on whether the parents share this goal."

Many parents do share this goal and have been working with the National Parent-Teacher's Association in offering advice on choosing programs, setting time limitations, and helping parents and children develop critical attitudes. One of their publications, *PTA Review Guide*, periodically reports the collected opinions of 6,000 parents and teachers concerning current television programming. In addition, they have recommended guidelines which include keeping a log of what programs and at what times children watch, helping in the selection of programs, setting reasonable limits, joining children in watching their programs, and asking and answering questions about the positive and negative content of them.

As Linda Lombardi has pointed out, "In the 1950s many parents felt they were depriving their children of something important if they didn't give them a TV set. Today, we're beginning to realize we're doing our children a favor when we take the TV set away, at least for a while every day."

Discussion

1. How does the opening sentence of this reading selection catch the attention of the reader?
2. What are the main points in the selection, and how are they supported? Can you accept all of the results of the studies mentioned?
3. What do the authors point out about the relation between TV viewing and school performance?
4. Since this is a college text, what techniques are used to make the information objective? Although the selection is objective, it is also interesting. Why?
5. What stylistic technique is used in the conclusion to leave a final message with the reader?
6. What do you think about the advice given to parents with regard to children's viewing of television?
7. The author presents some startling figures about the amount of TV viewing that takes place in the home. How much time do you and other members of your family spend before the TV set?

Reading 2

Why TV Won't Let Up on Violence

Sally Bedell Smith

This is the first half of a feature article that appeared in The New York Times. *This half presents the main points made by the writer; the second half elaborates on these points.*

    Read to discover what the writer has to say about violence on TV. Note especially the studies drawn on to support the view that a link exists between TV violence and aggressive and violent behavior in children.

Length of summary: Approximately 200 words

"Violence is alive and well on television," Steven Bochco, executive producer of "Hill Street Blues," said in a recent interview. Mr. Bochco, whose award-winning dramatic series has been praised for its sensitive, albeit gritty depiction of the world of urban police, was speaking partly in jest. But his words are as true as they have ever been.

Yet, there appears to be a difference in the quality, variety and pervasiveness of today's televised violence. Some observers believe that as a result of more than three decades of television, viewers have developed a kind of immunity to the horror of violence. By the age of 16, for example, the average young person will have seen some 18,000 murders on television. One extension of this phenomenon may be an appetite for more varied kinds of violence on television. "On the basis of the amount of exposure, certain things that initially would have been beyond the pale become more readily accepted," says David Pearl, director of the National Institute of Mental Health's project on television violence.

In this television season, violence has been more prevalent than in recent years, in large measure because there are fewer situation comedies and more action series—with the addition of such shows as "Hunter" and "Miami Vice" on NBC, "Cover Up" on CBS and "Street Hawk" on ABC. But also because 25 million of the nation's 84.9 million homes with television now receive at least one of the four principal pay cable services—Home Box Office, Cinemax, Showtime and The Movie Channel—which routinely show uncut feature films containing graphic violence as early as 8 in the evening.

However, observers have also noted changes in the way violence is depicted on network television programs. On the one hand, more violent acts in television programs today occur with machine guns and other sophisticated weaponry than they once did, and even on critically acclaimed shows such as "Hill Street Blues" violence now occurs with a greater intensity and realism than in shows of a decade ago. In addition, more action series these days are laced with jokes or gags that occasionally crop up in juxtaposition with violent acts. There is also less distinction between heroes and villains, and more violent acts are committed by people with psychological problems. And on cable television, an increasing number of feature films intertwining sex and violence are finding their way into the home.

Moreover, a new form of television, the music video—rock music illustrated by video images—is also being examined by social scientists who say they detect a new form of violence without even the tenuous dramatic context of many standard television series. According to researchers, many such videos—laregly seen on MTV Music Television, the 24-hour cable channel, but available on broadcast programs as well—are saturated with images of menace, cruelty and implied brutality as well as detached and often cold portrayals of violence against people and property.

Documentation of some shifts in the character of violence on the three broadcast networks is emerging from a new study of 500 television programs over the past 30 years by the Center for Media and Public Affairs, a nonprofit research center in Washington, D.C., that is underwritten by a number of educational institutions, including Columbia University and Smith College. "The data are preliminary, but we are finding that in the past three decades the nature of violence on television has changed," says Linda Lichter, co-director of the center.

These trends are coming to the fore two years after the National Institute of Mental Health issued its report stating that a connection exists between the viewing of media violence and aggressive and violent behavior in children. Only last September, the Attorney General's Task Force on Family Violence concluded that "the evidence is becoming overwhelming that just as witnessing violence in the home may contribute to normal adults and children learning and acting out violent behavior, violence on TV and movies may lead to the same result."

In October, Senator Arlen Specter, Republican of Pennsylvania and chairman of the Subcommittee on Juvenile Justice, held hearings on the effect of television violence on children. Once again, new studies were presented that pointed to a link between televised violence and real-life violence.

Even Hollywood producers acknowledge that a problem exists. In a 1983 survey of 100 top television writers and producers conducted by the Center for Media and Public Affairs, 60 percent of the respondents said they thought there was too much violence on television.

Yet, ABC, CBS and NBC continue to counter that while some aggressive behavior has been linked to television viewing, violent behavior has not and that television cannot be singled out in an environment that includes films, books and other influences. The networks' position is backed by some in the research community who contend that only young boys with certain predispositions could be made aggressive by televised violence; other social scientists support the networks by saying that watching violence can be cathartic in its providing a vicarious outlet for hostile impulses.

Discussion

1. What technique is used at the beginning of the article to catch the attention of the reader?
2. What kind of support is given for the points that are made? Are sources always identified?
3. According to the author, why is there more violence on TV than there used to be? How is violence depicted today?
4. Do you agree or disagree with any point made by the author?
5. The author refers to the new forms of violence in music videos. Do you feel these shows contain even more violence than on the network shows?
6. Can you find any explanation in this article about why TV producers will not "let up on" (reduce) the amount of violence on their programs?
7. Do you think that too much viewing of TV causes youngsters to become violent themselves?

Reading 3

Story Suitability

Herbert J. Gans

This excerpt comes from a book on TV news programs and news magazines. It gives the reader an insight into how TV news is produced. Note what the author says about how much of a TV news story is narrated and how much is shown on film.

Herbert J. Gans, "Story Suitability." From *A Study of the CBS Evening News, NBC Nightly News, Newsweek, and Time.* Copyright © 1979. Reprinted by permission of Pantheon Books.

Television journalists see themselves as providing a headline service, which is meant to supplement the newspapers; but their main purpose and competitive weapon is the offer of "immediacy," bringing the viewer "into" or near important and interesting events through the use of film. Consequently, all suggested stories are automatically judged for whether they lend themselves to filming; and when top producers compile their lists of selected stories, they always begin with, and give most thought to, the films they hope to run that day. At this point, however, quality considerations also come into play, for producers want good film rather than any film, and the prime measure of quality is "action." Action is "something happening," "an incident not a situation," such as a battle, an interpersonal conflict, or people struggling against nature. Action is also emotion, either a display of anger or other strong feelings, or an activity that evokes an emotional response, such as pity. Conversely, producers eschew undramatic film and they prefer to avoid "talking heads," that is, interviews or discussions. Even so, for an important story, dull film is better than no film at all.

As a result, television has been accused of emphasizing news that lends itself to filming. The truth, however, is more complicated. When film is not available, the news is presented as a tell story, although then producers worry that the "opposition" has filmed the same story. More important, words are as essential as film. The "text" with which a reporter narrates the film is often the real story, with the film chosen to accompany and illustrate the text, just as still pictures accompany magazine text. Television news, therefore, has rightly been described as visual radio. Also, tell stories are an intrinsic part of the news program. They supply news which producers are unable or unwilling to film, and they complement or update the film story. In fact, a film story is often chosen to fit the tell story, thus becoming its appendage. Since the anchorperson is thought to attract a significant number of viewers, almost a third of the program is given over to independent tell stories, unrelated to available film....

To be sure, television news is dominated by film, but film is chosen after substantive considerations are applied. Exciting film cannot be used if the story for which it provides immediacy is unimportant (of course, when exciting film is available, producers try to convince themselves of the story's importance, or else they look for an important tell story that justifies the use of the film, even if the connection is tenuous at times). However, using action film that is unimportant is condemned as sensationalism.

The charge against television news is accurate in one respect. Immediacy often requires producers to film dramatic highlights that may be parenthetical to a story's importance, which in turn requires the reporter's narrative "standupper," or the accompanying tell story, to supply the important news. For example, television reported the unrest of the 1960s through films of demonstrations and riots; and important economic news is almost always accompanied by films that feature supermarket cash registers or vignettes of victims of inflation and unemployment.

Television news can be criticized for accompanying important text with unimportant film, but the significant question is whether viewers pay closer attention to the text or the film. Television journalists defend the use of film as the best method of attracting and holding viewer attention, and some studies show that when viewers are asked to state a general preference, they choose film over tell stories. Still, in practice, they may pay as much attention to text as to film, particularly since many are eating dinner or are engaged in other activities while they are watching the news.

Discussion

1. According to the author, what do TV newscasters consider their main purposes to be?
2. What do TV producers look for when they choose the film for a news story?
3. Why has TV news been described as visual radio?
4. What use of film for a news story does the author condemn?
5. What are examples of film used to provide dramatic highlights to a news story that is being told?
6. What is meant by a "tell story" and "talking heads" on TV?
7. Do TV viewers pay closer attention to the text or to the film? What do the viewers say in one study, and what does the author think actually happens?
8. What do you think of TV news programs? Do you agree with criticisms of such programs as superficial, jumping quickly from one subject to another, without going into any story in depth, and sometimes moving from a very serious subject to a very trivial one? And do you feel, as some have said, that TV presents news stories merely as entertainment? Have you found some TV news programs that are informative and also go into a story in depth?

Reading for Further Ideas

The selections in this section are intended not only to give you additional information about the subject of the composition, but to continue to sharpen your reading skills, and in addition, to give you practice in preparing for essay examinations.

After you have skimmed through each selection and underlined the main points, make an outline from memory. Then check the reading selection again and make a more exact outline. This time, make a one-sentence summary of the main idea.

With this preparation, write a question for each selection that you think might be given on an essay examination. Without concentrating on details, make the question as comprehensive as possible. (You may also ask a question comparing the selection with others on the same subject.) Then write the answers and check them against the reading selection.

In writing your question, keep in mind the date and source of the selection (newspaper or magazine, textbook or other kind of book). Such sources often have different purposes and may therefore affect the way your questions might be asked.

Reading 1

The De-Massified Media

Alvin Toffler

The author of the following selection is a prominent writer and futurist. He offers challenging ideas in his best sellers, Future Shock *(1970) and* The Third Wave *(1980), from which this excerpt is taken. The three waves he talks about are stages of civilization. The First Wave is the agricultural revolution, which caused nomadic peoples to settle on the land they cultivated. The Second Wave is the Industrial Revolution, which brought centralization and standardization—mass production, mass housing, mass education, and mass information. The Third Wave is beginning to break up this kind of massing in all areas of life into smaller and more individualized units.*

In his chapter "The De-Massified Media," Toffler talks about the breaking up of information messages in the mass media—the newspapers, the newsmagazines, the radio, and finally, in the excerpt that follows, in television.

As you read, note the developments that are causing the "de-massing" of the TV messages. Also, observe the elements of style and content that you think contribute to making The Third Wave *a best seller.*

Since Toffler wrote The Third Wave, *the QUBE two-way programming mentioned in this excerpt has been discontinued because of lack of viewer interest in this system and the expense involved.*

Not until 1977 . . . did the Second Wave media suffer their most startling and significant defeat. For a generation the most powerful and the most "massifying" of the media has, of course, been television. In 1977 the picture tube began to flicker. Wrote *Time* magazine, "All fall, broadcast and ad executives nervously peeked at the figures . . . they could not believe what they were seeing. . . . For the first time in history, television viewing declined."

"Nobody," mumbled one astonished ad man, "*ever* assumed that viewership would go down."

Even now explanations abound. We are told the shows are even more miserable than in the past. That there is too much of this and not enough of that. Executive heads have rolled down the network corridors. We have been promised this or that new type of show. But the deeper truth is only beginning to emerge from the clouds of tele-hype. The day of the all-powerful centralized network that controls image production is waning. Indeed, a former president of NBC, charging the three main U.S. television networks with strategic "stupidity," has predicted their share of the prime-time viewing public would drop to 50 percent by the late 1980s. For the Third Wave communications media are subverting the dominance of the Second Wave media lords on a broad front.

Cable television today already reaches into 14.5 million American homes and is likely to spread with hurricane force in the early 1980s. Industry experts expect 20 to 26 million cable subscribers by the end of 1981, with cabling available to fully 50 percent of U.S. households. Things will move even faster once the shift is made from copper wires to cheap fiber optic systems that send light pulsing through hair-thin fibers. And like short-run printing presses or Xerox copiers, cable de-massifies the audience, carving it into multiple mini-publics. Moreover, cable systems can be designed for two-way communication so that subscribers may not merely watch programs but actively call various services,.

In Japan, by the early 1980s entire towns will be linked to light-wave cable, enabling users to dial requests not only for programs but for still photographs, data, theater reservations, or displays of newspaper and magazine material. Burglar and fire alarms will work through the same system.

In Ikoma, a bedroom suburb of Osaka, I was interviewed on a TV show on the experimental Hi-Ovis system, which places a microphone and television camera on top of the TV set in the home of every subscriber, so that viewers can become senders as well. As I was being interviewed by the program host, a Mrs. Sakamoto, viewing the program from her own living room, switched in and began chatting with us in broken English. I and the viewing public saw her on the screen and watched her little boy romping around the room as she welcomed me to Ikoma.

Hi-Ovis also keeps a bank of video cassettes on everything from music to cooking to education. Viewers can punch in a code number and request the computer to play a particular cassette for them on their screen at whatever hour they wish to see it.

Though it involves only about 160 homes, the Hi-Ovis experiment is backed by the Japanese government and contributions from such corporations as Fujitsu, Sumitomo Electric, Matsushita, and Kinetsu. It is extremely advanced and already based on fiber optics technology.

In Columbus, Ohio, a week earlier, I had visited Warner Cable Corporation's Qube system. Qube provides the subscriber with thirty TV channels (as against four regular broadcast stations) and presents specialized shows for everyone from preschoolers to doctors, lawyers, or the "adults only" audience. Qube is the most well-developed, commercially effective two-way cable system in the world. Providing each subscriber with what looks like a hand-held calculator, it permits him or her to communicate with the station by push button. A viewer using the so-called "hot buttons" can communicate with the Qube studio and its computer. *Time*, in describing the system, waxes positively rhapsodic, noting that the subscriber can "voice his opinions in local political debates, conduct garage sales and bid for *objets d'art* in a charity auction. . . . By pressing a button, Joe or Jane Columbus can quiz a politician, or turn electronic thumbs down or up on a local amateur talent program." Consumers can "comparison-shop the local supermarkets" or book a table at an Oriental restaurant.

Cable, however, is not the only worry facing the networks.

Video games have become a "hot item" in the stores. Millions of Americans have discovered a passion for gadgets that convert a TV screen into a Ping-Pong table, hockey rink, or tennis court. This development may seem trivial or irrelevant to orthodox political or social analysts. Yet it represents a wave of social learning, a premonitory training, as it were, for life in the electronic environment of tomorrow. Not only do video games further de-massify the audience and cut into the numbers who are watching the programs broadcast at any given moment, but through such seemingly innocent devices millions of people are learning to play with the television set, to talk back to it, and to interact with it. In the process they are changing from passive receivers to message senders as well. They are manipulating the set rather than merely letting the set manipulate them.

Information services, fed through the TV screen, are now already available in Britain where a viewer with an adapter unit can push a button and select which of a dozen or so different data services he or she wants—news, weather, financial, sports, and so forth. This data then moves across the TV screen as though on ticker tape. Before long users will no doubt be able to plug a hard-copier into the TV to capture on paper any images they wish to retain. Once again there is wide choice where little existed before.

Video cassette players and recorders are spreading rapidly as well. Marketers expect to see a million units in use in the United States by 1981. These not only allow viewers to tape Monday's football match for replay on, say, Saturday (thus demolishing the synchronization of imagery that the networks promote), but lay the basis for the sale of films and sports events on tape. (The Arabs are not asleep at the proverbial switch: the movie *The Messenger*, about the life of Muhammad, is available in boxed cassettes with gilt Arabic lettering on the outside.) Video recorders and players also make possible the sale of highly specialized cartridges containing, for example, medical instructional material for hospital staff, or tapes that show consumers how to assemble knockdown furniture or rewire a toaster. More fundamentally, video re-corders make it possible for any *consumer* to become, in addition, a *producer* of his or her own imagery. Once again the audience is de-massified.

Domestic satellites, finally, make it possible for individual television stations to form temporary mini-networks for specialized programming by bouncing signals from anywhere to anywhere else at minimal cost, thus end-running the existing networks. By the end of 1980 cable-TV operators will have one thousand earth stations in place to pick up satellite signals. "At that point," says *Television/Radio Age*, "a program distributor need only buy time on a satellite, presto, he has a nationwide cable TV network...he can selectively feed any group of systems he chooses." The satellite, declares William J. Donnelly, vice-president for electronic media at the giant Young & Rubicam advertising agency, "means smaller audiences and a greater multiplicity of nationally distributed programs."

All these different developments have one thing in common: they slice the mass television public into segments, and each slice not only increases our cultural diversity, it cuts deeply into the power of the networks that have until now so completely dominated our imagery. John O'Connor, the perceptive critic of the *New York Times*, sums it up simply. "One thing is certain," he writes. "Commerical television will no longer be able to dictate either what is watched or when it is watched."

What appears on the surface to be a set of unrelated events turns out to be a wave of closely interrelated changes sweeping across the media horizon from newspapers and radio at one end to magazines and television at the other. The mass media are under attack. New, de-massified media are proliferating, challenging—and sometimes even replacing—the mass media that were so dominant in all Second Wave societies.

Reading 2

Why TV Audiences Love to Play Games

Sandra Salmans

The following, the first part of a feature article, gives some background on the original game shows on TV and mentions those that are most popular today. Note what one study has revealed about who watches game shows and why. See whether you agree with the findings of this study.

Note: *The term* syndication *in this excerpt refers to the availability for purchase of series (such as "M*A*S*H") that are no longer being produced.*

Game-playing is becoming a way of life on television. Between its daytime and early-evening audiences, the "Wheel of Fortune" game show is seen daily by 43 million viewers, more than any other program. And while "Wheel" is an acknowledged phenomenon, it leads a pack of game shows, many of which have recently surged onto the home screen. From 9 A.M. to 8 P.M., in fact, the games barely stop. They fill the networks' schedules until noon or 12:30 P.M., when they are superseded by soap operas, then switch over to the independent stations and cable networks for several hours. At 7:30 P.M., after the evening news in the New York City area, Channel 2 offers "Wheel" and Channel 4 has "Family Feud."

Along with soap operas and reruns of situation comedies, game shows have been a fixture on the networks' daytime lineup for two decades. When they made their debut 30 years ago, it was in the evening, and they tended to be panel shows with celebrity contestants and a format that was equal parts talk and game.

"There were men in black tie, ladies in gowns and no neon lights," said Mark Goodson of Goodson-Todman Productions, which produced many of the shows, including "What's My Line?" "If they did it today, the panel would be brought in on a revolving table, or there would be a filmclip illustrating the person's occupation." Some of those programs evolved into quiz shows, culminating in the national scandal surrounding the "$64,000 Question" when it was learned that contestants had been coached before airtime.

Today, game shows still tend to test a contestant's knowledge of trivia and esoterica, but do so amid colorful sets blazing with flashing lights. "The Wheel of Fortune," for instance, is basically the old game of guessing letters to complete a phrase, with an enormous roulette wheel added to determine the stakes; all of this is played before three glittering revolving platforms that showcase prizes. Digital "bank accounts" continually tally each contestant's winnings.

Since the 1980's, the game shows have been relegated to the 9 A.M.-to-noon period. Now, however, enhanced with higher prizes and bigger budgets than ever, game shows are blossoming throughout the schedule. Increasingly, they are cropping up as syndicated programs on independent stations in the afternoon, and on network affiliates in prime-access time—the period between 7:30 and 8 P.M. in New York, for example, during which affiliated stations are not allowed to broadcast programming shown previously on the networks. Starting this autumn, "The Price Is Right" will join "Wheel of Fortune" and "Family Feud" in that time slot, said Mr. Goodson, whose company owns the show.

Furthermore, the shows are drawing sizable audiences. According to the most recent Nielsen report, 8 of the 20 top-rated daytime shows on the networks are game shows. ("The Price Is Right" trails number one-rated "General Hospital," followed by "Wheel," another half-hour of "The Price is Right," "Scrabble," "$25,000 Pyramid," "Press Your Luck," "Sale of the Century" and "Super Password.") Game shows also account for 5 of the 25 top-rated syndicated shows. ("Wheel," which leads even "M*A*S*H," is followed by "Jeopardy," "Family Feud," "Name That Tune" and "Sale of the Century.") That marks an increase from four game shows in 1984 and three in 1983.

"On the networks, a consistent number of game shows have been top-rated for several years," said David Poltrack, vice president of research for the CBS network. In syndication, he added, "the game shows' performance is as strong as it's been in a while."

While the number of viewers has grown, they remain predominantly older women, and the same attractions that drew them to game shows in the 1960's probably still prevail, according to Kathryn Montgomery, a professor of television at U.C.L.A., whose graduate students have been researching the phenomenon. For one thing, she noted, game shows, unlike soap operas, do not require constant attention, so the audience can interrupt its viewing for household chores.

On a more psychological level, Professor Montgomery said, 'There is speculation that people watch because they get a sense of power or omniscience. Often the show is structured so they know the answer before the contestant.'

As for the lavish prizes, she said, the programs "display products in a context of happiness and wish-fulfillment. And the contestants are chosen in such a way that they can be identified with by viewers, who can dream about having that money."

Reading 3

Soap Operas

Edward J. Whetmore

The following excerpt is from a book on the mass media. It explains the appeal that soap operas have for their audience. Note the kind of interaction soap operas have with their audience.

From *MediaAmerica: Form, Content and Consequences of Mass Communication*, 2nd edition, by Edward J. Whetmore, © 1982 by Wadsworth Publishing Company, Belmont, California 94002.

Though dozens of different daytime formats have been tried, daytime TV is still pretty much *soap operas* and *game shows*. The soaps were introduced from radio when daytime TV first begin, deriving their name from the soap products that were often sponsors. The soap opera format was brought intact from radio and it's changed little over the years. Protagonists are put into conflict situations, usually involving close friends or relatives, and must make decisions to resolve those conflicts. Some soaps, like *The Guiding Light* and *The Edge of Night,* boast 20 or more years on daytime TV and a loyal audience.

The soap opera depends so much on human interaction that we may use the term to describe our own conflicts. ("Gee, my father isn't speaking to me, my sister is getting an abortion, and I'm flunking out of school. My life is really like a soap opera!") In reality, few lives are as troubled and confused as those on the soaps. As with much of TV, our real lives are dull by comparison.

Soap opera characters are carefully created for the mass audience. They are usually young (25–35), well dressed, and financially comfortable. Leading men are doctors and lawyers. Leading women are attractive and well manicured. Indoor sets are unusually large and boast wall-to-wall carpeting, plush drapes, and built in wet bars. Soap opera characters tend to be very sophisticated and do a lot of eating, drinking, and arguing.

Regular viewers can name all the characters in a given soap and describe their history in detail. The casual observer gets lost in the plot, which has more twists and turns than a mountain highway:

Let's see...John's son is getting married today to the woman who used to be his father's wife, who was recently divorced from the doctor who delivered his illegitimate daughter. That illegitimate daughter is really Bill's mother, Nell, whose father was a doctor where Bill was in medical school. We know that Bill never graduated but came to town and set up practice anyway. Things were going great until he and Nell got divorced, but then she found out she was his mother and....

Unlike prime-time shows, soaps are often shot only a day or two before they are aired. This five-show-a-week schedule takes its toll on cast and crew. There is usually little budget for retakes, and sometimes missed cues and blown lines must be aired. It really keeps the cast on their toes. One advantage to the schedule is that the soap script may incorporate recent news events, while prime-time shows, shot as much as six months in advance, cannot.

Critics contend that all soaps are nauseatingly similar, but actually each is aimed at a special segment of the audience. Although 70 percent of that audience is women, there are different age groups. One hit among young viewers during the late 1970s was *The Young and the Restless.* It featured young characters and concentrated on presenting the latest fashions along with the plot.

Soap operas often set clothing and fashion trends. Most are taped in New York, and many fashion designers across the country keep an eye on the soaps to see what is happening. "What's in vogue in the soaps today will be in the shops tomorrow" is a standard saying.

Of more significance, soap operas are a fascinating study of audience-character relationships. There is no other media audience so involved with its programs and so devoted to its characters. When soap characters have an on-camera birthday, they can expect lots of cards from fans. If they are sick, thousands of viewers write and send get-well greetings. If a popular character "dies," viewers protest. And, unlike the prime-time audience, soap watchers tend to have a good handle on what they receive from their programs. The desire to believe in romantic love, the desire to see evil punished and virtue rewarded, and the desire to see others make mistakes are often cited by the viewers themselves. Soap characters are usually good or evil, positive or negative, with well-defined personalities.

Extra Discussion and Writing

Journal Entry

Write down your feeling about the differences between the television programs in your native country and those in the United States. Write freely, since you are the only one who will see this entry.

Letters

1. Write a letter to one of your teachers in your native country pointing out these same differences between the television programs. However, this time revise the journal entry for the letter so that it is more carefully controlled and correct. But keep the letter friendly, since you know the teacher.
2. Write a letter to a member of your family who is still in your native country telling about some features of American television that you like and some you do not like.
3. Write a letter to a newspaper complaining about some aspect of American television. Tell which type of newspaper you are writing to. For a more serious newspaper like *The New York Times*, use a more formal tone and greater detail. For a less formal newspaper, write a shorter letter and use a more conversational and emotional tone.

Sayings

We have a saying, "One picture is worth a thousand words." Explain how this saying can be applied to the presentation of the news on television, as opposed to the presentation of the news in a newspaper.

Reactions

Reading 1

What Soap Operas Are Trying to Tell Us

Carolyn See

The following article was written by a professor, at the University of California at Los Angeles, a book reviewer, and novelist (Golden Days, 1987). The article appeared first in TV Guide *in America, Canada, Australia, and South Africa.*

This article is quite different from the one by Edward Whetmore on pp. 146–148. Write a comparison between these two articles. You may refer to what you found more interesting or informative, what you liked or didn't like, what you agreed or disagreed with.

More people watch *General Hospital* than any other daytime show and many a nighttime show. This information can be "played" any number of ways. *Newsweek*'s cover story on *General Hospital* mentioned other soaps, but last Christmas season the cute boutiques in Beverly Hills immediately sold out of "I ♥ General Hospital" coffee cups and were left with an embarrassing backlog of *Ryan's Hope* paraphernalia. Other "experts" muddy the waters by calling *Dynasty* and *Dallas*, even *Upstairs, Downstairs*, nighttime soaps, a contradiction in terms. (Or is anything about people instead of crime and cars a "soap"?)...

What are the soaps trying to tell us? First, that Dan Rather doesn't matter. He can dress up like an Afghan all he wants. It doesn't matter what awful chemicals the Russians may be using or how many Polish miners perish underground. *No news matters.* The larger world doesn't matter. Port Charles is a large city, but there has never been a strike there or a cyclone. That snowstorm existed only in relation to Monica's baby.

Culture is largely a vehicle, on the sidelines. A professor noodles on the piano he keeps in his office while he worries about a domestic problem. But did you ever see a concert violinist on a soap? Did you ever see Lesley with her nose in a book? Did you ever see anyone in the daytime holding a record album? Or painting a picture (unless with an ulterior motive)?

Sports don't matter much. Who goes to the homecoming game matters, but that's all.

On the other hand, Christmas matters; Easter matters. So do parties, dates, engagements, sickness (naturally), and—don't forget this—who murdered whom, who's in a coma, and who's in jail for a crime he/she didn't commit.

What soaps are trying to tell us is appallingly simple: People matter more than all the other stuff. The rest of it is window dressing. A soap opera confirms that one person is important. In fact, the soaps may be seen as an inner refutation of almost every other thing we see on commerical *and* public television. Forget the Cosmos! Forget the Bomb. But remember what it feels like to be in love, accused, betrayed. Remember what it's like to feel. Remember what strange fun it was when something you thought was one way in the world turned out to be another way entirely. (When Stephen on *Dynasty* turns out to be not quite as homosexual as he thought. When the emerald necklace is made of paste—or is it? When Fallon almost sleeps with her own father by mistake—no, wait!) Remember pain. Neighbors are impossible. People lie and cheat. Living hurts. Soaps refute the cliché that Americans care only about happy talk....

Beyond all this, twinkling in the creamy, benevolent success of most of the soaps, *General Hospital* suggests daily to a large public—and to its own cast, to actors, writers, directors—that it's *possible*, even now, to have fun.

Why is it the most successful show on daytime television? Because it arrives at a perfect time. You watch it after a respectable morning's work, before the kids are home, long before it's time to start dinner. At work, you take a fashionably late lunch. In college, your morning classes are over. Afternoon workouts not yet begun.

Of course, there's a lot of sex on soap operas, more than on nighttime programs. For students—men and women—watching soap operas is a social activity accompanied by cheers and laughter. Some colleges have incorporated watching *General Hospital* into their curricula, and New Jersey's Monmouth College offers a course in the psychology of the soap opera.

The direction on *GH*, the writing, the character development, are nearly flawless. Many daytime soaps still content themselves with two-shots in living rooms and a lugubrious underwater pace; *General Hospital* is all over the place, with crowds, yachts, Richard Simmons. *GH* people talk like humans—perkily.

The dialogue sounds good. Villains don't content themselves with one spiteful, doleful note. For as long as she was on, Tracy Quartermaine, with her turbans and manicures and thin, exasperated smiles, was a perfect bellwether of awfulness, her rage perfectly motivated—a combination of material greed and surprise at how continuously stupid good people could be.

Then the secret ingredient (optional, like the dollop of brandy in boeuf bourguignon), what *GH* took a chance with when other soaps hung back, what *Dynasty* flirts with but hasn't quite embraced—fun....

Crime, yes. Freezing to death, why not? Adultery, *bien sûr!* But staying alive by being interested in "daily life" to the point of fanaticism, to the point of love, hate, fun—that's the message of the soaps.

Reading 2

Children's TV Viewing

Jane E. Brody

An article in The New York Times *points out that, according to the findings of research studies, too much TV viewing has damaging effects on children. Based on your own observation of television viewing, state whether you agree or disagree with the findings of these studies, as stated below. Give your reasons.*

[Too much TV viewing can] undermine children's health, resulting in obesity, lack of physical fitness, poor eating habits and behavioral problems. The passive nature of television viewing may also interfere with the development of imagination. And time spent in television viewing often detracts from reading and other active learning skills.

Excerpt from "Guidelines for Parents on Children's TV Viewing," *The New York Times,* January 21, 1987, p. C8.

Reading 3

To Tell the Truth, the Price Is Right

Stephanie Harrington

In the following article on game shows, the author expresses her feelings about such shows. Tell why you agree or disagree with her point of view. Write a comparison between this selection on game shows and the one on pp. 144-146. Consider the ideas, the style, the attitude, and the tone of each.

To critics, game shows are a vulgar expression of American materialism. To an enthusiast, they are a passion that drives someone in its throes to appear on national television dressed as a baked Alaska in hopes of winning a Vega Hatchback or a color TV or, at least, a nuclear-powered potato masher by AEC, Inc., and a week's supply of Blue Luster Carpet Shampoo. To broadcasters, this low-budget format is such an inexpensive schedule filler that, during daytime and early evening hours, they have given viewers little else to choose from. And the game shows' ratings are more than healthy enough to indicate that millions of viewers seem to find them an entertaining way to pass the time.

What is the appeal of game shows? One of the least charitable explanations has been offered by a man who has made millions from some of the most exploitive examples of the genre, independent producer Chuck Barris, who has given us "The Newlywed Game," "The Dating Game" and "The New Treasure Hunt." Barris, an assiduous *enfant terrible*, who has referred to himself as "the King of Slob Culture," told a *TV Guide* interviewer that the elements of a game show are "emotions and tensions...you must bring out those hidden hostilities in your contestants. You can actually watch them temporarily lose their sanity on the air. We prompt them to do that. Thus, audiences are being entertained, whether in awe or shock or horror or joy, over someone going bananas in public."

But perhaps the most profound manipulative aspect of the game-show business is the kind of financial calculation that leads broadcasters and producers not just to offer enough game shows to satisfy audiences who enjoy them but to blanket certain stretches of viewing time with game shows to the point that television consumers have little other choice. As one former network programer, who now works for an independent producer, observed, "It isn't really a public demanding a trend, but responding to a trend in offerings." And what is being offered is:

"Wheel of Fortune," on which contestants spin a roulette wheel to win guesses at the letters in a word puzzle, and winners must use their cash earnings to "shop" among "showcases" of prizes. Richard, winner of the *largest three-day total* in the program's *history* (more than $16,000), is beaming and rubbing his hands and saying, "I gotta go shopping." "That video cassette is really fabulous," volunteers host Chuck Woolery, who has been pushing the video cassette as if his brother-in-law had manufactured it. "Or do you want another car?" "For $170 I'd love the camera," says Richard, "and the wine and cheese for $50 and the Tiffany gift certificate for $1,000." Losers so home worse than bankrupt, with the consolation promise of a generous supply of Days Ease Air Freshener and Tabby Treat, "every meal a banquet for your cat."

And then there is the hardcore experience of fun and games in the consumer society, "The Price Is Right," which demands neither more nor less than precise knowledge of the famous Speigel mail-order catalogue, containing more than 50,000 quality items. If, as sociologist David Riesman observed, childhood in America is being a consumer trainee, "The Price is Right" is the final exam.

On this show, contestants compete to see who can come closest to guessing the retail value of merchandise without guessing higher than the exact price. Here, the chance to win a front-loading portable dishwasher, a refrigerator-freezer with activated-charcoal air filter and "meat keeper" temperature control, and a heavy-duty garbage compactor-disposer with one-half-horsepower motor depends on the contestant's certain knowledge that the retail price of four sets of "thick and thirsty famous St. Mary's towels," plus the retail price of a craft set plus the retail price of 15 cans of Lucite paint add up to more than the retail price of a Sunbeam 1,000-watt hair dryer with four speed settings and styling stand plus the retail price of a Schick Fresh Air Machine plus the retail price of a leather bag plus the price of a pollinium-proof pollywog terrarium with infrared heating device and southern exposure. With this kind of information, you can price your way to a shot at pricing—and thereby *winning—the Don Quixote Showcase!* Which includes "a trip to the land of Don Quixote," where you will stay in the *Eurobuilding Hotel* "in the heart of Madrid's Generalissimo Quarter!"

This side of that supershowcase in the sky, what could match this brand of Dionysian transport, except maybe a weekend at Friendly Frost, or dressing up like a macaroon to be sure you will be noticed and picked out of the studio audience to be a contestant on "Let's Make a Deal," which is such a big deal that admission to the studio audience is booked up for the next two years and host-producer Monty Hall was elected honorary Mayor of *Hollywood.* Here you can compete with the couple dressed in matching his and hers Lhasa Apso skins and the guy in the skirt who is supposed to be a cheerleader and the couple impersonating a pair of shoes and waving a sign that says, "Let's lace up a deal." Here you can experience the ecstasy of selling Monty the contents of your grungy old handbag for $150 and then agreeing to spend the $150 on a box, the contents of which you do not know, but which turns out to be...a *$759.95 refrigerator-freezer stocked with $25 worth of Breakstone's Cottage Cheese! And a $479.75 sewing machine!* Which means that you've traded *$150* and an old purse for a *deal,* the total retail value of which is *$1,264.70!* And you can compound your ecstasy by being smart enough *not* to trade it all back for your old purse and whatever amount of money Monty has put in it (which turns out to be a measly 27 bucks), or for the solid wall of frozen chopped chives from Armanino and the real clunker of a prize behind it. And then, after all this...the *agony* of *not* knowing when to stop and trying for the really *big* deal by agreeing to trade your $1,264.70 deal in for whatever is behind Door No. 3. Which turns out to be three bicycles and a $50 gift certificate to Dairy Queen.

But when it comes to sheer sado-masochism, the master of the medium is Barris, whose "The New Treasure Hunt" opens with the boast that it is the show that offers "more prizes and more cash than any other show in the world." (It is also a show that, according to Barris, grosses at least $2 million a year.) A stripped-down witless version of "Let's Make a Deal," "New Treasure Hunt" reached a pitch of manipulative frenzy with one contestant who traded in a prize of $1,850 for one clunker after another (each related to the word "tire")—a unicycle, a bicycle, the humiliating experience of being tied up on stage by four human *ti-ers.* Her emotions were pushed and pulled until she was crying and pleading like a victim in a trap. When at last she was presented with a Rolls-Royce, she fainted. (Later she had to sell the Rolls to pay the taxes on it.)

Barris amuses himself with fantasies about a game show he would call "Greed." "As I see it," he explains, "you would have this horrendous situation in which an arthritic 85-year-old man would come in on crutches and contestants would bid down to see how little money they would take to kick the crutches out...." But he is not beyond turning irony on himself. He is writing a novel in which a failing game-show producer, in a desperate effort to boost his ratings, figures out a way to kill contestants on the air.

Reading 4

TV Commercials

Walter Dean Burnham

The following selection, from a textbook on American government and politics, gives the author's view about the influence of commercials on TV programming. State whether you agree or disagree with the author, and give your reasons. What is your opinion of the commercials on TV?

People watch TV more to escape the strain of everyday existence than to come to terms with the world, but even as they escape, TV socializes them into the attitudes and behaviors suitable to members of a high consumption society. Watching J.R. and his friends and enemies, life and love on a cruise ship, a football game, or a police thriller takes viewers away from their own burdens and responsibilities as they watch others cope with theirs in exotic environments. Actors portray roles (tycoon, football player, private investigator, waitress) with which viewers can identify in ways that reinforce the structure of reality, though it has little to do with most viewers' lives.

The fundamental objective of TV entertainment is to deliver viewers to sponsors whose commercials—scrupulously crafted at costs even higher than those of TV production in general—tirelessly stimulate wants and hawk the products that will satisfy them. Because the networks must ensure that their programs do not inadvertently trivialize or diminish the sponsor's message, they steer clear of thought-provoking subjects. The majority of people are most comfortable with familiar, unchallenging ideas; and so, to prevent their defecting to another channel, the networks, as a rule, avoid topics such as business, labor, politics, white-collar crime, students, the elderly, or mental illness. There is little room in the entertainment business for thought-provoking fare.

Walter Dean Burnham, *Democracy in the Making: American Government and Politics*, 2nd ed. Copyright © 1986 by Prentice-Hall, Inc.

Reading 5

"I'm Walking"

This cartoon from the New Yorker *makes a devastating comment on the effect of television on the family. What is the cartoon saying, and what is your reaction to the cartoon?*

"I'm walking!"

Drawing by Sempé; ©1986 The New Yorker Magazine, Inc.

CHAPTER 6

Democracy

Composition
Vocabulary and Usage
Reading for Summary Writing
Reading for Further Ideas
Extra Discussion and Writing

Composition

Procedures for Discussion
Writing the Composition
Revising the Composition

Requirements for a Home Composition

1. Use white $8\frac{1}{2}'' \times 11''$ paper; write on one side only.
2. Type your composition double spaced on unlined paper (if handwritten, the paper should be clearly written on every other line). A typewritten page, double-spaced, is about 250 words.
3. Indent each paragraph, use wide margins ($1''$ to $1\frac{1}{4}''$), and number each page in the upper right-hand corner.
4. Include a separate page with the title, the thesis sentence, and the outline.

Procedures for Discussion

The teacher writes this heading on the board:

Meaning of Democracy

Students are then asked to contribute ideas about the topic, and the teacher lists the ideas on the board, in phrases, in the random order in which they are given.

At the end of the discussion, the teacher asks how the smaller points on the board may be organized under broader headings, and whether even more comprehensive headings can be added as the basis for greater unity.

Writing the Composition

Write a 500 to 600 word composition on the meaning of democracy.

Suggestions for the Content and Organization

Consider the possible classification of minor points under broader ones. (The subject of democracy can often be considered under two main classifications.) Then narrow down the subject—find a thesis or a point of view. The thesis can often come out of the broadest classifications, under which all the smaller points can go.

Here are some suggested approaches to a thesis:

Theory versus practice—in your country or elsewhere
Rights and responsibilities in a democracy
Form of government and individual rights in a democracy
Advantages and disadvantages of a democracy
Equality in a democracy (human rights)
Freedom in a democracy (human rights)
Comparison between one country that has democracy and one that
    does not
The ideal democracy
Favorable conditions for democracy (economic, political, social)
Abuses of democracy (in the United States or elsewhere)
Democracy as government of the people, by the people, for the people

Try to support the generalizations you make by using some of these techniques for making meaning clearer: example, comparison and contrast, cause-effect, division (on a logical basis), historical development, negative definition (saying what democracy is *not*).

Guide for the Outline and the Composition

The following guide will help you in preparing to write your composition. On the left side of the guide is the outline with suggestions for handling the introduction, transitions, and the conclusion of this composition. On the right side are general comments about how introductions, transitions, and conclusions may be written. (If you are accustomed to writing a first draft from rough notes, use this guide for your second and succeeding drafts.)

Outline

Title

General Comments

Use initial capital letters for all words except articles, short prepositions, and short conjunctions. Try to use an interesting title that reflects your thesis.

Introduction

This can include a dictionary definition, but use only as much of this definition as you will need for your interpretation of democracy.

It can also include a quotation. Or it can be a belief that you will argue against.

Purpose of the introduction:
 to catch the reader's interest
 to give a general idea of the subject

An introduction may include:
 a quotation
 a story, perhaps personal
 a rhetorical question (which you will
  answer)
 a definition
 a statement of a belief you will argue
  against
 a surprising or shocking fact
 a statement of a serious problem

Transitional lead-in

This gives the point of view from which you will discuss democracy and suggests how you will develop it.

Usually at the end of the introduction. Gives an indication of the central idea and the way it will be developed (may be in the form of a question).

I. First main point

This is the first support for your interpretation of democracy.

   A. First supporting detail

   B. Second supporting detail
            etc.

New paragraph. The first sentence: (1) mentions the general idea of the paragraph (from the important word[s] in the outline); (2) relates this sentence to what was said before.

Should be related to the preceding subpoint.

Note: Long subpoints may begin new paragraphs.

(Continue with your other main points and their supporting details.)

(Follow the suggestions given for the first main point.)

For each main point, give another support for your interpretation of democracy.

Conclusion

This can go back to something from your introduction. It can sum up your main points about democracy in an interesting way.

The conclusion should round out the composition in a strong and satisfying way, perhaps by referring again to whatever you used to introduce the composition.

Notes: (1) The conclusion should not add any new ideas that need further development. (2) If your last point ends on a strong note that points up your thesis, you may not need to add a conclusion.

Support for the points you make can come from your own beliefs and experience or from the readings in this chapter and elsewhere. (Be sure to identify your sources and to use quotation marks around the exact words of an author.) The support can be in the form of examples, current facts and figures, or authoritative opinion. Use enough support to make your point convincing to the reader.

Finally, keep in mind that this composition represents your own opinions. By stating them honestly and strongly, you will have a composition that the reader will find interesting enough to continue reading.

Revising the Composition

In succeeding drafts, try to sharpen your thesis and show more clearly how each main point contributes to the development of the thesis. Try writing down the opening sentences of your paragraphs on a separate sheet of paper to see if they make a clear sentence outline. Go over the reading selections again for further ideas or additional support.

Consult the Revision and Editing Checklist for guidance on organization, paragraphing, and sentences. You can get needed help with vocabulary in the vocabulary section that follows. Make a final check with the Symbol Chart for Correction of Compositions for the grammatical structures and usage in your composition.

Evaluation

If there is an exchange of student compositions, the Revision and Editing Checklist can serve as a guide in the evaluation of another student's composition. Use the following procedure in checking for the writer's organization and development of ideas.

1. Without looking at the other student's outline page, make an outline and a one-sentence summary of the central idea (or thesis) of the whole paper. Can you find a clear line of development? Do your summary sentence and your outline agree with those of the writer?
2. Find the support for each point made in the writer's paper. Is the support adequate and convincing?
3. Write on the student's paper what you consider the good points of the composition and what needs to be improved.

Vocabulary and Usage

Vocabulary
Usage Notes
Word Forms

Vocabulary

The following words may be useful to you in talking and writing about the subject of democracy.

Democracy

civil rights (always used in the plural)   Individual rights guaranteed by law—freedom of speech, the press, religion, assembly, etc. (The United States guarantees these civil rights in the first ten amendments to the Constitution, called the Bill of Rights.)

coalition   A temporary union of political parties to form a government; usually found in a parliamentary democracy.

diversity   A wide range of differences in customs, beliefs, attitudes, etc.

municipal   Relating to the local government or institutions of a town or city.

PACs (Political Action Committees)   In the United States, lobbying groups representing unions, businesses, professional organizations, and trade associations; political groups that help to finance candidates and to influence legislation.

pluralism   Political power shared by many groups with different interests and beliefs.

representative government—the republican system   In this system, the chief executive is a president who is elected by the people and serves for a specified length of time (four years in the United States), with or without the support of a majority of members of the legislature.

representative government—the parliamentary system   In this system, a prime minister is the chief executive. "The prime minister or premier must be an elected member of the legislative body (parliament).... Usually he or she is the head of the largest political party, or coalition of parties, in the legislature. The prime minister holds office only as long as he or she has the support of a majority of the lawmakers, but as prime minister is also the chief executive, performing most of the same functions as the American president." (*American Government and Politics Today*, Charles P. Sohner and Helen P. Martin, 2nd ed., p. 25.)

Voting and Elections

ballot   The list of candidates running for election.

candidate   A person who runs for government office. If the candidate already holds office and is running for re-election, he or she is also called the **incumbent**.

constituents   All the voters represented by an elected official.

the electorate   All those who are eligible (qualified) to vote.

majority   More than half the total number of votes.

plurality   More votes than those of any other of three or more candidates.

platform   The policies and issues (important questions) that a political party or a candidate will advocate. (These issues may be stated in **slogans**.)

the polls (always plural)   A voting place. (**A poll** is a questionnaire to elicit people's opinions.)

primary   In the United States, voters registered under a certain party may elect the candidates who will run in the regular elections. In some states, candidates are chosen at party conventions.

proportional representation   Representation of all parties in a legislature in proportion to their popular vote.

suffrage   The right to vote.

universal suffrage   The right to vote regardless of color, religion, sex, or property. In most countries there are restrictions of age (18 years in the United States) and citizenship.

Branches of Government (United States)

the executive branch   The branch that carries out the laws. The chief executive of the national (or federal) government is the president; the chief executive of each state is the governor; the chief executive of a city is usually the mayor.

the legislative branch   The branch that makes the laws. The national legislative branch in the United States is the Congress, which consists of two houses. The Senate has 2 senators for each of the 50 states, regardless of size or population, for a total of 100. The House of Representatives has 435 members, with the distribution by state, based on population.

the judicial branch   The branch that interprets and applies the law to disputes and crimes.

checks and balances   The power of each of the three branches to limit the power of the others.

veto   The privilege of a chief executive to refuse to sign a law passed by the legislature. A two-thirds majority vote of the legislature is then required to override the veto so that the bill can become law.

impeachment   The power of the legislature to put a chief executive on trial for misconduct in office.

Usage Notes

Democracy may be used in two senses: as an abstract concept and as a concrete noun. As an abstract concept, the word is noncountable and is used without an article.

>   *Democracy* first developed in rich countries.

As a concrete form of government, the word is countable and requires an article in the singular.

>   The United States is a *democracy*.

The article *the* is used with names of political parties:

>   *the* Republican Party

It is also used with names of the branches of government:

>   *the* executive branch
>   *the* legislative branch
>   *the* judicial branch

The is used with *polls*:

>   *the polls*

Do not use *the* with these expressions: *universal suffrage, proportional representation, free enterprise, capitalism.*

Word Forms

Use the correct forms for the words in parentheses.

The answers are on p. 355. If you need help with this exercise, refer to the explanations under Word Forms in Appendix A.

1. In a (democracy) _____ government, the law guarantees (free) _____ and (equal) _____ for all.

2. In a democracy, the (legislate) _____ branch makes the laws, the (execute) _____ branch carries them out, and the (judge) _____ branch interprets the laws.

3. The place where laws are made is the (legislate) _____; the people who make the laws are the (legislate) _____; the laws themselves are the (legislate) _____.

4. (Elect) _____ are held every year in the United States.

5. In a (parliament) _____ system, the country's chief (execute) _____ is chosen by the (elect) _____ (represent) _____, not by the (vote) _____.

6. In elections, a (major) _____ means more than half the total number of votes; a (plural) _____ means more votes than those of any other of three or more candidates.

7. In the United States Congress, the Senate consists of two (senate) _____ from each state; the number of (legislate) _____ in the House of (Represent) _____ is determined by the size of the (populate) _____.

8. The particular people represented by a (legislate) _____ are called his or her (constitute) _____.

9. A democracy permits (diverse) _____ of opinion.

10. A citizen in a democracy has certain rights and certain (response) _____.

11. A democracy usually guarantees (equal) _____ before the law, but it cannot guarantee (economy) _____ (secure) _____.

12. (History) _____, democracy first developed in (capital) _____ countries.

13. A basic (assume) _____ in a democracy is that people will obey the laws and (regulate) _____.

14. At a (politics) _____ convention, candidates are chosen as (represent) _____ of the party.

15. The U.S. Congress is (compose) _____ of two houses, the Senate, (represent) _____ each of the fifty states, regardless of population; and the House of Representatives, whose (represent) _____ depends on the number of people in each state.

16. (Theory) _____, a (democracy) _____ government treats everyone (equal) _____ before the law.

17. To guarantee the (exist) _____ of a democracy, steps must be taken to prevent the (tyrant) _____ of a dictatorship.

Reading for Summary Writing

For the following three reading selections, prepare a brief outline for class discussion before you write the summary. After the class discussion of each selection, you will write:

1. A longer, revised outline of the reading selection, using an alternation of numbers and letters.
2. A one-sentence summary of the selection that includes the central idea and the main points used to develop this idea (from the outline).
3. A summary of the selection. The length assigned in the text will determine the amount of detail you can include in the outline and summary.

Guidelines for Writing (Review)

1. For the outline, use the alternate number-letter system for main points and subpoints. The phrases you underlined in the opening sentences of paragraphs usually become the main points and subpoints in the outline.
2. For both the summary and the outline, follow the same order as the reading. However, you may begin the summary with a reference to the source of the selection (author, publication) and to its central idea.

3. Keep a sense of proportion. Write more about the points the author devotes more attention to.
4. Concentrate more on the main points than on examples or other supporting details.
5. Use proper transitions between the main points and the subpoints of your summary. Your summary must have an organization of its own.
6. Use your own words as much as possible, except for key phrases. You may quote important phrases or sentences.
7. Be careful not to overload any of the sentences with so much information that the sentence is hard to read.
8. Be consistent in your use of verb tenses. Use all present tense (the author states, feels) or all past tense (the author stated, felt). The present tense is more common in a summary.
9. Do not include your own ideas or your own attitude or interpretation. The summary should be an objective restatement of what the author has said.

Reading 1

Modern Democracy

Carl Becker

The author of this selection, Carl Becker, is a distinguished American historian who taught history at several American universities and wrote a number of books on history. The excerpt is from his Modern Democracy, *published in 1941, and was originally part of a lecture given at an American university in 1940.*

This selection is an example of extended definition. Some techniques used in extended definition to make the meaning of a concept clear are example, comparison and contrast, cause-effect, analysis (logical divisions), historical development, and negative definition (saying what something is not).

As you read, try to determine which techniques of extended definition receive most attention here. Also, note the paragraph that states the author's main idea.

Length of summary: Approximately 250 words

One of the presuppositions of modern thought is that institutions, in order to be understood, must be seen in relation to the conditions of time and place in which they appear. It is a little difficult for us to look at democracy in this way. We are so immersed in its present fortunes that we commonly

From Carl Becker, *Modern Democracy*, pp. 9–15. New Haven: Yale University Press, 1941. Copyright © 1941, Yale University Press. Reprinted by permission.

see it only as a "close-up," filling the screen to the exclusion of other things to which it is in fact related. In order to form an objective judgment of its nature and significance, we must therefore first of all get it in proper perspective. Let us then, in imagination, remove from the immediate present scene to some cool high place where we can survey at a glance five or six thousand years of history, and note the part that democracy has played in human civilization. The view, if we have been accustomed to take democratic institutions for granted, is a bit bleak and disheartening. For we see at once that in all this long time, over the habitable globe, the great majority of the human race has neither known nor apparently much cared for our favorite institutions.

Civilization was already old when democracy made its first noble appearance among the small city states of ancient Greece, where it flourished brilliantly for a brief century or two and then disappeared. At about the same time something that might be called democracy appeared in Rome and other Italian cities, but even in Rome it did not survive the conquest of the world by the Roman Republic, except as a form of local administration in the cities of the empire. In the twelfth and thirteenth centuries certain favorably placed medieval cities enjoyed a measure of self-government, but in most instances it was soon replaced by the dictatorship of military conquerors, the oligarchic control of a few families, or the encroaching power of autocratic kings. The oldest democracy of modern times is the Swiss Confederation, the next oldest is the Dutch Republic. Parliamentary government in England does not antedate the late seventeenth century, the great American experiment is scarcely older. Not until the nineteenth century did democratic government make its way in any considerable part of the world—in the great states of continental Europe, in South America, in Canada and Australia, in South Africa and Japan.

From this brief survey it is obvious that, taking the experience of mankind as a test, democracy has as yet had but a limited and temporary success. There must be a reason for this significant fact. The reason is that democratic government is a species of social luxury, at best a delicate and precarious adventure which depends for success on the validity of certain assumptions about the capacities and virtues of men, and upon the presence of certain material and intellectual conditions favorable to the exercise of these capacities and virtues. Let us take the material conditions first.

It is a striking fact that until recently democracy never flourished except in very small states—for the most part in cities. It is true that in both the Persian and the Roman empires a measure of self-government was accorded to local communities, but only in respect to purely local affairs; in no large state as a whole was democratic government found to be practicable. One essential reason is that until recently the means of communication were too slow and uncertain to create the necessary solidarity of interest and similarity of information over large areas. The principle of representation was well enough known to the Greeks, but in practice it proved impracticable except in limited areas and for special occasions. As late as the eighteenth century it was still the common opinion that the republican form of government, although the best ideally, was unsuited to large countries, even to a country no larger than France. This was the view of Montesquieu, and even of Rousseau. The view persisted into the nineteenth century, and English conservatives, who were opposed to the extension of the suffrage in England, consoled themselves with the notion that the American Civil War would confirm it— would demonstrate that government by and for the people would perish, if not from off the earth at least from large countries. If their hopes were confounded the reason is that the means of communication, figuratively speaking, were making large countries small. It is not altogether fanciful to suppose that, but for the railroad and the telegraph, the United States would today be divided into many small republics maneuvering for advantage and employing war and diplomacy for maintaining an unstable balance of power.

In modern times democratic institutions have, generally speaking, been most successful in new countries, such as the United States, Canada, and Australia, where the conditions of life have been easy for the people; and in European countries more or less in proportion to their industrial prosperity. In European countries, indeed, there has been a close correlation between the development of the industrial revolution and the emergence of democratic institutions. Holland and England, the first countries to experience the industrial revolution, were the first also (apart from Switzerland, where certain peculiar conditions obtained) to adopt democratic institutions; and as the industrial revolution spread to France, Belgium, Germany, and Italy, these countries in turn adopted at least a measure of democratic government. Democracy is in some sense an economic luxury, and it may be said that in modern times it has been a function of the development of new and potentially rich countries, or of the industrial revolution which suddenly dowered Europe with unaccustomed wealth. Now that prosperity is disappearing round every corner, democracy works less well than it did.

So much for the material conditions essential for the success of democratic government. Democracy implies in addition the presence of certain capacities and virtues in its citizens. These capacities and virtues are bound up with the assumptions on which democracy rests, and are available only so far as the assumptions are valid. The primary assumptions of democratic government is that its citizens are capable of managing their own affairs. But life in any community involves a conflict of individual and class interests, and a corresponding divergence of opinion as to the measures to be adopted for the common good. The divergent opinions must be somehow reconciled, the conflict of interests somehow compromised. It must then be an assumption of democratic government that its citizens are rational creatures, sufficiently so at least to understand the interests in conflict; and it must be an assumption that they are men of good will, sufficiently so toward each other at least to make those concessions of individual and class interest required for effecting workable compromises. The citizens of a democracy should be, as Pericles said the citizens of Athens were, if not all originators, at least all sound judges of good policy.

Discussion

1. Discuss the two techniques of extended definition used by the author.
2. Which type of extended definition does the introductory paragraph prepare the reader for? What conclusion does the author come to at the end of this first paragraph?
3. Where did democracy appear in previous eras? In modern times?
4. Which paragraph states the central idea of this selection? According to the author, what two kinds of conditions are necessary for democracy to exist?
5. Which conditions does the author discuss first? What are the two sub-points under this type?
6. Which sentence tells us that the discussion of the first type of condition is being concluded?
7. What assumptions does the author say are necessary for a democracy to exist?
8. What elements of content or style do you find in this selection that are characteristic of a more formal use of English?
9. Did you find the selection interesting? Why or why not?
10. Did you learn any facts that broadened your understanding of democracy?

Reading 2

The Genius of Democracy

R. M. MacIver

This selection was written by a well-known professor of sociology at New York's Columbia University. He uses a technique for extended definition different from those of the first selection. Watch for the way the author's points are developed as he makes clear what he considers the true meaning of democracy to be. Note the transitions MacIver uses as he goes from one subpoint to another. Note also the ending of the first main point, which prepares the reader for the second main point.

Length of summary: Approximately 250 words

Some Misunderstandings

There must be some universal appeal in the name of democracy, for even its destroyers proudly claim possession of its soul. Fascist writers announce that theirs is the genuine democracy and that so-called democracy is only a sham.

Reprinted by permission of Louisiana State University Press from *Leviathan and the People* by R. M. MacIver. Copyright © 1939.

Soviet spokesmen assert that they have now the most democratic constitution on earth, and Stalin himself declared that the 1937 elections in Russia were "the most democratic the world has seen." Not to be outdone, the Nazis, who can also point exultantly to their unanimous plebiscites, profess, as one of their leaders put it, that "the National Socialist form of state, as authoritarian dictatorship of the people, is, in truth, the most modern form of democracy in history." . . .

We may smile, sarcastically or sadly, at these professions coming from lands where men fear to whisper a word of criticism of their government, where it is perilous even to listen in to foreign radio stations. But we ourselves are often very careless in our definitions of democracy, and sometimes, as when we identify it with majority rule, we define it in ways which would actually justify such preposterous claims. It is highly important that we clear up this notion of democracy, so as to see precisely wherein it differs from dictatorship. . . .

. . . There are those who think that democracy means giving everyone equal authority, so that no man has any more power than another. This scheme would assure, not the presence of democracy, but the absence of government—in short, chaos, the "state of nature." There are others who think it is democratic to take a vote in order to decide the merits of plays or pictures or cigarettes or movie actresses, as though there were some necessary relation between merit and popularity.

. . . There are [some] organizations that propose to establish democracy by handing things out all round. . . . In ancient Athens . . . [it was believed] that there was something peculiarly democratic in the rotation of office, and they created so many offices that practically every citizen had his turn in one of them. To make the principle complete and give every man an equal chance they decided to use the lot instead of the ballot.

A more important confusion is that which equates democracy with the government of the many, opposed to the government of the few. The many in this sense never actually govern. They never do and never can decide the specific issues of policy that governments are always facing. . . . They can broadly decide the general direction of governmental policy and little more.

Nor can we say that democracy is any system under which the majority of the people support the existing government. Apart from the mere technical difficulty that it is sometimes not easy to say whether a democratically elected government still holds a majority or not—though no doubt Mr. Gallup is of great service to us here—there is the glaring fact that a dictatorship may have support of a majority, and any definition that will not enable us to distinguish democracy from dictatorship is worse than useless. Assuredly that is not what any intelligent defender of democracy means. We must carefully avoid the definition of democracy as simply majority-rule. Democracy does involve one form of majority-rule, a form in which there is no fixed majority entrenched against the processes and tides of free opinion that could reduce it again to a minority. But a majority-system that silences all opposition and censors all contrary opinion is emphatically not to be named a democracy.

* * *

There is one further confusion about the nature of democracy which we must seek to dispel before we turn to its positive character. Democracy first expressed itself in a certain type of representative system, a parliamentary system, and on the whole it is still associated with that system. But it is quite possible to conceive of democracy as existing without parliamentary institutions in the traditional sense; that is, apart from a central assembly composed of the elected representatives of the people, an assembly which debates in public, by majority vote, and constitutes the decisive and central organ of government. Historically the growth of democracy was the growth of parliamentary institutions, and it remains true that parliamentary institutions are impossible without democracy, without the free expression of opinion as the basis of national policy. But we must not assume that the free play of public opinion *must* register itself in parliamentary forms. Historical evolution may reveal an endless train of yet undreamed-of modes of government, adaptations to changing needs and changing demands. Democracy is on the whole a recent development. Parliamentary institutions arose when the problems of government were simpler than they are today, when public opinion was more homogeneous, less diversified by specialized corporate interests, when representation of localities or areas had a meaning that now it has for the most part lost, when agriculture was the predominant occupation of men and the relation to the land everywhere the paramount relation. All that is changed. Already, in every democracy, important activities of regulation are outside the direct control of parliaments. Everywhere the necessities of administration have created boards and commissions, controls and corporate functions, devoted to fundamental national tasks. If this process continues, parliaments and congresses may cease to be the main centers of national life. But if freedom continues, democracy will still prevail. Still the free tides of opinion will determine who shall govern, who shall be entrusted with power. The mechanism of democracy must always change if conditions change and the principle of liberty abides.

Positive Character of Democracy

If then the institutions of democracy are subject to change and must be forever readapted to changing conditions and changing needs, must we give up the attempt to discover the political form of democracy and seek instead to identify it by its spirit? I would rather not resort to that refuge. It is too inconclusive. It is also dangerous, since even its enemies may, and indeed do, claim for themselves whatever we assign as the spiritual quality of democracy. I must still define it by its form or structure, though realizing that only a congenial spirit, only an appropriate set of attitudes, can sustain that structure. I believe the problem is solved by the distinction between the form of *government* and the form of the *state* itself. No form of government is permanent, but there are abiding forms of state. Democracy is such a form, and wherever it has existed in the past or exists in the present, it can be identified by two simple criteria....

The two are as follows. (1) *Democracy puts into effect the distinction between the state* [i.e., the government] *and the community* [i.e., the individuals in the society]. Among other things this implies the existence of constitutional guarantees and civil rights which the government is not empowered to abrogate. (2) *Democracy depends on the free operation of conflicting opinions.* Among other things this implies a system under which any major trend or change of public opinion can constitutionally register itself in the determination both of the composition and of the policies of government.

Discussion

1. What purpose does the introduction serve in the development of the author's first main point? Where does the author refer again to the need to distinguish between true democracy and the false claims made in dictatorships?
2. Under misunderstandings of democracy, the author mentions one that is really an extension of democracy to daily life rather than a characteristic of a democratic government. What is this misunderstanding?
3. What does the author say about the support of the majority in relation to democracy? About majority rule?
4. Which confusion about democracy does the author devote most attention to? Why do you think he does this?
5. What does the author say are the essentials of parliamentary government?
6. Why, according to the author, did parliamentary government work well in earlier times? Why does it work less well now?
7. What distinction does the author make between the form of the government and the form of the state? How does the author explain what he means by the form of the state?
8. What are the two criteria that the author claims are necessary for true democracy? How does he explain each of the two criteria?
9. Would you add any other criteria for democracy to the two that the author gives?
10. What do you think of the author's suggestion that new forms of government might be needed in the future? Can you propose another form of government for the future that might give its people the kind of rights and freedoms the author discusses?

Note: You might be interested in reading Alvin Toffler's suggestions for new forms of democratic government for the future. Following his thesis in

The Third Wave of the breakup of elements of our present-day mass society, he says that the traditional system of democracy as representative government no longer works well because it is too difficult to arrive at the consensus of opinion that is needed to govern. He recommends the following new ways of governing in order to achieve democracy in the twenty-first century: (1) minority power rather than majority rule, through temporary modular parties; (2) semi-direct democracy, in which knowledgeable or involved segments of society can be asked for their opinions, possibly through two-way TV; (3) division of decision making, since with information overload, more and more political decisions at all levels will have to be shared.

Reading 3

Democracy as a Political Order

William Ebenstein and Edwin Fogelman

The following reading selection comes from a popular college text in political science. In this passage the authors give a narrow interpretation of what they mean by political democracy. As you read, note what they say political democracy is and what it is not.

Length of summary: Approximately 250 words

The classical formulation of political democracy as government by the people is applicable only in a community that is small enough to let each individual be heard in public assembly and vote there on specific policies and laws. Such direct democracy has functioned in the small city-states of ancient Greece and in the small towns of Switzerland and New England. In larger communities—nations, states, provinces, and cities—there has to be a division of labor. Some persons have to make the important political decisions for the whole society, and specially trained administrators and civil servants have to perform the tasks of management and administration for society as a whole. It makes a great deal of difference how the political decision makers and administrators are selected. Are they to come from royal families or aristocratic classes, in which case birth is the main criterion of selection? Are they to come from a small oligarchy of self-appointed rulers who have acquired their position by the gun and perpetuate their power by the threat of the gun? There is another method: political democracy.

From *Today's Isms: Communism, Fascism, Capitalism, Socialism*, 9th edition. Copyright © 1985, pp. 169–172. Reprinted by permission of Prentice-Hall, Inc., Englewood Cliffs, New Jersey.

In a large society, in which direct self-government is not feasible, political democracy may be defined as a political order in which adult citizens freely choose representatives in regularly scheduled competitive elections. While citizens in the direct democracy of small communities decide specific policies through their own votes in public assemblies, citizens in the indirect democracy of representative government of large communities express their preferences for a cluster of policies by voting for representatives who favor similar policies. In the large-scale political democracy of nation, state, or city, citizens participate in the political process in many ways other than through voting (involvement in party activities, campaign contributions, adherence to civic groups), but voting is the central act in influencing policy formation.

The election of representatives—of the political leadership—is indispensable to political democracy, but not every political system is democratic just because it holds elections. In making choices, the citizen must be free: free from governmental coercion to vote in a particular way, and free to obtain all the pertinent information about the various candidates and parties. Freedom of choice implies freedom of speech, assembly, radio, television, and the press. A free choice also implies a competitive election—that is, there have to be at least two parties or candidates vying for the vote.

This concept of political democracy as a political order in which the citizens freely choose their government in competitive elections states only *how* public policies are arrived at but says nothing about their content. Political democracies may pursue economic policies of laissez faire, state intervention, social welfare, or progressive nationalization of the means of production. In the field of education, political democracies may provide a college education for the majority of high school graduates or for only a small minority. In religion political democracies may adopt a basic policy of strict separation of state and church, or a policy supporting all religions, or they may favor one particular church. In regulating family relations and sexual morality, political democracies may adopt restrictive or permissive policies regarding divorce, abortion, and pornography. In foreign policy political democracies may be isolationist, internationalist, or imperialist.

Not only do differences and contradictions regarding specific policies exist between democratic systems of different nations, but the same democratic political order may enact specific policies today that totally contradict policies of yesteryear. The question of whether such policies are democratic can be answered with reference not to their content but only to the method by which they are made. Some persons find this limitation of political democracy to method and procedure unsatisfactory and seek to incorporate into its meaning such broad terms as "the good society," "liberty," "equality," "justice," and the like.

However, such broad terms do not lend themselves to empirical verification. There are as many conceptions of the good society as there are persons holding them. What seems to one person to be the good society may appear to another as barely tolerable or outright repugnant. By contrast, the meaning of political democracy in procedural terms can be easily verified: A political system that allows only one party and little or no freedom of speech and the press, that holds infrequent or no elections, that coerces citizens to vote in a particular way, or that punishes political opposition as a crime is not a political democracy, regardless of the content of its policies.

Those who favor political democracy cannot do so on the illusionary ground that it is absolute perfection, utopia here and now, or that it will ever approach utopia. Still, the inherent limits and imperfections of political democracy can be accepted on the pragmatic ground that the shortcomings of an undemocratic system in which the preferences of a minority prevail over those of the majority are even more serious.

Yet the very criterion that limits political democracy most seriously— the fact that it is a set of methods and procedures governing *how* policies are to be arrived at rather than *what* policies are to be effected—is also the source of its greatest strength. Precisely because the rules of the democratic political order relate to no one specific social or economic issue, they potentially affect all issues. Experience has shown that the political procedures of democracy, if practiced over any length of time, lead to their application to social, economic, educational, and religious issues. In the eighteenth century democracy pursued objectives that were essentially political in character, such as the broadening of the suffrage to all social classes and the elimination of restrictions on the basic political freedoms of speech, assembly, and the press. But from the middle of the nineteenth century on, the procedures of political democracy have been increasingly used to broaden the concept of democracy from the realm of government to that of society.

Finally, the nature of democracy as a set of methods and procedures also enables it to adapt to many kinds of political and economic institutions. Democracy is compatible, as experience has shown, with republican and monarchical forms of government; with two-party and multiparty systems; with more or less capitalism, socialism, or the welfare state; with varying types of religious belief and nonbelief; and with divergent levels of educational attainments and economic well-being.

Discussion

1. The first paragraph prepares the reader for the general subject of political democracy. What is the definition of political democracy that the authors give in the second paragraph? Do you feel this definition is broad enough for your interpretation of political democracy?
2. How do the authors explain what they mean by freedom in relation to elections?
3. Because of the way the authors are defining political democracy, what are the limits they impose on this kind of political democracy?
4. Why do they impose these limits?

5. How do they say that political democracy in the end actually can overcome these limits?
6. What is their conclusion about political democracy? Do you agree with this conclusion?

Reading for Further Ideas

The selections in this section are intended not only to give additional information about the subject of the composition, but to continue to sharpen your reading skills, and in addition, to give you practice in preparing for essay examinations.

After you have skimmed through each selection and underlined the main points, make an outline from memory. Then check the reading again and make a more exact outline. This time, make a one-sentence summary of the main idea.

With this preparation, write a question for each selection that you think might be given on an essay examination. Without concentrating on details, make the question as comprehensive as possible. (You may also ask a question comparing the selection with others on the same subject.) Then write the answers and check them against the reading.

In writing your question, keep in mind the date and source of the selection (newspaper or magazine, textbook or other kind of book). Such sources often have different purposes and may therefore affect the way your questions might be asked.

Reading 1

I Have a Dream

Martin Luther King, Jr.

The following selection is quite different from the preceding selections, which are careful analyses of the meaning of democracy. It is an impassioned speech made by a black civil rights leader, asking that the blacks be given the same civil rights as the whites in American society.

On August 23, 1963, King led a march of 200,000 people in Washington, D.C., from the Washington Monument to the Lincoln Memorial, where he delivered this deeply moving speech as millions of others watched on television. As you read the speech, note both what King is asking for and the kind of language he uses. Note especially the emotional impact of his use of repetition and of metaphor. See if you can find any literary sources that he draws on (see, for example, Lincoln's Gettysburg Address, p. 190).

Martin Luther King, Jr., was an ordained minister and, like the Indian leader Mahatma Gandhi, was a believer in nonviolent resistance. King was assassinated in 1968. His birthday, January 15, has been declared a national holiday.

Five score years ago, a great American, in whose symbolic shadow we stand, signed the Emancipation Proclamation. This momentous decree came as a great beacon light of hope to millions of Negro slaves who had been seared in the flames of withering injustice. It came as a joyous daybreak to end the long night of captivity.

But one hundred years later, we must face the tragic fact that the Negro is still not free. One hundred years later, the life of the Negro is still sadly crippled by the manacles of segregation and the chains of discrimination. One hundred years later, the Negro lives on a lonely island of poverty in the midst of a vast ocean of material prosperity. One hundred years later, the Negro is still languishing in the corners of American society and finds himself an exile in his own land. So we have come here today to dramatize an appalling condition.

In a sense we have come to our nation's capital to cash a check. When the architects of our republic wrote the magnificent words of the Constitution and the Declaration of Independence, they were signing a promissory note to which every American was to fall heir. This note was a promise that all men would be guaranteed the unalienable rights of life, liberty, and the pursuit of happiness.

It is obvious today that America has defaulted on this promissory note insofar as her citizens of color are concerned. Instead of honoring this sacred obligation, America has given the Negro people a bad check, a check which has come back marked "insufficient funds." But we refuse to believe that the bank of justice is bankrupt. We refuse to believe that there are insufficient funds in the great vaults of opportunity of this nation. So we have come to cash this check—a check that will give us upon demand the riches of freedom and the security of justice. We have also come to this hallowed spot to remind America of the fierce urgency of *now*. This is no time to engage in the luxury of cooling off or to take the tranquilizing drugs of gradualism. *Now* is the time to make real the promises of Democracy. *Now* is the time to rise from the dark and desolate valley of segregation to the sunlit path of racial justice. *Now* is the time to open the doors of opportunity to all of God's children. *Now* is the time to lift our nation from the quicksands of racial injustice to the solid rock of brotherhood.

It would be fatal for the nation to overlook the urgency of the moment and to underestimate the determination of the Negro. This sweltering summer of the Negro's legitimate discontent will not pass until there is an invigorating autumn of freedom and equality. 1963 is not an end, but a beginning. Those who hope that the Negro needed to blow off steam and will now be content will have a rude awakening if the nation returns to business as usual. There will be neither rest nor tranquillity in America until the Negro is granted his citizenship rights. The whirlwinds of revolt will continue to shake the foundations of our nation until the bright day of justice emerges.

But there is something that I must say to my people who stand on the warm threshold which leads into the palace of justice. In the process of gaining our rightful place we must not be guilty of wrongful deeds. Let us not seek to satisfy our thirst for freedom by drinking from the cup of bitterness and hatred. We must forever conduct our struggle on the high plane of dignity and discipline. We must not allow our creative protest to degenerate into physical violence. Again and again we must rise to the majestic heights of meeting physical force with soul force. The marvelous new militancy which has engulfed the Negro community must not lead us to a distrust of all white people, for many of our white brothers, as evidenced by their presence here today, have come to realize that their destiny is tied up with our destiny and their freedom is inextricably bound to our freedom. We cannot walk alone.

And as we walk, we must make the pledge that we shall march ahead. We cannot turn back. There are those who are asking the devotees of civil rights, "When will you be satisfied?" We can never be satisfied as long as the Negro is the victim of the unspeakable horrors of police brutality. We can never be satisfied as long as our bodies, heavy with the fatigue of travel, cannot gain lodging in the motels of the highways and the hotels of the cities. We cannot be satisfied as long as the Negro's basic mobility is from a smaller ghetto to a larger one. We can never be satisfied as long as a Negro in Mississippi cannot vote and a Negro in New York believes he has nothing for which to vote. No, no, we are not satisfied, and we will not be satisfied until justice rolls down like waters and righteousness like a mighty stream.

I am not unmindful that some of you have come here out of great trials and tribulations. Some of you have come fresh from narrow jail cells. Some of you have come from areas where your quest for freedom left you battered by the storms of persecution and staggered by the winds of police brutality. You have been the veterans of creative suffering. Continue to work with the faith that unearned suffering is redemptive.

Go back to Mississippi, go back to Alabama, go back to South Carolina, go back to Georgia, go back to Louisiana, go back to the slums and ghettos of our northern cities, knowing that somehow this situation will be changed. Let us not wallow in the valley of despair.

I say to you today, my friends, that in spite of the difficulties and frustrations of the moment I still have a dream. It is a dream deeply rooted in the American dream.

I have a dream that one day this nation will rise up and live out the true meaning of its creed: "We hold these truths to be self-evident; that all men are created equal."

I have a dream that one day on the red hills of Georgia the sons of former slaves and the sons of former slaveowners will be able to sit down together at the table of brotherhood.

I have a dream that one day even the state of Mississippi, a desert state sweltering with the heat of injustice and oppression, will be transformed into an oasis of freedom and justice.

I have a dream that my four little children will one day live in a nation where they will not be judged by the color of their skin but by the content of their character.

I have a dream today.

I have a dream that one day the state of Alabama, whose governor's lips are presently dripping with the words of interposition and nullification, will be transformed into a situation where little black boys and black girls will be able to join hands with little white boys and white girls and walk together as sisters and brothers.

I have a dream today.

I have a dream that one day every valley shall be exalted, every hill and mountain shall be made low, the rough places will be made plain, and the crooked places will be made straight, and the glory of the Lord shall be revealed, and all flesh shall see it together.

This is our hope. This is the faith with which I return to the South. With this faith we will be able to hew out of the mountain of despair a stone of hope. With this faith we will be able to transform the jangling discords of our nation into a beautiful symphony of brotherhood. With this faith we will be able to work together, to pray together, to struggle together, to go to jail together, to stand up for freedom together, knowing that we will be free one day.

This will be the day when all of God's children will be able to sing with new meaning

> My country, 'tis of thee,
> Sweet land of liberty,
>   Of thee I sing:
> Land where my fathers died,
> Land of the pilgrims' pride,
> From every mountain-side
>   Let freedom ring.

And if America is to be a great nation this must become true. So let freedom ring from the prodigious hilltops of New Hampshire. Let freedom ring from the mighty mountains of New York. Let freedom ring from the heightening Alleghenies of Pennsylvania!

Let freedom ring from the snowcapped Rockies of Colorado!

Let freedom ring from the curvaceous peaks of California!

But not only that; let freedom ring from Stone Mountain of Georgia!

Let freedom ring from Lookout Mountain of Tennessee!

Let freedom ring from every hill and molehill of Mississippi. From every mountainside, let freedom ring.

When we let freedom ring, when we let it ring from every village and every hamlet, from every state and every city, we will be able to speed up that day when all of God's children, black men and white men, Jews and Gentiles, Protestants and Catholics, will be able to join hands and sing in the words of the old Negro spiritual, "Free at last! free at last! thank God almighty, we are free at last!"

Reading 2

The Power of PACs

This selection comes from a special column in the New Republic, *a weekly magazine of news and commentary. It discusses the activities of the large number of political action committees (PACs), which are lobbying organizations in Washington, D.C., for special interest groups in practically every industry, trade, and profession. The article draws attention to a troublesome situation in a democracy— the influence of moneyed organizations on legislators: "Money talks." Since the* New Republic *is a journal of opinion, its writers express their own beliefs and feelings in its columns. Note the style used in this column.*

On February 14, 1988, The New York Times *reported on a study of PACs made by an organization that studies political trends. After interviewing officials of fifty PACs, the researchers found that lawmakers expected—and even demanded—financial contributions from PACs because of their need for large amounts of money for political campaigns. The PAC officials claimed they gave the money in order to gain access—that is, to have the chance to present their views*

views when a lawmaker had to make a decision. Legislative bills to limit the amount of money a PAC can contribute have been defeated time after time in Congress. It is worth noting that another kind of PAC has come into existence, one of whose purposes is to decrease the power of PACs.

Big Business is running things again in Washington. It was in charge in the old days before the stock market crash in 1929, and then, for half a century or so, the political parties stepped back in and took over. Now the parties are losing influence again, and power is being taken over by the new tool, the Political Action Committee....

...As Mark Green recently pointed out in this journal ("Political Pac-Man," TNR, December 13), and as Elizabeth Drew confirms in a two-part article, in *The New Yorker*, PACs are indeed taking over. "Increasingly, the shape and nature of our politics is being determined by the interests that have the money to contribute and the technicians who instruct the candidates in how to raise it and use it," Miss Drew writes. "Increasingly, the question of who gets funds is a decision made within Washington, by people who have an eye on some piece of the national agenda."

This is a technical-sounding matter, hard for the average voter to focus on. The voter is finding politics increasingly dull anyway. Our awful two-year election process has now begun. In 1984 we will have thirty or so primaries to struggle through. For five straight Presidential elections the percentage of voters has gone down. In 1980 only 54 percent of the American public voted, as opposed to 75 percent in Canada. In Canada and in other parliamentary countries politics is more exciting. You see the prime minister and the leader of the minority party going after each other hammer and tongs, face to face. Here you can hear President Reagan give his weekly five-minute explanation of public affairs on radio. Unlike any parliamentary system, there is no provision to call an immediate election when the House defeats him on issues like the MX missile.

In its October 25 cover story, *Time* showed how the PACs work: "Today the power of PACs threatens to undermine America's system of representative democracy," it warned. Increasingly, big corporations or smaller interest groups band together to raise campaign funds, which they hand out to sympathetic politicians. In theory there's nothing wrong with that; it just separates the political parties from the legislators who do the voting. "There is a growing sense that the system is getting out of hand," says Missouri Democrat Richard Gephardt....

...Let Elizabeth Drew pick up the story. Acquisition of campaign funds has become "an obsession on the part of nearly every candidate for federal office," she says. "The obsession leads the candidates to solicit and accept money from those most able to provide it....There are ostensible limits on how much can be contributed to the candidates for the House and the Senate, but these limits are essentially meaningless. The only limits are those on ingenuity." Yes, certainly, trade unionists have their PACs, too; in fact it was the unions that started the thing. But as the authority of political parties declined, other groups joined the fray, and the unions are far outdistanced now. Here's a case in point. The Federal Trade Commission issued a requirement that used-car dealers list known major defects of an automobile. Dealers didn't like it, and they were important: they had spent $675,000 in the 1980 campaign—they had bought "access." The House voted to kill the regulation; of the 286 members who voted against it, 242 had received money from the car dealers. Corruption? No; few disputes in Washington are settled on lofty moral grounds, but this is an ongoing process, and more and more the interest groups are intervening. It has led to the institutionalization of the Washington fundraiser. Congress finally voted to pay for Presidential campaigns, but not for Congressional campaigns. These are being increasingly centralized in Washington by the technicians and the money men. Democracy is taking a strange turn.

Reading 3

The Declaration of Independence

The Declaration of Independence was mostly the work of Thomas Jefferson, one of America's most distinguished statesmen, who later became the country's third president. The Declaration set forth the many grievances of the thirteen colonies against Great Britain and proclaimed their independence from the mother country. The document was signed by the members of the Continental Congress on July 4, 1776. Since then, July 4 has been celebrated in the United States as Independence Day, or more simply the Fourth of July.

You will note that near the beginning of this document, the "inalienable rights" of man are mentioned—"Life, Liberty and the pursuit of Happiness." The statement of these rights was revised from those mentioned first by John Locke, the British philosopher whose work influenced Jefferson's thinking. Locke gave these rights as "Life, Liberty, and the pursuit of Property."

As you read, you will note that the style of this document, written more than two hundred years ago, is quite different from today's. However, the Declaration is still greatly admired for its forthright tone and its eloquent presentation.

When in the course of human events, it becomes necessary for one people to dissolve the political bands which have connected them with another, and to assume among the Powers of the earth, the separate and equal station to which the Laws of Nature and of Nature's God entitle them, a decent respect to the opinions of mankind requires that they should declare the causes which impel them to the separation.

We hold these truths to be self-evident, that all men are created equal, that they are endowed by their Creator with certain unalienable Rights, that among these are Life, Liberty and the pursuit of Happiness. That to secure these rights, Governments are instituted among Men, deriving their just powers from the consent of the governed. That whenever any Form of Government becomes destructive of these ends, it is the Right of the People to alter or to abolish it, and to institute new Government, laying its foundation on such principles and organizing its powers in such form, as to them shall seem most likely to effect their Safety and Happiness. Prudence, indeed, will dictate that Governments long established should not be changed for light and transient causes; and accordingly all experience hath shown, that mankind are more disposed to suffer, while evils are sufferable, than to right themselves by abolishing the forms to which they are accustomed. But when a long train of abuses and usurpations pursuing invariably the same Object evinces a design to reduce them under absolute Despotism, it is their right, it is their duty, to throw off such government, and to provide new Guards for their future security. Such has been the patient sufferance of these Colonies; and such is now the necessity which constrains them to alter their former Systems of Government. The history of the present King of Great Britain is a history of repeated injuries and usurpations, all having in direct object the establishment of an absolute Tyranny over these States. To prove this, let Facts be submitted to a candid world.

He has refused his Assent to Laws, the most wholesome and necessary for the public good.

He has forbidden his Governors to pass Laws of immediate and pressing importance, unless suspended in their operation till his Assent should be obtained; and when so suspended, he has utterly neglected to attend to them.

He has refused to pass other Laws for the accommodation of large districts of people, unless those people would relinquish the right of Representation in the Legislature, a right inestimable to them and formidable to tyrants only.

He has called together legislative bodies at places unusual, uncomfortable, and distant from the depository of their Public Records, for the sole purpose of fatiguing them into compliance with his measures.

He has dissolved Representative Houses repeatedly, for opposing with many firmness his invasions on the rights of the people.

He has refused for a long time, after such dissolutions, to cause others to be elected; whereby the Legislative Powers, incapable of Annihilation, have returned to the People at large for their exercise; the State remaining in the mean time exposed to all the dangers of invasion from without, and convulsions within.

He has endeavoured to prevent the population of these States; for that purpose obstructing the Laws for Naturalization of Foreigners; refusing to pass others to encourage their migration hither, and raising the conditions of new Appropriations of Lands.

He has obstructed the Administration of Justice, by refusing his Assent to Laws for establishing Judiciary Powers.

He has made Judges dependent on his Will alone, for the tenure of their offices, and the amount and payment of their salaries.

He has erected a multitude of New Offices, and sent hither swarms of Officers to harass our People, and eat out their substance.

He has kept among us, in time of peace, Standing Armies without the Consent of our Legislature.

He has affected to render the Military independent of and superior to the Civil Power.

He has combined with others to subject us to jurisdiction foreign to our constitution, and unacknowledged by our laws; giving us Assent to their acts of pretended Legislation:

For quartering large bodies of armed troops among us:

For protecting them, by a mock Trial, from Punishment for any Murders which they should commit on the Inhabitants of these States:

For cutting off our Trade with all parts of the world:

For imposing Taxes on us without our Consent:

For depriving us in many cases, of the benefits of Trial by Jury:

For transporting us beyond Seas to be tried for pretended offences:

For abolishing the free System of English Laws in a Neighbouring Province, establishing therein an Arbitrary government, and enlarging its boundaries so as to render it at once an example and fit instrument for introducing the same absolute rule into these Colonies:

For taking away our Charters, abolishing our most valuable Laws, and altering fundamentally the Forms of our Governments:

For suspending our own Legislatures, and declaring themselves invested with Power to legislate for us in all cases whatsoever.

He has abdicated Government here, by declaring us out of his Protection and waging War against us.

He has plundered our seas, ravaged our Coasts, burnt our towns, and destroyed the Lives of our people.

He is at this time transporting large Armies of foreign Mercenaries to compleat the works of death, desolation and tyranny, already begun with circumstances of Cruelty & perfidy scarcely paralleled in the most barbarous ages, and totally unworthy the Head of a civilized nation.

He has constrained our fellow Citizens taken Captive on the high Seas to bear Arms against their Country, to become the executioners of their friends and Brethren, or to fall themselves by their Hands.

He has excited domestic insurrections amongst us, and has endeavoured to bring on the inhabitants of our frontiers, the merciless Indian Savages, whose known rule of warfare is an undistinguished destruction of all ages, sexes and conditions.

In every stage of these Oppressions We have Petitioned for Redress in the most humble terms: Our repeated petitions have been answered only by repeated injury. A Prince, whose character is thus marked by every act which may define a Tyrant, is unfit to be the ruler of a free People.

Nor have We been wanting in attention to our British brethren. We have warned them from time to time of attempts by their legislature to extend an unwarrantable jurisdiction over us. We have reminded them of the circumstances of our emigration and settlement here. We have appealed to their native justice and magnanimity and we have conjured them by the ties of our common kindred to disavow these usurpations, which would inevitably interrupt our connections and correspondence. They too have been deaf to the voice of justice and of consanguinity. We must, therefore acquiesce in the necessity, which denounces our Separation, and hold them, as we hold the rest of mankind, Enemies in War, in Peace Friends.

We, therefore, the Representatives of the United States of America, in General Congress, Assembled, appealing to the Supreme Judge of the world for the rectitude of our intentions, do, in the Name, and by Authority of the good People of these Colonies, solemnly publish and declare, That these United Colonies are, and of Right ought to be Free and Independent States; that they are Absolved from all Allegiance to the British Crown, and that all political connection between them and the State of Great Britain, is and ought to be totally dissolved; and that as Free and Independent States, they have full power to levy War, conclude Peace, contract Alliances, establish Commerce, and to do all other Acts and Things which Independent States may of right do. And for the support of this Declaration, with a firm reliance on the protection of Divine Providence, we mutually pledge to each other our lives, our Fortunes and our sacred Honor.

Reading 4

The American Constitution

The following tables are intended to give a quick overview of the American Constitution. They are taken from a chapter in a college text entitled "The American Federal Experience: The Development of Constitutional Democracy." The first table is an outline of the original Constitution. The second table outlines the twenty-six amendments, the first ten of which are known as the Bill of Rights.

An Outline of the Original Consitution

Preamble	**Attributes Consitution to "We the People"** States purposes of Constitution Contains no enforceable provisions
Article I	**Legislative Branch** Bicameral Congress: Senate and House of Representatives Membership and methods of selection Legislative procedures Powers and limitations on powers Limitations on state governments
Article II	**Executive Branch** President and vice-president Selection by electoral college Conditions of service Powers
Article III	**Judicial Branch** Supreme Court and provision for lower courts Selection and service of judges Powers Trial by jury guaranteed Treason defined
Article IV	**Intergovernmental Relations** Obligations of states to one another Admission of new states Obligations of national government to states
Article V	**Amendment Procedures**

Article VI   **Supremacy of Constitution and Miscellaneous**
Basis for judicial review
Assumption of prior debts
Prohibition of religious qualifications for public office

Article VII   **Procedure for Ratifying Constitution**

An Outline of Amendments to the Constitution

Amendment	Subject	Year of ratification
1	Guarantees freedom of expression and of religion	1791
	Prohibits establishment of state religion	
2	Protects states' power to maintain armed militias (national guard)	1791
3	Prohibits housing soldiers in private homes	1791
4	Protects right to privacy from unreasonable searches and seizures	1791
5	Limits criminal prosecution (grand jury)	1791
	Prohibits two trials for same crime (double jeopardy)	
	Prohibits forced confessions (self-incrimination)	
	Guarantees due process of law	
	Limits power to take private property (eminent domain)	
6	Criminal trial procedures guaranteeing rights:	1791
	To a speedy and public trial	
	To an impartial jury	
	To cross-examine witnesses	
	To subpoena witnesses	
	To legal counsel	
7	Guarantees jural trial in civil cases	1791
8	Prohibits excessive bail and fines	1791
	Prohibits cruel and unusual punishments	
9	Guarantees to the people rights not otherwise listed	1791
10	Protects powers reserved to the states	1791
11	Reduces judicial power of national courts, modifying Article III (adopted to counteract Supreme Court decision)	1798
12	Changes method of electing vice-president, modifying Article II	1804

After Amendment 12, more than 60 years elapsed before the 3 Civil War amendments were adopted, largely to protect black people against oppressive legislation passed by white-controlled state legislatures.

13	Prohibits slavery	1865
14	Establishes citizenship by birth in U.S.	1868
	Guarantees due process of law against state interference, incorporating most of Bill of Rights as limitations upon state as well as national power	
	Prohibits denial by states of equal protection of the laws (adopted partially to counteract Supreme Court decision)	

| 15 | Prohibits denial of right to vote because of race | 1870 |

After another 40 years, Amendments 16 through 19 were adopted within 7 years. Although dissimilar in content, they were all products of the Progressive movement which early in this century urged reform in all levels of government.

16	Permits national income tax levied without regard to state population, modifying Article I (adopted to conteract Supreme Court decision)	1913
17	Requires U.S. senators be elected directly by voters, modifying Article I	1913
18	Prohibits manufacture, sale, or transportation of alcoholic beverages	1919
19	Prohibits denial of right to vote because of sex	1920
20	Reduces period of time between election and start of term for national officials	1933
	Repeals Amendment 18	1933
22	Limits president to two terms	1951
23	Gives Washington, D.C., electoral votes in presidential elections	1961
24	Prohibits denial of right to vote because of failure to pay poll taxes	1964
25	Establishes procedure to select vice-president to fill vacancy in that office	1967
	Establishes procedure for vice-president to become acting president in the event of presidential disability	
26	Prohibits denial of right to vote because of age to those 18 or more	1971

Extra Discussion and Writing

Journal Entry

If you were keeping a journal for yourself, what would you write about your impressions of the U.S. democratic system? Since you are the only one reading this entry, write freely and say what you honestly think.

Letters

Write a letter to one of your teachers in your native country giving your impressions of American democracy in action. Revise the journal entry for the letter so that it is more carefully controlled and correct, but keep the letter friendly since you know the teacher.

Sayings

1. *The dignity and worth of man.* This phrase has been used to express an assumption about the citizens in a democracy. Explain what this assumption is and how it relates to democracy.
2. *Government of the people, by the people, for the people.* These phrases from Lincoln's Gettysburg Address have often been quoted in discussions of democracy. Explain how each of the prepositions—*of, by, for*—involve the people in a democracy.
3. *Money talks.* This cynical expression sometimes relates to the influence of moneyed organizations on representatives. Explain what this expression implies about the legislators in a democracy as they vote for or against certain laws.
4. *Your freedom ends at the tip of my nose.* What does this expression suggest about the limits of personal freedom?

Political Speech

You are running for high political office (president, mayor) in your country or in the United States. In your campaign, you are going to give a speech to persuade people to vote for you. Before you write the speech, (1) identify your audience: large, small, those with special interests (farmers, urban residents). Then (2) determine the issues you will discuss and the promises you will make. Here are some examples:

> The audience's personal interests: more jobs, higher standard of living, improved housing, justice before the law, better educational opportunities, right to own land, government help for farmers, reduction of crime, fairer distribution of goods and services.
>
> The country's interests: improved economy, greater technological progress, greater military strength, reduction of inflation.

Try to appeal to both the audience's reason and their emotions. To appeal to their emotions, you may employ various types of slanting—the selection of certain details, distortions, favorable or unfavorable words.

You may begin the speech with one of these salutations: <u>Ladies and gentlemen</u> (formal), <u>Fellow countrymen, Fellow New Yorkers</u> (for a local audience). It's best to end on a very strong note of promise or great hope for the future if you are elected.

Reactions

Reading 1

The Gettysburg Address

Abraham Lincoln

The Gettysburg Address, one of the shortest and most famous speeches in American history, was made at the dedication of the national cemetery in Gettysburg, Pennsylvania, on November 19, 1863. One of the decisive battles of the American Civil War (1861–65) had been fought at Gettysburg, with great loss of life on both sides.

As you read the speech, note the style that made the speech so famous that many American schoolchildren can recite it from memory. Note especially the use of parallel structures (similar grammatical forms), which lend eloquence to the speech.

Fourscore and seven years ago our fathers brought forth on this continent a new nation, conceived in liberty, and dedicated to the proposition that all men are created equal.

Now we are engaged in a great civil war, testing whether that nation, or any nation so conceived and so dedicated, can long endure. We are met on a great battlefield of that war. We have come to dedicate a portion of that field as a final resting-place for those who here gave their lives that that nation might live. It is altogether fitting and proper that we should do this.

But, in a larger sense, we cannot dedicate—we cannot consecrate—we cannot hallow—this ground. The brave men, living and dead, who struggled here, have consecrated it far above our poor power to add or detract. The world will little note nor long remember what we say here, but it can never forget what they did here. It is for us, the living, rather, to be dedicated here to the unfinished work which they who fought here have thus far so nobly advanced. It is rather for us to be here dedicated to the great task remaining before us—that from these honored dead we take increased devotion to that cause for which they gave the last full measure of devotion; that we here highly resolve that these dead shall not have died in vain; that this nation, under God, shall have a new birth of freedom; and that government of the people, by the people, for the people, shall not perish from the earth.

Reading 2

Constituents Voice
Opinions on Major Issues

*Because elected officials in the United States are often far removed from the people
who elected them (their constituents), a number of legislators have begun sending
questionnaires to their constituents to find out how they stand on certain issues.
The following opinion poll shows the results of a legislative questionnaire sent out
by the U.S. representative from a Manhattan district in 1987.*

   *What do you think about this means of getting the opinions of constituents
on important local and national issues? Do you think the poll results should affect
the way the legislator will vote in the House of Representatives? Should representatives vote according to what they themselves believe, or according to what their
constituents believe?*

More than 8,000 constituents responded to the legislative questionnaire
that I mailed to residents of the 17th Congressional District earlier this year.

This was an informal poll and not a scientific sampling of opinion, but I
believe the response generally reflects the views of the 17th District.

Opinion polls are one of the most effective means of monitoring the
district's range of opinion on major issues. I would like to express my appreciation to all those who completed and returned the questionnaire.

The results are printed below:

	For	Against	Not sure
1. Are you for or against stricter trade measures to reduce U.S. trade deficits?	39%	34%	27%
2. Are you for or against a federal law prohibiting discrimination on the basis of affectional or sexual orientation?	70%	23%	7%
3. Are you for or against legislation requiring employers to grant leave to employees for care of a new-born or newly adopted child, or seriously ill child or dependent parent?	74%	13%	13%
4. Are you for or against home-porting seven Navy ships, capable of carrying nuclear weapons, in New York Harbor?	23%	67%	10%

From *Congressman Ted Weiss Reports*, Vol. XI, No. 2, 1987. Reprinted by permission.

Are you for or against the following measures to reduce the federal budget deficit?

5. Reducing funding for social programs.	16%	78%	6%
6. Reducing military spending.	83%	12%	5%
7. Raising taxes.	29%	54%	17%
8. Continued enforcement of the Gramm-Rudman balanced budget law.	35%	37%	28%

Are you for or against the following approaches to the drug abuse problem?

9. Mandatory drug testing in the workplace.	29%	60%	11%
10. Increased funding for drug education and rehabilitation.	82%	11%	7%
11. Tougher penalties for drug dealers.	85%	8%	7%

Are you for or against the following campaign finance reform measures?

12. Public financing of congressional campaigns.	46%	35%	19%
13. Limits on total campaign expenditures.	89%	5%	6%
14. Stricter limits on contributions from PACs.	85%	7%	8%

Are you for or against the following proposed changes in the Medicare program?

15. Requiring doctors to accept the Medicare rate when treating Medicare patients.	71%	13%	16%
16. Expanding Medicare to cover catastrophic medical expenses in return for a premium of $59 a year.	80%	6%	14%

Recent U.S. policy in Central America has been highly controversial. Are you for or against the following?

17. U.S. military assistance to the contras who are fighting to overthrow the government of Nicaragua.	15%	74%	11%
18. Attaching strong human rights conditions to military aid to the government of El Salvador.	72%	14%	14%
19. Prohibiting the use of U.S. armed forces for combat in Central America.	67%	23%	10%

Are you for or against the following proposals in U.S. policy toward the Middle East?

20. A freeze on new Israeli settlements on the West Bank.	52%	24%	24%
21. Self-government by the Palestinians, in association with Jordan, on the West Bank and Gaza Strip.	49%	18%	33%
22. Negotiations between Israel and the PLO if the PLO recognizes Israel's right to exist.	78%	10%	12%

Are you for or against the following arms control and foreign policy initiatives?

23. Continued funding of the President's Star Wars missile defense system.	22%	67%	11%
24. President Reagan's decision to scrap U.S. compliance with the SALT II arms control treaty.	17%	69%	14%
25. A ban on nuclear tests in the United States so long as the Soviet Union abides by such a ban.	80%	13%	7%

26. Complete disinvestment in South Africa by U.S. corporations and individuals while that government maintains its policy of apartheid.   67%   20%   13%
27. The sale of weapons to Iran for the purpose of improving U.S. relations with that country.   8%   84%   8%
28. U.S. assistance to rebel forces fighting to overthrow the government of Angola.   17%   61%   22%
29. U.S. military and financial support for the Chilean government.   7%   68%   25%
30. Increasing U.S. economic development aid to poorer nations.   60%   22%   18%

CHAPTER 7

Newspapers

Composition
Vocabulary and Usage
Reading for Summary Writing
Reading for Further Ideas
Extra Discussion and Writing

Composition

Procedures for Discussion
Writing the Composition
Revising the Composition

Requirements for a Home Composition
_____

1. Use white $8\frac{1}{2}'' \times 11''$ paper; write on one side only.
2. Type your composition double spaced on unlined paper (if hand-written, the paper should be clearly written on every other line). A typewritten page, double-spaced, is about 250 words.
3. Indent each paragraph, use wide margins ($1''$ to $1\frac{1}{4}''$), and number each page in the upper right-hand corner.
4. Include a separate page with the title, the thesis sentence, and the outline.

Procedures for Discussion

Students are first assigned to bring a local newspaper to class. They are told to be prepared to discuss:

1. The general purposes of a newspaper
2. These aspects of their newspaper:
   a. The format (physical arrangement)
   b. The treatment of the news
   c. The language used
   d. The special features
   e. The advertising

After discussing each of these points in class, the teacher asks students to determine what kind of reader their particular paper is intended for.

Writing the Composition

This composition will be written in answer to one of the following two essay questions. The composition may be assigned to be written at home or at the next class meeting. Write on either 1 or 2:

　　1. Discuss a local newspaper in terms of the kind of reader it is intended for. You may consider any or all of the following: the treatment of the news, the language used, the special features, and the advertising. Use specific examples from your newspaper, but maintain a balance between general statements and examples.

　　2. What do you think the ideal newspaper should contain? Consider its purpose, its treatment of the news, its advertising, and whatever else you think is important in such a newspaper.

　　Read the question you choose carefully. Underline first the words that point to the central idea; then underline its parts. All these parts should be developed in your composition in terms of the central idea.

Suggestions for the Content and Organization

Whether you write your answer to this essay question at home or in class, consider the following advice.

　　You may use your central idea to provide a transitional means of connecting each of your main points.

　　　Example:　1. *The New York Times* reader expects, looks for
　　　　　　　　2. The *ideal newspaper* should, is, has

In question 1, you may bring out the points you want to make about your newspaper by comparing it with another paper, but you must put more emphasis on the paper you are writing about, so that the reader knows that this paper is really your subject.

If you write the composition in class, you may not have time to write a formal outline. Your composition should be a reasonable length, determined by the amount of time of the class session, rather than by the number of words. Write from notes that have some kind of organizational structure, and that indicate how you will handle the introduction and conclusion.

Write carefully, since you may not be able to rewrite. Time yourself so that you can write about each point listed in your notes and still have time at the end to look over your paper.

Guide for the Outline and the Composition

If you write the composition at home, or if you rewrite the class composition, the following guide should help you. On the left side of the guide is the outline with suggestions for handling the introduction, transitions, and the conclusion of this composition. On the right side are general comments about how introductions, transitions, and conclusions may be written. (If you are accustomed to writing a first draft from rough notes, use this guide for your second and succeeding drafts.)

Outline	*General Comments*
Title	Use initial capital letters for all words except articles, short prepositions, and short conjunctions. Try to use an interesting title that reflects your thesis.

Introduction
This can set a specific scene that will lead into your central idea.
Or it can be general—the importance of being informed; the newspaper in comparison with other mass media; the purposes of a newspaper.
	Purpose of the introduction:
	    to catch the reader's interest
	    to give a general idea of the subject
	
	An introduction may include:
	    a quotation
	    a story, perhaps personal
	    a rhetorical question (which you
	        will answer)
	    a definition
	    a statement of a belief you will
	        argue against
	    a surprising or shocking fact
	    a statement of a serious problem

Transitional lead-in
This lets the reader know that your discussion will be in terms of:
an intended reader, or
an ideal newspaper

Usually at the end of the introduction. Gives an indication of the central idea and the way it will be developed (may be in the form of a question).

I. First main point
This is the first point about: (1) what the reader of the paper looks for, or (2) what an ideal newspaper should be.

New paragraph. The first sentence: (1) mentions the general idea of the paragraph (from the important word[s] in the outline); (2) relates this sentence to what was said before.

  A. First supporting detail

  B. Second supporting detail

      etc.

Should be related to the preceding subpoint.

Note: Long subpoints may begin new paragraphs.

(Continue with your other main points and their supporting details.)

Begin each point with a reminder that you are talking about: (1) a particular kind of reader, or (2) your ideal newspaper

(Follow the suggestions given for the first main point.)

Conclusion
This can summarize the main points you made in an interesting way. Or it can return to some point made in the introduction.

The conclusion should round out the composition in a strong and satisfying way, perhaps by referring again to whatever you used to introduce the composition.

Notes: (1) The conclusion should not add any new ideas that need further development. (2) If your last point ends on a strong note that points up your thesis, you may not need to add a conclusion.

Support for the points you make can come from your own beliefs and experience or from the readings in this chapter and elsewhere. (Be sure to identify your sources and to use quotation marks around the exact words of an author.) The support can be in the form of examples, current facts and figures, or authoritative opinion. Use enough support to make your point convincing to the reader.

Finally, keep in mind that this composition represents your own opinions. By stating them honestly and strongly, you will have a composition that the reader will find interesting enough to continue reading.

Revising the Composition

In succeeding drafts, try to sharpen your thesis and show more clearly how each main point contributes to the development of the thesis. Try writing down the opening sentences of your paragraphs on a separate sheet of paper to see if they make a clear sentence outline. Go over the reading selections again for further ideas or additional support.

Consult the Revision and Editing Checklist for guidance on organization, paragraphing, and sentences. You can get needed vocabulary help in the vocabulary section that follows. Make a final check with the Symbol Chart for Correction of Compositions for the grammatical structures and usage in your composition.

Evaluation

If there is an exchange of student compositions, the Revision and Editing Checklist can serve as a guide in the evaluation of another student's composition. Use the following procedure in checking for the writer's organization and development of ideas.

1. Without looking at the other student's outline page, make an outline and a one-sentence summary of the central idea (or thesis) of the whole paper. Can you find a clear line of development? Do your summary sentence and your outline agree with those of the writer?
2. Find the support for each point made in the writer's paper. Is the support adequate and convincing?
3. Write on the student's paper what you consider the good points of the composition and what needs to be improved.

Vocabulary and Usage

Vocabulary
Usage Notes
Word Forms

Vocabulary

The following words may be useful to you in talking and writing about newspapers.

The Newspaper Itself

cartoon   A drawing satirizing some action or person, often through caricature.

circulation   The number of copies of a periodical that are distributed or sold.

classified ad (advertisement)   A short advertisement in a newspaper, often involving individual sales or purchases, or jobs.

column   An article that appears regularly in a newspaper or magazine.

columnist   The writer of such a column.

comics (sometimes called **cartoons**, or very informally, **the funnies**)   Strips showing a series of drawings about humorous events or adventures, sometimes with continuing characters and a story.

editorial   The opinion of the publisher or editor as expressed in a special column of a newspaper.

feature story   A story often related to a current event but with human interest appeal. May give background information—the story behind the news.

format   The general arrangement (or **layout**) of a publication. Includes the size of the paper, the print and headlines, the colors, the pictures, the columns.

headline   A large heading at the top of a newspaper article. May stand by itself on the front page.

obituary   A notice in a newspaper of someone's death.

op ed page (for opposite editorial page)   A page opposite the editorial page that contains articles and letters from readers expressing personal viewpoints.

periodical   A publication, such as a newspaper or magazine, that is published at regular intervals.

special feature   Any feature included in a newspaper that is not a news story: editorials, special columns, cartoons, crossword puzzles, etc.

syndicated feature   A column or other feature bought from an agency for simultaneous publication in different newspapers.

tabloid   A newspaper, usually half-size, with short, often sensational news stories, and many pictures.

People Involved in Newspaper Publication

correspondent   A person employed by a periodical to supply news or articles regularly from a distance.

editor   A person who supervises or prepares material for publication.

journalism   The profession of being a journalist.

journalist   A person who collects, writes, edits, or publishes news for a newspaper.

publisher   The head of a newspaper. May be the owner or someone representing the owner.

reporter   Someone who collects and reports news for a newspaper.

Things Newspapers Write About

catastrophe   Any sudden and great disaster.

gossip   Informal talk or rumor, often of a personal or sensational nature.

scandal   Any wrongdoing that is morally offensive and leads to disgrace (**scandalous** = adjective).

sensational (news)   News that arouses a strong emotional reaction or intense interest; news producing a shock effect (**sensationalism** = noun).

Language Used in Newspapers

colloquial language   More conversational, everyday language. The tone may be playful and familiar. May also include some slang.

formal language   Language with a wide range of vocabulary that maintains a serious tone. Sentences are long and complex.

slang   Language of greatest informality. Adds color, humor, feeling. Usually not acceptable in formal writing.

Usage Notes

Use *the* with the name of a newspaper. Capitalize *the* if it is part of the name:

> *The* New York Times.

The word *news* is a singular noncountable noun. Use a singular adjective (*much, this*) and a singular verb. If a plural is desired, use *news stories*.

> This news is very good.

Other words that are singular noncountable nouns are:

> information
> slang—*but* slang words
> vocabulary—*but* vocabulary words
> gossip
> advice
> entertainment

Advertisement vs. *advertising. Advertisement* refers to a concrete thing that exists. It is countable and can be made plural:

> That newspaper carries many *advertisements*.

Advertising is an abstract idea. It is noncountable.

> That newspaper carries much *advertising*.

Use *on* with *page*

> *on* the front page

Medium is the singular form; *media* is the plural form.

> The newspaper is a *medium* of communications.

> The newspaper is one of the mass *media*.

Few vs. *a few*. *Few* is a quantity that represents *almost none*. It stresses the *absence* of something.

> There are *few* major newspapers here.

A few is a quantity that represents *some,* but *a small amount*. It stresses the *presence* of something.

> There are *a few* major newspapers here.

Each and *every* require singular verbs.

> *Each* of these papers *is* different.

A number vs. *the number*. *A number* specifies *some, many*. Use a plural verb.

A number of newspapers *have failed*.

The number specifies the amount. Use a singular verb.

> *The number* of newspapers in this town *is* small.

When referring to socioeconomic class, use *the:*

> *the* lower class
> *the* middle class
> *the* upper class
> *the* white-collar class
> *the* blue-collar class

A general statement with the word *newspaper* can be made in the singular or the plural.

> *The newspaper* can provide entertainment as well as information.
> *Newspapers* can provide entertainment as well as information.

Use quotation marks around the names of newspapers. (But in research papers, use underlining for the names of newspapers as well as other publications.)

Do not use *on* after the verb *emphasize:*

> This newspaper *emphasizes* important world news.
> This newspaper *places emphasis on* important world news.

Word Forms

The answers are on p. 355. If you need help with this exercise, refer to the explanations of Word Forms in the Appendix. Use the correct forms for the words in parentheses.

1. Most newspapers in the United States are (private) _____ owned

   and (operate) _____.

2. (Circulate) _____ provides one-fourth of a newspaper's in-

   come in the United States. (Advertise) _____ provides the

   other three-fourths of the paper's income.

3. Stores place (advertise) _____ in newspapers to increase their

   business. Individuals place (classify) _____ ads in papers for

   (employ) _____, real estate, cars and other (person)

   _____ matters.

4. Newspapers express their opinion about the news in their (edit)

   _____ columns.

5. Many newspapers have special (finance) _____ and (culture)

   _____ sections.

6. Some people want the news to be merely (inform) _____; others

   want the news to be (entertain) _____ as well.

7. Someone who reports the news is a (report) _____; someone

   who prepares the news for (publish) _____ is an (edit)

   _____; and someone who reports the news from a distance is

   a (correspond) _____.

8. The word tabloid (usual) _____ refers to the smaller size of a

   newspaper. However, tabloids have become (associate) _____

   with the (report) _____ of important news in (abbreviate)

   _____ form and with a more (extend) _____

   (cover) _____ of (sensation) _____ news.

9. Greater (emphasize) _____ in tabloids is (place)

   _____ on (scandal) _____ events such as (bribe)

   _____, (corrupt) _____, murder, (rob)

_____, (burglar) _____, (kidnap) _____ etc.

10. The tabloids also concentrate more (heavy) _____ on local news than on (nation) _____ or foreign news.

11. Language (appeal) _____ to the emotions is often used in tabloids. Such language is called (connote) _____ language. Language that is (emotion) _____ neutral is called (denote) _____ language.

12. A feature story is a (time) _____ story that is more (length) _____ than a news story and has a greater human interest appeal.

13. A news story is supposed to be (object) _____ rather than (subject) _____. It gives the who, when, where, what, how, and why of an event.

14. Hobby columns such as bridge and stamp (collect) _____, and games such as crossword puzzles offer (recreate) _____ for the reader.

15. Individuals and organizations often send press releases to newspapers (give) _____ news of their current (active) _____ and (incident) _____ hoping to get some free (public) _____.

Reading for Summary Writing

For the following three reading selections, prepare a brief outline for class discussion before you write the summary. After the class discussion of each selection, you will write:

1. A longer, revised outline of the reading selection, using an alternation of numbers and letters.
2. A one-sentence summary of the reading selection. The sentence should include the central idea and the main points used to develop this idea (from the outline).
3. A summary of the reading selection. The length assigned in the text will determine the amount of detail you can include in the outline and summary.

Guidelines for Writing (Review)

1. For the outline, use the alternate number-letter system for main points and subpoints. The phrases underlined in the opening sentences of paragraphs usually become the main points or subpoints in the outline.
2. For both the summary and the outline, follow the same order as the reading selection. However, you may begin the summary with a reference to the source of the selection (author, publication, etc.) and to its central idea.
3. Keep a sense of proportion. Write more about points the author devotes more attention to.
4. Concentrate more on the main points than on examples or other supporting details.
5. Use proper transitions between the main points and the subpoints of your summary; your summary must have an organization of its own.
6. Use your own words as much as possible, except for key phrases. You may quote important phrases or sentences.
7. Be careful not to overload any of the sentences with so much information that the sentence is hard to read.
8. Be consistent in your use of verb tenses. Use all present tense (the author states, feels) or all past tense (the author stated, felt). The present tense is more common in a summary.
9. Do not include your own ideas or your own attitude or interpretation. The summary should be an objective restatement of what the author has said.

Reading 1

Where Is the News Leading Us?

Norman Cousins

The author of this article is a former editor of the Saturday Review of Literature. *The article is an example of persuasive writing. Cousins cites a definition of*

Norman Cousins, "Where Is the News Leading Us?" in *Today's Education* 66 (March–April 1977), p. 27. By permission of Norman Cousins and *Today's Education*. National Education Association.

news *that he finds unsatisfactory; he then goes on to give his own expansion of the meaning of* news.

Note which introductory technique the author uses to catch the attention of the reader. Note also the technique used to conclude the article.

Length of summary: Approximately 200 words

Not long ago I was asked to join in a public symposium on the role of the American press. Two other speakers were included on the program. The first was a distinguished TV anchorman. The other was the editor of one of the nation's leading papers, a newsman to the core—tough, aggressive, and savvy in the ways and means of solid reporting.

The purpose of the symposium, as I understood it, was to scrutinize the obligations of the media and to suggest the best ways to meet those obligations.

During the open-discussion period, a gentleman in the audience addressed a question to my two colleagues. Why, he asked, are the newspapers and television news programs so disaster-prone? Why are newsmen and women so attracted to tragedy, violence, failure?

The anchorman and editor reacted as though they had been blamed for the existence of bad news. Newsmen and newswomen, they said, are only responsible for reporting the news, not for creating it or modifying it.

It didn't seem to me that the newsmen had answered the question. The gentleman who had asked it was not blaming them for the distortions in the world. He was just wondering why distortions are most reported. The news media seem to operate on the philosophy that all news is bad news. Why? Could it be that the emphasis on downside news is largely the result of tradition—the way newsmen and newswomen are accustomed to respond to daily events?

Perhaps it would be useful here to examine the way we define the word *news*, for this is where the problem begins. *News* is supposed to deal with happenings of the past 12 hours—24 hours at most. Anything that happens so suddenly, however, is apt to be eruptive. A sniper kills some pedestrians; a terrorist holds 250 people hostage in a plane; OPEC announces a 25 percent increase in petroleum prices; Great Britain devalues by another 10 percent; a truck conveying radioactive wastes collides with a mobile cement mixer.

Focusing solely on these details, however, produces a misshapen picture. Civilization is a lot more than the sum total of its catastrophes. The most important ingredient in any civilization is progress. But progress doesn't happen all at once. It is not eruptive. Generally, it comes in bits and pieces, very little of it clearly visible at any given moment, but all of it involved in the making of historical change for the better.

It is this aspect of living history that most news reporting reflects inadequately. The result is that we are underinformed about positive developments and overinformed about disasters. This, in turn, leads to a public mood of defeatism and despair, which in themselves tend to be inhibitors of progress. An unrelieved diet of eruptive news depletes the essential human energies a free society needs. A mood of hopelessness and cynicism is hardly likely to furnish the energy needed to meet serious challenges.

I am not suggesting that "positive" news be contrived as an antidote to the disasters on page one. Nor do I define *positive news* as in-depth reportage of functions of the local YMCA. What I am trying to get across is the notion that the responsibility of the news media is to search out and report on important events—*whether or not* they come under the heading of conflict, confrontation, or catastrophe. The world is a splendid combination of heaven and hell, and *both* sectors call for attention and scrutiny.

My hope is that the profession of journalism will soon see its responsibility in a wider perspective. The time has come to consider the existence of a large area of human happenings that legitimately qualify as news. For example, how many news articles have been written about nitrogen-fixation—the process by which plants can be made to "fix" their own nitrogen, thus reducing the need for fertilizer? Scientists all over the world are now pursuing this prospect in the hope of combating famine. How much is known about the revolutionary changes being made in increasing the rice harvest in the Far East? There are literally dozens of similar important developments in the world that are worthy of inclusion in any roundup of major news stories.

The anchorman and editor were right in saying that newsmen and women are not responsible for shaping the world. But they *are* responsible for affecting our attitudes. We are only what we think we are; we can achieve only those goals we dare to envision. News people provide us with the only picture we have of ourselves and of the world. It had better be a true portrait—and not a caricature—for it is this picture on which we will base our decisions and around which we will plan our future.

The journalist, to paraphrase Walter Lippmann, is the public's philosopher. "The acquired culture," Lippmann wrote, "is not transmitted in our genes. The good life in the good society, though attainable, is never attained and possessed once and for all. What has been attained will again be lost if the wisdom of the good life in a good society is not transmitted."

With an accurate report of the good life in the good society, we can begin to use the news as Bernard de Chartres suggested we use history—boosting ourselves up on our experiences, "like dwarfs seated on the shoulders of giants," enabled, thus, "to see more things than the Ancients and things more distant."

Discussion

1. What is the occasion that serves as a springboard for the comments the author makes in this article?
2. Why does the author think the newsmen had not answered the question that was asked in the open-discussion period?

3. What is the definition of *news* given in the article?
4. What does the author think is wrong with this view of what news is?
5. What does the author see as the real responsibility of the news media? Do you agree?
6. Note that the author concludes with not one but two quotations. The first relates the purpose of the journalist to that of the philosopher. What is this purpose? The second quotation relates the goal of the journalist to that of history. What is this goal?
7. What do you think of the two final quotations, especially the figure of speech that concludes the article?
8. What is your opinion of the way the news is presented in the American newspaper you generally read?
9. Do you think that the scope of journalism has been expanded since Cousins wrote this article? If you think so, give examples.

Reading 2

The Newspaper Story: Its Construction

F. Fraser Bond

The following selection is an excerpt from a chapter in a popular book on journalism. The selection gives the traditional manner of constructing a news story. Although the book was written in 1954, the requirements for constructing a news story have not changed substantially. Note what the author says about the three parts of the newspaper story.

Length of summary: Approximately 200 words

The newspaper story in America has evolved to meet the requirements of everyday life as lived by everyday readers. It relies on the elements of novelty, directness, pace and variety, and it strives to convey its information in the form most in keeping with the tempo of our times. It aims to state its facts quickly and clearly.

We can divided the newspaper story as it strikes our eye on the newspaper page into three parts:

1. The headline.
2. The first paragraph.
3. The remainder of the story.

The headline first attracts us. It stands out in bold black type. Its message is terse, abrupt and often startling. It makes up stop and look. It tells us quickly what the story covers. Its primary function is to attract our attention. It corresponds to the beat of the drum outside the side show. But we will not consider the nimble art of headline writing here. As we have seen, headline writing belongs to the copyreader's province and not to the reporter's.

The First Paragraph or Lead

It would be difficult to overstate the importance of the opening paragraph or lead. Always this lead remains the primary concern of the newspaper writer. In any form of writing the writer tries to put his best foot foremost. In journalistic writing, this first stride has unique importance.

Because the present-day reader resembles the man who both runs and reads, present-day newspapers seek to facilitate his getting his information quickly. The convention has developed of telling the main facts of a news story in its first lead paragraph. Read any American or Canadian newspaper today, and you will find that by glancing at the headlines and through each lead you get, substantially, all the important news, although you may miss many interesting details.

This convention requires that in the lead the reporter answer the questions which would occur to any normal person when confronted with the announcement of an event. These questions, called the five W's, are:

Who?
What?
When?
Where?
Why?
and   How?

Suppose the news story concerns a fire. In writing his lead the reporter would answer the question, What? "Fire broke out," he would write. He would answer the questions, Who? and Where? by telling whose premises were burned and giving their location. He would answer When by telling the time the fire broke out and how long it lasted. Why? In this case, the cause, the inevitable carelessly tossed cigarette butt. Our reporter can answer the How in this story in several ways—by describing the type of fire, "flames fanned by a stiff breeze," or by answering How much? Here he would estimate the probable financial loss and find out to what extent the premises had been covered by insurance.

This simple illustration shows us some of the things which a good lead is required to do. It summarizes the story for the reader. It identifies the persons concerned. In this case it gives the full name of the owner of the premises and the address of his property. It fixes the locale of the story. It gives the reader the latest available information—in this case probably the extent of the damage. Yet so far, it has neglected another very important function of the lead. It has failed so far to stress the story's news "feature."

What is a story's news feature? It is that angle or twist which differentiates the story from any other of its particular type. Let us illustrate. Our fire story so far appears merely as a run-of-the-mill item. Blazes of this kind unfortunately happen everywhere, every day. But, suppose the burned premises temporarily housed important works of art which likewise went up in smoke and were lost to the world; or suppose the building was the property of some well-known person, a statesman, a Hollywood star, a baseball hero; or suppose again that next door to the burning premises stood a theatre, crowded at the time by people unaware of the danger. Each of these suppositions would satisfy as the story's news feature. Each would supply the necessary element of uniqueness.

But whether it be run-of-the-mill or outstanding in its impact, the lead should cover the story's essential facts. The city editor enunciated the alpha and omega of the craft when he shouted to his inquiring cub reporter:

"Spill the whole story in the first paragraph, and maintain the interest for the rest of the column."

The best-written lead not only satisfies the reader's initial curiosity, but whets his appetite to read more. Summing up, we may say then that the newspaper writer must see to it that his lead does five things: presents a summary of the story; identifies the persons and the places concerned; stresses the news feature; gives the latest news of the event; and, if possible, stimulates the reader to continue the story. And the present-day tendency is to achieve all this as quickly and as briefly as possible.

Discussion

1. What kind of information does the author say should go into the first paragraph of a newspaper story? What is the purpose of this first paragraph?
2. What goes into the rest of the story?
3. How does the author define the news feature of a story? What examples does he give of news features?
4. Since this selection comes from a book on journalism, it contains elements of style that make it easily readable. What are these elements?

Reading 3

To Inform, to Influence, to Serve...

Ernest C. Hynds

The following selection is from a volume in a series called Studies in Media Management. This selection details the many functions of a newspaper, including a recent additional function. Like the article by Norman Cousins, this selection takes up a definition of news *and expands the scope of the definition.*

Since the book from which this excerpt comes deals with various research findings, many additional notes about the author's sources are given at the end of each chapter. The notes that are included with this selection notes will give you some idea of the kinds of information that require sources in documented research work. (In another style, these notes are placed at the bottom [or foot] of each page and so are called footnotes.*)*

Length of summary: Approximately 250 words

Traditionally, the newspaper's basic roles have been to inform, influence, entertain, and foster the development of the nation's economy through advertising; these roles are still important. But changing audiences, and potential audiences, have suggested the addition of a fifth basic function: to serve people and help make their lives better. Serving readers has always been a function of newspapers, but the demands of increasingly self-focused readers with multiple needs and the pressures of competition for their time and money give a new urgency to reader service.

Of these basic roles, dissemination of information is most vital. Complete, accurate information is essential to clear thinking, and clear thinking is necessary to making sound judgments, whether the information receivers are electing a president, voting on a school bond issue, or selecting a product to purchase. The basis for our newspapers' protection under the First Amendment is their role in informing the public of matters important to the public welfare. Opinion polls over the years suggest that newspapers have not always succeeded in this goal. A major fault for being uninformed must lie with those who make little or no effort to become informed. But blame must also lie with newspapers and other media for not providing adequate information, motivating people to read that information, or both.

Newspapers should consider themselves to be in the business of transferring information from sources to readers and seek better ways to gather, process and distribute information. In particular, they need to learn more about the persons with whom they are seeking to communicate and adjust their presentations accordingly. As one publisher phrased it, newspapers must think of themselves as "information providers" serving "information consumers."[1] They must think in terms of meeting consumer needs for information. If newspapers adopt this approach, they should be able to produce more successful products now and adjust more easily to the challenges of new technology and possibly new media in the future.

Much of the information that newspapers transmit which does not deal with advertising is characterized by an emphasis on timeliness and human interest and is described as news. Broadly defined, news is any information which a receiver has not previously received; but most news stories deal with events or situations of the immediate past, the present or the future that interest large numbers of persons. What the Governor said about taxes today, not last month, is news. The nearness of an event or situation to the reader and its significance for him also help determine its news value. The local school bond issue is important because it might raise the reader's taxes or affect the education of his children. The arms limitation treaty is significant because of its far-reaching effects regardless of where it may be signed.

Sensational events such as crimes and natural disasters and unusual events of all kinds have been emphasized by many newspapers, and they still are by some who contend that reader interest in them remains high. The bank official who embezzles funds, the hurricane that takes lives and destroys homes, or the kitten whose best friend is a big dog all make news in the eyes of many editors. But many newspapers today are looking more to situations than single events to report; more editors are placing greater weight on the significant than the sensational. The rash of local robberies is news; the causes for the outbreak, perhaps involving drug addicts seeking money for their addiction, and what the police are doing about it are even more newsworthy. Good newspapers today are making an effort to show how current happenings fit into a continuing story.

Although news of crimes and disasters is at times overplayed, the amount of space allotted to such coverage is probably much less than many believe. A content study conducted as part of the Newspaper Readership Project in the late 1970s showed that only 7% of the articles included in the sample dealt with crime and only 2% with accidents and disasters. By contrast, 12% dealt with state and local news, 4% with domestic U.S. news, 6% with international news, 14% with sports, 14% with features, and 17% with other general interest news.[2]

What is considered news will, of course, vary with the publication involved and the editor providing the definition. The appointment of a new bank president in a small town may be big news to the newspaper located there, but it may receive only a paragraph or two on an inside page of a nearby metropolitan daily. A lengthy account of some metropolitan problem in that same daily might not be included in the small-town papers nearby. Alternative publications often view news differently than do other newspapers; some may stress politics while others cover the subculture they serve. All specialized newspapers stress specialized information for their particular audiences whether they are made up of businessmen, sports enthusiasts or members of a women's liberation group.

Newspapers traditionally have sought to answer six basic questions about the stories they cover; they still do. But since radio and television frequently report the *who, what, when* and *where* of major news stories first, newspapers often concentrate on telling the *why* and *how* of these stories and explaining what they mean to the individual reader. The *who* and *what* elements may still be emphasized in the many local stories that the broadcast media cannot include or emphasize in their limited time segments.

News can be placed into categories according to geography, subject matter and perhaps other criteria. Most daily newspapers carry at least some international, national and regional news as well as state and local news. Many have special editors, and sometimes departments, to handle news of sports, business, education, family matters and other special interests. Experience indicates that people do like to read about events they witnessed or in which they participated; experience confirms the need of newspapers and other media to appeal to basic human drives such as love, recognition, new experiences and security in news stories as well as in advertising.

A study of *How the Public Gets Its News*, sponsored by the Newsprint Information Committee in the late 1970s, found that news remains the most important component of a newspaper, even for the infrequent readers who are attracted to features. More than half the respondents, 59%, said if they had to choose between an all-news paper and one that gave a news summary and consisted mostly of entertainment features, they would choose all-news.[3]

Research conducted in recent years suggests, however, that the reader's definition of news may be expanding. The "new" definition includes news of the world, the government, and the most recent accident or crime. But it also includes news of the theater, movies, art, lifestyles, and a comparatively new beat which Dr. Ruth Clark, senior vice-president of Yankelovich, Skelly, and White, refers to as "self." The "self" beat covers a wide range of topics, including such things as psychology, self-understanding, physical well-being and physical self-enhancement.[4] The definition of news could be modified further in the future by an increasing emphasis on relevance. David L. Bowen, vice-president and director of communications of Associated Press, told a 1979 seminar on "The Newspaper of the Year 2000" that future readers might well look only for the news that is relevant to their personal needs.[5]

Information that could not be classified as news because it lacked timeliness or some other vital ingredient has been referred to as feature material. Such features may involve advice columns on human relations, health and other topics; human interest stories of various kinds; reviews of books, plays and other art forms; comics, and other items. Editorials, political cartoons, political columns and letters to the editor also help newspapers perform their information function; but they usually also contain opinions and are placed together on an opinion or editorial page.

Information is the staple of any good newspaper. But most hope to influence their readers as well as inform them. If read, newspapers probably exert some influence regardless of their intentions. How much influence they exert and what kind is not easy to assess. Laboratory situations to measure such influence cannot easily be created. Other types of documentation also are difficult to obtain. Still a few hypotheses, if not generalizations, can be advanced.

First, it is evident that newspapers exert influence through their total presentations and their image in the community and not through their advocacies alone. The human interest stories about the plight of the individual prisoner may evoke as much support for penal reform as the carefully documented argument of the editorial writer, perhaps more. The newspaper's coverage of an election may have far more influence on the outcome than its advocacy of a particular candidate....

Second, newspapers have helped bring reforms in government and other areas by focusing public attention on existing needs and problems. They have exposed corruption in government at all levels, revealed deplorable conditions in mental health institutions, prisons and slums, and pointed out needs in health, education, transportation and other areas. Many instances can be cited where remedial action was taken after problems were pointed out by newspapers.

Third, newspapers may have at least an indirect influence on elections at all levels through what has been described as "agenda setting." They help determine what issues, or non-issues, the candidates will discuss by the questions they ask, or do not ask. Newspapers help voters decide what issues are important in making decisions by their emphasis, or lack of it, on those issues.

Fourth, it appears that the influence of editorial endorsements in newspapers is dependent on the amount of information that the reader has about the candidate or issue being endorsed. If the reader has little or no information, or if his information is contradictory and he has no particular bias against the newspaper, its editorial may help him reach a decision. Since undecided voters are the ones most likely to be influenced by editorials and since undecided voters often swing elections, the influence of endorsements may be greater than generally believed. Candidates still seem to want them. It should be noted, however, that party affiliation, the physical appearance of candidates, the economic condition of the country or community, the weather and various personal biases may influence voter decisions more than arguments or information.

Fifth, it seems likely that the greatest influence of newspapers and other media is of a long-range cumulative nature. The effect of reading one article or editorial may be limited unless it is the reader's only source of information about the topic. But the effect generated by reading a newspaper over a long period of time may be considerable. Such reading can contribute to the reader's storehouse of information and ideas and help shape his perceptions and stereotypes. The newspaper cannot fully control what information the reader gets. He chooses what he will read. But newspapers can help those who seek information. They can help focus attention on community problems such as poor highways or inefficiency in government, and they can help keep public officials in the spotlight. Unfortunately, the influence of newspapers on government has not always been positive. At times they may have caused confusion by omissions, condensations or inaccurate reports.

Sixth, it is possible that newspapers exert influence through a chain reaction process. Influential persons in various groups rely on the mass media, and especially newspapers and magazines, for information. These persons receive data from the newspapers, structure it to suit their own needs, then share it with others.

Finally, it seems certain that newspapers exert some influence by providing an account of what takes place in society, what people think about it and how they react to it. Present concepts of what is going on in the community and the world are shaped to a large degree by what the mass media, including newspapers, say is going on....

Although most newspapers seek primarily to inform and influence their readers, many seek also to entertain them. Radio and subsequently television have preempted many of the entertainment responsibilities once held by both newspapers and magazines. Their serials, variety programs and situation comedies provide many opportunities for individual entertainment, escape and vicarious living. But many newspapers still devote a substantial part of their non-advertising space to human interest stories, advice columns, comics, crossword puzzles and other entertainment features. Some newspapers devote as much space to comic strips as they devote to editorials, letters and political columnists combined. Information and entertainment should not be regarded as mutually exclusive, however. Many features admirably combine the two elements, and some influence their readers as well. A comic character may speak more aptly to some issues than a renowned columnist. But the criticism that some newspapers devote too much space to entertainment has validity in some cases. Editors normally seek to justify an entertainment emphasis by pointing to the results of readership surveys. The people get a great deal of what they say they read.

Substantial changes in American lifestyles and values during the past fifteen years require that newspapers give increased emphasis to serving the diverse needs of readers in the 1980s and beyond. They always have served in a general way by providing information, guidance, entertainment, and advertising. But society's new emphasis on self, self-improvement, and self-fulfillment demands more specific efforts to help readers as individuals. This demand is discussed in a Newspaper Readership Project study of *Changing Needs of Changing Readers*, published in 1979. Dr. Ruth Clark, the study report author, describes today's readers as "more sophisticated, better educated, less accepting and literally saturated with information." She says they still want newspapers to tell them what is important, including hard news about national and international events and governmental actions that affect them. But they also want attention paid to their personal needs, help in understanding and dealing with their problems, news about their neighborhoods, and advice on how to cope. They want newspapers to be more attentive to their personal needs, more caring, more warmly human, and less anonymous. This study contends that there is a serious gap between editors and readers that goes beyond a simple difference of opinion between what editors think is new and interesting and what people want in their newspapers.[6]

Even before the Newspaper Readership Project study cited above, many newspapers had started to give more emphasis to serving diverse needs of readers. The fundamental premise of the Total Newspaper concept developed by the International Newspaper Promotion Association in the 1970s is "Newspapers Serve People." Under this marketing concept, readers and advertisers are asked periodically what expectations they hope to see fulfilled by their newspapers and all departments work together to produce a product that meets those expectations to the extent feasible. Individual newspapers have added a variety of special sections to provide information and advice on health, home repairs, shopping, taxes, investments, dining out, grooming, and other consumer interests.

Notes

1. Robert G. Marbut in a speech on "The Future of Newspapers" to the 50th Production Management Conference of the American Newspaper Publishers Association Research Institute in St. Louis, Missouri, June 8, 1978. Marbut is president and chief executive officer of Harte-Hanks Communications, Inc.
2. Leo Bogart, "How the Public Gets Its News," *Newspaper Readership Report*, Vol. 2, No. 1 (January, 1978), 2.
3. Leo Bogart in a speech to the Associated Press Managing Editors in New Orleans, Louisiana, October 27, 1977, commenting on a study titled *How the Public Gets Its News*, underwritten by the Newsprint Information Committee.
4. Ruth Clark in a speech to the 49th Annual Production Management Conference of the ANPA Research Institute in 1977. The speech was reprinted in ANPA/RI Bulletin No. 1265.
5. "Changes in the Communications Industry," *SNPA Special Bulletin: The Newspaper of the Year 2000* (March 26, 1979), 1.
6. Ruth Clark, *Changing Needs of Changing Readers...* (Reston, Va., May, 1979), 2–3. This is a report of a study by Yankelovich, Skelly & White, commissioned by the American Society of Newspaper Editors as part of The Newspaper Readership Project.

Discussion

1. What do you think about the author's listing as a basic role of newspapers "to foster the development of the nation's economy through advertising"? (Note what the author says later on about the function of advertising.)

2. Why does the author feel that the dissemination of information is so important?

3. What is the broad definition of news given by the author? What are many newspapers now including under the category of news?

4. What is your reaction to the statistics that come from the Newspaper Readership Project?

5. What are the six basic questions that newspapers have traditionally tried to answer in their stories? Which two questions does the author say are now given greater attention by newspapers, and what is the reason for this emphasis?

6. What is the new kind of news that Ruth Clark refers to as "self"?

7. According to the author, information in newspapers that cannot be classified as news is referred to as feature material. What is included under features?

8. The author says it is very difficult to do research studies on the influence of newspapers on readers. However, he gives seven hypotheses about sources of influence. What are these sources?

9. What kinds of features does the author say are sources of entertainment in newspapers? Why do some newspapers justify the amount of space they devote to entertainment?

10. According to the results of the study *Changing Needs of Changing Readers*, what are the many new needs that today's readers want a newspaper to meet?

11. The author has added notes to give the additional information about sources that is required in research writing. Which of the following reasons explains why the author used each of these notes?
    a. The results of a special study are given—either statistics or conclusions drawn from the study.
    b. The opinions of authorities are cited—whether directly quoted or stated indirectly.
    c. Special definitions or interpretations are given by authorities.
    d. Terms are used by authorities in an unusual sense (these may be given within quotation marks).

Reading for Further Ideas

The selections in this section are intended not only to give you additional information about the subject of the composition, but to continue to sharpen your reading skills, and in addition, to give you practice in preparing for essay examinations.

After you have skimmed through each selection and underlined the main points, make an outline from memory. Then check the reading again and make a more exact outline. This time, make a one-sentence summary of the main idea.

With this preparation, write a question for each selection that you think might be given on an essay examination. Without concentrating on details, make the question as comprehensive as possible. (You may also ask a question comparing the selection with others on the same subject.) Then write the answers and check them against the reading selection.

In writing your question, keep in mind the date and source of the selection (newspaper or magazine, textbook, other kind of book). Such sources often have different purposes and may therefore affect the way your questions might be asked.

Reading 1

Factors Determining News Value

F. Fraser Bond

The following excerpt is taken from a chapter entitled "The Nature of News." Earlier in the chapter, Bond gives this definition: "News is a timely report of anything of interest *to humanity and the best news is that which* interests *the most readers." Note the stress on interest rather than importance.*

In this selection, the author explains clearly and succinctly what news events are considered newsworthy by most writers and editors.

Four main factors determine the value of news.

We have already mentioned the first one: *Timeliness.*

The reader wants his news to be new. That is why he buys his paper or listens to the broadcast. The miracle of present-day communication frequently makes the announcement of the news almost coincide with the instant of its happening.

Another is: *Proximity.*

The reader finds more interest in a minor event close at hand than in a more important event miles away. James Gordon Bennett, Jr., when he first published his Paris Edition of *The Herald*, gave his reporters this principle in the epigram, "A dead dog in the Rue de Louvre (the paper's address) is of

Reprinted by permission of Macmillan Publishing Company from *An Introduction to Journalism* by F. Fraser Bond. Copyright 1954 by Macmillan Publishing Company; renewed 1982 by R. H. Nichols.

more interest than a flood in China." Today news of purely local concern is the bedrock on which the publishers of American newspapers outside the largest cities build their circulation, and surveys show that news of international importance, except major events, is of interest to only 10 percent of readers in large communities and to so small a proportion of readers in the small cities that no percentage figures have been worked out.

The third factor is: *Size.*

The very small and the very large attract attention. We find interest in minuteness as well as in magnitude—but chiefly in magnitude. Accordingly, when we hear of an accident or a catastrophe, we ask for the number of lives lost and the extent of the damage done. We want to know the amount of the philanthropist's bequest and the dimensions of the new airliner.

The fourth factor is: *Importance.*

Is the news reported important or in any way significant? We might naturally think that this factor should head our list, but news practice decrees otherwise, for the touchstone, as noted before, is interest. The trivial story, if imbued with interest, frequently ranks in newsworthiness above announcements which are important and significant, but dull. This is no new thing. Away back in 51 B.C. Cicero complained that his professional news correspondent was giving him too much of sporting events and not enough about the political situation. Editors get the same complaint today from their thoughtful readers. They know they can't satisfy everyone. They know, also, that "interesting" news, which encompasses much that is trivial, attracts the mass audience, while the merely important is addressed to a small public. Nevertheless, the better papers and the better newscasts seek to give news that holds significance and importance its proper place and treatment.

Elements of News Interest

History never actually repeats, but it does seem to repeat tendencies. Similarly, news stories never duplicate each other, but they do have a way of falling into definite categories. Analyzing them as we read them from day to day or listen to them as they come over the radio, we can easily discern elements of news interest which recur constantly. Sometimes a story will contain several of these interest-provoking elements, sometimes but one. In each instance the dominant element present gives us the clue to that story's type and category. Here are some of the chief elements of news interest:

1. Self-interest. Topics related to the individual reader or listener, to his affairs, his family, his hobbies and his well-being make the strongest appeal to his interest.

2. Money. The love of money may be the root of all evil; it certainly lies at the root of much news interest. Stories with economic appeal attract us, rich and poor alike.

3. Sex. Sex curiosity stimulates interest from childhood on. It draws us to many crime stories, as well as to those with a more wholesome romantic appeal.

4. Conflict. Struggle always secures our interest. Big news is news of battle, of flying fists. It is hard to hold readers with an account of a love feast. Many types of stories have conflict as their underlying element—the struggle against odds.

Here are several of these types:

1. Man's struggle with Nature.
2. Struggle between individual and organized society.
3. Struggle between political and economic groups:
   a. Wars
   b. Campaigns
   c. Strikes

5. The unusual. Novelty, strangeness, incongruity form the basis of much that we consider news. Departures from the expected fascinate us. Variations from the norm often amuse us. This element led the editors of the Minneapolis *Morning Tribune* to print this item from a city far away:

REVEALING ACCIDENT

Boston, Mass.—Struck by a motor-cycle, 8-year-old Timothy Todd was taken to a hospital where doctors discovered he had: 1. Possible fractures of the nose and knee; 2. Chickenpox.

6. Hero worship and fame. Big names not only make news, they are news themselves. We all find interest in what a well-known person does or thinks or says. Under this head fall stories of the "success" and achievement type, as well as many interviews and personality sketches.

7. Suspense. Stories which make us wonder what will happen excite a continuing interest. Here we find those stories involving the rescue appeal—will or will not the trapped miners survive?—stories of adventure and exploration.

8. Human interest. News of fellow human beings or of animals which touch our emotions come under "human interest." Such stories have a way of appealing to such primary emotions as love, pity, horror, fear, sympathy, jealousy, sacrifice.

9. Events affecting large organized groups. We are all "joiners" to a certain extent and accordingly find interest in any item that concerns our political party, our church, our fraternity, our scout troop. These groups may be:

1. International.
2. National.
3. State.
4. Civic.

10. Contest. The struggle to win allies itself with the conflict element was previously noted but deserves an individual listing, for it forms the basis of much of the appeal of the sports page. It also enters into accounts of danger and daring where man pits his strength against great obstacles.

11. Discovery and invention. "Eureka!" exlaimed Archimedes. "News!" says the editor.

12. Crime. Wrongdoing holds a fascination for saint and sinner alike. Frequently we hear editors criticized for publishing "too much crime news." Too much or too little, they wouldn't publish it at all unless readers found absorbing interest in it. The "best" crime stories, from the news point of view, unite many of the foregoing elements such as sex, conflict, suspense, human interest and sometimes even big name and fame appeal.

The four factors of news value and the dozen or more elements that stimulate reader and listener interest play their parts in determining an item's newsworthiness.

Reading 2

Transition to the Modern Mass Media: 1880–1920

Walter Dean Burnham

The following selection is from a section in a textbook headed "The History of Media and Politics in America." The excerpt begins with the early 1880s and ends with the early 1990s. Note the way the author relates the growth of the American newspaper to the political and economic developments of the time. Note also what the author has to say about objectivity in American newspapers, yellow journalism, and the expanded scope of the newspapers' contents and functions.

Note: *The* American Heritage Dictionary *defines* yellow journalism *as "Journalism that exploits, distorts or exaggerates the news to create sensations and attract readers. [Said to be short for* Yellow Kid Journalism, *an allusion to the "Yellow Kid" cartoons in the* New York World, *which was noted for sensationalism and vulgarity.]"*

The emergence of a mass audience and a real national political market, complete with parties, conventions, organizers, bosses, and a fully mobilized electorate, could not occur until the late 1820s, during the "democratic revolution" associated with Andrew Jackson. The most democratizing elements of all were probably improvements in transportation and communication.

Construction of adequate roads, turnpikes, canals, and (after 1828) railroads powered by steam engines drastically curtailed the time needed for domestic news to reach its audiences. Establishment of regular transatlantic steamship lines in 1838 just as dramatically reduced the time needed for European news to reach this country. The invention of the telegraph in 1844 was another giant leap forward, though it took nearly another generation before the country was fully equipped to use this first electric device for transmitting information. During the 1830s, the so-called penny press dramatically reduced the costs of newspapers (by four-fifths in many cases) and substantially increased circulations. Much of the earlier press had been strongly partisan, but its reach was limited. With the penny-press revolution and the founding of mass-circulation political papers such as James Gordon Bennett's New York *Herald* (1835) and Horace Greeley's New York *Tribune* (1841), mass communications media emerged, fully able to shape national opinion. The price/circulation revolution was consolidated by major reductions in newsprint, heavy reliance—for the time—on advertising and the introduction of much more efficient, steam-powered presses....

During the golden age of the party system, probably more than three-quarters of the press were partisan. Associated with press giants such as Joseph Pulitzer and William Randolph Hearst, new styles of news coverage and reporting developed at this time. For members of the new generation such as Pulitzer, journalistic standards of comprehensiveness, accuracy, and elimination of partisan slanting of the news were the strategy of the day. For Hearst and many imitators, a key to success was sensationalizing the news and, where possible, creating media events that could lend themselves to sensationalism. Perhaps the greatest coup for this *yellow journalism* was its work in paving the way for the Spanish-American War (1898) and the occupation of Cuba and the Philippines that followed. It should be stressed, however, that many of the founders of great newspaper chains in this period—including Pulitzer, Hearst, and Roy Howard—were crusaders whose papers frequently attacked, and exposed not only corrupt political bosses but the buccaneering capitalism of the era. On the other hand, political conservatives, such as Adolph Ochs of *The New York Times*, could and did succeed as well. The key to success, ultimately, was the creation of a product that commanded strong loyalty among subscribers. In that day, that meant first and foremost an emphasis on news itself.

Underlying all these journalistic developments were fundamental shifts in the American economic and social system, specifically the rise of corporate capitalism and an increase in consumption as affluence and urbanization burgeoned. Producing a fat Sunday paper was an expensive business by 1900, and newspapers needed large volumes of advertising. Then, as now, advertising rates were tied to audience size, which newspapers attempted to increase by curtailing their partisanship and adding a variety of features: sports, comics, homemaking, and rotogravure and magazine sections. Eventually, however, the news business became heavily concentrated. Horace Greeley, a poor farm boy from New Hampshire, had been able to start up the *Tribune* in 1841 with a few thousand dollars at most, but a similar effort required hundreds of thousands if not millions of dollars well before 1900.

Extra Discussion and Writing

Journal Entry

Compare an American newspaper with one in your country. Consider a number of the points that have been discussed in this chapter—for example, the reporting of the news, the special features, the advertising. Consider also the ownership of the newspapers. Write freely, since you are the only one who will see this entry.

Letters

1. Write a letter to one of your teachers in your country about the same subject as the journal entry. However, this time revise the journal entry for the letter to make it more carefully controlled and correct, but keep the letter friendly since you know the teacher.
2. Write a letter to your school newspaper about some situation or event on your campus. Express strong approval or disapproval.

Sayings

The newspaper is the average person's university. Explain the ways in which a newspaper can be educational.

Reactions

Reading 1

New York Post Meets Deadline

Part of the success of the national newspaper USA Today *comes from the attractiveness of its format and the ease of readability. After examining the following page from the February 22, 1988, issue, write an analysis of the way the statistics expanding the story of the* New York Post *are presented to make the data eye-catching as well as informative.*

   USA Today *was one of the first newspapers to use color to add to the eye appeal of its stories. On this page, the box containing the words "today's tip-off" has a green background; the section headed by "N.Y.* Post *meets deadline" has an orange background.*

TODAY'S TIP-OFF

The Commerce Department . . . this week launches a nationwide program — 'Export Now!' — to recruit execs of exporting firms to help educate small and medium-size businesses about export opportunities.

A House committee . . . will vote Wednesday on a bill that would increase the minimum wage from $3.35 an hour to $4.65 an hour over three years. Critics claim that would increase unemployment and inflation.

'N.Y. Post' meets deadline

New York real estate developer Peter S. Kalikow will face stiff competition from two tabloids and the venerable *New York Times* when he takes over the money-losing *New York Post* March 7. A look at the competition:

BILLIE BOGGS WANTS A BABY
NEW YORK POST
LAST PHOTOS OF JENNIFER

Date launched: 1801
Employees: 1,200
Circulation[1]: 690,915[2]
Loss: $17M

THE NEW YORK DAILY NEWS
GUARDS SNUFF REVOLT AT RIKERS
PANEL: BOOT BIAGGI

Date launched: 1919
Employees: 4,000
Circulation[1]: 1.29M
Loss: $5M to 7M

Newsday
It Wasn't Meant To Be

Date launched: 1985
Employees: 3,550[3]
Circulation[1]: 139,087
Loss: $15M

The New York Times

Date launched: 1851
Employees: 5,000
Circulation[1]: 1.02M
Profit: $200M

1 – as of 9/30/87; *New York Newsday* circulation doesn't include Long Island *Newsday* circulation of 502,276
2 – The *New York Post* circulation has slipped since 9/30/87 to less than 500,000 partly because of fewer editions
3 – total of employees from *New York Newsday* and Long Island *Newsday*

Reading 2

A Word from Readers

Ann Landers

Like her sister, Abigail Van Buren, Ann Landers has a syndicated column of advice in many newspapers. The letters from readers that she prints are carefully selected either because they are interesting or because they appeal to the emotions. (These letters often come across as entertainment.)

The following letter to her readers sums up the results of her survey of reader opinion on a question she had asked, and the column contains some reader responses. Give your reaction to the kind of question asked in her survey, and to the way she analyzed the replies.

Although Ann Landers says she received 50,000 replies, she printed only a few of them. What do you think about the replies she selected for her column?

Dear Readers: Yesterday I printed the results of the survey. The question I asked my readers was: If you had it to do over again would you marry the person to whom you are now married?

Over 50,000 people wrote in. The results were tabulated by professionals. There were two sets of responses—those who signed their cards and letters and those who did not. From the signed mail, I got these answers: 70 per cent said YES—30 per cent said NO. From the unsigned mail: Forty-eight per cent said YES—52 per cent NO.

Seventy per cent of the respondents did NOT sign. Many who signed gave their addresses, also.

Of the signed mail, 80 per cent came from females and 20 per cent from males. The unsigned mail was 70 per cent from females and 30 per cent from males.

I received 42 postcards from homosexuals. They were all "very happy" and voted YES.

Several readers pointed out a fact that could have influenced many women. The survey column appeared on Valentine's Day.

From San Jose, a wife wrote: "I may feel different tomorrow but tonight I am voting NO. It's Valentine's Day and this clown to whom I've been married for 15 years (five children) didn't even give me a card."

A man in Pittsburgh sent two dozen cards (unsigned). On each card he wrote (in green ink). "I vote NO. SHE'S MURDER."

A woman from San Francisco wrote a letter saying. "I voted NO yesterday. I was drunk. My husband is an angel—a lot better than I deserve. Please change my vote to YES."

From Davenport, Iowa: "Female, married 27 years. We are the happiest couple in town. I vote YES." At the bottom of the card, hastily scrawled in pencil, was a word from her husband, who obviously had been asked to drop the card in the mailbox. He wrote, "That's what SHE thinks. I vote NO."

A reader from Phoenix: "I DID do it all over again—married the same person—three times. My marriage to Thelma was annulled by her parents because she was under-age. When she turned legal we were married by a justice of the peace. Two years later we were married by a Catholic priest. She's terrific."

From Akron: "I am 12 years old. I read your column every day. My parents got into a fight tonight over how to vote in your survey. My mother said she was voting NO because my dad spends too many nights playing backgammon. Dad said their marriage was a lot better than most—even with her griping about him playing so much backgammon. He said he would vote YES. The conversation suddenly turned to how much my mother's brother cost my dad in business. I think you'd better put them both down as NO."

From Oklahoma City: "Dear Ann: In the 32 years we've been married my husband never once told me he loved me—even though I asked him several times. He always answered, "I'm not the mushy type." Tonight he clipped out your column and wrote across it, 'YES. She is a beautiful person. I'm a lucky man.' I cried like a baby. Make that two YESSES from O. City."

Reading 3

Mad **Magazine's "Newspaper Department"**

The following selections come from one issue of Mad, *a magazine that satirizes the mass media. One selection is satirizing an influential gossip columnist, Louella O. Parsons (1881–1972), who reported on Hollywood celebrities. Her column was read in hundreds of newspapers around the world. Another is a satirical editorial supposedly by William Randolph Hearst (1863–1951), who established a vast newspaper empire through the use of sensational news reporting.*

For purposes of satire, the style of each selection is exaggerated. Discuss the style of these selections, noting their particular slant or bias.

> Billy Poobah, son of Mr. & Mrs. Jim Poobah, took a bicycle ride yesterday. But imagine his surprise when he returned home to find his father waiting for him with a hairbrush. It seems that the bike Billy took for a ride wasn't his. It belonged to the little boy next door.

The other day, while perusing the pages of a little-known weekly paper called "The Abeline Gardening Club and P.T.A. Gazette," we ran across the above story...and it started us thinking. What if this story were picked up by all those wire-services like UP, AP, and URRP, and sent around the country? What would happen to it? Here then is MAD's version of how some newspapers, magazines, and columnists would treat the very same....

HOLLYWOOD HIGHLIGHTS

Epic Crime To Be Movie Epic

By LOUELLA O. PARSONS

Motion Picture Editor, International News Service

SNAPSHOTZ OF HOLLYWOOD COLLECTED AT RANDOM...Well folks, all Movieland is agog. Because underneath all that tinsel and glamour, people here are just like folks. What I'm trying to tell you is William Wyler stopped by my house this morning on the way to the studio because, as Bill put it, he couldn't wait to tell me the happy news.

So here is the exclusive news Bill told me over a cup of coffee in the kitchen. He has purchased the exclusive rights to the "Billy Poobah Story." That was the story you will recall, of the little boy out of Joplin, St. Louis, who stole a bicycle and did all those terrible things. Bill also wanted me to know exclusively that he has lined up Sal Mineo to play Billy, and, of course, June Alyson will play Billy's mother. Charles Bickford, that wonderful old character actor, will play Billy's bicycle.

DAILY NEWS

Billy (The Kid) Yields in Daylight Nab

Abeline, Aug. 16—For sex hours today, citizens of Abeline, shocked by one of the most bizarre crimes committed in these parts since the bawdy, sexy, early frontier days, waited for the capture of the hopped-up, sex-crazed bicycle-thief, sex-year-old Billy Poobah.

The self-styled badman, wearing a Davy Crockett cap and a pair of faded, hand-me-down levis, was finally nabbed in his tree-house hideout along with several accomplices. (Latest reports fail to implicate any of these in the actual theft, although they are all being held as material witnesses.)

Gives up without a fight

Exhibiting the crooked sneer of the incorrigible juvenile delinquent, Billy Poobah was dragged, screaming, into his father's bedroom. (See photos in center fold). Through wild eyes, red-rimmed with debauchery, he looked out on what promised to be his last view of outside faces for at least sex days.

Sheriff refuses comment

The Sheriff's Office refused comment on whether or not Poobah was thought to be the mastermind behind a series of bicycle thefts and sex crimes which have terrorized Abeline for the past sex weeks.

JOURNAL AMERICAN

"The end of everything is the beginnig of nothing."
—William Randolph Hearst

An Open Letter to Billy Poobah

WE'VE NEVER met you, Billy. You may be short, or tall, or fat, or thin, or all those things. We don't know. We may even like you. Someday.

BUT NOT TODAY!

NO, BILLY. Not today. For today, you are an angry man, full of the stone-headed UNREASONABLENESS that has cursed all the angry men who have gone before you.

THE NAPOLEONS, THE HITLERS, THE STALINS, THE ROOSEVELTS!

WE KNOW your crime, Billy. And somehow, we feel that tomorrow, you will regret that crime. AT LEAST WE HOPE YOU DO! For stone-headed UNREASONABLENESS can never contend with TRUTH and HONESTY and AMERICANISM.

NOT FOR LONG!

SO TRY, Billy. Try for a moment to look across your narrow road, and see what's on the other side. See what you've done to the people on the other side of that road. See how you have hurt those people…PEOPLE WHO LOVE YOU, IN SPITE OF THAT HURT.

WE'VE NEVER met you, Billy. But someday, we may even like you.

THE AMERICAN PEOPLE

THE NEW YORK TIMES

BOY, THREE, HELD IN BIKE THEFT

Abeline Youth is Accused of Stealing New Bicycle by Neighbor's Boy

By Robert Buck
Special to The New York Times

ABELINE, Kan., Aug. 16—It is alleged to have been reported by hitherto reliable but as yet unconfirmed sources, that a young man was indicted in Abeline, Kan., on a charge of third degree petty larceny. His name is being withheld, presumably pending investigation by proper authorities. This report has been neither confirmed nor denied by local officials.

TIME

For Billy, No Santa Claus

Out on the hot, hard, dirt-caked streets of Abeline, Kansas, there was sadness today. For the first time in his brief life, little Billy Poobah (rhymes with Poo-Bah) knew the meaning of fear. Billy, who is short (2′6″), partly bald, and old beyond his thirty-seven months, was taken into custody on a charge of small theft. There, in the hot, hard, dirt-caked bedroom of his small Kansas farmhouse, Father Poobah prepared Billy for his Armageddon. (For Billy's reaction, see DOMESTIC AFFAIRS.)

Comparing Two Editorials

The function of newspaper editorials is to express the opinions of editors and publishers. One important purpose of such editorials is to argue for social, political, and economic reform, often on the local level. In the two editorials that follow, the tabloid *Daily News* (February 18, 1987) and the more formal *New York Times* (March 3, 1988) are asking for the same thing—repeal of a law that has resulted in waste and corruption in New York City.

Note: Donald Trump, who is mentioned in *The New York Times* editorial, is a private builder who succeeded in just a few months in repairing the Wollman Skating Rink after city contractors had spent years and a considerable amount of money on the project, without success.

In about 250 words, write a composition that points out the differences between the two editorials in format (physical design), language and tone, use of details, and the way the argument is presented.

Construction Graft Is Killing Housing

At the heart of New York City's drive to build affordable housing is the construction industry. A cancer is eating at that industry—the cancer of corruption. The graft is notorious—outrageous!—yet largely ignored by city's politicians and the industry itself.

The corruption adds billions to the expense of building in the city—and of living and working here; ultimately, the cost is passed along to the public in sky-high rents or mortgages.

Enough is enough! It's long past time for New York's leadership to smash this crooked business. The fight is crucial if the city is going to end the appalling shortage of affordable housing that threatens the city's future. Here are the targets:

✓   **Abolish the Wicks Law.** Wicks is a state statute. It dictates that on large public construction jobs there must be *four* major contractors—general, electrical, plumbing, heating/ventilation. That flies in the face of common sense—and standard practice in private industry. The only people who love it are the contractors and the unions—it adds millions to their annual take.

The results are horrendous. At most public sites, confusion and waste abound. For instance, masons will finish a wall without knowing—or caring—that the plumbing behind it is unfinished. The chaos is tailor-made, of course, for ripoffs.

Mayor Koch estimates that abolishing this nightmarish condition will save the city at least $100 million a year—possibly as much as *$300 million*. No single act Cuomo and the Legislature can take in 1987 will do more to spur desperately needed housing in New York than *abolishing the Wicks Law.*

✓   Overtime, featherbedding and no-show jobs are built into the work rules. Example: Every union site that works under lights must have one electrician assigned *just to throw the on-off switch.*

✓   Many major payrolls carry ghost workers who are, in fact, organized crime soldiers. If they show up, it's only to book bets or play loanshark.

✓   Theft and vandalism are popular sports. So is installing fixtures by day—destroying them at night. To create more work. Or blackmail the owner.

✓   Bid-rigging by contractors and suppliers is widespread. Concrete is one of the most outrageous examples. Until recently, the price per cubic yard in Manhattan was *50% higher* than in Westchester County.

✓   The city has an army of inspectors to watchdog construction work. Bribing them is a major, corrupting pastime. U.S. Attorney Rudy Giuliani has run stings to nail dozens of crooked inspectors. He told writer Nicholas Pileggi: "I was amazed at how easy cases were to make." In any investigation of sewer inspectors, Giuliani said, "*Nobody* turned us down" when bribes were offered. He added: "The businessmen we caught paying bribes said this was the way of doing business in New York.... You couldn't do business if you didn't pay off."

The solution is obvious: hard-headed public policies and relentless law enforcement. The greatest enemy is the attitude that says it's cheaper to go along with corruption than to fight it. That's a big lie. It must be rejected:

Stop caving in. The city and state are just as afraid as private contractors to buck a corrupt system. Example: The Battery Park City Authority hired a $20,000 "consultant" with mob ties to keep "labor peace." Public agencies spend billions annually. If they refuse to do business with the crooks, they can strike a mighty blow at corruption.

Prosecute. Treat construction graft as a major felony and go after everybody relentlessly—the fixers *and* the politicians and white-collar people they fix.

Attack featherbedding. Both Congress and the New York Legislature should make featherbedding a felony—for no-show workers, for union officials and for contractors who knowingly give in to it.

Screen bids. Contractors who are notorious bunglers—or worse—are accepted time and time again on public jobs. Scandalous: The city and state must keep a joint registry of firms and their work records. They must be given the power to reject bids from contractors with established patterns of incompetence and/or corruption.

Next: An Action agenda for housing.

This Is the Year to Kill the Wicks Law

Over the next decade, New York City plans to spend $16 billion on major capital construction projects. Count at least $1.6 billion as needless waste. The reason? The state Wicks Law, which bars use of a general contractor on public construction jobs. Common sense cries out for repeal of this weight around the taxpayer's neck. Legislators who resist repeal invite being held regularly and repeatedly accountable for the waste.

In private industry, construction jobs are generally awarded by low bid to a general contractor responsible for hiring and supervising subcontractors. That same system is used by the Federal Government and by 44 states. New York's Wicks Law, enacted 67 years ago, requires separate bids for plumbing, electrical, heating and ventilation work. No single contractor is in charge. The idea was to increase competition and reduce building costs. The result is the opposite.

The inevitable coordination problems caused by multiple contracting scare off responsible bidders while inviting big overruns, shoddy work and endless litigation. The result can be embarrassing fiascoes, like the city's repeated failures to fix problems with the Wollman Skating Rink in Central Park before turning the job over to Donald Trump. A 1987 study by the state budget office found the law added as much as 30 percent to the cost of building prisons, fire stations and academic buildings.

Subcontractors respond that the law protects against corruption. They are refuted by the state's Organized Crime Task Force. It finds that multiple contracting actually fosters collusive bidding.

Past efforts to repeal the Wicks Law have been blocked by plumbers, electricians and other craft unions. With tenacious lobbying and campaign gifts, they wield disproportionate power in Albany.

In his State of the State Message in January, Governor Cuomo pledged to put real political muscle behind Wick Law repeal. Success will test his leadership. The issue involves conquering senseless waste, and more—the public's right to honest, competent government.

Political Cartoon

The following cartoon satirizes a common practice of some public officials. The term junket *has been given to such a trip.*

What is this practice, and what comment is the cartoonist making about it?

Patrick Crowley, Copley News Service, P.O. Box 190, San Diego, CA 92112. Reprinted by permission.

CHAPTER 8

Capital Punishment

Composition
Vocabulary and Usage
Reading for Summary Writing
Reading for Further Ideas
Extra Discussion and Writing

Composition

Procedures for Discussion
Writing the Composition
Revising the Composition

Requirements for a Home Composition

1. Use white $8\frac{1}{2}'' \times 11''$ paper; write on one side only.
2. Type your composition double spaced on unlined paper (if hand-written, the paper should be clearly written on every other line). A typewritten page, double-spaced, is about 250 words.
3. Indent each paragraph, use wide margins ($1''$ to $1\frac{1}{4}''$), and number each page in the upper righthand corner.
4. Include a separate page with the title, the thesis sentence, and the outline.

Procedures for Discussion

The teacher writes this question on the board:

Should We Have Capital Punishment?

Under the question, the teacher sets up two columns:

Yes, we should   No, we shouldn't

Then the teacher asks for arguments for either side and lists the arguments in phrases in the appropriate column in the random order they are given. Whenever possible, when an argument for one side is listed, the argument for the other side (the rebuttal) should be solicited from students and listed in the opposite column.

Writing the Composition

Write a 750- to 800-word composition of argument about capital punishment.

Suggestions for the Content and Organization

You may organize all your arguments, for or against, under one or two broad classifications (for example, justice, deterrence, fairness). Then try to narrow down your answer to one position. You may admit there is some justification for the other side, but you believe your position has greater weight. (In a composition of argument or opinion, there is often no "right" answer. The decision is made according to your viewpoint.)

Consider using one of the following patterns of argument:

1. Presenting only the arguments on your side, regardless of those on the other side. (This pattern is acceptable for a short paper.)
2. First giving all the arguments for the other side, then in the second part of the paper, giving all your answers to the same arguments (the rebuttal).
3. Taking up your arguments one at a time. For each argument, you may give the other side first, then yours (the rebuttal). Or you may reverse the procedure, giving your own argument first, then meeting the objections of those opposed to this viewpoint. These are the more common forms of development.
4. Developing your strongly favored position in any of the ways above (for or against), but concluding with some reservations (for example, you are mostly against capital punishment, with some exceptions).

Whatever pattern you follow, develop each argument separately (for example, justice, deterrence) in the body of the composition. Do not mix several arguments in one paragraph.

Since the assignment is fairly short for a controversial subject like capital punishment, you need to find your best arguments, the ones you feel most strongly about, and present them logically and clearly. You can use your own ideas for support, but the more support you use from authoritative sources that come from your readings, the stronger your arguments will be. (Also, drawing on readings for this composition will prepare you for writing the research paper, which is based almost entirely on readings.) In your composition, choose current sources that have the greatest reliability and identify the source (author, publication).

Finally, keep in mind that this composition represents your own opinions. By stating them honestly and strongly, you will have a composition that the reader will find interesting enough to continue reading.

Warning: Since this chapter has more, and longer readings than those in the other chapters, it is important that you write your first draft without looking at the readings in order to avoid temptation of copying too much from them. As you rewrite each draft, add the support from the readings.

Guide for the Outline and the Composition

The following guide will help you in preparing to write your composition. On the left side of the guide is the outline with suggestions for handling the introduction, transitions, and the conclusion of this composition. On the right side are general comments about how introductions, transitions, and conclusions may be written. (If you are accustomed to writing a first draft from rough notes, use this guide for your second and succeeding drafts.)

Outline	*General Comments*
Title	Use initial capital letters for all words except articles, short prepositions, and short conjunctions. Try to use an interesting title that reflects your thesis.
Introduction This can describe a scene or tell a story. Or it can list the kinds of crime deserving capital punishment. Or it can refer to the rising crime rate in the United States or to the fear in our streets.	Purpose of the introduction: to catch the reader's interest to give a general idea of the subject An introduction may include: a quotation a story, perhaps personal a rhetorical question (which you will answer)

a definition

a statement of a belief you will argue against

a surprising or shocking fact

a statement of a serious problem

Transitional lead-in

This indicates your position and the basis for this position.

Usually at the end of the introduction. Gives an indication of the central idea and the way it will be developed (may be in the form of a question).

I. First main point

This is your first argument for or against capital punishment.

A. First supporting detail

B. Second supporting detail
etc.

New paragraph. The first sentence: (1) mentions the general idea of the paragraph (from the important word[s] in the outline); (2) relates this sentence to what was said before.

Should be related to the preceding subpoint.

Note: Long subpoints may begin new paragraphs.

(Continue with your other main points and their supporting details.)

For each main point, remind the reader that you are presenting another argument for or against capital punishment.

(Follow the suggestions given for the first main point.)

Conclusion

This can be a suggestion for preventing capital crimes (gun control, social reform, etc.). Or it can be an alternative punishment.

The conclusion should round out the composition in a strong and satisfying way, perhaps by referring again to whatever you used to introduce the composition.

Notes: (1) The conclusion should not add any new ideas that need further development. (2) If your last point ends on a strong note that points up your thesis, you may not need to add a conclusion.

Support for the points you make can come from your own beliefs and experience or from the readings in this chapter and elsewhere. (Be sure to identify your sources and to use quotation marks around the exact words of an author.) The support can be in the form of examples, current facts and figures, or authoritative opinion. Use enough support to make your point convincing to the reader.

Finally, keep in mind that this composition represents your own opinions. By stating them honestly and strongly, you will have a composition that the reader will find interesting enough to continue reading.

Revising the Composition

In succeeding drafts, try to sharpen your thesis and show more clearly how each main point contributes to the development of the thesis. Try writing down the opening sentences of your paragraphs on a separate sheet of paper to see if they make a clear sentence outline. Go over the reading selections again for further ideas or additional support.

Consult the Revision and Editing Checklist for guidance on organization, paragraphing, and sentences. You can get needed vocabulary help in the vocabulary section that follows. Make a final check with the Symbol Chart for Correction of Compositions for the grammatical structures and usage in your composition.

Evaluation

If there is an exchange of student compositions, the Revision and Editing Checklist can serve as a guide in the evaluation of another student's composition. Use the following procedure in checking for the writer's organization and development of ideas.

1. Without looking at the other student's outline page, make an outline and a one-sentence summary of the central idea (or thesis) of the whole paper. Can you find a clear line of development? Do your summary sentence and your outline agree with those of the writer?
2. Find the support for each point made in the writer's paper. Is the support adequate and convincing?
3. Write on the student's paper what you consider the good points of the composition and what needs to be improved.

Vocabulary and Usage

Vocabulary
Usage Notes
Word Forms

Vocabulary

The following words may be useful to you in talking and writing about the subject of capital punishment.

capital punishment or **the death penalty**   By law, punishment by death for a serious crime. The execution (putting to death) in the United States may be by the electric chair, firing squad, hanging, or lethal (causing death) injection.

Kinds of Crime

homicide   Killing, murder.

arson   The intentional burning of property (**arsonist**, noun).

rape   Sexual attack on a person (usually a woman) (**rapist**, noun).

assassination   Deliberate murder of an important person, especially a political figure (**assassin**, noun).

hijacking   Stealing goods from a moving vehicle (**hijacker**, noun).

skyjacking   Taking over an airliner (**skyjacker**, noun).

terrorism   The use of violence to achieve political goals (**terrorist**, noun).

espionage   Spying (**spy**, noun).

drug trafficking   Dealing in drugs (**drug trafficker**, noun).

kidnaping (also kidnapping, British)   Seizing a person by force and holding that person for ransom or some other demand (**kidnap(p)er**, noun).

burglary   Breaking into a building, usually to steal (**burglar**, noun).

robbery   Stealing, with the use of force (**robber**, noun).

assault   A violent attack.

treason   Betrayal of one's country by giving away its secrets (**traitor**, noun).

sabotage   The deliberate damaging of property or the obstruction of production in a factory (**saboteur**, noun).

Degrees of Crime

offense   A violation of a law or rule, a crime (**offender**, noun).

felony   A serious crime, punishable by a heavy sentence—for example, murder, arson (**felon**, noun; **felonious**, adjective).

misdemeanor   A less serious offense than a felony.

manslaughter   The unlawful killing of a person without intent to do harm.

Being Charged with a Crime

arrest   Seize a person by legal authority.

bail   Security (money or property) given as a guarantee that an accused person will return for his or her trial.

grand jury   A group of citizens that determines whether there is enough evidence to bring an accused person to trial.

indictment   Being charged by the law with an offense.

arraignment   The act of summoning an accused person before a court because of the charges in an indictment.

prosecute   To institute and conduct a legal action against an accused person. The prosecuting attorney (or prosecutor), as a representative of the law, makes the charges against the accused person in a trial.

trial   A formal hearing to decide a case in a court of law. For a serious case, a trial includes the judge, the jury (in the United States, usually twelve citizens, who will decide whether the accused person is innocent or guilty), the accused person, the defense attorney, the prosecuting attorney, witnesses for and against the prosecution.

verdict   The decision of the jury regarding the innocence or guilt of an accused person in a court trial. If the verdict is guilty, the judge usually gives the sentence—the punishment—for the accused.

convict (verb)   Find a person guilty of an offense (**a convict** is a prisoner).

parole   The conditional release of a prisoner before his or her sentence ends. A **parolee** must report to a **parole officer**.

commute   Reduce a punishment to one that is less severe. (In the case of the death penalty, it is usually the governor who commutes the punishment.)

Other Vocabulary

deterrent   Something that discourages a person from doing something for fear of punishment (**deterrent**, adj., **deterrence**, noun, **deter**, verb).

rehabilitation   Restoration to useful life (especially to acceptable social behavior) through education and therapy.

discrimination   Prejudice (**discriminatory**, adj.).

mandatory   Required by law (without exception).

discretionary   Having the power to make decisions according to one's own judgment (thus allowing for exceptions).

mitigating circumstances   Circumstances that contribute to making a punishment less severe.

aggravating circumstances   Circumstances that contribute to making a punishment more severe.

retribution   A punishment that is deserved. (Because the word can be interpreted as a just punishment administered by a higher authority, it has a good, or neutral connotation.)

revenge   Punishment inflicted in return for some harm, often personal. (Usually, in discussions of capital punishment, **revenge** has a negative connotation, as resulting from our lower instincts.)

capricious   Tending to change one's mind unpredictably for no apparent reason.

arbitrary   Determined by individual judgment rather than by a guiding principle or law.

opponent   A person who is against something or someone.

proponent   A person who is for something.

inhuman   Lacking pity, brutal, heartless.

inhumane   Not caring for others, without sympathy.

Usage Notes

Use *the:*

> *the death penalty*

but do not use *the:*

> *capital punishment*

Do not use *the:*

> go to prison
> go to jail

Do not add *-s:*

> the poor, the rich, the underprivileged

These adjectives used as nouns require plural verbs:

> (the) blacks, (the) whites

Do not add *-es* to research:

> do research

A number is plural (= some, man); *the number* is singular.

> *A number* of studies *reveal* that the rate of crime is increasing.
> *The number* of crimes is increasing.

Prepositions used with words about argument:

> (dis)agree *with* someone that capital punishment can deter criminals
> (dis)agree *with* someone *about* the power of capital punishment to deter
>   criminals
> argue *for* or *against*
> be *in* favor *of* = favor
> be *against* = be opposed *to* (or oppose)

Word Forms

Use the correct forms for the words in parentheses.

The answers are on page 355. If you need help with this exercise, refer to the explanations under Word Forms in Appendix C.

1. Capital (punish) _____ has become a very (controversy)

   _____ issue.

2. In the Western world, a person is presumed to be (innocence)

   _____ until proven (guilt) _____.

3. To avoid the (caprice) _____ application of the death penalty,

   some states make the death sentence (mandate) _____ for

   certain crimes.

4. (Oppose) _____ of the dealth penalty object to its (discriminate)

   _____ application; (propose) _____ are in

   favor of it for (murder) _____ who kill (intention)

   _____ rather than (accident) _____.

5. Some people feel that (crime) _____ are victims of their

   (inherit) _____ and their (surround) _____ and that

   their antisocial (behave) _____ can be changed through

   (rehabilitate) _____.

6. If there is a (suspect) _____ that a crime has been (commit)

   _____, the (suspect) _____ is (arrest)

   _____ and (arraign) _____. If there is enough

   (evident) _____ of (crime) _____ action, an

   (indict) _____ is brought against the (accuse) _____

person, who will then become the (defend) _____ in a court

(try) _____.

7. In a (try) _____, the twelve (jury) _____ will listen

to the (evident) _____ and make a (decide) _____

whether the (accuse) _____ is (guilt) _____ or

(innocent) _____.

8. Most people feel that all (murder) _____, (rape)

_____, (arson) _____, (terror) _____,

and (kidnap) _____ should be (severe) _____

punished.

9. Some people feel that capital punishment can act as a (deter)

_____ to criminals; other feel it does not prevent (felon)

_____ acts.

Reading for Summary Writing

For the following *three* selections, prepare a brief outline for class discussion
before you write the summary.

After the class discussion of each selection, you will write:

1. A longer, revised outline of the selection, using an alternation of numbers and letters.
2. A one-sentence summary of the selection. The sentence should include
the central idea and the main points used to develop this idea (from the
outline).
3. A summary of the selection. The length assigned in the text will determine the amount of detail that can be included in the outline and summary.

Guidelines for Writing (Review)

1. For the outline, use the alternate number-letter system for main points
and subpoints. The phrases you underlined in the opening sentences of
paragraphs usually become the main points or subpoints in the outline.
2. For both summary and outline, follow the same order as the reading
selection. However, you may begin the summary with a reference to the
source of the selection (author, publication, etc.) and to its central idea.

3. Keep a sense of proportion. Write more about points the author devotes more attention to.
4. Concentrate more on the main points than on examples or other supporting details.
5. Use proper transitions between the main points and the subpoints of your summary. Your summary must have an organization of its own.
6. Use your own words as much as possible, except for key phrases. You may quote important phrases or sentences.
7. Be careful not to overload any of the sentences with so much information that the sentence is hard to read.
8. Be consistent in your use of verb tenses. Use all present tense (the author states, feels) or all past tense (the author stated, felt). The present tense is more common in a summary.
9. Do not include your own ideas or your own attitude or interpretation. The summary should be an objective restatement of what the author has said.

Reading 1

Death and Justice: How Capital Punishment Affirms Life

Edward I. Koch

The following article was written by the mayor of New York City. It is a strong argument in favor of capital punishment.

Note the development of the arguments. Koch takes up the arguments against capital punishment one at a time, using numbers and italics for greater emphasis. Then, after each opposing argument, he refutes it with support for his own position.

*Note also the way Koch introduces this article by quoting from two killers on the morality of killing. As you read, watch for the way Koch relates the key concepts in his title—*justice *and* affirmation of life—*to capital punishment.*

Length of summary: Approximately 300 words

The New Republic, April 15, 1985, pp. 12–15. Copyright © 1985 by *The New Republic*. Reprinted by permission.

Last December a man named <u>Robert Lee Willie,</u> who had been convicted of raping and murdering an 18-year-old woman, was executed in the Louisiana state prison. In a statement issued several minutes before his death, Mr. Willie said: <u>"Killing people is wrong.... It makes no difference whether it's citizens, countries, or governments. Killing is wrong."</u> Two weeks later in South Carolina, an admitted killer named <u>Joseph Carl Shaw</u> was put to death for murdering two teenagers. In an appeal to the governor for clemency, Mr. Shaw wrote: <u>"Killing is wrong when I did it. Killing is wrong when you do it. I hope you have the courage and moral strength to stop the killing."</u>

It is a curiosity of modern life that we find ourselves being lectured on morality by cold-blooded killers. Mr. Willie previously had been convicted of aggravated rape, aggravated kidnapping, and the murders of a Louisiana deputy and a man from Missouri. Mr. Shaw committed another murder a week before the two for which has was executed, and admitted mutilating the body of the 14-year-old girl he killed. <u>I can't help wondering what prompted these murderers to speak out against killing as they entered the death-house door.</u> Did their newfound reverence for life stem from the realization that they were about to lose their own?

Life is indeed precious, and I believe the death penalty helps to affirm this fact. <u>Had the death penalty been a real possibility in the minds of these murderers, they might well have stayed their hand.</u> They might have shown moral awareness before their victims died, and not after. Consider the tragic death of Rosa Velez, who happened to be home when a man named Luis Vera burglarized her apartment in Brooklyn. "Yeah, I shot her," Vera admitted. "She knew me, and I knew I wouldn't go to the chair."

During my 22 years in public service, I have heard the pros and cons of capital punishment expressed with special intensity. As a district leader, councilman, congressman, and mayor, I have represented constituencies generally thought of as liberal. Because I support the death penalty for heinous crimes of murder, I have sometimes been the subject of emotional and outraged attacks by voters who find my position reprehensible or worse. I have listened to their ideas. I have weighed their objectives carefully. I still support the death penalty. The reasons I maintain my position can be best understood by examining the arguments most frequently heard in opposition.

(1) *The death penalty is "barbaric."* Sometimes opponents of capital punishment horrify with tales of lingering death on the gallows, of faulty electric chairs, or of agony in the gas chamber. Partly in response to such protests, several states such as North Carolina and Texas switched to execution by lethal injection. The condemned person is put to death painlessly, without ropes, voltage, bullets, or gas. Did this answer the objections of death penalty opponents? Of course not. On June 22, 1984, *The New York Times* published an editorial that sarcastically attacked the new "hygienic" method of death by injection, and stated that "execution can never be made humane through science." <u>So it's not the method that really troubles opponents. It's the death itself they consider barbaric.</u>

Admittedly, capital punishment is not a pleasant topic. However, one does not have to like the death penalty in order to support it any more than one must like radical surgery, radiation, or chemotherapy in order to find necessary these attempts at curing cancer. Ultimately we may learn how to cure cancer with a simple pill. Unfortunately, that day has not yet arrived. Today we are faced with the choice of letting the cancer spread or trying to cure it with the methods available, methods that one day will almost certainly be considered barbaric. But to give up and do nothing would be far more barbaric and would certainly delay the discovery of an eventual cure. The analogy between cancer and murder is imperfect, because murder it not the "disease" we are trying to cure. The disease is injustice. We may not like the death penalty, but it must be available to punish crimes of cold-blooded murder, cases in which any other form of punishment would be inadequate and, therefore, unjust. If we create a society in which injustice is not tolerated, incidents of murder—the most flagrant form of injustice—will diminish.

(2) *No other major democracy uses the death penalty.* No other major democracy—in fact, few other countries of any description—are plagued by a murder rate such as that in the United States. Fewer and fewer Americans can remember the days when unlocked doors were the norm and murder was a rare and terrible offense. In America the murder rate climbed 122 percent between 1963 and 1980. During that same period, the murder rate in New York City increased by almost 400 percent, and the statistics are even worse in many other cities. A study at M.I.T. showed that based on 1970 homicide rates a person who lived in a large American city ran a greater risk of being murdered than an American soldier in World War II ran of being killed in combat. It is not surprising that the laws of each country differ according to differing conditions and traditions. If other countries had our murder problem, the cry for capital punishment would be just as loud as it is here. And I daresay that any other major democracy where 75 percent of the people supported the death penalty would soon enact it into law.

(3) *An innocent person might be executed by mistake.* Consider the work of Adam Bedau, one of the most implacable foes of capital punishment in this country. According to Mr. Bedau, it is "false sentimentality to argue that the death penalty should be abolished because of the abstract possibility that an innocent person might be executed." He cites a study of the 7,000 executions in this country from 1893 to 1971, and concludes that the record fails to show that such cases occur. The main point, however, is this. If government functioned only when the possibility of error didn't exist, government wouldn't function at all. Human life deserves special protection, and one of the best ways to guarantee that protection is to assure that convicted murderers do not kill again. Only the death penalty can accomplish this end. In a recent case in New Jersey, a man named Richard Biegenwald was freed from prison after serving 18 years for murder; since his release he has been convicted of committing four murders. A prisoner named Lemuel Smith, who, while serving four life sentences for murder (plus two life sentences for kid-

naping and robbery) in New York's Green Haven Prison, lured a woman corrections officer into the chaplain's office and strangled her. He then mutilated and dismembered her body. An additional life sentence for Smith is meaningless. Because New York has no death penalty statute, Smith has effectively been given a license to kill.

But the problem of multiple murder is not confined to the nation's penitentiaries. In 1981, 91 police officers were killed in the line of duty in this country. Seven percent of those arrested in the cases that have been solved had a previous arrest for murder. In New York City in 1976 and 1977, 85 persons arrested for homicide had a previous arrest for murder. Six of these individuals had two previous arrests for murder, and one had four previous murder arrests. During those two years the New York police were arresting for murder persons with a previous arrest for murder on the average of one every 8.5 days. This is not surprising when we learn that in 1975, for example, the median time served in Massachusetts for homicide was less than two-and-a-half years. In 1976 a study sponsored by the Twentieth Century Fund found that the average time served in the United States for first-degree murder is ten years. The median time served may be considerably lower.

(4) *Capital punishment cheapens the value of human life.* On the contrary, it can be easily demonstrated that the death penalty strengthens the value of human life. If the penalty for rape were lowered, clearly it would signal a lessened regard for the victims' suffering, humiliation, and personal integrity. It would cheapen their horrible experience, and expose them to an increased danger of recurrence. When we lower the penalty for murder, it signals a lessened regard for the value of the victim's life. Some critics of capital punishment, such as columnist Jimmy Breslin, have suggested that a life sentence is actually a harsher penalty for murder than death. This is sophistic nonsense. A few killers may decide not to appeal a death sentence, but the overwhelming majority make every effort to stay alive. It is by exacting the highest penalty for the taking of human life that we affirm the highest value of human life.

(5) *The death penalty is applied in a discriminatory manner.* This factor no longer seems to be the problem it once was. The appeals process for a condemned prisoner is lengthy and painstaking. Every effort is made to see that the verdict and sentence were fairly arrived at. However, assertions of discrimination are not an argument for ending the death penalty but for extending it. It is not justice to exclude everyone from the penalty of the law if a few are found to be so favored. Justice requires that the law be applied equally to all.

(6) *Thou Shalt Not Kill.* The Bible is our greatest source of moral inspiration. Opponents of the death penalty frequently cite the sixth of the Ten Commandments in an attempt to prove that capital punishment is divinely proscribed. In the original Hebrew, however, the Sixth Commandment reads, "Thou Shalt Not Commit Murder," and the Torah specifies capital punishment for a variety of offenses. The biblical viewpoint has been upheld by

philosophers throughout history. The greatest thinkers of the 19th century—
Kant, Locke, Hobbes, Rousseau, Montesquieu, and Mill—agreed that natural
law properly authorizes the sovereign to take life in order to vindicate justice.
Only Jeremy Bentham was ambivalent. Washington, Jefferson, and Franklin
endorsed it. Abraham Lincoln authorized executions for deserters in wartime. Alexis de Tocqueville, who expressed profound respect for American
institutions, believed that the death penalty was indispensable to the support
of social order. The United States Constitution, widely admired as one of the
seminal achievements in the history of humanity, condemns cruel and inhuman punishment, but does not condemn capital punishment.

(7) *The death penalty is state-sanctioned murder.* This is the defense with
which Messrs. Willie and Shaw hoped to soften the resolve of those who sentenced them to death. By saying in effect, "You're no better than I am," the
murderer seeks to bring his accusers down to his own level. It is also a popular argument among opponents of capital punishment, but a transparently
false one. Simply put, the state has rights that the private individual does not.
In a democracy, those rights are given to the state by the electorate. The
execution of a lawfully condemned killer is no more an act of murder than is
legal imprisonment an act of kidnapping. If an individual forces a neighbor
to pay him money under threat of punishment, it's called extortion. If the
state does it, it's called taxation. Rights and responsibilities surrendered by
the individual are what give the state its power to govern. This contract is the
foundation of civilization itself.

Everyone wants his or her rights, and will defend them jealously. Not
everyone, however, wants responsibilities, especially the painful responsibilities that come with law enforcement. Twenty-one years ago a woman named
Kitty Genovese was assaulted and murdered on a street in New York. Dozens
of neighbors heard her cries for help but did nothing to assist her. They
didn't even call the police. In such a climate the criminal understandably
grows bolder. In the presence of moral cowardice, he lectures us on our supposed failings and tries to equate his crimes with our quest for justice.

The death of anyone—even a convicted killer—diminishes us all. But
we are diminished even more by a justice system that fails to function. It is an
illusion to let ourselves believe that doing away with capital punishment re-
moves the murderer's deed from our conscience. The rights of society are
paramount. When we protect guilty lives, we give up innocent lives in exchange. When opponents of capital punishment say to the state: "I will not let
you kill in my name," they are also saying to murderers: "You can kill in your
own name as long as I have an excuse for not getting involved."

It is hard to imagine anything worse than being murdered while neighbors do nothing. But something worse exists. When those same neighbors
shrink back from justly punishing the murderer, the victim dies twice.

Discussion

1. What do you think of Koch's introducing this article against capital pun-ishment by referring to the words of killers who had been condemned to die? How would you characterize the author's attitude in using such an introduction?

2. How does Koch use the analogy between the death penalty and curing cancer? Why does he insist that this analogy is imperfect? What does he say is the "disease" that the death penalty is supposed to cure?

3. What statistics does Koch cite to explain why the crime situation in the United States is different from those in other countries? What percent of the American people support capital punishment?

4. What study does Koch draw on to prove that the execution of an inno-cent person rarely happens? (A recent article in *The New York Times** reports more specific findings on what seems to be the same study Koch refers to, a study by Hugo Bedau and Michael Radelet. This article states that researchers found "that 350 innocent men have been sentenced in the 20th century and 23 have been executed." And the researchers felt that these figures were conservative; "they were based on cases in which the real murderer was found or the state admitted a mistake.")

5. What statistics does Koch give for the average length of time served for murder in the United States?

6. What does the author say about the affirmation of life in relation to capital punishment?

7. How does the author refute the arguments of opponents who quote the Biblical commandment, Thou shalt not kill?

8. What does Koch mean by his concluding remark, "When neighbors shrink back from justly punishing the murderer, the victim dies twice"? What example does he use in relation to this point?

9. Koch repeatedly uses the term *justice* throughout his article. Find exam-ples of this use. What does he mean by justice in relation to crime?

10. Which of the author's arguments do you think are strong, and which are weak? Give the reasons for your answer.

11. If you believe in capital punishment, what crimes do you think deserve such punishment?

12. Do you have capital punishment in your country? If so, for what kinds of crimes? Is there much violent crime in your country?

13. Many crimes in the United States are committed with guns. Does your government allow private citizens to have guns? Are guns easily availa-ble in your country?

---

*Peter Applebome, "Rise in Executions Widening Debate," *The New York Times*, November 1, 1987.

Reading 2

An Eye for an Eye

Kurt Andersen

The following article about capital punishment in Time *Magazine is accompanied by pictures: a full-page picture of an electric chair, and throughout the article, photographs of other means of execution. Omitted here are the stories of individuals on death row that run alongside the text of the article. These stories are presented in such a way that the reader feels either hate or sympathy for the criminals. This selection also does not include the opening verbal description of the electric chair with a person in it ready for execution. In addition, some details of lurid crimes have been omitted.*

As you read, note that the support given for points made in the article includes statistics and authoritative opinion. But note that other kinds of opinion are also used.

Because this article is presented in terms of human interest rather than as a carefully reasoned argument, you may have some trouble making a neat outline and summary.

Length of summary: Approximately 300 words

The national death-row population today is 1,137. That is 200 more than a year ago, twice as many as in 1979, and larger, moreover, than ever before. Florida alone has 189 death-row prisoners, Texas has 153, Georgia and California 118 each. The inmates include about a dozen teen-agers, 13 women (five of them in Georgia) and six soldiers. Half of the condemned are white.

The long-building public sentiment to get tough with violent criminals, to kill the killers, seems on the verge of putting the nation's 15 electric chairs, nine gas chambers, several gallows and *ad hoc* firing squads back to regular work. In addition, five states have a new and peculiarly American technique for killing, lethal anesthesia injections, which could increase public acceptance of executions. Experts on capital punishment, both pro and con, agree that as many as ten to 15 inmates could be put to death this year, a total not reached since the early 1960s. "People on death rows are simply running out of appeals," says the Rev. Joe Ingle, a prison activist and death-penalty opponent. "I fear we are heading toward a slaughter."

For years, the capital-punishment debate has been sporadic and mainly intramural—professor *vs.* professor, lawyer *vs.* lawyer—as executions took place only once or twice annually at most. Says Florida's Governor Robert Graham, who signed Spenkelink's death warrant in 1979: "We haven't enforced the death penalty much, so we've been able to avoid all the responsibilities that go with that experience."

But now an old array of tough questions—practical, legal, moral, even metaphysical—is being examined. Is the death penalty an effective, much less a necessary, deterrent to murder? Is it fair? That is, does it fall equally on the wealthy white surgeon represented by Edward Bennett Williams and the indigent black with court-appointed (and possibly perfunctory) counsel? Most fundamental, is it civilized to take a life in the name of justice?

Fear, pure and simple, is behind the new advocacy of the death penalty. Between 1960 and 1973, the U.S. homicide rate doubled, from 4.7 murders per 100,000 people to 9.4. The rate has leveled off considerably and stands at 9.8 per 100,000 today. (Other countries' rates are, by U.S. standards, amazingly low: England, 1.1, and Japan, 1.0, are typical). No more precipitous increases are expected this century: criminologists believe that the murder spree of the '60s and early '70s was mostly the doing of World War II baby-boom children passing through their crime-prone years of adolescence and young adulthood. As it happened, the number of young people and cheap, readily available handguns burgeoned at the same time. Handguns are used in 50% of U.S. murders.

But a U.S. public that has felt terrorized by murderers and thugs is unreceptive to promises that the worst may be over and understandably finds the current level of violent crime intolerable. According to a Gallup poll last fall, 72% of Americans now favor capital punishment, up from just 42% in 1966. "People are frightened and upset about crime in the streets," says William Bailey, a Cleveland State University sociologist. "Nothing seems to be done to solve the problem, so the feeling grows that if we can't cure murderers, something we *can* do is kill them." Jim Jablonski, 44, a Chicago steelworker, speaks for a lot of furious citizens. "Murderers got to pay," he says. For him the next sentence follows self-evidently: "I say, fry the bastards."

Execution by injection may be too new to have its tough-guy slang like "fry." But last month outside the prison at Huntsville, Texas, the sentiment was the same. As Charlie Brooks waited to be injected, a crowd of 300 gathered to celebrate. Some of the pro-execution revelers, mostly college students, carried placards; KILL 'EM IN VEIN, said one. "Most of the people I know are for capital punishment," declared Paula Huffman, 21, a Sam Houston State University senior at the deathwatch. "And so am I. Definitely." Nevertheless, when the moment arrived, just after midnight, she and the rest of her shivering, smiling chums suddenly turned quiet and grave.

Historically, American executions were public, the last in Kentucky in 1936. Hanging was standard for 200 years, through the 1800s. More primitive means—burnings in particular—were extreme rarities even in the 17th century. Up until 1900, nearly all executions were carried out by local jurisdictions; lynchings were as frequent as legal hangings. But by the start of the Depression, state authorities had mostly taken over the grim chore....

The dilemma of whether to kill the killers comes up in only a small fraction of all U.S. homicides. The criteria for capital murder vary from state to state and even, inevitably, from case to case. In general, there must be "aggravating circumstances." These can be as specific as the murder of a fireman or one by an inmate serving a life sentence; as common as a homicide committed along with a lesser felony, like burglary; and as vague as Florida's law citing "especially heinous, atrocious or cruel" killings. It is estimated that about 10% of U.S. homicides currently qualify, or some 2,000 murders last year. Those killings are the ones the threat of capital punishment is mean to prevent.

The idea of deterrence can be quickly reduced to very personal rudiments: *If I know I will be punished so severely, I will not commit the crime.* The logic is undeniable. Yet in the thickets of real life and real crime, deterrence, while central to practically all punishment, is often very uncertain, and its effect on prospective murderers is especially unclear. Unfortunately, public discussion usually consists of flat-out pronouncements. Capital punishment, says Conservative Commentator William F. Buckley, "is a strong, plausible deterrent." No, declares New York Governor Cuomo, "there has never been any evidence that the death penalty deters." Neither is altogether wrong, but the stick-figure oversimplifications on both sides do a disservice to a complicated question.

The scholarly evidence is not quite as unequivocal as some abolitionists claim. But it does not make much of a case for deterrence. The most persuasive research compared the homicide rates of states that did and did not prescribe the death penalty. For instance, Michigan, which abolished capital punishment in 1847, was found to have had a homicide rate identical to adjacent states, Ohio and Indiana, that were executing. Similarly, Minnesota and Rhode Island, states with no death penalty, had proportionately as many killings as their respective neighbors, Iowa and Massachusetts, which had capital punishment. In 1939 South Dakota adopted and used the death penalty, and its homicide rate fell 20% over the next decade; North Dakota got along without capital punishment for the same ten years, and homicides dropped 40%.

Similar before-and-after studies in Canada, England and other countries likewise found nothing to suggest that capital punishment had deterred murderers any better than the prospect of long prison terms. And in Britain during the 1950s, a typical "lifer" actually served only about seven years, compared with a much tougher average U.S. "life" term today of 20 years. A comprehensive study in the U.S., by the National Academy of Sciences in 1978, also found that the death penalty had not proved its worth as a deterrent.

Were it not for the work of Economist Isaac Ehrlich, the deterrence debate would be entirely one-sided. Using econometric modeling techniques to build a "supply-and-demand" theory of murder, Ehrlich argued in a 1975 paper that capital punishment prevents more murders than do prison sentences. Because of the 3,411 executions carried out from 1933 to 1967, Ehrlich speculates, enough potential murderers were discouraged so that some 27,000 victims' lives were saved.

That stunning conclusion drew immediate attacks. Critics, and they are legion, cite a variety of defects: Ehrlich did not compare the effectiveness of the death penalty with that of particular prison terms; his formula does not work if the years between 1965 and 1969 are omitted; and in accounting for the increase in homicides during the '60s, he neglects the possible influences of racial unrest, the Viet Nam War, a loosening of moral standards and increased handgun ownership.

To work at all, deterrence requires murderers to reckon at least roughly the probable costs of their actions. But if a killer is drunk or high on drugs, that kind of rational assessment might be impossible. Passions are often at play that make a cost-benefit analysis unlikely. Most killers are probably not lucid thinkers at their best. Henry Brisbon Jr. may be legally sane, but he is by ordinary standards demented enough to make a mess of any theory of deterrence. Says New York University Law Professor Anthony Amsterdam: "People who ask themselves those questions—'Am I scared of the death penalty? Would I not be deterred?'—and think rationally, do not commit murder for many, many reasons other than the death penalty."

Former Prosecutor Bernard Carey, until 1980 state's attorney for Cook County, favors capital punishment, sparingly used. Yet he says, "I don't think it's much of a deterrent because the kinds of people who commit these crimes aren't going to be deterred by the electric chair." Some might be encouraged. "For every person for whom the death penalty is a deterrent," says Stanford Psychiatry Professor Donald Lunde, "there's at least one for whom it is an incentive." Such murderers, says Amsterdam, "are attracted by the Jimmy Cagney image of 'live fast, die young and have a beautiful corpse.' "

The arguments for capital punishment are usually visceral or anecdotal. Ernest van den Haag, professor of jurisprudence and public policy at Fordham University, says flatly, "Nobody fears prison as much as death." Florida's Governor Graham, who has signed 45 death warrants, cites the case of a restaurant robbery seen by a customer. "Afterward," recounts Graham, "he was the only witness. So the two guys took him out to the Everglades and shot him in the back of the head. If they had felt that being convicted for robbery and first-degree murder was sufficiently different, they might have had second thoughts."

In a sense, death's deterrent power has never really been given a chance in the U.S. Even during the comparative execution frenzy of the 1930s, hardly one in 50 murderers was put to death, a scant 2%. Reppetto estimates that if

25% of convicted killers were executed, 100 a week or more, there might be a deterring effect. But it is unthinkable, he agrees, that the U.S. will begin dispatching its villains on such a wholesale basis. Even at a rate of 100 executions annually, an implausibly high figure given today's judicial guarantees, a killer's chances of getting caught, convicted and executed would for him still be comfortably low: 250 to 1.

Even if executions were on television, there is no guarantee that prospective murderers would pay heed. As Camus noted in his 1957 essay against capital punishment: "When pickpockets were punished by hanging in England, other thieves exercised their talents in the crowds surrounding the scaffold where their fellow was being hanged."

But U.S. society is not unprotected just because it lacks weekly or daily executions. "The issue is not whether we slay murderers or free them," notes University of Michigan Law Professor Richard Lempert. "It is whether we send them to their death or to prison for life." Prison is a far more manageable weapon than death, and the U.S. is not at all hesitant to put criminals behind bars: the population there has doubled since 1970, to 400,000. "One trouble with the death penalty," says Henry Schwarzschild, an A.C.L.U. official, "is that it makes 25 years seem like a light sentence."

Opponents of capital punishment feel that prison terms without parole would deter as many potential murderers as the death penalty. Says Amsterdam: "The *degree* of punishment is not necessarily a deterrent even to someone who thinks rationally. What deters people from crime is the *likelihood* of getting caught and undergoing punishment." Reppetto agree: "I always favor something that will get tough with a lot of offenders instead of getting very tough with just a handful."

To diehard proponents of the death penalty, deterrence hardly matters anyway. Declares Buckley: "If it could be absolutely determined that there was no deterrent factor, I'd still be in favor of capital punishment." Taking the lives of murderers has a zero-sum symmetry that is simple and satisfying enough to feel like human instinct: the worst possible crime deserves no less than the worst possible punishment. "An eye for an eye," says Illinois Farmer Jim Hensley. "That's what it has to be. People can't be allowed to get away with killing." Counters Amsterdam: "The answer can hardly be found in a literal application of the eye-for-an-eye formula. We do not burn down arsonists' houses." The scriptures do preach mercy as well as retribution. Last Saturday, in fact, Pope John Paul II sweepingly recommended "clemency, or pardon, for those condemned to death." . . .

Capital punishment, says L.D.F. Lawyer Joel Berger "attempts to vindicate one murder by committing a second murder. And the second murder is more reprehensible because it is officially sanctioned and done with great ceremony in the name of us all." Not simply just as bad, but worse: this may be the central emotional truth for those who most passionately disapprove of executions. The cretinous killer or the seething psychopath is a loose cannon.

But the well-orchestrated modern execution, careful, and thoroughly consid-ered, is horrible because of its meticulous sanity. Executions are worse, in the abolitionists' moral scheme, because the government is always in control; it knows better, but kills anyway.

Proponents see the distinction between murder and state-sanctioned executions in a different light. "One is legal, the other is not," Van den Haag says. "If I take you and put you in a room against your will, it is called kidnap-ing. If I put on a uniform and put you in a room against your will, it's called arrest."

What was once perhaps the most potent argument against capital pun-ishment arises less often these days....In the U.S. today, as death rows swell and the pace of executions quickens, the risks of such a mistake grows. "You know there are going to be some," warns Michael Millman, a California state public defender. Abolitionist Sanford Kadish, a leading authority on criminal law, is less worried. Says he: "The chances are exceedingly remote."

Kadish puts his trust in the exhaustive system of judicial review that is now required in capital cases. Today no death-row inmate will be executed until his case has been brought to the attention of his state's highest court, a federal district court, a federal circuit court of appeals and the U.S. Supreme Court. The process is properly slow. In California it takes an average of three years after conviction for a capital case to work its way through the state court system alone. The improbably named James Free, 27, is on death row in Illi-nois for a double murder. Confesses Free: "I will use every appeals route I can dream up. That will buy time, maybe five or ten more years."

In 1953, by contrast, a pair of Missouri kidnapers were executed only eleven weeks after their crime. A quarter of the people executed during the 1960s had no appeals at all, and two-thirds of their cases were never reviewed by any federal court.

The historic decision came in 1972, after five years without an execu-tion, and just as fierce public majorities were forming in support of capital punishment. In *Furman* vs. *Georgia*, the Supreme Court nullified all 40 death-penalty statutes and the sentences of 629 death-row inmates, declaring that judges and juries had intolerably wide discretion to impose death or not. This lack of standards made the death sentence "freakishly imposed" on "a capri-ciously selected random handful" of murderers, wrote Justice Potter Stewart. "These death sentences are cruel and unusual in the same way that being struck by lightning is cruel and unusual." Within a few years, 37 state legisla-tures had passed statutes designed especially to meet the court's objections.

Most of the new laws went too far, mandating death for certain murders regardless of circumstances, and were overturned by the court. But the stat-utes adopted by Georgia, Florida and Texas were ruled acceptable. Death is a constitutional punishment, the court decided, not cruel or unusual as long as the judge and jury have given due consideration to the murderer's character and the particulars of his crime, the "mitigating factors."* Against these are weighed the aggravating factors that distinguish capital murder from ordinary homicide.

The court's decisions since have essentially been refinements and tidying addenda. Last January in *Eddings* vs. *Oklahoma*, for instance, the Justices ruled that the judge or jury must consider any mitigating factor the convict claims. Yet to many observers, that sounds like a return toward uncontrollable discretion, the very flaw the court prohibited in 1972. Says former L.D.F. Lawyer David Kendall: "We're right back to *Furman*."

Abolitionists hope so, anyway. They are now arguing a subtle paradox. The prudence and selectivity required by the court, they say, means that executions will be carried out only rarely, and thus will remain arbitrary and freakish, a sort of death lottery. There is always caprice along the way to death row. Prosecutors have great leeway in deciding which homicides to try as capital murders. A killer can be persuaded to testify against an accomplice to save his own life. Brooks was convicted and executed; for the same murder his partner must serve only eight more years in prison.

The Supreme Court's refusal last month to stay Brooks' execution does not give abolitionists much hope for a new landmark ruling in their favor. "We've become technicians," says L.D.F's Berger of his small litigious corps. "The great moral issues have been removed from the legal arena."

At the time of *Furman* it was widely recognized that the system was unquestionably stacked against black defendants, especially in the "death belt" of the South. Some of the racism has been wrung out. Yet clear bias remains, much attributable to prosecutorial choices. A recent study of homicide cases in Houston's Harris County is troubling. In cases where a black or Chicano had killed a white, 65% of defendants were tried for capital murder; only 25% of whites who killed a black or Chicano faced the death penalty. "I don't think it's overt racism," says University of Texas Law Professor Ed Sherman. But prosecutors want to win, and they "perceive that a Texas jury is more likely to give the death penalty to a black who killed a white." A similar South Carolina study found an almost identical pattern: local prosecutors over four years sought death sentences in 38% of homicides involving a white victim and black killer, but only 13% when a white had killed a black.

A serious problem is the quality of legal help for murder defendants. The Texas study, conducted by the Governor's judicial council, found that three-quarters of murderers with court-appointed lawyers were sentenced to death, against about a third of those represented by private attorneys. Amsterdam, who has argued eight capital cases before the Supreme Court, contends that "great lawyering at the right time would save virtually everybody who is going to be executed." Scharlette Holdman, director of Florida's Clearinghouse on Criminal Justice, persuades volunteer lawyers to represent

---

*Of the nine on today's Supreme Court, only Thurgood Marshall and William Brennan believe that the death penalty itself is unconstitutional.

death-row inmates. "Every person sentenced to die comes from a case fraught with errors," she says. "If you're adequately represented you don't get death. It's that simple."

Aside from public defenders, there are only about a dozen attorneys working full time on behalf of the condemned. Court-appointed lawyers in most states are not required to stay on a murderer's case after a conviction. "Drunk lawyers, lazy lawyers, incompetent layers, no lawyers," says Holdman. "You can have all the correct issues for appeal, but if you don't have a good lawyer to raise them, they don't mean a damn thing." Of 2,000 death sentences imposed during the post-*Furman* decade, about half have been reversed or vacated by the courts.

The careful legal course demanded by the Supreme Court is expensive. Last year the New York State Defenders Association estimated the trial costs for a typical capital-punishment case: a defense bill of $176,000, about $845,000 for the prosecution and court costs of $300,000. The total: $1.5 million, and this before any appeal is filed. Getting a writ before the Supreme Court, just one appellate step, might cost $170,000.

It is often argued, with blithe inhumanity, that there are good fiscal reasons for executing murderers: prison is too costly. It is cheaper to send a student to Stanford for a year than it is to keep a con in nearby San Quentin ($10,000 *vs.* $20,000). But imprisoning one inmate for 50 years would require less than $1 million in New York, not bad compared with the costs of the painstaking appeal process.

Everyone seems afraid of imposing bona fide life sentences, however, and for reasons unconnected with expense. Seventeen states have laws providing for life without parole for those convicted of murdering a robbery victim. Abolitionists say such a sentence is excessive. Statistics show that fewer than 1% of freed murderers kill again after their release from prison, in part because of their advanced age. But if capital punishment is abandoned, it may make sense, politically and economically, to permit the public some vengeful satisfaction. Life without parole is unimaginably harsh. But it would be a way occasionally to formalize the revulsion at Charles Manson and his ilk. As it is, Manson will be eligible for parole in 1985.

If not for the Bittakers (and Judys, Gacys, Mansons, Specks and Starkweathers), the capital-punishment debate might already have been decided in the abolitionists' favor. Bittaker's prosecutor had an apt beyond-the-pale phrase for Bittaker and his partner: "mutants from hell." Can they be human? Without killers in this league, more of America's logic and instinctive sense of mercy could prevail. There might be more electorates like Michigan's and more Governors like New York's who declare that capital punishment is unworthy of a decent society.

Administration of the death penalty perhaps cannot be made fair enough. As a deterrent, it is probably not necessary. But public passions are inflamed by the inevitable monsters. Civil reason is suspended in the face of what looks like evil incarnate. "It's an emotional issue. It's not a rational issue." Says who? Lawrence Bittaker, an emotional man, whose life is very hard to save.

   Note: The story of Lawrence Bittaker's henous crimes was included with this article.

Discussion

1. How many prisoners were on death row at the time this article was written? What percent were white and what percent were black? (*Note:* The number of death row inmates has now increased to almost 2,000.)
2. According to a Gallup pole in 1982, what percent of Americans favor capital punishment? What was the percent in 1966?
3. Why does the author say more people are advocating the death penalty now?
4. How do other countries compare with the United States in the number of murders? What percent of murders are committed in the United States by handguns?
5. Today, the states are responsible for making and executing the laws about capital punishment. Up to 1900, what other jurisdiction carried out the death penalty?
6. What evidence does the author give that the chances of an innocent person's being executed are extremely unlikely now?
7. What does the author say about the 1972 Supreme Court decision (*Furman* vs. *Georgia*)? How many states now have capital punishment laws according to the article?
   Note: The number has increased since this article was written. In 1976, another important decision was made by the Supreme Court about capital punishment. The decision was that the application of capital punishment could be constitutional if the court could prove "beyond a reasonable doubt" that "aggravating factors," such as the heinousness (horribleness, hatefulness) of a crime outweighed the "mitigating factors," such as mental incapacity or lack of a criminal record.
8. What do you think of the use of the econometric argument as proof that capital punishment is a deterrent to murder?
9. According to the author, how much does it cost the law as a death sentence appeal goes through the various courts? How much does it cost to keep someone in prison for a year?
10. Describe the different kinds of evidence used to support the points made in the article.
11. How can you describe the author's style? Do you find the style readable? If so, what techniques make it readable? (Consider the title, "An Eye for an Eye.")
12. What do you think is the author's position on capital punishment—for or against? Find proof in the article for your answer.

Reading 3

Deterrence

James Q. Wilson

The following selection is from Chapter Ten, "The Death Penalty," in Thinking About Crime. *In this passage, Wilson cites a number a studies made to determine the deterrent effect of capital punishment.*

Elsewhere in his book, Wilson has come to the conclusion that the only basis on which to argue about capital punishment is not deterrence but justice—does the punishment fit the crime?

The notes from the end of the chapter have been included to illustrate the degree of authoritative support given in this scholarly argument about the deterrent effect of capital punishment.

Length of summary: Approximately 200 words

Perhaps the first serious effort in this country to assess the deterrent effect of the death penalty was that of Thorsten Sellin, an opponent of capital punishment. In his first study, he did four things.[1] First, he compared homicide rates between adjacent states with and without the death penalty. The crude rates for homicide in these groups of states appeared to be about the same and to change in the same ways, regardless of whether a state did or did not have the death penalty on the books. Second, he compared homicide rates within states before and after they abolished or restored the death penalty. The rates did not change significantly after the legal status of the penalties changed. Third, he examined homicide rates in those cities where executions occurred and were presumed to have been publicized. . . . There was no difference in the homicide rate before and after the executions. (Similar studies, with similar results, were done by Robert Dann, Leonard D. Savitz, and William Graves.[2] Graves even uncovered evidence in California that led him

1. Thorsten Sellin, *Capital Punishment* (New York: Harper & Row, 1967), esp. pp. 135–160.
2. Robert H. Dann, "The Deterrent Effect of Capital Punishment," Bulletin 29, Friends Social Service Series (Philadelphia, 1935); Leonard D. Savitz, "A Study in Capital Punishment," *Journal of Criminal Law, Criminology, and Police Science* 49 (1959): 338–341; William E. Graves, "A Doctor Looks at Capital Punishment" in *The Death Penalty in America*, ed. Hugo Adam Bedau (Chicago: Aldine, 1964), pp. 322–332. See also David F. Phillips, "New Evidence on an Old Controversy," *American Journal of Sociology* 86 (1980): 139–147.

to speculate that there was in increase in the number of homicides on the days immediately preceding an execution.) Finally, Sellin sought to discover whether law-enforcement officers were safer from murderous attacks in states with the death penalty than in those without it. He found that the rate at which police officers were shot and killed in states that had abolished capital punishment was the same as the rate in states that had retained the death penalty. Donald R. Campion reached the same conclusion after studying the deaths of state police officers.[3]

It is sometimes argued in rejoinder to these findings that while executions may not deter murderers generally, they will help protect prison guards and other inmates from fatal assaults by convicts who "have nothing else to lose." Sellin compiled a list of fifty-nine persons who committed murders in state and federal prisons in 1965. He concluded that it is "visionary" to believe that the death penalty could reduce the "hazards of life in prison." Eleven of the prison murders were found in states without capital punishment and forty-three were in states with it. (The other five were in federal prisons.)

All these studies have serious methodological weaknesses. One problem is the degree of comparability of states with and without the death penalty. Sellin tried to "match" states by taking contiguous ones (for example, Michigan, Indiana, and Ohio), but of course such states are not really matched at all—they differ not only in the penalty for murder but in many other respects as well, and these other differences may offset any differences resulting from the form of punishment.

Another problem lies in the definition of a capital crime. What should be studied is the rate of crimes for which capital punishment is legally possible. I am not aware of any data on "murder rates" that distinguish between those homicides (like first-degree murder) for which death may be a penalty and those (like second-degree murder or nonnegligent manslaughter) for which it may not. Sellin's studies compare homicide rates, but no one knows what fraction of those homicides are first-degree murder for which execution is possible, even in the states that retain capital punishment.

Finally, and perhaps most important, it is not clear from many of these studies what is meant by "the death penalty." If what is meant is simply the legal possibility of execution, then "the death penalty" may be more fiction than fact. In many states that had the death penalty on the books, no executions were in fact carried out for many years. The majority members of a legislative commission in Massachusetts, for example, reported in 1968 that the death penalty is no deterrent to crime, but the minority members pointed out that no one had been executed in the state since 1947, and therefore no one could say whether the legal possibility of execution was or was not a

---

3. Donald R. Campion, "Does the Death Penalty Protect State Police?" in Bedau, *The Death Penalty*, pp. 301–315.

deterrent. Indeed, in 1960 there were only fifty-six executions in the entire country, more than half of these occurring in the South; in 1965 there were only seven; between 1968 and 1976 there were no executions; since 1977 there have been (as of mid-1982) four.

Discussion

1. The first study made by Thorsten Sellin is often cited in arguments about the deterrent effect of capital punishment. What four things did he study? On the basis of Sellin's findings, what conclusions can be reached about the deterrent effect of capital punishment?
2. What does the author say are the three methodological weaknesses of studies such as those made by Sellin?
3. What does the author mean by "most murders are 'unsuccessful' assaults"?
4. Do you think it is actually possible to measure the deterrent effect of capital punishment by means of special studies? Can you think of a more reliable way of studying the deterrent effect of the death penalty than those mentioned in this selection?
5. How would you compare the styles of each of the three selections in this summary writing section? Keep in mind that Koch presents his arguments from an empirical (practical) point of view (as someone responsible for executing the law); the authors of "An Eye for an Eye" write from a human interest point of view; and Wilson writes from a scholarly point of view.

Reading for Further Ideas

The reading selections in this section are intended not only to give you additional information about the subject of the composition, but to continue to sharpen your reading skills, and in addition, to give you practice in preparing for essay examinations.

After you have skimmed through each selection and underlined the main points, make an outline from memory. Then check the reading selection again and make a more exact outline. This time, make a one-sentence summary of the main idea.

With this preparation, write a question for each selection that you think might be given on an essay examination. Without concentrating on details, make the question as comprehensive as possible. (You may also ask a question comparing the selection with others on the same subject.) Then write the answers and check them against the reading selection.

In writing your question, keep in mind the date and source of the selection (newspaper or magazine, textbook or other kind of book). Such sources often have different purposes and may therefore affect the way your questions might be asked.

Reading 1

Death Penalty Update

The following editorial is from a conservative journal. As you read this editorial, see if you can find evidence that it is for or against capital punishment.

Reference is made in the selection to Norman Mailer's book The Executioner's Song, *which is about the execution of Gary Gilmore in the late 1970s for the murder of two men in separate holdups. The case attracted national and international attention because it was one of the first executions to be scheduled after a period of years during which the states waited for Supreme Court decisions on capital punishment. Many people who opposed capital punishment protested Gilmore's execution.*

Jack Henry Abbott, a convicted murderer, was released from prison under the sponsorship of Norman Mailer, who admired Abbott's literary talent. Soon after his release, Abbott killed again. (The slang expression laid an egg *means "resulted in a serious mistake.")*

Charles Manson was a notorious cult killer in the late 1960s. Sirhan Sirhan assassinated Robert Kennedy in Los Angeles during the presidential campaign of 1968.

The fact that executions have moved off the front pages and out of prime-time excitement reflects progress—i.e., capital punishment, having been the subject of extended public discussion and long litigation, has begun to fade as a major issue. About the current situation, a few observations.

Virtually all of those on death row have committed abominable crimes, a measure of the continuing reluctance to imposed the death sentence. Nevertheless, a gradual shift in focus from the perpetrator to the victim has undoubtedly occurred. Norman Mailer's *The Executioner's Song* (1979) may represent the last generally acclaimed celebration of a murderer for some time to come; Mailer's later sponsorship of murderer Jack Henry Abbott laid a serious egg; and *Newsweek*'s extended feature on J. D. Autry, recently executed in Huntsville, Texas, evoked little sympathy for Autry, and a considerable amount for his casually murdered victims.

National Review, May 4, 1984. © 1984 by National Review, Inc., 150 East 35th Street, New York, N.Y. 10016. Reprinted with permission.

Execution has numerous kinds of significance, but a principal one is the role of society as surrogate for the victim. Had the murdered cashier shot Autry before he put a bullet between his eyes, it would have been self-defense. Autry's execution corrects the error in timing.

Many murderers have been living on death row for years as a result of long legal delays. As the legal points are settled, the pace of executions will speed up, though some still more baroque appeals are yet in store. Attorneys for men convicted of murder are preparing to argue that capital punishment discriminates against males; i.e., since 1930 3,313 men have been executed, as against only thirty women. Even granting that men commit more murders, the courts do appear to have been more lenient with the fair sex. The remedy, of course, is not to spare the male killers but to treat their fair-sex counterparts equally.

Many egregious killers will survive because of our prolonged period of moral and legal confusion. Charles Manson and Sirhan Sirhan continue to live at taxpayers' expense in California, as do many others across the nation. Richard Herrin, the rejected lover who beat Bonnie Garland to death with a hammer as she slept in her bed, will be a free man in a few years.

But sanity appears to be returning to the processes of justice, and the death rows are being cleaned out.

Reading 2

Capital Punishment: No Deterrent

George Harsh

The following selection, which appeared in The New York Times *in December 1971, was written by the author of* Lonesome Road, *the story of Harsh's twelve years on a Georgia chain gang to which he had been sentenced for murder. The headline, "Capital Punishment: No Deterrent," gives Harsh's side of the argument immediately.*

The article is written with great feeling since it is based on Harsh's own experience. Study the way he presents his arguments and see if you agree with them, especially the argument that most people would prefer execution to life imprisonment.

An author was once said to be qualified as an expert on murder and capital punishment because he had "talked with over one hundred murderers." I too have talked with over a hundred murderers. Therefore, I submit that I too am an expert on murder and capital punishment.

Not only have I talked with over one hundred murderers, but I have slept alongside them, I have eaten with them, laughed and cried with them and spent six months in the death cells with many of them.

I am a convicted murderer.

While still in my teens I was convicted of a senseless crime and sentenced to die in the electric chair. This sentence would have been carried out had I not come from a white, wealthy and influential family. As it was I spent twelve years in prison working alongside other murderers and during those years I gained some insight into why some of us go tick while others go tock. And from my experiences I can state unequivocally that capital punishment is not a deterrent to murder.

The vast majority of all murders are committed under one of four conditions:

(1) It is an act of explosive passion during which the killer is oblivious to and uncaring of the consequences of his acts.

(2) It is a crime carefully thought out, planned and plotted wherein the perpetrator is certain he will not be caught.

(3) It is an act of panic committed during the carrying out of a lesser crime.

(4) It is the act of a mad person whose mind is walled off from reality anyway.

To further disprove the deterrent theory, stop any ten people at random and pose the question: "Would you rather be executed or spend the remainder of your life in prison?" All will invariably opt for the quick death of execution rather than the lingering death of life in prison.

There are those who will say, "Yes, but send a man to prison for life and within a few years he will again be out walking the streets." It happens. In fact 90 per cent of those we send to prison are eventually released. But those of us who have heard the clang of prison doors shutting behind us and have faced a life in prison have no way of knowing whether we will be among that 90 per cent. So, if there is a deterrent, prison is the greater.

Capital punishment is a law zeroed in on the poor, the underprivileged, the friendless, the uneducated and the ignorant. How many rich men have ever been executed in this country? It is not likely any ever will be. With sufficient money a capital case can be kept in the courts until the defendant dies of old age. Among those wise and experienced in such matters is a saying, "You can't hang a million dollars." This is not cynicism: It is truth. And I am living proof of the validity of this colloquialism.

It would be instructive and of sociological significance to see a breakdown of the 648 cases of the men awaiting execution in the death cells of this country. How many of these people are white, and how many are black? How many of them are so poor they were unable to hire competent legal help to insure themselves a fair trial? How many of them, all their lives, have been denied opportunity and hope? And how many of them are rich? Or even moderately well-to-do?

This law of capital punishment represents a sickness of the human spirit. This Mosaic law of death is drawn from the worst of all human motives—revenge. And no amount of self-deception, such as claiming it to be a "deterrent," can effectively hide this fact.

In the near future the Supreme Court of the United States will render its decision as to whether the death penalty represents cruel and unusual punishment and is therefore unconstitutional.

At the very outset the decision will spell life—or death—for the 648 people awaiting the verdict. But of even more lasting effect the verdict will serve as a road sign as to the direction we as a nation are to take. If the death penalty is upheld then we shall continue to perpetuate the lie by which all men throughout history have administered their criminal law; i.e., capital punishment is a deterrent to murder. If, on the other hand, the death penalty is erased it will serve notice that we as a people intend to take a long stride on the road toward eventual maturity and civilization.

What is important here is the undeniable fact that when we stoop to the debasing act of putting to death, in cold blood, a fellow human being who is completely at our mercy, we as a society decrease our own humanity to the exact extent of that wretch's death.

Let us therefore be merciful unto ourselves and abolish the self-brutalizing violence of capital punishment.

Reading 3

Public Figures Join Killer's Fight to Live

Jeane DeQuine

The following article takes up the famous case of Willie Darden, who insisted for the fourteen years he was on the Florida death row that he was innocent of the crimes he was accused of. The evidence supporting his guilt was the testimony of two of the surviving victims of these crimes—the wife who was sexually assaulted while her husband lay dying and the young neighbor who was shot three times.

Darden's six appeals went through the state courts and all the way up to the U.S. Supreme Court. His seventh appeal was denied, and on the morning of March 15, 1988, he was executed. He thus became the 96th person to be executed since 1976, the year the Supreme Court restored the death penalty.

The article is headed by a photo of Darden, handcuffed, in a fighting posture. Three smaller pictures also appear in the article. One is of the actress Margot Kidder, with the caption: "It is wrong when citizens kill citizens, and it is wrong when governments kill citizens." The second photograph is of Florida Governor Bob Martinez, with the caption: "I agree that the innocent should not be punished. However, I believe Willie Darden is not innocent." The third photo is of Soviet dissident Andrei Sakharov, and is captioned: "The death penalty is an inhuman institution....After an execution, an injustice or a mistake cannot be corrected."

This article was written from a human interest point of view. Note the details that make the reader feel sympathy for Darden as a human being. From this article, decide whether you think that Darden was innocent and, even if he was guilty, whether he had the possibility of being rehabilitated so that he could have become a good citizen in society. Finally, as you read, try to find evidence of whether the writer of the article is for or against the death penalty.

Convicted killer Willie Darden has become an international symbol and cause during 14 years on Florida's death row here.

Courts have stopped his execution six times—more than any other death-row inmate—for a 1973 killing.

Now, he's mounting a campaign to get the U.S. Supreme Court—which reconvenes today—to grant him a new trial in the killing of a Lakeland store owner. Darden says he didn't commit the crime.

"I'm going to holler until I can't holler no more," Darden, 54, says in an interview. "I'm going to do that as long as I have breath in my body."

Fueling Darden's drive: supporters around the world, including Soviet dissident Andrei Sakharov, Michigan Democratic Rep. John Conyers Jr., actress Margot Kidder, British rock star Peter Gabriel and Amnesty International.

Supporters have asked Gov. Bob Martinez to grant clemency. They cite affidavits from a minister and a woman that Darden could not have been at the scene of the killing.

"Perhaps if the governor is made aware that people in many countries around the world are outraged at the prospect of this execution," Gabriel says, "then the sum total might begin to influence him and he might reconsider the appeal" for clemency.

Martinez has rejected their appeals. He says the death penalty was appropriate for individuals "who choose to disregard the most sacred element of human rights—the right to life."

Darden was on a weekend furlough from prison—where he was jailed for rape—when the store owner was killed, his wife sexually assaulted and a 16-year-old boy wounded.

Darden still claims he was far from the crime scene.

"I haven't been such a good fellow over the years," Darden says. "But I haven't been such a violent fellow, either."

Darden came within seven hours of execution in 1985, and last month avoided his sixth death warrant when the Supreme Court went into a recess without considering a bid to reopen his case.

In 1986, Darden's conviction was affirmed by the Supreme Court in a 5–4 decision. His lawyers have asked the court to reopen the case because of the new testimony.

Darden says he's the victim of racism. He points to trial remarks by the prosecutor, who called him an "animal" who "shouldn't be let out of his cell unless he has a leash on him."

These days, Darden passes time along with 279 other death-row inmates by spending 16 hours a day writing letters in his defense.

He rises at 4 a.m., drinks a cup of coffee, smokes a Hav-a-Tampa cigar and answers about 50 letters daily out of the 300 he says he receives. He reads the Bible, prays for his life and hopes his opponents will stop badgering him. "I hate it when someone calls me a killer."

As he speaks, Darden wears handcuffs and a yellow T-shirt, the color-coded dress for death-row inmates. He says he tries not to think of death.

"You know that you're facing death and you know there are people who are trying to kill you," Darden says. "You feel like you are in a vacuum and you are sucked in."

Reading 4

The Need for Gun Control Legislation

Edward M. Kennedy

The following selection is an argument on an issue often related to capital punishment. Kennedy introduces his argument with the alarming statistics about the number of deaths caused by guns.

Edward M. Kennedy, "The Need for Gun Control Legislation." From *Current History* (July–August 1976). Copyright © 1976 by *Current History*. Reprinted by permission.

As you read, note the form of the argument. Kennedy first quickly presents the views of his opponents, using numbers for each of their arguments. Then he systematically answers each of these opposing views, using the same number in order to make his reasoning easy to follow.

The case for effective firearms legislation can be logically and clearly explained on the basis of the daily tragedies reported in our nation's newspapers. Over 25,000 Americans die each year because of shooting, accidents, suicides and murders caused by guns, primarily because too many Americans possess firearms. When guns are available, they have proved to be a far too easily accessible tool for the destruction of human life. Because of the senseless deaths and injuries caused by guns I strongly support the public demand for legislation to provide a uniform, nationwide system to control the abuse and misuse of firearms. A brief review of the conditions involving firearms in this country makes it clear that the proliferation of firearms, particularly handguns, must be halted.

My interest in the need for effective firearms legislation goes back at least to 1963. I have introduced firearms bills in the Senate on several occasions. I offered gun control amendments to pending legislation on the Senate floor. Since I have been in the Senate, I have heard much of the testimony presented by nearly 200 witnesses, during more than 40 days of hearings on gun control. The issues never change. The arguments never vary. The statistics never recede. In 1963, handgun murders totaled 4,200. Eleven years later, in 1974, handguns were used to murder 11,000 Americans. The tragic toll of handgun suicides and accidental handgun deaths pushes the annual figures well beyond reasonable limits for a society that claims to respect life and personal security.

Gun manufacturers produce more guns each year, and American gun deaths increase right along with the output of firearms. Advocates for stronger controls are understandably alarmed by production figures showing that the annual output of handguns increased from 568,000 in 1968 to over 2.5 million in 1974.

Many experts insist that a gun, and particularly a handgun, is such a viciously lethal weapon that no citizen deserves to wield the awesome power of a gun. Our complex society requires a rethinking of the proper role of firearms in modern America. Our forefathers used firearms as an integral part of their struggle for survival. But today firearms are not appropriate for daily life in the United States.

The arguments used to oppose gun controls are old and hackneyed. The same lament has been used in one of the following forms time and time again.

First. Gun controls cannot limit the supply of guns enough to reduce violence. *Second.* The Constitution protects the citizen's right to bear arms. *Third.* There is no need to ban guns because guns are not killers: people do the killing. *Fourth.* Criminals will always find a way to obtain guns. Thus, controls will only disarm those who obey the law. *Fifth.* Registration and licensing procedures are so cumbersome and inconvenient that they would create unfair burdens for legitimate gun owners.

Opponents of effective gun controls believe that these objections are valid. But a thorough examination of each of these claims reveals that not one of them is well founded.

First, can laws limit the supply of guns enough to reduce violent crime?

Of course, such laws, properly enforced, can reduce the availability of handguns. In 1968, when importers anticipated the enactment of a new gun law, about 1.2 million handguns were rushed into the American market. In 1969, pistol and revolver imports fell to less than 350,000 and have not risen substantially above that total since then.

Today, nearly three million new handguns enter the American market every year because handgun parts are still legally imported and because American manufacturers are still authorized to produce them. The legislation I have introduced would not only reduce the number of handguns assembled from imported parts, but it would also drastically curtail the output of domestically manufactured handguns.

In June, 1934, President Franklin D. Roosevelt signed the National Firearms Act, which outlawed civilian ownership of machineguns. Perhaps this is the law that best illustrates the way in which legislation can effectively restrain the availability of firearms. Since enactment of that measure over 40 years ago, machineguns have been virtually eliminated in the United States. Obviously, a machinegun has no legitimately useful place in a civilized society. Easily concealed pistols and revolvers are also out of place in today's highly urbanized and complex society.

Opponents of handgun control insist that it is impossible to prevent a criminal from obtaining a handgun. But if a criminal has to steal a gun before he can use a gun, he will use a gun much less frequently.

An effectively enforced ban on the output of these deadly devices is the most direct way to reduce the deaths and injuries caused by guns.

Second, it is claimed that the second amendment to the constitution protects the citizen's right to bear arms. Anyone who believes that "the right to bear arms" is guaranteed in the Constitution has conveniently ignored the language of the second amendment, which provides that: "A well regulated militia being necessary to the security of a free state, the right of the people to keep and bear arms shall not be infringed."

The United States Supreme Court has repeatedly said that this amendment has nothing to do with the right to personal ownership of guns but only with the right of a state to establish a militia.

In perspective, the purpose of the second amendment emerges clearly. Debates in the first and second Congresses were naturally affected by the recently won independence of the new government. And in Massachusetts it was bitterly recalled that the British Crown had quartered its troops but forbade the organization of a colonial militia. Congressional debates of early Congresses support the view that the second amendment was designed to protect and preserve the state militias. No mention was made of any individual's "right" to possess, carry, or use arms, and there is no indication of any concern with the need to do so. The new government was far more interested in maintaining state militias to defend the hard-won liberty. That fledgling government feared the establishment of a federal standing army as a threat to the basic authority of the several states.

Indeed, in December 1791, when the Bill of Rights was ratified, all but one of the 14 states of the Union adopted a constitution or a declaration of rights under which their people were governed.

Rhode Island still operated under its charter of 1663, which authorized the colony to organize a militia. But there was no mention of any "right" to bear arms.

Eight states—Delaware, New Jersey, Connecticut, Georgia, South Carolina, Maryland, New Hampshire, and New York—operated under constitutions that made no mention of any "right" to bear arms, although each authorized a state militia.

Three states—Massachusetts, North Carolina, and Virginia—expressly recognized the right of the people to bear arms for the defense of the state.

Two states—Pennsylvania and Vermont—included language in their constitutions which acknowledged that: "The people have a right to bear arms for the defense of themselves and the State."

However, that sentence was included in a paragraph that was concerned with the prohibition against a standing army and the guarantee of civilian control of the militia. Considering the history of the right to bear arms, reason defines the phrase "defense of themselves" as referring only to collective defense. That phrase did not include individual defense.

It appears, therefore, that both the states and the Congress were preoccupied with the distrust of standing armies and the importance of preserving state militias. It was in this context that the second amendment was written and it is in this context that it has been interpreted by the courts.

Third, a common refrain against firearm controls is that "guns do not kill, people do." This argument contends that people who use guns to commit crimes should be dealt with severely but that efforts to control weapons are not necessary. Yet, a glance at the statistics and common sense tell us that it is when guns are in hand that two-thirds of the people who kill other people do so; it was when guns were in hand that over 250,000 robberies were committed in 1973; it was when guns were in hand that one-fourth of the nation's 400,000 aggravated assaults were committed in 1973.

Murder is usually committed in a moment of rage. Guns are quick and easy to use. They are also deadly accurate, and they are all too often readily accessible. It is estimated that there are over 35 million handguns in private ownership in this country. Each year, 2.5 million new handguns are introduced into the marketplace for civilian use. Because handguns are available people use them.

An attacker makes a deliberate choice of a gun over a knife. But because the fatality rate of knife wounds is about one-fifth that of gun wounds, it may be concluded that using a knife instead of a gun might cause 90 percent fewer deaths.

Fourth, others argue that because criminals have guns, gun control will simply disarm law-abiding citizens. Lawless citizens, according to that argument, will not feel obliged to abide by gun restrictions.

Perhaps there is truth in this argument. And for this reason, I am convinced that gun restrictions can be effective in limiting the wholesale misuse of firearms. Strict gun restrictions will aid in disarming anyone who fails to register his weapons or to obtain a license for ownership. Indeed, the enforcement of licensing and registration laws will isolate precisely those citizens who flaunt the law, because such legislation makes it a crime merely to possess an unregistered firearm. The commission of a crime with such weapon compounds the wrong of any criminal action.

Fifth. It may be that the greatest number who protest gun controls do so because the administrative requirements for registration are cumbersome and inconvenient. Since 1969, Congress has attempted several times to remove the 1968 gun control law's record-keeping requirements with regard to sales of .22 caliber ammunition.

I have repeatedly objected to any move that would eliminate the requirement that sales of such ammunition must be recorded. Between six billion and seven billion rounds of ammunition are produced in this country each year. At least 85 percent of those bullets are .22 caliber. Records maintained to control the sale of ammunition may be useful in restricting access to those gun owners who intend to use their weapons for legitimate purposes.

I believe that any measure that will substantially reduce the misuse of firearms will at the same time enhance whatever pleasures may be derived from the so-called recreational pursuits of gun ownership.

Among the nations of the world, the United States stands in the bloodiest pool of deaths by gunfire. Americans are not only ranked No. 1, but No. 2 lags so far behind that a tally of gun deaths in all civilized nations probably would not equal the excessive fusillade Americans train on their fellow citizens.

In 1973, the total gun murder rate in the United States was 6.2 per 100,000 population. And the handgun murder rate was 4.9. Thus, even the United States handgun murder rate was 62 times the rate in Scotland, the Netherlands, and Great Britain and Japan, 31 times the rate in Denmark, France, Sweden, and Switzerland, and 20 times the rate in New Zealand, Germany, and Italy.

Among civilized societies that have acted to control guns the United States is a glaring exception. In Italy, West Germany, France, Britain, and the Soviet Union, "the right to bear arms" is a strictly regulated privilege. In Japan, private gun ownership is all but prohibited. Five European countries totally prohibit the private possession of handguns. A 1968 State Department survey of 102 of its diplomatic posts revealed that 29 European countries require either a license to carry a firearm or registration of the ownership or sale of each privately owned firearm, or both.

Legislation to control the violence caused by firearms is essential in a national campaign to reduce handgun deaths. At the same time, public education and ongoing research in the relationship between firearms and violence is also important.

The gun mystique fascinates and excites the imagination. Films, novels and dramatic presentations that depict gun violence are enjoyed and readily understood by all members of our society. The role of the handgun in American society has been distorted. A complete reform of the role of the handgun is needed. It is clearly not a weapon of entertainment, and only rarely is it used for sporting purposes. Many Americans insist that a handgun provides comfort and security in a menacing environment where assailants threaten the weak, the helpless, and the lonely. Yet the proliferation of handguns seems to involve a vicious cycle that sees more and more people buying guns to protect themselves from more and more people who have guns.

I am convinced that this national evil of handgun roulette must be interrupted before the two-gun family becomes as common as the two-car family. In April, 1976, the House of Representatives' Subcommittee on Crime reported a bill to begin to establish controls on the use of handguns. If this measure if enacted, it will establish the foundation for a full system of controls that can stem the unbridled flow of firearms violence. From other sources, it has also been recommended that handgun production quotas must be imposed upon the nation's firearms producers. Because the American people have repeatedly expressed the demand for an end to firearms violence, I look forward to the enactment of effective and enforceable controls on the use of firearms.

Extra Discussion and Writing

Journal Entry

Give your reaction to the amount of violent crime in the United States, much of it committed by guns. Do you find it surprising that there should be so much controversy in the United States about the death penalty? What do you think about the availability of guns in this country? Write freely, since you are the only one who will see this entry.

Letters

1. Write a letter to a newspaper in your country discussing the same things as in your journal entry. But this time, since you are now writing a formal letter, revise the journal entry for the letter so that it is more carefully controlled and correct.
2. Write a letter home discussing the kind of crime you see in the United States, where many people are afraid to be out on the streets after a certain hour. Compare this situation with the one in your country.

Saying

An Eye for an Eye is an expression from the Old Testament of the Bible. What does it mean? Do you agree with what it stands for?

Debate

Prepare a short debate on capital punishment. Decide which issues the debate will concentrate on, both for and against: justice, cost, fairness, and so on.

Reactions

Reading 1

A Brother's Murder

Brent Staples

One of the arguments against capital punishment is that society is to blame for the antisocial behavior of those who commit crimes. The following selection, the first part of an essay by an editor of The New York Times Book Review, *gives us an*

*insight into the kind of poverty-stricken surroundings that breed despair and vio-
lence—places where gunplay is an everyday occurrence in their idle street life, and
where life and death mean nothing.*

*After you read this selection, discuss whether you think society is to blame for
criminal behavior and whether you think the young men like the author's brother
can be rehabilitated once they are in prison.*

It has been more than two years since my telephone rang with the news
that my younger brother Blake—just 22 years old—had been murdered. The
young man who killed him was only 24. Wearing a ski mask, he emerged from
a car, fired six times at close range with a massive .44 Magnum, then fled. The
two had once been inseparable friends. A senseless rivalry—beginning, I
think, with an argument over a girlfriend—escalated from posturing, to
threats, to violence, to murder. The way the two were living, death could have
come to either of them from anywhere. In fact, the assailant had already
survived multiple gunshot sounds from an incident much like the one in
which my brother lost his life.

As I wept for Blake I felt wrenched backward into events and circumstances that had seemed light-years gone. Though a decade apart, we both
were raised in Chester, Pa., an angry, heavily black, heavily poor, industrial
city southwest of Philadelphia. There, in the 1960's, I was introduced to mor-
tality, not by the old and failing, but by beautiful young men who lay wrecked
after sudden explosions of violence. The first, I remember from my 14th
year—Johnny, brash lover of fast cars, stabbed to death two doors from my
house in a fight over a pool game. The next year, my teenage cousin, Wesley,
whom I loved very much, was shot dead. The summers blur. Milton, an angry
young neighbor, shot a crosstown rival, wounding him badly. William, another teen-age neighbor, took a shotgun blast to the shoulder in some urban
drama and displayed his bandages proudly. His brother, Leonard, severely
beaten, lost an eye and donned a black patch. It went on.

I recall not long before I left for college, two local Vietnam veterans—
one from the Marines, one from the Army—arguing fiercely, nearly at blows
about which outfit had done the most in the war. The most killing, they
meant. Not much later, I read a magazine article that set that dispute in a
context. In the story, a noncommissioned officer—a sergeant, I believe—said
he would pass up any number of affluent, suburban-born recruits to get hard-
core soldiers from the inner city. They jumped into the rice paddies with
"their manhood on their sleeves," I believe he said. These two items—the
veterans arguing and the sergeant's words—still characterize for me the circumstances under which black men in their teens and 20's kill one another
with such frequency. With a touchy paranoia born of living battered lives,
they are desperate to be *real* men. Killing is only *machismo* taken to the extreme. Incursions to be punished by death were many and minor, and they
remain so: they include stepping on the wrong toe, literally; cheating in a

drug deal; simply saying "I dare you" to someone holding a gun; crossing territorial lines in a gang dispute. My brother grew up to wear his manhood on his sleeve. And when he died, he was in that group—black, male and in its teens and early 20's—that is far and away the most likely to murder or be murdered....

Reading 2

Made in the U.S.A.; Works Every Time

The following selection, published on the op-ed page of The New York Times *on January 15, 1976, is excerpted from* Fortune News. Fortune News *is a publication of Fortune Society, an organization of ex-convicts and other individuals. The excerpt records the answers by several former convicts about their use of guns in street crimes. The headline, "Made in the U.S.A.; Works Every Time," refers to the illustration of a gun and its parts which heads the article.*

As you read, note the power that the possession of a gun has given to the men quoted in this excerpt. What would you suggest could be done for released ex-convicts who would like to become law-abiding citizens? They come out of prison with little money and a prison record that makes employers reluctant to hire them.

Note: All names in the excerpt have been omitted to protect the identity of those men who are quoted.

I had two guns on me, a .38 revolver and a double-barrel sawed-off, 12-gauge shotgun. I used it a few times when I was a drug dealer. I shot one guy with a pistol when I was dealing and he was a user. Both guns I got for nothing. They were as a result of favors which people owed me. Addicts would get me guns as a result of my getting them drugs. I also would rent out those pieces to addicts. With a gun, I felt like a big shot. I felt superior.

When you're doing drugs and its big business, somebody is looking to rip you off. I'm in favor of gun control if they take them off of everybody, including the cops. If they couldn't pass a law taking guns off the cops *on-duty*, then they should not be permitted to carry them off-duty. There are a lot of off-duty cops, sitting in gin-mills, with guns strapped to them.

An automatic handgun was my weapon on the streets. I did show it in holdups but I never had to fire it. People must have seen a look in my face. There were various places to get a gun. I got mine on the street in a transaction which cost me about $50.

When I had a gun, I felt good. There's a lot of power in a gun. If you feel like you're nothing, a gun can make you feel like a king.

There should be stricter gun controls but it is not going to really solve the problem. Why should there be guns manufactured at all? I would rather see guns not made than to try to control them after they are made.

I had a small handgun which was carried in my pocket during stick-ups. I showed the gun during the commission of a robbery and used it as a power symbol. It was never fired while in my possession.

It was always easy to get a gun from street merchants. The going price was about $60 for me. It stimulated my ego to carry a weapon. I carried it with me all the time, even when not planning a robbery. It stimulated power within me (a misconception) and enhanced my ego.

I believe in universal disarmament, the elimination of all guns. Guns are an indication that there has been a breakdown in communications. They are the end result of the failure to communicate.

I used a .22. It was in my possession and I used it and shot a man I was living with in California. He was O.K., not seriously hurt from the wound. I loved the power of the gun. To me, the gun represented power. I purchased it from some guy in a bar in L.A. for $30.

I'm not sure if gun control would do any good, unless you stop manufacturing them. Most of the people buy their guns illegally. A lot of the wrong people carry guns for the wrong reasons—and that is on both sides of the law.

Usually, I carried a .25 automatic, a P-38 Walther and a .39 police positive. Generally, I carried the .25 around with me all the time. If I thought there was going to be trouble, I'd carry a bigger piece.

I used it once—while being chased, and fortunately it misfired. There's a lot to it, when you carry a gun. It made me feel as if I were in command of any situation. It gave me a sense of power, not power but a sense of power. It made me feel that I was larger than I was. I felt like God and that I could determine life and death.

I feel that the average citizen should have the right to carry a gun. If we are going to give law-enforcement officers the power of life and death, then all citizens should have the same right. That may be an oversimplification but it is a starting point. Now that I'm a law-abiding citizen, there should be some mechanism for me to defend myself.

CHAPTER 9

The Research Paper

Defining the Research Paper

With the research paper (also called a term paper), you are moving from the shorter compositions, where you have used readings to support your points, to a longer paper supported almost entirely by readings.

The research paper is *not* a book report based on one source. It is a formal paper in which you draw on many sources to present a small area of a larger subject in some depth. These sources provide reliable facts and authoritative opinion to support a point of view or an opinion, to present an argument, to give a historical perspective, or to analyze or explain. Since most of the information in the research paper comes from your readings, the sources need to be acknowledged at specific points in the text and in the bibliography (the list of sources at the end of your paper).

Here is your own contribution to the paper:

1. You give the subject a focus (the thesis).
2. You give organization to the paper.
3. You choose the sources of information and the way you use them.
4. You make general statements at the beginning or the end of the paper.
5. You present your own conclusions.

Although the research paper is a formal paper, it should be written so that it will be interesting and informative not only to the instructor who will read it, but to other students. It should not be a patchwork of scattered bits of information with no theme holding them together.

The research paper you will be asked to write for this class can serve as a model for the term papers you will have to write for other courses. It is customary in this kind of class for the teacher to assign a paper that ranges in length from 6 to 20 pages, with 8 to 10 pages on average. The number of sources of information you will be required to consult also varies. (For your other classes, your papers may not need such tight documentation as for this class.)

The style of documentation given here for the research paper is the one that was simplified in 1984 by the Modern Language Association (MLA). In this simplified form the traditional footnotes used to indicate the source of a piece of information have been replaced by a brief parenthetic reference in the text to the source (now called a citation).

Possible Subjects

Unless your teacher assigns a subject (or choice of subjects) for the research paper, you may select your own. Choose one that is interesting to you, either in your major field or in another field that you might not otherwise have the opportunity to investigate. Avoid highly technical subjects or those you cannot narrow down effectively in the assigned length. The following list offers suggestions that may help you choose a subject.

Liberal Arts

history: current or earlier events
biography: of a famous person
literature: an author and/or his or her work
art: an artist and/or his or her work (a sculptor, composer, musician)
music: a particular school (jazz, rock) or the music of a particular country or group
religion and ethics
education: theories, psychology
language: historical development of a particular language
communication, propaganda

mass media: radio, television, newspapers, magazines
theater, dance, movies
archeology, anthropology
utopias
politics: political theories, forms of government
economics, business
   inflation (price-wage spiral)
   strikes
   labor unions
   unemployment
   government controls
   business cycle (prosperity, recession, depression, recovery)
   labor-management relations
revolution: Russia, China, other countries, other times
economic theories: Keynes, supply-side, monetary policy

Social Sciences

social change: in your country or in the United States
the family (extended vs. nuclear), marriage, divorce
economic problems: in your country or in the United States
population shift (from country to city)
urban development
problems of cities: growth, deterioration
pollution
armaments
superstition
population explosion
poverty: in your country or in the United States
birth control, abortion
drug abuse, alcoholism
homosexuality
problems of the adolescent
suicide (teenagers and others)
retirement
problems of the aging
mercy killing (euthanasia)
health, disease
problems of minorities: in your country and in the United States
juvenile delinquency

Science/Technology

developments in medicine: new drugs, techniques
computers: artificial intelligence (robots, robotics)
reproduction: genetic engineering, cloning, artificial insemination, test
   tube babies

superconductivity
evolution
space travel, satellites
black holes, quarks
alternate sources of energy: solar, geothermal, tides

Other

agriculture
transportation
advertising, publishing
sports
hobbies

In addition to these suggestions, you may use one of the composition subjects in Chapters 2–8 if you use a different thesis and add a number of new sources.

Research Sources

There are a number of places where you can check to find sources of information for your research paper. If you want to know which books in the library might have information about your subject, check the main catalog. If you want to know which magazine articles might be useful, refer to one of the periodical indexes (lists of articles) that tell where and when articles were published. You may also check for articles in newspaper indexes and in encyclopedias or other reference books.

You should become acquainted with the resources of your library. And because of the increasing amount of information now found in libraries, you should feel free to ask a librarian to help you locate what you need for your research.

Books

All books in a library are listed in a main catalog in alphabetical order. The catalog may be the traditional card catalog, a microform catalog, or a computer catalog. For each book in the library, the catalog contains at least three entries: one under the author's name, one under the title of the book, and one or more under the subject. For your research paper, you will probably refer to the subject entry. You might need to check more than one related subject before you find the one that is closest to your topic.

If your subject is fairly new, you might want to check the Subject Guide of *Books in Print*. It is published annually and includes all subjects except literature.

Articles in Periodicals

The indexes which list articles in magazines and newspapers are usually found in the reference room of a library. Under the subject heading in an index you will find out which periodical contains articles you might want to read. Some specialized indexes also contain abstracts (short summaries) of articles. Since indexes are issued periodically, you may have to check several volumes to get the information you need. Because indexes include current articles, they are especially useful for topics of more recent interest and discovery—for example, space exploration, cloning, miniaturized chips for computers.

Magazine Articles

GENERAL MAGAZINES

One of the most useful indexes is the *Reader's Guide to Periodical Literature* (usually shortened to the *Reader's Guide*). It covers articles in more than 200 popular magazines—for example, *Time, Business Week, Reader's Digest, National Geographic*. Articles are listed alphabetically in two places: under the name of the author and under the subject. The *Reader's Guide* includes reviews of literature and of the performing arts. Because the Guide has a cumulative index covering many years, you may find it easier to check the cumulative volume before you check individual volumes.

Your library may also have a microfilm index of articles in general magazines. For example, the *Magazine Index*, put out by Information Access, lists articles from 400 popular magazines and is constantly updated for the last four years. This index displays the lists of articles in alphabetical order on a microfilm reader, and has the advantage of enabling you to check quickly for the most recent articles on your subject.

SPECIALIZED JOURNALS

Indexes for these journals list articles in scholarly journals that relate to a particular field. There are indexes for agriculture, art, education, business, engineering, music, public affairs, and many others. You may find these specialized indexes more useful for the kind of research you are doing because the articles they list can offer more authoritative support than those in the more general popular magazines.

In most of these specialized indexes, it is best to check under a subject heading, especially since the indexes differ as to whether they include separate entries for authors and titles.

ABSTRACTS

Abstracts cover scholarly articles in such specialized fields as psychology, biology, chemistry, and history. They not only tell where an article may be found, but give a short summary of the article. Some abstracts are highly specialized within a field—for example, *Criminal Justice Abstracts, Personnel Management Abstracts, Genetics Abstracts, Environment Abstracts, Ergonomics Abstracts.*

Newspaper Articles

The index of newspaper articles found in most libraries is *The New York Times Index*, which goes back to 1851. Another newspaper index most libraries have is *The Wall Street Journal Index*, which starts with 1958.

Your library may also carry the *National Newspaper Index* put out by Information Access. This microfilm index includes articles that are constantly updated for the last three years from *The New York Times, The Wall Street Journal, The Christian Science Monitor, The Washington Post*, and *The Los Angeles Times.* Like the *Magazine Index*, the articles, arranged alphabetically, are projected on a microfilm reader.

Locating Periodicals

After you have learned from the indexes which articles you would like to look at, the next step is to find out where those held by the library are located. Magazines and journals may be listed in the main catalog along with the books, or in a separate periodical catalog, or in special books. Copy down the call number and try to locate the periodical(s) you want. If you are having difficulty, ask a librarian to help you. (It is possible that your library does not carry all the periodicals listed in the indexes you consulted.)

Older copies of magazines are usually bound in volumes and may be placed on the shelves along with the books, or they may be on microfilm or microfiche. Older newspapers are placed on microfiche and need to be amplified on a screen for viewing. Recent newspapers and magazines are usually in a special periodical room or section.

Reference Works

For articles on your subject other than those in periodicals, you may consult the following types of reference works. They are usually found in the library's reference room.

Encyclopedias

For encyclopedia articles, note the date of the edition you are using. If the edition if an old one, some of the information may be out of date.

GENERAL ENCYCLOPEDIAS

> *Encyclopaedia Britannica*
> *Encyclopedia Americana*
> *Encylopedia International*
> *Collier's Encyclopedia*
> *The World Book*
> *Compton's*

SPECIALIZED ENCYCLOPEDIAS

These are available in such fields as history, literature, philosophy, psychology, music, social sciences, science and technology, banking and finance, music.

Dictionaries

The standard dictionaries are:

> *American Heritage Dictionary*
> *Webster's New World Dictionary*
> *Webster's Collegiate Dictionary*
> *The Random House Dictionary*

There are also dictionaries of usage, slang, synonyms, science and technology, and so on.

Yearbooks

These sources provide easy access to current statistics, historical information on current heads of government, and so on.

> *Information Please Almanac*
> *World Almanac and Book of Facts*
> *Facts on File*
> *Reader's Digest Almanac*

Biography

Among the better known reference works are these:

Contemporary Authors
Current Biography
Dictionary of American Biography
Dictionary of National Biography (British)
Who's Who (British)
Who's Who in America
Who's Who in the World

Reference works on biography are especially useful if you need to get some quick information about the life of a well-known historical person.

Literature

There are many reference works on literature. Some of the standard ones are these:

Cambridge History of American Literature
Cambridge History of English Literature
Oxford Companion to American Literature
Oxford Companion to Classical Literature
Oxford Companion to English Literature

Preparation for the Research Paper

Preliminary Reading

To do your preliminary reading, you might start with some of the articles in the general or specialized encyclopedias, especially if your subject deals with historical events, biography, or scientific or technological developments. Such reading can give you a broad perspective on your subject and help you decide whether you are interested enough to continue working on the topic. Begin your reading well before the paper is due in case you will want to change your subject.

When you have decided on a general subject for your paper, gather many more references than you will need so that you will still have enough in case some turn out to be unavailable or not useful. Write down the name of the author, the title and/or the publication, the date, and any other information that will help you locate the book, including the call number. Using 3 by

5″ cards will make it easier for you to alphabetize the cards later for the bibliography.

For your final list of references, make sure that you have a good distribution of books and articles (if your subject is very current, you may need to rely almost entirely on articles). Use sources that are as up to date as possible. Avoid a heavy reliance on encyclopedia articles; many of these articles may be outdated or too general. Also avoid using sources that you have to translate. You may have trouble putting the source material into proper English.

Preparing the Outline

After you have done some of the preliminary reading, make a list of your ideas on the topic in the order in which they occur to you. Then try to state in one sentence what seems to be the general direction of your thinking on the subject. In this sentence, your thesis sentence, the subject contains the general topic you are writing about; the predicate contains what you say about this topic.

You may find that your thesis sentence will require you to write a very long paper or to treat your subject superficially. If this happens, narrow down the scope of the sentence to the point where you can develop supporting points adequately within the assigned length of the paper.

Once you have your central idea expressed in a thesis sentence, you are ready to prepare a preliminary outline (or a rough draft). The following procedures are useful in setting up the outline based on your central idea.

1. Eliminate from the preliminary outline or draft the points that do not contribute to the central idea. Add others that might strengthen the central idea.
2. Organize minor points under broader headings, making sure that none of the points overlap. At this stage you may need to add even more general headings under which you can put some of the smaller points.
3. Arrange the main points and their subpoints in the most effective order. Some common types of order are by time or space, by logical divisions, or by a progression from less to more important.

To show clearly what your main points and their subpoints are, use the standard outline form you have been using for compositions.

I. (First main point)
  A. (First subpoint)
    1. (Further subdivision)
      a. (Further subdivision)
    2.
  B.
II.

Note that a period is placed after the number or letter and that the first word of all main points and all subdivisions begins with a capital letter.

All the items in the outline can be written either as phrases or as full sentences, but the same form should be followed throughout. Also, there should be at least two items under each subdivision (a single item can be included with the main heading).

In later outlines, some changes can be made. You might want to eliminate or add items, or you might want to modify your thesis.

If, for each point and subpoint in the outline, you add a note about the source of the support, you will have a clear picture of how to develop your paper. You will also see whether you are relying too heavily on one source.

In the final form of your outline, try to consider whether a reader can see clearly how the main points support your thesis. For a short research paper like this one, it is best not to include too many main points and to keep them simple and clear.

Preparing the Outline: An Example

Let us suppose you choose to write a paper on pollution. After your preliminary reading on the general subject, you decide to limit your paper to the various kinds of pollution. Then you might put down the following points in random order:

> Chemical wastes discharged in the water
> Herbicides and pesticides used in agriculture
> Auto emissions
> Sewage
> Smoke from factories and other buildings
> Radioactive waste
> Garbage disposal

As you look for ways of organizing many of these points under broader headings, you find that they can be classified roughly under the headings of air pollution, water pollution, and land pollution.

I.   Air pollution
   A. Auto emissions
   B. Smoke from factories and other buildings
II. Water pollution
   A. Chemical wastes
   B. Sewage
III. Land pollution
   A. Herbicides and pesticides used in agriculture
   B. Radioactive waste
   C. Garbage disposal

This outline gives you an orderly way to present your information.

At this point there are two crucial decisions to make: how much of your general subject to cover, and what your emphasis will be. You can deal exclusively but superficially with all three main points, or you can confine yourself to one or two of them, or even to one in order to cover the subject in some depth. Once you have determined the limits of your subject, you will then have to decide on how you will treat it—that is, what your thesis will be. The emphasis can be on causes, effects, solutions to problem, or some combination of these.

If you consider carefully what your broader headings are, and if you have a definite thesis, it will be easier to make clear transitions in the opening sentences of paragraphs and easier for the reader to follow your line of development or argument.

Further Reading

Once you have set up a tentative outline, you will continue to read for specific support for the points in the outline. In reading a book, check the contents and the index to see what you can use for your paper. Avoid the temptation to read too much, especially if you have a limited amount of time in which to prepare. If you read rather widely, you may write much more than is required, and you may not focus your subject narrowly enough. Also, you may not leave yourself enough time to write the paper.

You will need to use some judgment in evaluating the reliability of each source of information and the amount of weight you will give to it. In checking for reliability, consider these points:

1. *The reputation of the author.* Does the writer's position indicate that he or she is qualified to speak with authority on the subject? Is the writer objective? Keep in mind that a writer's personal bias may lead to deliberate distortion of facts to prove a point.
2. *The reputation of the periodical.* Obviously, information from a scholarly journal will provide more authoritative support than information from a popular magazine.
3. *The date of the book or article.* If the article was written some time ago, the information may be out of date. This is especially true for statistics.

Taking Notes

The recommended procedure for taking notes is to use 3 × 5″ (or 4 × 6″) cards for each bit of information you think you will need. An alternative procedure is to use regular size paper, but to leave enough space between each piece of information so that you can later cut up the paper to separate each note. Using cards or small pieces of paper will make it easier to organize your information.

For each note you take, be sure to put down the number from your outline that the information is to support, a shortened form of the source from which it comes, and the page number. Putting this information down at the notetaking stage will save you a lot of trouble later when you are ready to write. There is nothing more frustrating or time-consuming than trying to remember where you found a fact or an idea.

Since the writing of the research paper is your own work, the notes you take should be in your own words: you should *paraphrase* (restate) or *summarize*. Do not copy down the exact words unless you think the wording is very important for your point and you may want to quote it. Words taken directly from your source of information should be placed within quotation marks *as you are taking notes*, and the source and page number should be labeled clearly in case you actually use the quotation in the paper. Using the exact wording from sources without quotation marks and a citation is considered plagiarism. This is a serious offense in a research paper because you are presenting as your own work passages that have been written by someone else. Teachers usually know when writing is plagiarized because the style is so much more correct and complex than the student's writing. Also, plagiarized material often includes the author's transitional expressions that do not belong with the student's development of his or her ideas.

During the notetaking stage, you may want to photocopy pages for possible later use. Underline, on the photocopy only, what you think you may want to use, with a note in the margin to show where the information belongs in your paper.

Writing the Research Paper

The paper should be typed double spaced on unlined $8\frac{1}{2}''$ × $11''$ white paper. Use $1''$ or $1\frac{1}{4}''$ margins on all four sides. Place the page numbers in the upper right corner, $\frac{1}{2}''$ from the top.

Setting Up the Research Paper

The research paper should include these parts:

> *Title page.* This contains the title, your name, your teacher's name, the number and section of the course, and the date.
> *Outline page(s).* This includes a one-sentence statement of your central idea. This thesis sentence should account for all the main points on your outline.

Text of the research paper. (The numbering of pages begins with page 1 and continues through the bibliography.)

Note page (if notes are used for the information that is not closely related to the text). Footnote numbers are raised slightly and are numbered consecutively. Indent five spaces, then return to the left margin for the second line. Use double space.

Bibliography page(s) (also called *Works Cited* or *References*). Items are arranged in *alphabetical order*, according to the first item, usually the author's last name. Begin at the left margin, then indent five spaces for the second line. Use double space.

In addition, you might want to add an appendix containing a sketch, a diagram, or a chart that will provide clarification of a point or points made in the paper.

Selecting a Title

The title should indicate what your thesis is. For example, if you are researching Mozart's death, your title should not be simply "Mozart," but "Mozart's Death," or even more specifically, "The Mystery of Mozart's Death." Sometimes a thesis can be reflected in a subtitle: "Capital Punishment: The Question of Justification."

Writing from the Outline

One of the first steps in using the outline to write a research paper is deciding which points should be developed through broad generalizations and which should be developed through specific details with intensive support from readings. The more sweeping generalizations are usually made at the beginning. Their purpose is to provide the broader perspective into which you will fit your subject. For example, if you are dealing with a historical event, you might want to summarize some of the events that preceded it. If you are dealing with biography, you should include only those parts of the life that are relevant for your thesis. Avoid the temptation to begin with the person's birth and end with his or her death.

Keep in mind that you need to maintain a sense of proportion. Do not get so involved in the introductory remarks that lead up to your thesis that you have little space left for effective development of the thesis. Most of your paper should be devoted to the points on your outline that support your thesis.

Introductions, Conclusions, and Paragraphing

The following is a recap of the guidelines that have already been given for writing introductions and conclusions and for developing paragraphs.

Introductions

The introduction looks forward to what will be discussed. A good introduction should:

> Give a general idea of what you are going to talk about.
>
> Prepare the reader for the specific subject (the thesis). (Actual details should not be included here but should be held for their proper place in the outline.)
>
> Anticipate the way the thesis will be developed (your organization).
>
> Catch the attention of the reader, possibly through a question that will be answered, an argument that will be refuted, a quotation, or an anecdote.

Sometimes it's best to write your introduction after you have finished the paper, so that any changes or sharpening of your focus can be accounted for.

Conclusions

The conclusion looks back to what has been said in the main part of the paper. A good conclusion should:

> Open up from the narrower focus of the research paper to a broader perspective.
>
> Remind the reader of the thesis of the paper without giving just a summary of the main points.
>
> Be interesting and strong. The conclusion can be expressed as a hope, an opinion, a judgment, an attitude, a solution—possibly using a question or a striking quotation.

Paragraphing

As in most formal papers, the arrangement in each paragraph that supports the thesis will usually be from general to specific. Besides making a smooth transition from the preceding paragraph, the opening sentence of a paragraph should let the reader know which point of the outline is being developed.

The point being made by the opening sentence should be adequately supported by specific details from your readings. The details should be significant, authoritative, and up to date, and they should be clearly related to the point of the paragraph. For each point, you will need to decide which details from your readings can be summarized, which paraphrased, and which should be quoted because of their importance.

A check to see if you are writing clear opening sentences is to rewrite them on a separate sheet of paper and to observe whether they hold together and represent the main points from the outline. This check will also show whether you have used effective transitions.

Because you will be referring frequently to the opinions of others, you will need to make sure that the reader knows when you are actually stating your own opinion by prefacing it by a phrase such as *I believe* or *I feel*. (Except for the most formal doctoral dissertations, there is no need to avoid the use of *I*.)

Cautions

1. Allow yourself enough time for writing the paper. A good writer prepares a first draft and then puts it aside for a while, so that he or she can write the second draft with a fresh eye.
2. Keep a copy of the paper. Occasionally a student's paper is lost or mislaid.

Documentation

Citations, Footnotes, and Quotations

Here we must first draw attention to some recent changes in form and terminology with regard to documenting a research paper. The term *footnote* has been used traditionally for information placed at the bottom (or *foot*) of the page, giving references to sources of information or making additional comments. Such information has also been placed at the end of the paper, with the heading *Endnotes* or *Notes*. Now it is more customary to replace the footnote references with shortened references, called *citations*, inserted in the text itself, and to put only the additional comments on a separate page at the end. This change avoids the earlier repetition of the full references in both the footnotes and the list of books and articles at the end of the paper (the *bibliography*).

Citations

In the kind of tightly documented research paper you are being asked to write, where most of the information comes from reading, you will need to use many citations. Use citations for whatever information you have paraphrased or summarized from sources. Citations are especially necessary for all quoted material, for all facts and figures, and for all authoritative opinion. However, there is no need to cite information that is common knowledge, such as well-known dates (1492) or historical facts (Columbus discovered America).

Citations are placed at the end of the information that comes from your sources, or at the end of the quotation you have used. If the information for a whole paragraph comes from the same source, put the citation at the end of the paragraph.

Notes

Notes, numbered consecutively, are used for information, either your own or from sources, that does not fit logically into the development of the paper and that will be explained further on the notes page.

Information in the notes may consist of a definition or an explanation of a special term, a reference to another source (or to other sources), a reference to an opposing point of view, or a brief explanation of procedures followed in a particular study mentioned in the text of the paper.

Quotations

Quotations are used for what is said uniquely and cannot be restated easily in your own words. Quotations can lend a great deal of authority to your paper if they are used sparingly and chosen wisely. Quotations are not for ornament, but to make your point more convincing. Avoid quoting merely to have a restatement in an author's words of what you have already said. Quotations should be tightly incorporated within the text of your paper.

Information that is quoted should be in the exact words of the author and should have a citation at the end. If you quote only a phrase within a sentence, the phrase should fit into the grammatical structure of your sentence, with the punctuation and capitalization required by the sentence.

Words that have been omitted from the original are indicated by ellipsis points (…) within a sentence; four points (….) are used at the end of a sentence. If more than four typed lines are quoted, they should be indented ten spaces and double spaced, with no quotation marks. A quotation of four lines or less should not be separated from the rest of the paragraph.

When you are using a quotation, it is advisable to identify the author as an authority in the field. For example, you may introduce the quotation as follows:

> Eric Erikson, a well-known psychologist, had found [or revealed, claimed, expressed the view, suggested, stated] that....

If you are quoting from a study, you might introduce the study this way:

> According to a recent study [or a survey, or recent statistics].... Or: A recent study has shown [or revealed, indicated] that....

Documentation Styles

Citations

Citations are incorporated within the text. They appear in parentheses at the end of the information they refer to. They include only enough information to identify the source, usually *the last name of the author(s) and the page number* from a book or article.

Source: From Frank, Marcella. *Modern English: A Practical Reference Guide.* Englewood Cliffs: Prentice, 1972.

Citation: English nouns may be divided into common nouns and proper nouns (Frank 6).

Note that no comma or abbreviation for the word *page* separates the two items in the citation. The period comes after the citation.

If the author is identified in the text, only the page number is given in the citation:

Citation: In her grammar reference book, Marcella Frank explains that nouns may be divided into common nouns and proper nouns (6).

If there is more than one title by an author, a shortened form of the title is included.

For a quotation cited within one of your references, use *qtd. in* before the author of your reference. For an unsigned article in a newspaper or encyclopedia, cite the title (if short) or a shortened form of the title.

Source: From Brooks, Andree. "Repeated Remarriage: A Growing Trend." *The New York Times* 7 Feb. 1985, C1 + .

Citation: Brooks introduces her article with a quotation from Alvin Toffler's *Future Shock:* "Couples will enter into matrimony knowing from the start that the relationship is short-lived. And when the opportunity presents itself, they will marry again...and again...and again." (qtd. in Brooks C1+).

The bibliographic information about the original source may be provided in a numbered footnote.

Notes

The note number in the text should be raised slightly, with no space before it.

Source: From Francis, W. Nelson *The English Language: An Introduction.* New York: Norton, 1965.

Numbered
       note: W. Nelson Francis, a well-known linguist, points out the difference between standard English in the United States and standard English in Great Britain.[4]

Notes are placed in numerical order on a separate page at the end of the text (before the bibliography). The first line is indented five spaces, and the slightly raised number begins each entry, with a space after it.

Note on
Notes page: [4]Francis defines standard English as "that naturally used by more college-educated people who fill positions of social, financial, and professional influence in the community" (246).

GENERAL RULES

The entries in the bibliographical list of references are arranged alphabetically according to the last name of the author. If the bibliography contains two (or more) entries by the same author, use three hyphens (- - -) instead of repeating the name of the author.

A general principle is to begin the entry with a person's name. If you have the name of an author, put that name first; if you have only the name of an editor, put that name first. If you do not have any person's name, start the entry with the second item (do not consider articles like *a* or *the* in alphabetizing).

GENERAL ORDER OF BIBLIOGRAPHIC ITEMS

Author [last name first].[1] "Title of Article." *Title of Publication* [book, magazine, newspaper, encyclopedia]. Facts of Publication [the name of the publisher is often shortened].

Use periods and two spaces to separate the main items in each entry and use a period at the end of the entry. Beginning with the second line, indent five spaces.

---

[1]Information in square brackets represents an author's side remarks to the reader; the information is not part of the regular text.

Any additional information is given *after the title of the* publication:

> edition (abbreviated *ed.*)
> edited by (abbreviated *ed.*)
> translator (abbreviated *trans.*)
> volume: use Arabic numerals, without the abbreviation *vol.*)
> name of series: not underlined
> date of a hardcover edition, if a paperback reprint is used.

SPECIFIC RULES, BY TYPE OF PUBLICATION

Books

> Author. *Title of Book: Subtitle.* [any other information.] City: Publisher, Date [last copyright date].

If several cities are listed, give only the first one. The copyright date is usually on the back of the title page. Use the most recent date.

> Becker, Carl. *Modern Democracy.* New Haven, Yale UP, 1941.

For more than one author, only the name of the first author is reversed.

> Leggett, Glen, C. David Mead, and Melinda Kramer. *Prentice-Hall Handbook for Writers.* 9th ed. Englewood Cliffs: Prentice, 1985.

For more than three authors, *et al.* (meaning *and others*) is used after the first name.

For a *paperback reprint*, add the data of the original publication after the title.

> Toffler, Alvin. *The Third Wave.* 1980. New York: Bantam, 1981.

The name of the original publisher is usually not necessary, but it may be given in a numbered footnote.

Articles from a Book (Anthology)

Include the page numbers of the entire article.

> Rodriguez, Richard. "Aria: A Memoir of a Bilingual Childhood." *The Bedford Reader.* Ed. X. J. Kennedy and Dorothy M. Kennedy. New York: St. Martin's, 1987. 539–552.

Periodical Articles

Abbreviate the names of the months. Use the first three letters of the name (Apr., Oct.) except for September (Sept). Write out the four letter names (May, June, July).

Here is a *magazine* example:

Kramer, Jane. "Letter from Europe." *New Yorker* 26 Nov. 1984: 122–37.

Here is a *scholarly journal* example:

Clark, Herbert H., and Thomas H. Carlson. "Hearers and Speech Acts." *Language* 58 (1982): 332–73.

For *newspaper* articles, list the author (if known), then the title of the article. If there is no author, alphabetize by first word of title (excluding articles *a* and *the*).

Lewis, Paul. "Common Market to Discuss Entry of New Members." *The New York Times* 3 Dec. 1984, sec. A:1+ .

Encyclopedia Articles

List by author (if known); if not, by the title of the article. The volume or page number of an encyclopedia article is not necessary, but the year of the edition as well as the title of the article must be included.

"American Indian Languages." *New Columbia Encyclopedia.* 1975 ed.

Interviews, Speeches

If you use personal interviews or professors' lectures as sources of information, the following form may be used.

Name of person(s). Personal Interview. Date.
Name of professor. Lecture. Date.

PUNCTUATION OF INDIVIDUAL ITEMS

Underlining. For names of publications (books, magazines, journals, newspapers, pamphlets); also for the names of all performances (plays, radio and TV programs, operas, ballets).

Quotation marks. For divisions within publications (articles, chapters, poems). Quotation marks are not used for a title standing alone on a title page or at the top of the first page of a research paper.

Capitalization within titles. The first word and all other words except articles and short prepositions and conjunctions begin with a capital letter. Do not use the style of capitalization found in catalogs and indexes, where only the first word of the title of a book or article is capitalized.

ABBREVIATIONS

et al.	=	and others. Used when there are more than three authors; name only the first author.
col.	=	column (especially for newspapers)
ed.	=	editor, edited (by), edition
n.d.	=	no date
rev.	=	revised or revision
trans.	=	translator, or translated (by)
vol., vols.	=	volume, volumes

American Psychological Association (APA) Style of Documentation for Research Papers

The form given in this book for the research paper is the Modern Language Association (MLA) style generally used in the humanities, which includes language and literature. It is therefore the style taught in classes for which this book is intended. For the social, physical, and biological sciences, for business, and for education, a slightly different form of documentation may be used, that of the American Psychological Association (APA). The examples that follow point out some of the differences in style between the two.

Citations

MLA (author page):   ...(Sohner and Martin 77).
APA (author, year):   ...(Sohner, & Martin, 1980).

Note the use of the ampersand (&) with a comma before it.

The page number is added for a quotation, a paraphrase, a figure, a table. The number is preceded by a comma and "p." for one page or "pp." for more than one page:

...(Sohner, & Martin, 1980, p. 77).

Bibliography

> MLA: *Works Cited*
>
> APA: *References* or *Reference List*

BOOKS

> MLA: Sohner, Charles P. and Helen P. Martin. *American Government and Politics Today.* 3rd ed. Glenview, Ill.: Scott, Foresman, 1980.
>
> APA: Sohner, C. P., & Martin, H. P. (1980). *American government and politics today* (3rd ed.). Glenview, Ill.: Scott, Foresman.

Note these differences from the MLA style:

1. The use of initials only for first names for all authors.
2. The use of the ampersand (&) instead of and (preceded by a comma).
3. The reversal of order in the name of the second author (in this style, all names of authors are reversed).
4. The placement of the date in parentheses after the author(s) name(s).
5. The lowercase letters that begin every word in the title except the first word or proper names (a capital letter also begins the first word of a subtitle).
6. The use of parentheses for the edition.

In both styles, if the city of publication is not well known, the state or the country is included in abbreviated form.

In APA style, the names of organizations and university presses are spelled out in full—National Education Association, Yale University Press.

ARTICLES

For both styles, include the page numbers of the entire article.
When citing from a *book:*

> MLA: Rodriguez, Richard. "Aria: A Memoir of a Bilingual childhood." *The Bedford Reader.* Ed. X. J. Kennedy and Dorothy M. Kennedy. New York: St. Martin's, 1982. 522–544.
>
> APA: Rodriguez, R. (1982). Aria: A memoir of a bilingual childhood. In X. J. Kennedy & D. M. Kennedy (Eds.), *The Bedford Reader* (pp. 522–544). New York: St. Martin's.

For the book in APA style, note that:

1. *In* begins the entry.
2. The editors' names are given first, with no reversal, followed by (Eds.).
3. The page numbers are placed within parentheses after the name of the book.

When citing from a *magazine:*

MLA: Kantrowitz, Barbara. "The Parental Leave Debate." *Newsweek* 17 Feb. 1986: 74.

APA: Kantrowitz, B. (1986, February 17). The parental leave debate. *Newsweek*, p. 74.

Note these further differences between the two styles:

1. For the date, the year is given first, followed by the month, spelled out in full, and the day (if there is one).
2. No quotation marks are used around the name of the article.

When citing from a *journal:*

MLA: Clark, Herbett H., and Thomas H. Carlson. "Hearers and Speech Acts." *Language* 58 (1982): 332–73.

APA: Clark, H. H., & Carlson, T. H. (1982). Hearers and speech acts. *Language, 58*, 332–73.

When citing from a *newspaper:*

MLA: Salmans, Sandra. "Why TV Audiences Love to Play Games." *New York Times* 28 Apr. 1985, Sect. 2, p. 1+ .

APA: Salmans, S. (1985, April 28). Why TV audiences love to play games. *New York Times*, pp. 1, 25.

Sample Research Paper

The following is an example of a research paper written by a student using MLA documentation.

The Republican Campaign of 1984

Arisa Yoshida

Uses of Language 1

Professor: Dr. Marcella Frank

April 13, 1988

Outline

Thesis: The Republicans thoroughly capitalized on television in their 1984 "image campaign."

Introduction: The 1984 television-oriented presidential campaign

  I. Reagan's strength

    A. The favorable political and economic environment

    B. His personal advantages

 II. How Reagan overcame his disadvantages

    A. Some disadvantages he started with

    B. His breakthrough from these disadvantages

III. The Republican "image" campaign

    A. The disappearing issues

    B. The "image-over-substance" strategy

    C. The steps to victory

 IV. Television's role in the Republican strategy

    A. The "mood and image" television commercials

    B. The staging of campaign stops for the evening news

    C. The persuasive influence of television pictures

    Conclusion: The Republican campaign pointed toward the campaign strategies of the future.

Arisa Yoshida 1

On the cover of <u>Time</u> of October 22, 1984 there was a cartoon of Reagan, Mondale, Bush, and Ferraro as jockeys riding horses with television cameras for heads. This cartoon pointed up the essential character of the 1984 United States presidential campaign, a televised horse race. Many critics have claimed that the 1984 election campaign was a television-oriented image campaign in which the candidates did not fully confront each other despite their fundamental differences on issues. From this point of view, television news, with its gift for dramatic fragments of reality, changed the campaign into a popularity contest which consequently favored the president, who had been a professional actor. Is this true? If so, what strong advantages did Reagan have for his historic landslide victory, gaining 49 out of 50 states and the District of Columbia? How did the Republicans capitalize on television in their strategy?

In examining what happened in the Republican campaign, we must start with the Great Communicator, Ronald Reagan. As we look back, 1984 was unquestionably Reagan's year. From the beginning of the year he enjoyed the advantage of an incumbent running at a time of peace and buoyant economy after the serious recession in 1982, with low inflation, rising incomes and employment, all of which supported his popularity throughout the campaign and never disappeared until the day of the election.[1] The incumbency also guaranteed Reagan longer exposure on television as a strong leader and saved time and money for the primary battles while the Democrats continued to bitterly wound each other. The Democratic choice of their candidate also benefited Reagan. Walter Mondale, who had been the vice president in the Carter administration, was the easiest Democratic candidate to link with what Reagan incessantly portrayed as the failed Democratic policies of the past.

In addition to this favorable political and economic environment, Reagan had the ability of marvelous stage management on television. As Elizabeth Drew explains in her book <u>Campaign Journal,</u> he was a master performer adept at "making his case in his television speeches" and at "posing a rhetorical question that made it seem that only a fool could disagree with him" (573). Moreover, partly thanks to this excellent self-presentation, the polls showed the Reagan's score on leadership was consistently high even throughout the recession in 1980-81. According to the data of the Center for Political Studies, people sometimes seemed to be charmed when Reagan acted decisively regardless of what action he took.[2]

His amiable, photogenic looks and likability also became his political advantages;[3] his radio

trained voice was "among his most effective weapons" (Blumenthal 13). As one of his managers

boastingly said, it seemed true to some extent that "people like and trust him [Reagan], and

everything else is irrelevant..." (Defrank and Clift 20). Reagan's favorite rating, which was

about 60% throughout the campaign, was always higher than that accorded his policies. People

liked him regardless of his policies because, by repeatedly saying "America is back, standing

tall," he reminded them of the old America of strength, safety and pride.[4]

The outcome did not seem so inevitable at the start of the year, though. The Republicans

worried that many more voters identified themselves as Democrats (assumed to be 53% of the

electorate) than as Republicans (35%) (Drew 288). The hard-core anti-Reagan group was

concentrated in the biggest states ("Reagan's strategy...." 34). Other worries were in terms

of issues. The budget deficit had mounted to nearly $200 billion, three times as huge as that

of the Carter administration. And the polls showed a marked increase in the number of voters

who were anxious about the nuclear-arms race largely because of the cold relations with the

Soviet Union (Church 17).

Ironically, Mondale's announcement that he was going to raise taxes to solve the problem

of the budget deficit helped Reagan enormously. All Reagan had to do was to stress the fact that

his tax-cutting policies were already resulting in natural economic growth that would offset

the deficit. Over-optimistic as this claim might be, Reagan could label himself as a tax cutter

and Mondale as a tax raiser. In order to neutralize the old anxiety about his hawk image, Reagan

gradually toned down his right wing policies and came close to the political center. And even

the Soviet Union, which Reagan had called an "evil empire" through most of his political

career before the campaign, contributed to his cause by sending their foreign minister, Andrei

Gromyko, to meet with him, thus silencing the Democrats who had blamed him for being the first

president since Hoover not to have met with a Soviet leader.

In the 1984 campaign, issues strangely dropped out of sight. For the most part the

campaign was "a strange presidential race, peculiarly disengaged, almost disembodied"

(Morrow 30). Except for the debates there were few confrontations of the candidates. Evan

Thomas suggested in Time of November 5, 1984, that compared with Reagan, "an evangelical

politician" who always "talked long on parable but low on supporting evidence," Mondale seemed to have more support on the issues (20). But few listened to Mondale because, unlike

Reagan, he could not dramatize his presentation. Many critics noted that Mondale's problem was

not his message but his manner. By contrast, Reagan's triumph was "one of manner over matter"

(Blumenthal 13). Reagan, in fact, did not have to respond to Mondale. He did not even outline

clearly what he would do in his second term.

This policy is exactly what the Republicans intended. Reagan preferred hitting broad

themes to picking over details, and he was poor at extemporaneous discussion (Drew 175). To

exploit all assets and avoid all weaknesses of the president, therefore, the Republicans'

"image-over-substance" strategy in 1984 stressed broad themes over specific issues and the

party abandoned press conferences after the convention. Elizabeth Drew stated that the

Republicans' first strategy was "to have Reagan be 'Presidential' as long as possible"

because being nonpolitical was the best political strategy to keep making pictures on

television screens that touched the people's hearts (289-290). Based on this policy, Reagan

successfully played the role of a bipartisan and national statesman, making the trip to Red

China, participating in the summit in London and getting a political boost even from the

Olympics.

Throughout the 1984 campaign, the Republican strategy worked well. For example, while

developing public interest in the candidacy of the president, the Republicans picked up the

best timing to launch the re-election campaign at the end of January, just after the release of

the polls unanimously showing the overwhelming popularity of the president and after the

release of figures indicating sound economic growth. Reagan made a "bravura performance" at

the State of the Union Speech, and the final declaration of his candidacy was dramatized as

well. He came on "live on all three networks from the Oval Office in Washington at 10:55 p.m.

Sunday, a moment carefully chosen to put him on-screen at the end of prime time in the East and

the beginning of it on the Pacific coast" (Church 16). In March, Tuesday Team Inc., a Madison

Avenue advertising agency, was formed to tout Reagan's record and polish his media

manipulation. From the beginning, the campaign staff knew that, for a candidate like Reagan,

television was the most powerful political weapon as a forum for the image strategy of his

campaign.

In 1984 the Republicans, with the advice of Tuesday Team Inc., abandoned nearly all

Arisa Yoshida 4

aspects of the issue-oriented political commercials and ran "the most effective 'mood and image' commercials ever seen in a presidential campaign" (Blume 9). Reagan narrated most of his ads, in which he fostered nostalgia (Blumenthal 12). These bright commercials playing up feelings of patriotism and prosperity made a sharp contrast to Mondale's political commercials focusing on the serious issue, the deficit.[5] Standing alone, these commercials may have had a limited impact. But in 1984, as Blume pointed out, the Republicans seemed to "succeed in communicating the same 'message' through television evening news" (9).

All campaign stops were carefully coordinated to reinforce the images of the commercials. James Kelly in his article "Packaging the Presidency" in Time portrayed how skillfully the Republicans planned a scenario for Reagan on television news:

> Bedecked stage set between sunny crowds and smiling skies, . . . Reagan,
> standing against a blue backdrop and delivering in patented style. . . . Cut to
> the faces of his listeners, some aglow in admiration. . . . A band bursts into
> melody, balloons sail heavenward, and cheers erupt from a thousand throats
> (36).

Their staging worked so well that viewers often had trouble distinguishing the paid political commercials from the evening news. As Tom Collins pointed out in the Seattle Times, Reagan's campaign clips on the evening news were in a sense superior to commercials because they had "the verisimilitude of reality" (8). The presentation of the president through both commercials and news was so meticulously staged that television evening news looked like free political commercials.

From the networks' point of view, television did not consciously cause one candidate to triumph and another to fail, and sometimes the reporters on the screen made critical comments on the visual image strategy of blurring out issues. But according to some researchers, voters developed strong opinions about candidates "simply by watching them on television without hearing what they were saying" (Leo 37). When people do not hear the candidate, why is it expected that they will hear the reporters who are always attempting to cram in so much in a short time? As Blume analyzes, "In reports measured in seconds on the nightly news, if the image is powerful enough, it will be more convincing" than any narration (193). And the Republican strategists had learned very well how to take advantage of modern media opportunities. Their approach was to make Reagan visual but not vulnerable and to shield him from cross-examination while presenting him in an array of skillfully staged scenarios that were irresistible to the camera. The only thing that counted was getting such positive pictures. In fact television cameras were always after Reagan because he made good pictures.

In hindsight, according to Burnham in <u>Democracy in the Making,</u> Reagan's landslide had been preordained from the beginning (310). On the one hand, the Americans expressed satisfaction with what seemed to be a successful presidency in terms of economic growth and the nation's strength and pride. In short, they saw "no reason to change" (Mashek 24). On the other hand, thanks to Reagan's skill as a "performer," the Republican party created the most successful "image building" campaign on television, in which television itself became the crucial electoral process. The 1984 Republican campaign pointed the way toward the campaign strategies of the future.

Arisa Yoshida 6

Notes

[1]Whether Reaganomics really boosted the economy is another question. On Oct. 22, 1984, The New Republic argued in its editorial "Mondale for President" (7–12) that in fact the economic recovery had nothing to do with Reagan's policies.

[2]For further information, see "Not by Issues Alone" (Leo 37).

[3]For the media's preference for photogenic politicians, refer to the section on "The Media as Kingmakers" (Burnham 233–236).

[4]Bruce Bawer pointed out in his essay "Ronald Reagan as Indiana Jones [the film hero]" in Newsweek of Aug. 27, 1984, that many ordinary Americans appeared willing and eager to respond to such upbeat heroic images (14).

[5]For a more detailed analysis of the effect of Reagan's "image" commercials on television, see "The Reagan Millennium" (Blumenthal 12).

Arisa Yoshida 7

Works Cited

Blume, Keith. The Presidential Election Show. South Hadley, Mass.: Bergin & Garvey, 1985.

Blumenthal, Sidney. "The Reagan Millennium." The New Republic 19 Nov. 1984: 12–14.

Burnham, Walter Dean. Democracy in the Making 2nd ed. Englewood Cliffs: Prentice-Hall, 1986.

Church, George J. "There He Goes Again." Time 6 Feb. 1984: 16–20.

Collins, Tom. Seattle Times 19 Nov. 1984: 8.

Defrank, Thomas M., and Eleanor Clift. "Ronald Reagan's Magic." Newsweek 6 Feb. 1984: 20–
        24.

Drew, Elizabeth. Campaign Journal: Political Events of 1983–1984. New York: Macmillan,
        1985.

Kelly, James. "Packaging the Presidency." Time 12 Nov. 1984: 36.

Leo, John. "Not by Issues Alone." Time 12 Nov. 1984: 37.

Mashek, John W. "Reagan by a Mile." U.S. News & World Report 5 Nov. 1984: 24–26.

Morrow, Lance. "To the Polls at Last." Time 12 Nov. 1984: 30–32.

"Reagan's Strategy for a Tough Campaign." Business Week 13 Feb. 1984: 34–35.

Thomas, Evan. "The Goal: A Landslide." Time 5 Nov. 1984: 18–20.

APPENDIX A

Grammar and Usage

Sentence Structure

Independent (Coordinate) Clauses

Two sentences may be connected by a coordinate conjunction or a conjunctive verb.

Meaning	Coordinate Conjunction	Conjunctive Adverb*
addition	, and	; moreover(,)
result	, so	; therefore(,)
contrast	, but	; however(,)

*Synonyms for conjunctive adverbs expressing these relationships are: *in addition, for this reason, that's why, as a result, nevertheless, on the contrary.* Conjunctive adverbs expressing some other relationships are: *for example, that is, in other words, in fact, in short, meanwhile.*

Some of the explanations in this appendix are from Marcella Frank, *Modern English: Exercises for Non-Native Speakers, Part II: Sentences and Complex Structures,* 2nd ed. (Englewood Cliffs, N.J.: Prentice-Hall, 1986). Reprinted by permission.

Note that:

(1) A comma is used before a coordinate conjunction, especially if both parts of the sentence are long.

(2) A semicolon is used before a conjunctive adverb. A comma may also be used after the conjunctive adverb.

The two sentences with the added connectives may be kept separate with a period, especially if one or both sentences are long.

> *Example:* The train was speeding when the accident occurred. No one was seriously hurt.
> The train was speeding when the accident occurred, but no one was seriously hurt.
> The train was speeding when the accident occurred; however, no one was seriously hurt.

The conjunctive adverb may have other positions in the second independent clause:

> ; no one, however, was seriously hurt.
> , no one was seriously hurt, however. [This position is used only if the clause is short.]

Commas to set off the adverbs in these positions are optional. However, regardless of the position of the adverb, the semicolon remains in the position where the period was.

Exercise

The relationship between each of the following sets of sentences is addition, result, or contrast. Combine each set of sentences by using (1) a coordinate conjunction, and (2) a conjunctive adverb. See whether each conjunctive adverb can be moved.

> *Examples:* The pressure at work kept increasing.
> She decided to quit her job.
> The pressure at work kept increasing, so she decided to quit her job.
> The pressure at work kept increasing; therefore, she decided to quit her job. [or ; she therefore decided to quit her job.]
> This job requires hard work.
> You will also need to travel a lot. [omit *also*]
> This job requires hard work, and you will need to travel a lot.
> This job requires hard work; moreover, you will need to travel a lot. [or ; you will need, moreover, to travel a lot.]

1. She went to bed early.
   It took hours for her to fall asleep.
2. She wants to lose weight.
   She has gone on a strict diet.
3. The night air was very still.
   A light rain had also begun to fall. [omit *also*]
4. Her friend did her best to learn to cook.
   Nothing she prepared came out right.
5. Our team learned that the train would be very late.
   We decided to take the plane.
6. The girl can sing very well.
   She is also a talented actress. [omit *also*]
7. Their basement was damaged by the flood.
   They can't afford to fix it now.
8. My boss wants to live like a millionaire.
   He bought an expensive mansion in an exclusive area.
9. Their army lost the last few battles.
   They kept on fighting.
10. Capital punishment is often applied unfairly.
    A mistake is sometimes also made. [omit *also*]
11. The boy has been absent from class many times.
    The principal called him to his office for an explanation.

Dependent Subordinate Clauses

Dependent clauses contain subjects and predicates with full verbs. These clauses function as adverbs, nouns, and adjectives.

Adverbial Clauses

Adverbial clauses are introduced by subordinate conjunctions and *must be attached to the rest of the sentence.* The following are the most common introductory subordinate conjunctions:

Meaning	*Conjunctions*
cause	because, since, as
contrast	although, even though, though; while, whereas
condition	if, unless (= if...not), whether (for two choices), even if
time	before, after, when, until, since, while

Like adverbs, adverbial clauses may appear in initial position (at the beginning of the sentence), in final position (at the end of the sentence), or, less commonly, in midposition (between the subject and the verb of the sentence). Commas are more likely to be used with adverbial clauses at the beginning of a sentence, especially if the clause is long, than at the end.

Exercise

Combine each set of sentences so that *one of the sentences* becomes an *adverbial clause* beginning with one of the subordinate conjunctions. Make whatever changes are necessary, but preserve the logical relationship between each set of sentences.

Note: Some of the relationship expressions at the beginning of the second sentence will be replaced by the conjunction starting the adverbial clause. Also, not all subordinate conjunctions work equally well in some sentences, nor do all the adverbial positions.

Examples: They have a lot of money.
However, they give almost nothing to charity.
   Although [even though, though] they have a lot of money, they give almost nothing to charity. [or the clause may be at the end]

They'd better get here soon.
Otherwise they'll miss the plane.
   If they don't get [or Unless they get] here soon, they'll miss the plane. [or the clause may be at the end]

She made some good investments in the stock market.
She decided to retire early.
   Because [since, as] she made some good investments in the stock market, she decided to retire early. [or the clause may be at the end]

1. He disliked mathematics.
   But he decided to take a course in statistics.
2. We must pay our taxes.
   If we don't, we'll be fined by the government.
3. The doctor won the respect of all his patients.
   He was sincerely dedicated to his profession.
4. Their new house is being built.
   During this time, they are living at a hotel nearby.
5. The children were enjoying their outdoor picnic.
   A sudden downpour forced them indoors.
6. Their old car was starting to give them a lot of trouble.
   They decided to buy a new one.

7. Television appeared in people's homes in the fifties.
   Up to this time, the radio had been the chief source of home entertainment.
8. The city would like to complete the new subway.
   But it has run out of money for the project.
9. They had to take a passenger off the plane.
   She suddenly became very ill.
10. The family was decorating the Christmas tree.
    The fire alarm went off.
11. He got a new pair of eyeglasses.
    Already he has been able to see much better.
12. A lot of money has been spent on remodeling that old building.
    It still looks ugly.
13. Some people spend their leisure time reading books.
    Others prefer to watch television.
14. First he removed the old paint from the table.
    Then he painted it a bright red.
15. The defendant should have told the truth.
    If he had, he would have received a lighter sentence.
16. The house must be very quiet.
    Only then can he concentrate. [Note the reversal of word order after *only.*]
17. The soprano was singing a beautiful aria at the opera.
    Her tired companion was sleeping soundly.
18. Their long report will be finished in a few days.
    Even so, the report will be too late for the meeting.
19. The story may be true or it may be a false rumor.
    In any case, she caused great harm by repeating it.

Adjective Clauses

Adjective (or relative) clauses modify nouns or pronouns that precede them. These clauses are introduced by different relative pronouns or adverbs according to the noun that is being modified.

Noun Being Modified (antecedent)	Relative Pronoun, Adverb	Examples

a person	*who-whom-whose, that*
	    as subject:
	
	    as object of the verb:
		The man *who* [or *that*] *wants to see you* is over there.
		The man *whom* [or *who,* or *that,* or ——] *you want to see* is over there.

	as object of the preposition:	The man *to whom you were just speaking* is a scientist. or The man *whom* [or *who,* or *that,* or ——] *you were just speaking to* is a scientist.

a thing	*which, that*
	  as subject:
	
	  as object of the verb:
	
	  as object of the preposition:
		They enjoy movies *which* [or *that*] *have a happy ending.*
		The movie *which* [or *that,* or ——] *they are watching* has a happy ending.
		
		The movie *in which she is starring* has a happy ending.
		or
		The movie *which* [or *that,* or ——] *she is starring in* has a hapy ending.

a place	*where,* (also *in, on which*)	The school *where he is studying* is expensive.
a time	*when,* (also *on, at, in which*)	He is looking forward to the time *when he will graduate.*

If the adjective clause is not needed to identify the noun (the noun is already named), or to single out one (or some) from others, commas are placed around the clause. *That* cannot be used in nonrestrictive clauses that are set off by commas.

Examples:

restrictive clause:	A teenager *who* [or *that*] *had come to this country recently* won the science award.
nonrestrictive clause:	My friend Philip, *who had come to this country recently,* won the science award.

Exercise

Change the *second sentence* in each group into an *adjective clause* modifying the italicized noun(s) in the first sentence. The clause must come directly after its noun. Use commas around the clauses that do not identify or restrict their nouns.

> *Examples:* The *Mona Lisa* is in the Louvre in Paris.
> It was painted by Da Vinci.
>> The Mona Lisa, which was painted by Da Vinci, is in the Louvre in Paris.
>
> *The child* was found unharmed.
> The police were looking for her.
>> The child whom [who, that, ——] the police were looking for was found unharmed.

1. They returned *the lawnmower* to their neighbors.
   They had borrowed it.
2. *The country* will be decided on soon.
   The meeting will be held in this country.
3. *The song* has become very popular.
   He wrote that song.
4. *The World Trade Center* consists of two skyscrapers.
   It is located in New York City.
5. *The music* is the theme song of our new play.
   You are listening to it.
6. *The children* were delighted by the antics of the clown.
   Most of the children had never been to a circus.
7. He has already spent *all the money*.
   He inherited this money.
8. *Celia* has made her parents very angry.
   She has been coming home late many nights.
9. They are renovating *the apartment building*.
   The Johnsons live in this apartment building.
10. *Brazil* is famous for its carnival celebrations.
    They live in Brazil now.
11. No one is certain of *the exact day*.
    The revolution began on this day.
12. *Alice* is now recovering nicely.
    Her arm was hurt in an accident.

Noun Clauses

The types of noun clauses are shown in the chart below, along with the words that introduce these clauses.

Note that no commas are used with noun clause subjects or objects. Note also that noun clauses follow normal word order (subject-verb-object) rather than question order.

Noun Clause Derived from:	Introductory Conjuction	Function of Clause	Examples
a statement **Coffee grows in Brazil.**	**that**	subject subject after **it** subjective complement object of verb appositive	**That* coffee grows in Brazil** is well known to all. It is well known **that coffee grows in Brazil.** [less formal] My understanding is **that coffee grows in Brazil.** I know **that coffee grows in Brazil.** His belief **that coffee grows in Brazil** is correct.
a question expecting a *yes* or *no* answer **Will he get the money?**	**whether** (*or* **not**)**, if**	subject subjective complement object of verb object of preposition subject	**Whether (or not) he gets the money** doesn't concern me. **The question** is **whether he will get the money.** Do you know **whether** (*or* **if**) **he will get the money?** We were concerned about **whether he would get the money.** **How he gets the money** is his own affair.
interrogative word question **How will he get the money?**	*who, whoever, what, which, when, where, why, how*	subjective complement object of verb object of preposition	The question is **how he will get the money.** I don't know **how he will get the money.** We were concerned about **how he would get the money.**
a request **Write the letter soon.**	**that**	object of verb	He suggested **that I write the letter soon.**
an exclamation **What a pretty girl she is!**	**what how**	object of verb object of preposition	I hadn't realized **what a pretty girl she was.** We talked about **what a pretty girl she was.**

*The use of **the fact that** (rather than **that**) to introduce a noun clause subject emphasizes the factual nature of the subject.

Exercise

Combine the following sets of sentences so that the word *this* in one sentence is replaced by a *noun clause* made from the other sentence. (Observe the sequence of tenses: a past main verb usually requires a past form in the noun clause unless the noun clause is making a general statement.)

Examples: This was obvious to the scientists.
Progress was being made in their experiment.
That progress was being made in their experiment was obvious to the scientists.

or

It was obvious to the scientists that progress...in their experiment.

The manager asked the customer *this*.
How long have you been waiting?
The manager asked the customer how long she had been waiting. [sequence of tenses]

1. Will they give the dance or not?
   This was still uncertain.
2. She didn't notice *this*.
   She lost an earring.
3. The company didn't know this.
   Who made the terrible mistake?
4. Who stole the money?
   This person is a clever thief.
5. The management requests *this*.*
   All parcels must be checked.
6. The firefighters are amazed at *this*.
   How quickly the fire spread!
7. I don't know *this*.*
   Should I accept the invitation or not?
8. She inquired about *this*.
   Where is the library?
9. The deliveryman asked *this*.*
   Where should I deliver the merchandise?
10. The dentist asked me *this*.
    Which tooth is hurting me?
11. I didn't know *this*.*
    How can I correct the error?
12. The customer asked the salesclerk *this*.
    What time does the store close?

---

*These noun clauses can also have an infinitive structure: I don't know *whether to accept the invitation.*

Adverbial, Adjectival, and Nominal (Noun) Structures

Adverbial Structures

Adverbial structures have the same function as adverbs. However, they are more likely to modify verbs or the whole sentence than to modify adjectives or adverbs.

Exercise

Combine each set of sentences in as many ways as you can to produce adverbials. Make whatever changes are necessary (including additions or omissions), but preserve the logical relationship between the sentences. Note the possible position of the adverbials. Be careful of the punctuation.

Examples:	The room was long. They had plenty of wall space for pictures.	
	adverbial clause:	*Because the room was long,* they had.... [or the clause may be at the end of the sentence]
	prepositional phrase:	*Because of the great length of the room,* they had.... [or the phrase may be at the end of the sentence] Note the use of *great* for *very.*
	absolute construction:	*The room being very long,* they had....
	They are very wealthy now. They still live very modestly.	
	adverbial clause:	*Although they are very wealthy, they....*
	prepositional phrase:	*In spite of their great wealth, they....*

1. The road was icy.
   Some people had car accidents.
2. It was very dangerous.
   He rescued the child from the burning house.
3. The actress was very talented.
   She became a star very soon.
4. She was preparing dinner.
   At the same time she kept an eye on the children playing outside.
5. Stop smoking so much.
   You may get lung cancer.

6. It was raining heavily.
   The driver could barely see the road.
7. There was a lack of food during the war.
   People didn't complain.
8. He was driving along a dark road.
   A deer ran out in front of his car.
9. The company promised to hire the laid off workers soon.
   The company never did rehire them.
10. The government threatened to arrest all the demonstrators.
    They didn't follow through on the threat.
11. I might receive an overseas telephone call.
    In this case, transfer the call to me right away.
12. Some people like to eat meat.
    Other people are vegetarians.
13. First she washed the kitchen floor.
    Then she put a coat of wax on it.
14. It might rain.
    In this case, the picnic will be postponed.
15. They may come to the meeting or they may not.
    In either case, we'll start the meeting on time.

Adjectival Structures

Adjectival structures have the same function as adjectives: they modify nouns or pronouns.

Exercise

Change the sentences in parentheses into adjective structures that modify the italicized nouns before them. See which structures can be moved to the beginning of the sentence. Be careful of the punctuation. Use commas with an adjective structure that does not identify or limit further the noun it modifies.

> *Examples:*   The lamp (the lamp is standing on the table) is expensive.
> adjective clause: The lamp (*which* or *that*) *is standing on the table* is expensive.
> participial phrase: The lamp *standing on the table* is expensive.
> prepositional phrase: The lamp *on the table* is expensive.

1. *The people* (they live in this building) are complaining about the poor maintenance.
2. *Celia* (she was running to catch the bus) fell and hurt herself.

3. *The prisoners* (they were being held for political reasons) were released in a general amnesty.
4. *Our chairman* (he had eaten too much for lunch) almost fell asleep at the meeting.
5. *My best friend* (he had won a lot of money in the lottery) invited all his friends to a big celebration.
6. *The performance* (it was given yesterday) was brilliant.
7. *His youngest sister* (she is now in college) wants to become a physicist.
8. There have been many fires in *the building* (they live in the building).
9. Most of *the things* (the things were to be sold at the church bazaar) were donated by the church members.*
10. *The refugees* (some of them had not eaten for days) were overjoyed when the truckloads of food arrived.
11. *His neighbor* (his car had been stolen) reported the theft to the police.
12. *The monument* (you are looking at it now) is in honor of *those men* (they were killed in the last war).
13. The students are pleased with *their new teacher* (they all respect her).

Nominal Structures

Nominal structures have the same functions as nouns. These structures may be used as subjects, objects of verbs, objects of prepositions, subjective complements, and objective complements.

Exercise

Combine the sentences so that the word *this* is replaced by a *noun structure* formed from the other sentence. Make as many combinations as you can.

Examples:	He solved their legal problems quickly. This was surprising.	
	noun clause:	*That he solved their legal problems quickly* was surprising.
		It was surprising *that he solved their legal problems quickly.*
	gerund phrase:	*His solving their legal problems quickly* was surprising.
	infinitive phrase:	*For him to solve their legal problems quickly* was surprising.
	abstract noun phrase:	*His quick solution to their legal problems* was surprising. [Note that the adverb *quickly* becomes an adjective modifier of the noun.]

*An infinitive beginning with *to be sold* may also be used as an adjectival.

1. The company rejected his proposal.
   This was a great disappointment.
2. The city anticipated *this*.
   They might have trouble with the new subway cars.
3. She avoids all hard work.
   This is obvious.
4. Can you tell me *this*?
   Where is the dean's office?
5. The auto mechanic suggested *this*.
   I should replace all the old tires.
6. We must begin the project at once.
   This is very important.
7. The school is wondering about *this*.
   Should they buy more school buses?
8. The typewriter repairman recommends *this*.
   We should have the typewriters cleaned regularly.
9. He didn't pay his taxes.
   He was fined for *this*.
10. We overlook our faults.
    This is easy to do.
11. People consume too much sugar.
    This is not good for the health [omit *people*]
12. The problem for us is *this*.
    How can we get the president's approval?

Correcting Faults in Usage

Correcting Sentence Faults

Avoid faulty parallelism.

Incorrect: There is a great difference between dining out and to have a snack at home.

Correct: There is a great difference between dining out and having a snack at home.

[Structures joined by *and, or, but,* and sometimes *not* or *than* require the same grammatical form.]

Avoid dangling constructions.

Incorrect: After eating dinner, the table was cleared.

Correct: After eating dinner, she cleared the table. (or) After they ate dinner, she cleared the table.

[An introductory structure that does not have its own subject within it depends on the subject of the main clause for its agent.]

Avoid run-on sentences.

Incorrect: John was sick, he didn't come to school.

Correct: John was sick. He didn't come to school. (or) John was sick; he didn't come to school. (or) John was sick, so he didn't come to school. (or) Because John was sick, he didn't come to school.

[Sentences that are not joined by the coordinate conjunctions (*and, or, nor, but, so, for, yet*) require a semicolon or a period between them.]

Avoid sentence fragments.

Incorrect: She looks almost like her twin sister. The only difference being that she is a little taller.

Correct: She looks almost like her twin sister, the only difference being that she is a little taller. (or) She looks almost like her twin sister. The only difference is that she is a little taller.

[A dependent clause or phrase structure must be attached to the rest of the sentence. Do not cut it off with either a period or a semicolon.]

Exercise

Rewrite the following sentences, correcting faulty parallelism, dangling constructions, run-on sentences, and sentence fragments.

1. Capital punishment should not be legalized because of its immorality, injustice, and it violates our constitutional rights.
2. In visiting a city in Europe, the similarities which you can see are many.
3. Men and women were created equal, therefore women have the same right to work as men do.
4. Some newspapers have no advertising at all. Whereas others carry many advertisements.
5. It is said that equality works only if some changes are made. Changes like having good child-care centers for all economic classes.
6. Another purpose the newspaper should have is to serve the public, the classified ads in the paper help people find jobs and apartments.
7. In comparing my language with English, many differences become apparent.
8. The family's economy was dependent on the young people, moreover the nation's economy was dependent on them too.
9. Security comes from the sense of being needed and usefulness.
10. Youth has become an economic liability. Thus adding new emotional problems to those already present.
11. The sports section in this newspaper is on Monday, the science section is on Tuesday, and there is a food section on Wednesday.
12. The persons who should get capital punishment are murderers, drug dealers, and bank robbers. Because these types of persons are really harmful to society.
13. We should not use capital punishment for crimes such as stealing, kill somebody unintentionally, or do something one is forced to do.
14. In earlier years, most people lived on farms thus youth was needed for economic reasons.
15. Coming from South India, my native language is Tamil.
16. Crime in my country is almost unknown even misdemeanors are rarely heard of.
17. By putting a consonant before each vowel, various syllables begin to take shape.
18. My reasons for going to college are self-improvement, enjoyment, cultural stimulation, and to be prepared to face life.
19. Such situations will cause conflict and arguments. Finally ending with divorce or physical violence.
20. When using a dictionary to check up a word, English follows alphabetical order.
21. The punishment of death is not worse than life imprisonment. Although there is a difference between these two.

Improving Sentences

Avoid excessive or illogical coordination.

Incorrect: The title of this book is *The Scarlet Letter* and it is a story about a woman who commits adultery.

Correct: The Scarlet Letter is a story about a woman who commits adultery.

Avoid unnecessary complexity in grammatical structure.

Incorrect: If you sail a boat, it's fun.

Correct: Sailing a boat is fun.

Incorrect: In this book, it tells about the great improvement in computers.

Correct: This book tells about the great improvement in computers.

Avoid repetition of words that mean the same thing.

Incorrect: The people should be given choices in choosing a representative.

Correct: The people should be given a choice of representatives.

Avoid a shift in tense.

Incorrect: The author urges us to eat a balanced meal. He said that fruit and vegetables gave us the vitamins we needed.

Correct: The author urged us ....

Avoid a shift in pronouns used in general statements.

Incorrect: You never really know what love is until we experience it ourselves.

Correct: We really never know what love is until we experience it ourselves.

Exercise

Improve the following sentences for sentence structure, meaning, or shifts in tense or in pronouns.

1. With the freedom of choosing your own classes, college is our best chance to widen our horizon.
2. English words have one or more syllables, and they are really difficult to pronounce.
3. My native country is India. It has many diverse areas and languages.
4. Although it has been years since my grandmother passed away, but my mother still feels guilty about having a career.
5. As the woman walks toward the store, three strong men jumped out and attacked her.
6. The story is short and there are not many characters. However, the author was able to get his point across very well.
7. The death penalty should be applied all over the world, and it would certainly lessen the rate of crime and violence.
8. From one of the articles in this magazine, it tells how much the television programs encourage violence.
9. Only God alone can decide who will die.
10. According to this study, the author point out that the percentage of women who work after childbirth is increasing.
11. He is very wealthy and has no family except for a niece and she had tried to save his life.
12. Wherever you are, people must establish some rules in order to live. If not, we are going to have anarchy.
13. Swift wrote about the problems in Ireland in his masterpiece of irony which is called "A Modest Proposal."
14. When TV was invented, it was invented for many reasons.
15. Korean has its own alphabet, and there are ten vowels and fourteen consonants.
16. A democratic state is one which is governed by a democratic government consisting of elected representatives.
17. Capital punishment is legal execution by the law.

Subject–Verb Agreement

The form of the verb is singular or plural according to the subject. There are different forms for agreement of the verb only in the present tense, where *-s* is added for the third person singular verb.

> She loves her mother.
> They love their mother.

Irregular third person singular verbs also end in *-s: is, was, has, does.*
The following are specific rules for subject-verb agreement.

The verb agrees with the main word in the subject.	The *material* used for these dresses *is* the best that money can buy.
However, if the main word of the subject expresses a *part* (*some, all, most, half,* etc.), the verb agrees with the noun in a following *of* phrase.	Most of the *machinery has* already arrived. Most of the *machines have* already arrived.
If *each* or *every* is used with the subject, a singular verb must be used.	*Everybody* in the class *has* to write a term paper.
Two nouns joined by *and* take a plural verb.	My aunt and my niece are going to Disneyland.
However, if a preposition like *together with* or *as well as* is used instead of *and,* a singular verb is required in formal usage.	The plant supervisor, as well as the workers, wants greater safety measures to be taken.
A noncountable noun requires a singular verb. Examples of noncountable words are *coffee, gold, mathematics, advice, furniture, equipment, scenery, vocabulary, slang, knowledge.*	The information in this book is very interesting.
A subject whose main word is an *-ing* or *-to* form requires a singular verb.	Writing good letters takes a long time.
A *number* (= *some, many*) takes a plural verb.	A number of students are going home for the holidays.
The number takes a singular verb.	The number of students going home for the holidays is small.

Exercise

Correct the following sentences for subject-verb agreement.

1. There is a number of reasons why I am continuing my education in college.
2. The two most important elements making up democracy is the constitution and the system of government.
3. The contribution of the young people were important in establishing their security.
4. What kinds of crime is considered as deserving capital punishment?
5. Conventional rules about serving and eating food in our country differs from those in the past.
6. Evidence show that capital punishment is applied unfairly.
7. The information gathered about capital punishment are misleading.
8. The isolation of the child from adults have great educational value.
9. Tamil has some special letters which doesn't exist in any language in the world.
10. The majority of the words is spelled according to general rules.
11. Some of the Chinese punctuation are different from those in English.
12. There has been a lot of radical changes in women's social role.
13. Each of the languages have some similarities and some differences.
14. The number of newspapers in the United States have been decreasing.
15. There is no prepositions or articles in my language.
16. French, as well as English, add *-s* for the plural.
17. The Korean's sense of social distinctions have brought about a complete system of honorifics.
18. There has been studies of tribes where the man reared the children.
19. The writing style of the two languages are different.

Verbs: Auxiliaries

Use the correct verb form with auxiliaries:

be + *-ing* (progressive)	She *is* plant*ing* the seeds now.
	She has *been* plant*ing* the seeds all day.
	She will *be* plant*ing* the seeds soon.
be + *-ed* (passive)	The seeds *were* plant*ed* last week.
	The seeds are *being* plant*ed* now.

	The seeds will *be* plant*ed* next week.
	The seeds have already *been* plant*ed*.
have + -*ed* (perfect)	She *has* already plant*ed* the seeds.
	She will *have* plant*ed* the seeds before next week.
do + [no ending] (if there is no auxiliary in the positive statement)	*For questions: Did* she *plant* the seeds?
	For negatives: She *didn't plant* the seeds.
	For substitution: She planted the same kind of seeds as she *did* last year.

will-would
shall-should
can-could } + [no ending]
may-might
must

She *will* [or *should, may, must*] *plant* the seeds soon.

Use the correct form of irregular verbs with auxiliaries.	*Incorrect:* The lesson on verbs was teached yesterday.
	Correct: The lesson on verbs was taught yesterday. [For irregular verbs, the second principal part is the past tense; the third principal part is used with the auxiliary *have* for the perfect tenses, and with the auxiliary *be* for the passive forms.]
Do not omit a required auxiliary with the verb in the predicate.	*Incorrect:* While you walking on the street, you can see many magnificent buildings.
	Correct: While you are walking on the street, you.... [After

some conjunctions of time,
both the subject and the *be*
auxiliary may be omitted:
While *walking* on the street,
you....]

Do not add an auxiliary
incorrectly.

Incorrect: Water is consists of
hydrogen and oxygen.
Correct: Water consists of
hydrogen and oxygen.

Exercise

Correct the following sentences containing errors in verb forms.

1. The nuclear family is compose of only the parents and their children.
2. One block could be fill with rich people but the next block could be fill with very poor people.
3. The evil act of a rapist is deserve the death penalty.
4. Does he really lives a better life?
5. These words have repeated several times in the story.
6. The students have chose their class president.
7. The company is try to increase its production.
8. Many people watching too much television.
9. I needed my father's signature on some documents that required for a passport.
10. The committee has been meet all day.
11. On this holiday in my country, water is throwing on everyone.
12. Some people not care about others.
13. She would has helped her nephew if he had wanted her to.
14. He has wore his new suit only once.
15. The subjects I'm studying now are interest me very much.
16. We have three meals a day which served at regular times.
17. Her husband thinks only a mother supposed to take care of the children.
18. We often serve dinner outdoors, and so does our neighbors.
19. English uses a different writing system than Chinese has.
20. I born in Venezuela.
21. I move to the United States after my mother was died.
22. How much cost this book?
23. Many colloquial expressions have been use in this newspaper.
24. Some people only concerned about themselves and their family.

Verb Tenses

Use the correct tense.

Incorrect: In the past, people have traveled by horse and carriage.

Correct: In the past, people traveled by horse and carriage.

[Present perfect represents time that comes up to the present. It cannot be used with time that is definitely past.]

Incorrect: She writes a letter now.

Correct: She is writing a letter now.

[Use the present progressive for present verbs of action.]

Use the correct past tense forms of irregular verbs.

Incorrect: I seen him yesterday.

Correct: I saw him yesterday.

Use the correct form after *wish.*

Incorrect: They wish they could live in Europe now instead of in the United States.

Correct: They wish they lived....

Incorrect: I'm catching a cold. I wish I didn't go out in the rain yesterday.

Correct: I wish I hadn't gone out in the rain yesterday.

Use the correct verb form for unreal conditional sentences.

Incorrect: He would be very happy if he will pass the test.

Correct: He would be very happy if he passed the test.

Incorrect: He would have passed the test if he studied harder.

Correct: He would have passed the test if he had studied harder.

Use the correct form in future real conditions or time clauses.

Incorrect: When it will stop raining, we'll go for a walk.
Correct: When it stops raining, we'll go for a walk.

Incorrect: If I will go to the post office, I will get you some stamps.
Correct: If I go to the post office, I will get you some stamps.

Use the correct tense in sequence of tenses.

Incorrect: He asked me how long I have been waiting.
Correct: He asked me how long I had been waiting.
[A past main verb usually requires that a following verb, or its auxiliary, also have past form.]

Use the correct form after verbs of urgency like *suggest, recommend,* or after adjectives of urgency like *important, necessary.*

Incorrect: I suggest that you are very careful when you use this machine.
Correct: I suggest that you be very careful when you use this machine.
[After verbs or adjectives of urgency, the present subjunctive—the name of the verb, with no change—is used.]

Exercise

Correct the following sentences containing errors in verb forms.

1. He will not do anything until he will see a lawyer.
2. He pretended that he doesn't understand the question.
3. I wish it would be warmer outside now.
4. It is essential that a guard is on duty at all hours of the day.
5. They begun the construction last week.
6. We recommend that this bill is passed at once.
7. I wish you told me about this earlier.

8. She prepared dinner when a quarrel broke out among the children.
9. He had many difficulties since he came to this country.
10. After I will wash the dishes, let's have a game of cards.
11. We will take the train if the weather will be very bad.
12. I didn't notice whether she is wearing her wedding ring.
13. Now my office is very busy. I wish I took my vacation when I had the chance.
14. If I felt better yesterday, I would have gone shopping.
15. He requested that all the committee members would be on time.
16. Let's go inside. It begins to rain.
17. I wish I knew you when you were a child.
18. If you will see Robert, give him my regards.
19. These days she tries to prepare herself for the medical exam.
20. We just went to bed when the telephone rang.
21. If I knew more French last year, I would have lived in France.
22. It is required that every uniform fits properly.
23. In the past, many marriages have been arranged by matchmakers.
24. Her father teached her how to use the computer.
25. I wish I were with you yesterday.
26. He would help us if he would be here now.
27. It is necessary that everybody takes proper precautions to avoid accidents.
28. The company would have been more successful if they had more efficient management.
29. I was very tired after our hike, so I laid down to rest for a while.

Verbals

Verbs that follow other verbs should be in the correct form: either in *-ing* form or *to* infinitive form. (These verbs are listed before the exercise.)

Incorrect: He stopped to see his friend after a bitter quarrel they had.

Correct: He stopped seeing his friend after a bitter quarrel they had.

Incorrect: The doctor recommended him to take a long vacation.

Correct: The doctor recommended his taking a long vacation.

[The "subject" of the gerund is usually in possessive form: his.]

Verbs that follow prepositions should be in the *-ing* form.

Incorrect: After finish his work, he went to a movie to relax.
Correct: After finishing his work;...
Incorrect: I look forward to see you again.
Correct: I look forward to seeing you again.
[*to* after some verbs or adjectives is a preposition rather than the sign of the infinitive.]

Infinitives without *to* are used after such auxiliaries as *can, must, would rather, had better*.

Incorrect: I would rather to live in the suburbs than right in town.
Correct: I would rather live....

Infinitives without *to* are used after the verbs *make, have,* or *let* (someone *do* something).

Incorrect: His mother made him to do his homework before he could watch television.
Correct: His mother made him do his homework....

A verb modifying a noun before it should be in the correct *-ing* or *-ed* participial form.

Incorrect: A person run for political office has to spend a lot of money on a campaign.
Correct: A person running for political office....
[Another correction: A person who runs for political office....]

Verbs Followed by Infinitives or -ing *Forms (Gerunds)**

Verbs + *-ing* Forms
(*admit **doing** something*)

admit	finish	quit (= stop, *informal*)
anticipate	give up	recommend
appreciate	imagine	regret (*for the past*)[1]
avoid	keep (on)	remember (*for the past*)[2]
consider (= keep in mind)	miss	resent
delay	postpone	resist
deny	practice	risk
enjoy	put off	stop
		suggest

Verbs + either the infinitive or the *-ing* Forms
(*attempt **to do** or **doing** something*)

attempt	like
begin	love
continue	neglect
dislike	plan
hate	prefer
hesitate	start
intend	

Verbs + Infinitives
(*afford **to do** something*)

afford	hope
arrange	learn
consent	manage
decide	pretend
deserve	refuse
determine	swear
endeavor	threaten
forget	volunteer

[1]*Regret* is followed by the infinitive when it does not refer to past time: *We regret to inform you that the trip has been canceled.*
[2]*Remember* is followed by the infinitive when it means "remind oneself about something in the future": *We must remember to buy tickets for the ballet as soon as we arrive in town.*

*From Marcella Frank, *Writer's Companion* (Englewood Cliffs: Prentice-Hall, 1983), pp. 75–76. Reprinted by permission.

Verbs + Objects + Infinitives
*(advise **someone** to **do** something)*

advise	encourage	request
allow	expect[3]	require
beg[3]	forbid	teach
cause	force	tell
challenge	instruct	urge
command	invite	want[3]
convince	order	warn
dare (= challenge)	permit	wish[3]
desire[3]	persuade	would like[3]
enable	remind	

Exercise

In the following sentences, use the correct form of the verbals.

1. People are getting used to (watch) _____ violent scenes on TV.

2. Her employer always avoids (make) _____ an unpleasant decision.

3. These children are used to (get) _____ and not to (give) _____ .

4. It's getting late. We must (leave) _____ soon.

5. Dentists often recommend (brush) _____ our teeth after each meal.

6. I used (eat) _____ anything I wanted, but now I have to be careful.

7. I had my tailor (shorten) _____ the sleeves of my new jacket.

8. Many people are enjoying (watch) _____ television instead of (discover) _____ the world on their own.

9. People (commit) _____ terrible crimes such as murder should be legally executed.

10. They are accustomed to (go) _____ to the beach every summer.

11. The thief crept into the house without (be seen) _____ by anyone.

---

[3]These verbs can also be used without an object before the infinitive: *expect **to do** something.*

12. He is opposed to (turn) _____ the building into condominium apartments.

13. Many people (have) _____ different views ask why capital punishment should be abolished.

14. The bad weather prevented them from (continue) _____ with the construction.

15. Their mother never makes them (do) _____ anything they don't want to.

16. This method hasn't worked. I suggest your (try) _____ another method.

17. Let the cake (cool) _____ before (put) _____ on the icing.

18. The speaker kept on (talk) _____ even after most of the audience had left the hall.

19. Many people have objected to (pay) _____ the increased taxes on their homes.

20. There is a statistical study (indicate) _____ that the number of crimes has increased.

21. They have finally finished (build) _____ the new bridge.

22. He would rather (work) _____ on a farm than in an office.

23. It's very cold in here. Would you mind (close) _____ the window.

24. I'd better not (go) _____ to the movies. I have too much homework to do.

Word Order (1)

| Do not place an adverbial expression between a verb and its object. | *Incorrect:* I like very much English. *Correct:* I like English very much. |

Do not place a pronoun object after a separable (two-part) verb.

Incorrect: I don't know this word. I'll look up it in the dictionary.

Correct: .... I'll look it up in the dictionary.

Do not use a long adverbial between the two parts of a verb.

Incorrect: The flight attendants were all the time helping the passengers.

Correct: The flight attendants were helping the passengers all the time.

Use the proper order of adverbials after verbs.

Incorrect: I haven't seem him for a long time at school.

Correct: I haven't seem him at school for a long time. [Adverbials of time are usually placed last.]

Place limiting adverbs such as *only, even, hardly,* or *almost* directly before the words they refer to (formal usage).

Incorrect: This mistake appears almost on every page. [informal]

Correct: This mistake appears on almost every page. [formal]

Exercise

Correct the mistakes in word order in the following sentences.

1. They arrived on January 12, 1989, in New York.
2. Chinese is mostly written from top to bottom in columns.
3. The professor illustrates perfectly this struggle.
4. This television program presents more deeply the news.
5. He now speaks very well English.
6. These mountains almost cross the entire country.
7. Children need unquestionably a family with a mother's love.
8. We don't use in Russian the verb "to be."
9. We celebrate in the United States our Independence Day on July 4.
10. The airline may, if not enough tickets are sold, cancel the flight.
11. She is going to school to learn to speak more fluently English.
12. I only have seen stories about such women in the movies.
13. In the U.S.S.R. we hardly see any functioning Moslem mosques.
14. You will have never again a chance like this.
15. She misses still her native country.
16. We even learn to recognize automatically accents.

Word Order (2)

Use reversed subject-verb order in interrogative-word questions.

Incorrect: Why they are going to move?
Correct: Why are they going to move?
Incorrect: How much cost your umbrella?
Correct: How much did your umbrella cost?
[If the verb does not have an auxiliary, a form of the *do* auxiliary is needed unless the question word is the subject: Who bought the umbrella?]

Use normal word order in indirect questions (noun clauses).

Incorrect: He asked me how much did my umbrella cost.
Correct: He asked me how much my umbrella cost.
[Note that the *did* auxiliary is not used in the indirect question. If a form of *be* is in the question before a (pro)noun subject (How late *is* the train?), the verb will come after the subject in the indirect question: He asked me how late the train *was*.]

Use reversed question order in sentences or clauses beginning with negative adverbials, or with *only, so.* (As in questions, you will need to add a form of the auxiliary *do* to verbs that do not have any auxiliaries.)

Incorrect: Only with great reluctance he consented to address the audience.
Correct: Only with great reluctance did he consent to address the audience.

Incorrect: He likes the movies, and so his wife does.
Correct: He likes the movies, and so does his wife.

Exercise

Correct the mistakes in word order in the following sentences.

1. Only by a thorough examination one can understand the difference.
2. I'm not planning to publish books in philosophy. Neither I am trying to solve scientific problems.
3. The police want to know where does the accused person live.
4. When school will begin in the fall?
5. She likes to get up early, and so her husband does.
6. Under no circumstances an individual has the right to speak out against the political powers in the country.
7. So beautiful Snow White was that the Prince fell in love with her immediately.
8. Where we should go to register?
9. Their mother asked them what did they want for dinner.
10. She doesn't like vegetables, and neither her children do.
11. Very rarely parents take time to supervise what their children are watching on television.
12. Until what time the subway trains run?
13. I don't understand why is so expensive this dress.
14. When the factory closed down, not only he lost his job but his pension also.
15. Why you didn't come to my party?
16. Not only they have been discriminated against, but the accused have not been given good lawyers.

Word Forms

Use the correct noun ending.
Identifying nouns:
By position—
  before a verb as subject
  after a verb (as object or subjective complement)
  after a preposition
By preceding determiners
(*the, a, some, my, fourth*)

Incorrect: The reason for my homesick was that I missed my family very much.
Correct: The reason for my homesickness was that I missed my family very much.
[The noun *homesickness* appears after the preposition *for* and is preceded by the determiner *my*.]

Use the correct adjective ending.

Identifying adjectives:

By position—

before a noun

after a linking verb (*be, become, get, appear, look, seem*)

By preceding words like *very, quite, so*

Incorrect: In this country there is freedom for all religion sects.

Correct: In this country there is freedom for all religious sects.

[The adjective *religious* appears before the noun *sects*.]

Incorrect: My job is not interested at all.

Correct: My job is not interesting at all.

[For participial adjectives, the *-ing* ending has *active* meaning: The game was exciting; the exciting game. The *-ed* participle has *passive* meaning: The audience was excited; the excited audience.]

Use the correct adverbial ending.

Identifying adverbs:

By position—

initial, mid, final

before adjectives or other adverbs as modifiers

By preceding words like *very, quite, so*

(Many adverbs have *-ly* endings added to adjectives.)

Incorrect: The food in this restaurant is incredible good.

Correct: The food in this restaurant is incredibly good.

[The adverb *incredibly* appears as a modifier before the adjective *good*.]

Use the correct verb ending.

Identifying verbs:

By preceding auxiliaries

By *to* (for the infinitive)

Incorrect: To summary in one sentence, the United States owes much to its colonial heritage.

Correct: To summarize in one sentence, the United States owes much to its colonial heritage.

[The verb *summarize* is preceded by *to*.]

Exercise

In the following sentences, correct the mistakes in word forms.

1. Is deterrence a total futile argument?
2. Young people are aware that progress is depended on them.
3. Men are realizing that women should have more independent and free to choose their own careers.
4. Old people often suffer from a feeling of lonely and empty.
5. TV programs that are extremely realist and often violent should not be seen by children.
6. It is naturally that a man should not let a woman carry something heavy.
7. A person committed a murder deserves to be punished severely.
8. Originated thousands of years ago in Greece, democracy has appeared in many countries since.
9. Murders are committed because of a temporily lost of rationality by the killer.
10. I enjoy jobs that challenge my intelligent; I feel attractive to people who can talk about different subjects.
11. People are complaining about the unsafety environment.
12. Which points does the author emphasis most in her story?
13. She plans to give up her job after marry.
14. The flood ruined the crops and caused great destroy of property.
15. She and her brother have complete different temperaments.
16. She plays the piano very good.
17. He has a controlled interest in that bank.
18. The economical problems in my country are very great.
19. She's studying computer science and mathematic.

Prepositions (1)

Use the correct preposition after verbs.	*Incorrect:* I don't agree to the author's opinion.
	Correct: I don't agree with the author's opinion.
Use the correct preposition after adjectives.	*Incorrect:* Water is composed from hydrogen and oxygen.
	Correct: Water is composed of hydrogen and oxygen.

Use the correct preposition after nouns.	*Incorrect:* His resemblance with his father is very striking. *Correct:* His resemblance to his father is very striking.
Use the correct preposition to express adverbial meanings (time, place, cause) or in adverbial expressions.	*Incorrect:* Their national convention will take place on March. *Correct:* Their national convention will take place in March. *Incorrect:* She's going downtown to look at some dresses that are for sale. *Correct:* ...to look at some dresses that are on sale.
Use the correct prepositional form in two-part verbs.	*Incorrect:* We've just received our new computer. Would you like to try it on? *Correct:* .... Would you like to try it out?

Exercise

In the following sentences, supply the correct prepositions.

1. TV could be beneficial if the viewer were capable _____ choosing only the best programs.

2. Many old people are suffering _____ loneliness.

3. My country has been influenced by Western customs _____ many decades.

4. The point that the author brings _____ is that children often do not get enough supervision.

5. Great Britain consists _____ of England, Scotland and Wales.

6. She's interested _____ studying the customs of that African tribe.

7. She is married _____ a very rich man.

8. What were the conditions that brought _____ the civil war in that country?

9. She likes to go out to dinner very often. Her husband, _____ the other band, prefers to stay home and watch television.

10. Their bid was turned _____ because it was too high.

11. This report is based _____ many surveys.

12. My apartment is _____ the fifth floor.

13. Public opinion changes from time to time, depending _____ social conditions.

14. I prefer classical music _____ jazz.

15. In accordance _____ your request, we are canceling your order.

16. His present behavior is not consistent _____ his behavior in the past.

Prepositions (2)

Do not use a preposition in front of a subject.

Incorrect: By acting as a clown was his way of amusing children.
Correct: Acting as a clown was his way of amusing children.

If two parallel items cannot be used with the same preposition, each preposition should be included.

Incorrect: The long years of drought left many inhabitants without food and complete poverty.
Correct: ...without food and in complete poverty.

Do not use a preposition as a conjunction.

Incorrect: During I'm watching television, the commercials interrupt many times.
Correct: While I'm watching television,...
[The conjunction *while* permits a clause—a subject and a predicate—to follow it.]
or

	During the time that I'm watching television,... [The preposition *during* is followed by a noun object— *time*]
Do not omit a required preposition.	*Incorrect:* My uncle waited me at the airport for three hours. *Correct:* My uncle waited for me....
Do not use an unnecessary preposition.	*Incorrect:* He entered into the room so quietly that no one noticed him. *Correct:* He entered the room so quietly.... *Incorrect:* Most of Japanese are very polite. *Correct:* Most Japanese are very polite.

Exercise

In the following sentences, correct the faults in the use of prepositions.

1. Some tabloids emphasize on sex and violence.
2. For countries such as Greece, which once had a flourishing culture, now is a relatively weak nation.
3. High school seniors have a great interest and need for gathering information about different colleges.
4. Because of women are climbing step by step to better positions in the business world, they are spending less time at home with their children.
5. I explained them how South Korea was different from North Korea.
6. Children's behavior is shaped at home, not a day care center.
7. The third question concerns about the fairness of the law.
8. Recently, many of married women who don't have to work want to have careers.
9. Many young people lack of sympathy for older people.
10. In the Eighth Amendment of the Constitution states that there should be no cruel or unusual punishment.
11. The city in which I grew up in has changed very much.
12. Most of criminals have a poor family background.
13. More women are seeking for jobs than ever before.
14. Because of the readers of this newspaper don't have much money, the advertising section concentrates largely on inexpensive items.

15. By taking courses offered in my freshman and sophomore years can help me make a decision about my major.
16. With the movies shown on television make the viewers feel that they are living in a different world.
17. Let's ask to our teacher to explain the use of articles again.
18. The American colonists had a wide experience and knowledge about self-government.
19. Despite it was a new experience for me, I felt comfortable in the crowded streets of this new city.
20. He said me, "Come back again tomorrow."

Pronouns

Make sure that a pronoun that refers to a preceding noun has the same number (singular or plural) as that noun.	*Incorrect:* Women once stayed at home to take care of the children, but now she wants to work outside the home. *Correct:* ...but now *they* want to work outside the home.
Use the correct subject, object, or possessive form of pronouns.	*Incorrect:* He received a letter threatening he and his family. *Correct:* He received a letter threatening *him* and his family. [*Him* is the object of *threatening*]
Use the correct pronoun.	*Incorrect:* We have seen a change in today's woman, which wants to have a job outside the home. *Correct:* ...today's woman, *who* wants.... [In an adjective clause, *who* is used for a person, *which* for a thing. *That* may be used for a person or a thing if there is no comma before it.]
Do not use an unnecessary pronoun.	*Incorrect:* My friend, he told me the whole story. *Correct:* My friend told me the whole story.

Use the correct form of *other*.

Incorrect: He would like to make friends with many others Americans.

Correct: He would like to make friends with many *other* Americans.

[*Other* is used with a plural noun; *another* with a singular. (The) *others* is a plural pronoun standing alone: Some people like to vacation at the beach, while *others* prefer the mountains.]

Do not omit a pronoun beginning an adjective clause.

Incorrect: My country is located in Southeast Asia is a small one.

Correct: My country, which is located in Southeast Asia, is a small one.

[The adjective clause can be replaced by a participial phrase: My country, located in Southeast Asia, is a small one.]

Incorrect: Today there are more people are going to college than before.

Correct: Today there are more people who are going to college than before. (*or*) Today there are more people going to college than before. (*or better*) Today more people are going to college than before.

Use introductory *it* and *there* correctly.

Incorrect: It is too much pollution in big cities.

Correct: There is too much pollution in big cities.

[*There* is used mostly with a *noun* that follows (pollution). *It* is used with an *adjective* that follows: *It* is *common* to find pollution in big cities. Do not omit introductory *it*.]

Exercise

In the following sentences, correct the pronoun faults.

1. Hijacking and kidnaping are another examples of crimes that deserve capital punishment.
2. I like the news on television because they are very interesting.
3. In another words, the roles of the generations were reversed.
4. Inferences are not to be used in writing reports because it is a statement about the unknown made on the basis of the known.
5. They plan to build their new home theirself.
6. They form the legislative branch which duty it is to pass laws and to balance the executive and the judicial powers.
7. They believe that capital punishment kills people legally in cold blood is inhumane.
8. There are not many countries really give the power to the people to choose their own government.
9. Greek is a key language, which its roots appear in almost every other known language.
10. There weren't many educational programs that the audiences could learn from them.
11. If teachers have enough time, he can shape a student into a better tool for society.
12. There was a little boy jumped out the window in imitation of Superman.
13. Both parents should look after the children because they (the children) need special care when they are young. [Avoid a parenthetic explanation of a pronoun.]
14. The teacher who he had the greatest influence on me was my English teacher.
15. It is something wrong with our TV set.
16. He has always liked to meet people from others countries.
17. They invited my wife and I to the opening of their new play.
18. It is a lot of noise in this room.
19. This pen doesn't work too well. I'll try the another one.
20. It is no place like home.
21. The subject which I liked it the best in school was English.

Comparison

Use the correct form for the degree of comparison.
two units: *taller than, more beautiful than*
three or more units: *the tallest, the most beautiful*

Incorrect: He is the tallest of the two brothers.
Correct: He is the taller of the two brothers.

Use the required structure word or word form for comparison.

the same as
as ... as
different from
compared with
in comparison with

Incorrect: My country has the same problems than other developing countries.
Correct: My country has the same problems as other developing countries.

Use *like, alike* correctly.

Incorrect: English is alike my language in many ways.
Correct: English is like my language in many ways.
(or) English and my language are alike in many ways.

Use the required substitute word in comparison: *one(s), that-those*

Incorrect: The salaries we pay for this kind of work are higher than in other countries.
Correct: The salaries we pay for this kind of work are higher than those in other countries.

Exercise

In the following sentences, correct the mistakes in comparison.

1. Inflections of English adjectives are simpler than Korean.
2. The values of the young generation are different from the older generation.
3. The word forms in Spanish are different from that of English.
4. Comparing with the morning paper, our evening paper has more special features.
5. For English speakers, Greek is much more easier than Arabic or Japanese.
6. His grades are about the same than they were last year.
7. The life of a worker is often happier than his employer.
8. My city is quite different with New York.
9. In compare with Great Britain, the United States has very few dialects.
10. I think American television programs are worst than the French programs.
11. The word order of Spanish is similar to English.
12. My language, alike English, is written from left to right.
13. The cultural life of my city differs from it in New York in many respects.
14. In my country, this is the longest and enjoyable holiday season.

15. He is the best of the two students who won prizes.
16. The streets in my city are not that safe like they used to be.
17. The two sisters are alike each other in many ways.
18. American television programs are not really very different from the other countries.

Articles: General Rules

Use an article (*a* or *the*) with a singular countable noun, unless another determiner like *this, their, many, fourth* is used.

Incorrect: Author says that the divorce rate has been increasing rapidly.
Correct: The author says that the divorce rate has been increasing rapidly.

Do not use *the* with a noncountable noun that is not followed by a modifier.

Incorrect: The society expects us to conform to its traditional ways.
Correct: Society expects us to conform to its traditional ways.

Use *the* if a countable or a noncountable noun is narrowed down by a following modifier.

Incorrect: Society we live in is becoming more permissive.
Correct: The society we live in is becoming more permissive.

Incorrect: American corporations are trying to learn from Japanese style of management.
Correct: American corporations are trying to learn from the Japanese style of management.
[*of* = phrase modifiers usually require *the* before the noun, unless another determiner is used.]

Use *the* for singular class words in general statements.

Incorrect: Computer now has many uses in business and industry.

Correct: The computer now has many uses in business and industry. *(or)* Computers now have many uses in business and industry.

[The plural form without *the* can also be used as a class word in a general statement.]

Use *the* for known or familiar objects:

in the outside environment

Incorrect: Trees are now covered with snow.

Correct: The trees are now covered with snow.

[But: In northern climates, trees lose their leaves in the winter. *Trees* is a plural class word in a general statement.]

in the inside environment

Incorrect: Please put milk over there.

Correct: Please put the milk over there.

[But: Milk is good for children. *Milk* is a noncountable class word in a general statement.]

Use *a* with a singular noun having indefinite reference:

the person or thing is unknown to the speaker

Incorrect: Man is here to see you.

Correct: A man is here to see you.

the person or thing represents one member of a class

Incorrect: Elizabeth is doctor.

Correct: Elizabeth is a doctor.

Incorrect: Lion is a wild animal.

Correct: A lion is a wild animal.

[Also: *The* lion ... for the entire class.]

Use *the* with superlatives, ordinals, and other "ranking" words (the *first*, the *last*, the *next*, the *following*).

Incorrect: Please read second chapter for tomorrow.

Correct: Please read the second chapter for tomorrow.

[But: Please read Chapter 2 for tomorrow. *The* is not used with cardinal numbers.]

Incorrect: This is last week of
    registration.
Correct: This is the last week of
    registration.
[But: All classes ended last
    week. *Last* is a point in time.]

Use *the* in *of* phrases after
  expressions of quantity (*most
  of the*).

Incorrect: Most of Americans I
    know have television sets.
Correct: Most of the Americans
    I know have television sets.
    (*or*) Most Americans I know
    have television sets.

Use *the* with adjectives used as
  nouns.

Incorrect: French celebrate
    Bastille Day on July 14.
Correct: The French celebrate
    Bastille Day on July 14.

Use *such a, what a* with singular
  countable nouns.

Incorrect: What beautiful home
    they have!
Correct: What a beautiful home
    they have!

Exercise

In the blank spaces, use *a, an,* or *the.* If no article is required, place an X in the
blank space.

1. _____ money is not enough to bring us _____ happiness.

2. Follow _____ street over there until you get to _____
   subway.

3. _____ beautiful picture was hanging on _____ wall
   of _____ bedroom.

4. Please get _____ bread and _____ butter from
   _____ refrigerator and put them on _____ table.

5. _____ cattle are raised in many parts of this country.

6. _____ doctors recommend _____ aspirin for
   _____ colds.

7. She is studying _____ Spanish in _____ high school.

8. _____ British and _____ French fought many wars.

9. Kyoto has _____ large population.

10. _____ celebration of our country's independence takes place on July 4.

11. I read _____ story about _____ man living before the American Revolution. _____ man lived at _____ foot of _____ mountains.

12. Because of _____ superstitions, some buildings do not have _____ thirteenth floor.

13. One day I went to _____ friend's house and I noticed something new, _____ beautiful painting.

14. Such _____ small country cannot have _____ diversity of industry.

15. _____ population of Mexico City keeps increasing.

16. _____ automobile has contributed to _____ development of _____ suburbs.

17. He was lying on _____ ground, looking up at _____ moon and _____ stars.

18. This is _____ best book I have ever read.

19. _____ second paragraph gives _____ most important idea of _____ essay we are reading.

20. Most of _____ students in our class passed _____ examination.

21. _____ psychology teaches us a lot about _____ human nature.

22. I began to attend _____ college _____ last year.

23. She is quite _____ good teacher.

24. _____ housework has been made easier because of _____ modern conveniences.

25. In _____ past, it was hoped that _____ younger generation would create _____ new and better society.

26. Many of _____ people whose homes were flooded received

    _____ financial assistance in order to rebuild their homes.

27. _____ burning of trash indoors can be dangerous.

28. _____ people I have met so far have been very kind and warm.

29. What _____ beautiful weather we are having!

30. After many months, I finally got _____ visa.

31. In _____ last one hundred years, my city has become

    _____ very important center of _____ trade and

    _____ culture.

32. _____ Chapter Five is _____ most interesting one if

    our textbook.

33. Columbus discovered America in _____ fifteenth century.

34. _____ history teaches us that _____ same mistakes

    can occur again.

Articles: *The* in Names

USE *the*

With geographic names	
bodies of water, except lakes and bays	the Mediterranean Sea, the Pacific Ocean, the Nile River [But: Lake Erie, Hudson Bay]
names in *of* phrases	The Gulf of Mexico, the City of New York
names that end in a word for a political union	The British Commonwealth, the Soviet Union
plural names	The United States, the Philippines
names of general areas using points of the compass (the north, the east, the south, the west)	the Middle East, the South (in the U.S.) [But: Northern Europe, Southeast Asia (parts of continents)]
With names of historic events	The French Revolution, the Renaissance [But: World War Two]
With official titles	the President, the Prime Minister [But: President Lincoln—(the name accompanies the title)]

With names for government bodies	the Army, the Treasury Department, the police, the highway patrol
With names of organizations, institutions	the United Nations, the Girl Scouts
With names of political parties	the Labor party, the Republican party
With names of newspapers	*The New York Times*, the *Wall Street Journal*
With names of museums, libraries, buildings, hotels	the Metropolitan Museum, the Woolworth Building, the Hilton Hotel

DO NOT USE *the*

With geographic names	continents, most countries, states, cities, Africa, Poland, Texas, London
With names of parks, streets, avenues	Hyde Park, Fifth Avenue, Broadway
With names of colleges and universities that do not contain an *of* phrase in the name	Columbia University, the University of Pennsylvania
With names of holidays	Thanksgiving Day, Easter [But: the Fourth of July]
With names of most magazines	*Time, Glamour*

Exercise

Insert *the* where required. Use an X if *the* is not required.

1. _____ United States is bordered on _____ east by _____ Atlantic Ocean, on _____ west by _____ Pacific Ocean.

2. Mark Twain wrote about his experience as a river pilot on _____ Mississippi River.

3. _____ Middle Ages is the time in European history between the fifth and the fifteenth centuries.

4. In the United States, _____ President Washington is revered as the father of our country.

5. _____ Cancer Society does a lot of research which is designed to help cancer patients.

6. _____ Democratic party in the United States is known for being more liberal than _____ Republican party.

7. They live near _____ Geneva.

8. _____ Panama Canal is in _____ Central America.

9. They often go to _____ Highland Park to play handball.

10. On _____ Christmas Day, Americans often exchange presents.

11. _____ *Daily News* is a tabloid that concentrates on local news.

12. Karl Marx wrote much of *Das Kapital* in _____ British Museum.

13. _____ World Trade Center consists of two of the tallest buildings in the world.

14. _____ Dominican Republic is in _____ Caribbean Sea.

15. Most of the stores in this town are on _____ Main Street.

16. _____ Princeton University is one of the Ivy League schools.

17. In the United States, many parties are given on _____ New Year's Eve.

18. Another name for _____ Soviet Union is _____ USSR.

19. Right now she's studying at _____ New York University.

20. Trolley cars used to run on _____ 42nd Street.

21. Americans celebrate _____ Independence Day on July 4.

22. _____ prime minister is the chief executive of a parliamentary government.

23. Their son wants to join _____ marines.

24. _____ Scotland is a part of _____ British Isles.

25. Her favorite magazine for news is _____ *Newsweek*; for 25. fashion it is _____ *Vogue*.

26. _____ *Christian Science Monitor* is considered one of the best newspapers in the United States.

27. ＿＿＿＿＿＿＿＿＿ Persian Gulf is rich in oil.

28. ＿＿＿＿＿＿＿＿＿ Guggenheim Museum in New York was designed by Frank Lloyd Wright.

29. ＿＿＿＿＿＿＿＿＿ Industrial Revolution began in England in the late nineteenth century.

30. ＿＿＿＿＿＿＿＿＿ Philippines are in ＿＿＿＿＿＿＿＿＿ Southeast Asia.

31. ＿＿＿＿＿＿＿＿＿ U.S. Armed Forces consist of ＿＿＿＿＿＿＿＿＿ Army, ＿＿＿＿＿＿＿＿＿ Navy, and ＿＿＿＿＿＿＿＿＿ Air Force.

32. They're staying at ＿＿＿＿＿＿＿＿＿ Plaza Hotel.

33. To ＿＿＿＿＿＿＿＿＿ east of ＿＿＿＿＿＿＿＿＿ India is ＿＿＿＿＿＿＿＿＿ Bay of Bengal.

Answers to Exercises

Exercises in the Text

Chapter 2

1. definition(s) 2. Phonetics 3. punctuation 4. parentheses 5. alphabetically; alphabetic(al) 6. grammatically 7. exclamatory; exclamation; beginning 8. declension 9. conjugation 10. inflected 11. omission 12. comparison; emphasizes; differences; similarities 13. basically; pronunciation; irregularities 14. difficulty; hearing; distinguishing 15. Compared; relatively; inflections 16. comparing; totally

Chapter 3

1. illiteracy; heritage 2. centralized; regulated; operated 3. cultural; called; humanities 4. universal; compulsory 5. indoctrinate; questioning 6. elementary; primary; secondary 7. vocational; occupations 8. progressive; supposed; doing; reading 9. required; elective; optional 10. choice; specialize 11. stimulating; interested; depth; breadth 12. solutions; decisions; objectively 13. Adjusting; objectives 14. stimulation; growth 15. preparing; secondary

Chapter 4

1. responsibilities; tranquillity; stability 2. security; protection 3. expectations; satisfactorily 4. conveniences; lighten 5. financial; independence; boring; broaden 6. supervision; delinquency 7. economic; necessity 8. emotional; insecurity 9. controversial; emotional 10. morality; training 11. professionals 12. availability; abortion; choice 13. socialization; responsibility 14. leaving; jeopardize 15. educated; financial; equality 16. increasing 17. faced; having; taking

Chapter 5

1. affects 2. beneficial; chosen 3. distortion(s); occurrence; entertaining; informative 4. violence; hostility; aggressiveness; harmful 5. serialized; successive 6. fantasize; wealthy; powerful; beautiful 7. relaxation; recreation 8. influential 9. financial 10. viewing; passivity; creativity 11. comedians; successful; wealthy 12. criticism; depth 13. documentary; factual; viewer(s) 14. excitement; economical 15. criticized; emphasis; violence 16. watching; eating; getting

Chapter 6

1. democratic; freedom; equality 2. legislative; executive; judicial 3. legislature; legislators; legislation 4. Elections 5. parliamentary; executive; elected; representatives; voters 6. majority; plurality 7. senators; legislators; Representatives; population 8. legislator; constituents 9. diversity 10. responsibilities 11. equality; economic; security 12. Historically; capitalist 13. assumption; regulations 14. political; representatives 15. composed; representing; representation 16. Theoretically; democratic; equally 17. existence; tyranny

Chapter 7

1. privately; operated 2. Circulation; advertising 3. advertisements; classified; employment; personal 4. editorial 5. financial; cultural 6. informed; entertaining 7. reporter; publication; editor; correspondent 8. usually; associated; reporting; abbreviated; extensive; coverage; sensational 9. emphasis; placed; scandalous; bribery; corruption; robbery; burglary; kidnaping 10. heavily; national 11. appealing; connotative; emotionally; denotative 12. timely; lengthy 13. objective; subjective 14. collecting; recreation 15. giving; activities; incidentally; publicity

Chapter 8

1. punishment; controversial 2. innocent; guilty 3. capricious; mandatory 4. Opponents; discriminatory; proponents; murderers; intentionally; accidentally 5. criminals; inheritance; surroundings; behavior; rehabilitation 6. suspicion; committed; suspect; arrested; arraigned; evidence; criminal; indictment; accused; defendant; trial 7. trial; jurors; evidence; decision; accused; guilty; innocent 8. murderers; rapists; arsonists; terrorists; kidnapers; severely 9. deterrent; felonious

Appendix Exercises

Note: Choices of positions and choices of introductory words (conjunctions) have been omitted in the answers that follow.

Sentence Structure

Independent (Coordinate) Clauses

1. early, but/early; however (,) 2. weight, so/weight; therefore (,) 3. still, and/still; moreover (,) 4. cook, but/cook; however (,) 5. late, so/late; therefore (,) 6. well, and/well; moreover (,) 7. flood, but/flood; however (,) 8. millionaire, so/millionaire; therefore (,) 9. battles, but/battles; however (,) 10. unfairly (,) and/unfairly; moreover (,) 11. times, so/times; therefore (,)

Adverbial Clauses

1. Although he dislikes mathematics, 2. Unless we (If we don't) pay our taxes,
3. because he was sincerely...profession. 4. While their new house...built, 5.
While the children...picnic, or when a sudden downpour...indoors. 6. Because
their old car...trouble, 7. Until (or Before) television...the fifties, 8. Although the
city...subway, 9. ...plane when she suddenly...ill. 10. While the family...tree, or
the family...tree when the fire alarm went off. 11. Since he got...eyeglasses,
12. Although a lot of money...building, 13. ...books, while others....or While
some people...books, others.... 14. After he removed...table, he.... 15. If the
defendant had told the truth, he...sentence. 16. Only when the house is very quiet
can he concentrate. 17. While the soprano...opera, her.... 18. Even if their long
report is finished...days, it will be.... 19. Whether the story is true or false, she...
it.

Adjective Clauses

1. The lawnmower that (which or——) they had borrowed 2. country in which
(where) the meeting will be held 3. The song that (which or ——) he wrote 4. The
World Trade Center, which is located in New York City, 5. The music that (which or
——) listening to 6. The children, most of whom...a circus,.... 7. All the money
that (which or ——) he inherited 8. Celia, who has been coming...nights,....
9. The apartment building in which (where) the Johnsons live or that (which
or ——) the Johnsons live in 10. Brazil, where they live now, 11. The exact day on
which (when) the revolution began 12. Alice, whose arm was hurt in an accident,

Noun Clauses

1. Whether they would give the dance (or not) was still uncertain. or It was still
uncertain whether they would.... 2. notice that she had lost an earring.
3. ...know who had made the terrible mistake. 4. Whoever stole the money is a
clever thief. 5. ...requests that all parcels be checked. 6. ...amazed at how quickly
the fire (had) spread. 7. ...know whether I should accept the invitation (or not). or
...know whether to accept the invitation. 8. ...about where the library was (is).
9. ...asked where he should deliver the merchandise. or...asked where to deliver
the merchandise. 10. ...asked me which tooth was hurting me. 11. ...know how I
should (how to) correct the error. 12. ...asked the sales clerk what time the store
closed (closes).

Adverbial Structures

1. Because the road was icy,/Because of the iciness of the road,/The road being icy,
2. Although it was very dangerous,/In spite of the great danger, 3. Because the
actress was very talented,/Because of the actress' great talent [sometimes a participial
phrase may express cause: Being very talented,] 4. While (she was) preparing
dinner, 6. Unless you (If you don't) stop smoking so much, 6 Because it was
raining heavily/Because of the heavy rain, 7. Although there was a lack of food
during the war,/In spite of a lack of food during the war 8. While he was driving
along a dark road, a deer..../He was driving...when a deer ran out.... 9. Although
the company promised to hire the laid off workers soon,/In spite of the company's
promise (or the promise of the company) to hire.... 10. Although the government
...demonstrators, they didn't..../In spite of the government's threat 11. If I receive
an overseas telephone call, 12. While some people like to eat meat, other..../Some
people like to eat meat, while other people.... 13. Before she washed (or Before

washing) the kitchen floor,/She put a coat of wax on the floor after she washed it.
14. If it rains/In case of rain 15. Whether they come to the meeting or not,

Adjectival Structures

1. The people who (that) live in this building/The people living in this building
2. Celia, who was running to catch the bus/Celia, running to catch the bus 3. The
prisoners who (that) were being held for political reasons/The prisoners being held
...reasons 4. Our chairman, who had eaten too much for lunch,/Our chairman,
having eaten too much for lunch, 5. My best friend, who had won a lot of money in
the lottery,/My best friend, having won a lot of money in the lottery, 6. The
performance that (which) was given yesterday/The performance given yesterday/The
performance yesterday 7. His youngest sister, who is now in college,/His youngest
sister, now in college, 8. The building in which (where) they live/The building that
(which or ——) they live in 9. the things that (which) were to be...bazaar/the things
to be sold...bazaar 10. The refugees, some of whom had not eaten for days, 11.
His neighbor, whose car had been stolen, 12. The monument at which you are
looking now/The monument that (which or ——) you are looking at now 13. their
new teacher, whom they all respect.

Nominal Structures

1. That the company...proposal was a great disappointment/It was a great
disappointment that the company...proposal/The company's rejecting his proposal..../For the company to reject his proposal was..../The company's rejecting
(rejection of) his proposal was.... 2. ...anticipated that they might...
cars./anticipated having trouble...cars. 3. That she avoids hard work is obvious./It
is obvious that...work./Her avoiding (or avoidance of) hard work...obvious.
4. ...me where the dean's office is? 5. ...suggested that I (should) replace...tires./
...suggested my replacing...tires. 6. That we begin the project at once is very
important./It is very important that we...once./For us to begin the project at once is
very important./It is very important for us to begin...once. 7. ...about whether
they should buy (or whether to buy) more school buses. 8. ...recommends that we
(should) have...regularly./...recommends our having...regularly. 9. ...for not
paying his taxes. 10. That we overlook our faults is easy to do./It is easy to overlook
our faults./Overlooking our faults is easy to do. 11. Consuming (To consume, the
consumption of) sugar is not...health. 12. ...is how can we get (how to get) the
president's approval.

Correcting Faults in Usage

Correcting Sentence Faults

1. ...injustice, and violation of.... 2. ...Europe, you can see many similarities.
3. ...equal; therefore women.... 4. ...at all, whereas others.... 5. ...are made,
changes like.... 6. ...the public. The classified ads.... 7. ...with English, I find
many differences./A comparison of my language with English reveals many
differences. 8. ...people; moreover the nation's economy.... 9. ...of being needed
and useful. 10. ...liability, thus adding.... 11. ...on Tuesday, and the food section
is on Wednesday. 12. ...and bank robbers, because these types.... 13. ...stealing,
killing...or doing something.... 14. ...on farms; thus youth...reasons.
15. ...South India, I use Tamil as my native language. 16. ...unknown; even
misdemeanors.... 17. ...each vowel, we can form various syllables. 18. ...cultural
stimulation and preparation for (or to face) life. 19. ...arguments, finally ending

...violence. 20. ...a word, you will find that English follows alphabetical order. 21. ...life imprisonment, although there is....

Improving Sentences

1. ...choosing our own classes.... 2. ...syllables that are really...pronounce. 3. My native country, India, has...languages. 4. omit *although* or *but* 5. walked-jumped or walks-jumps 6. is-are, is able to 7. If the death penalty were applied all over the world, it would certainly lessen the crime rate./The application of the death penalty all over the world would certainly...rate. 8. One of the articles in this magazine tells how much...violence. 9. omit *only* or *alone* 10. The author of this study points out that...increasing. 11. ...family except a niece who had tried... life. 12. Replace *you* and *people* by *we* 13. ...irony, "A Modest Proposal." 14. TV was invented for many reasons. 15. ...alphabet of ten vowels and fourteen consonants. 17. omit *legal* or *by the law*

Subject-Verb Agreement

1. Change *is* to *are* 2. Change *is* to *are* 3. change *were* to *was* 4. change *is* to *are* 5. change *differs* to *differ* 6. change *show* to *shows* 7. change *are* to *is* 8. change *have* to *has* 9. change *doesn't* to *don't* 10. change *is* to *are* 11. change *are* to *is* 12. change *has* to *have* 13. change *have* to *has* 14. change *have* to *has* 15. change *is* to *are* 16. change *add* to *adds* 17. change *have* to *has* 18. change *has* to *have* 19. change *are* to *is*

Verbs: Auxiliaries

1. is composed of 2. could be filled, could be filled 3. deserves 4. live 5. have been repeated 6. have chosen 7. is trying 8. watch or are watching 9. that were required 10. has been meeting 11. is thrown 12. do not care 13. would have helped 14. has worn 15. now interest me 16. are served 17. is supposed to 18. so do our neighbors 19. Chinese does 20. was born 21. mother died 22. does this book cost 23. have been used 24. are only concerned

Verbs: Tenses

1. until he sees 2. didn't understand 3. it were warmer 4. a guard be on duty 5. began 6. this bill be passed 7. had told me 8. was preparing dinner 9. has had 10. After I wash 11. if the weather is 12. she was wearing 13. I wish I had taken 14. If I had felt better 15. members be on time 16. It is beginning 17. I wish I had known you 18. If you see 19. she is trying 20. We had just gone to bed 21. If I had known 22. every uniform fit properly 23. had been arranged 24. taught 25. I wish I had been 26. He would have helped us 27. everybody take 28. if they had had 29. I lay down

Verbals

1. watching 2. making 3. getting, giving 4. leave/be leaving 5. brushing 6. to eat 7. shorten 8. watching, discovering 9. committing 10. going 11. being seen 12. turning 13. having 14. continuing 15. do 16. trying 17. cool, putting 18. talking 19. paying 20. indicating 21. building 22. work 23. closing 24. go

Word Order (1)

1. They arrived in New York on January 12, 1989. 2. Chinese is written mostly
3. illustrates this struggle perfectly 4. presents the news more deeply 5. speaks
English very well 6. across almost the entire country 7. Children unquestionably
need a family 8. use the verb "to be" in Russian 9. In the United States we
celebrate 10. If not enough tickets are sold, the airline may cancel the flight. 11. to
speak English more fluently. 12. I have seen stories about such women only in the
movies. 13. we see hardly any functioning moslem mosques 14. You will never
again have a chance like this. 15. She still misses 16. to recognize accents
automatically

Word Order (2)

1. can one understand 2. Neither am I trying 3. where the accused person lives.
4. When will school begin 5. so does her husband 6. has an individual the right
7. So beautiful was Snow White 8. Where should we go 9. what they wanted for
dinner 10. neither do her children 11. Very rarely do parents take time 12. Until
what time do the subway trains run? 13. why this dress is so expensive 14. not only
did he lose his job 15. Why didn't you come 16. Not only have they been discriminated against

Word Forms

1. totally 2. dependent 3. independence, freedom 4. lonely, emptiness
5. realistic 6. natural 7. committing 8. Originating 9. temporary loss
10. intelligence, attracted 11. unsafe 12. emphasize 13. marriage
14. destruction 15. completely 16. well 17. controlling 18. economic
19. mathematics

Prepositions (1)

1. of 2. from 3. for 4. out 5. of 6. in 7. to 8. about 9. on 10. down 11. on,
upon 12. on 13. on, upon 14. to 15. with 16. with

Prepositions (2)

1. emphasize sex 2. omit *For* 3. interest in and need for 4. use *Because* instead of
Because of 5. I explained to them 6. at home, not in a day care center 7. concerned
the fairness 8. many married women 9. lack sympathy for 10. omit *In* 11. in
which I grew up/(which) I grew up in 12. Most criminals 13. seeking jobs 14. use
Because instead of *Because of* 15. omit *By* 16. omit *With* 17. ask our teacher
18. experience in and knowledge about 19. use *Although* instead of *Despite* 20. He
said to me

Pronouns

1. other examples 2. it is very interesting
3. In other words 4. because they are statements 5. themselves 6. whose duty it
is 7. capital punishment, which kills people 8. countries which (that) give power
9. whose roots (the roots of which) appear 10. that the audiences could learn
from 11. they can shape 12. boy who (that) jumped out 13. because children

need 14. the teacher who had 15. There is something wrong 16. from other countries 17. invited my wife and me 18. There is 19. the other one 20. There is no place 21. which I liked best

Comparison

1. simpler than those in Korean 2. different from those of the older generation 3. different from those of English 4. Compared with the morning paper 5. much easier than 6. the same as 7. happier than that of his employer 8. different from 9. In comparison with 10. are worse than 11. similar to that of English 12. like English 13. differs from that (or the one) in New York 14. the longest and the most enjoyable 15. the better of the two 16. not as (so) safe as 17. are like each other 18. different from those (the ones) in other countries

Articles: General Rules

1. X, X 2. the, the 3. A, the, the 4. the, the, the, the 5. X 6. X, X, X 7. X, X 8. the, the 9. a 10. The 11. a, a, The, the, the 12. X, a 13. a, a 14. a, a 15. The 16. The, the, the 17. the, the, the 18. the 19. The, the, the 20. the, the 21. X, X 22. X, X 23. A 24. X, X 25. the, the 26. the, X 27. the 28. The 29. X 30. a 31. the, a, X, X 32. X, the 33. the 34. X, the

Articles: The *in Names*

1. The, the, the, the, the 2. the 3. The 4. X 5. The 6. The, the 7. X 8. The, X 9. X 10. X 11. The 12. the 13. The 14. The, the 15. X 16. X 17. X 18. the, the 19. X 20. X 21. X 22. The 23. the 24. X, the 25. X, X 26. The 27. The 28. The 29. The 30. The, X 31. The, the, the, the 32. the 33. the, X, the

APPENDIX B

Punctuation and Spelling Rules

Punctuation Rules*

This section on punctuation deals mainly with specific marks of punctuation that are related to sentence structure. However, two warnings about the use of punctuation in general need to be made first.

1. No punctuation should be used at the beginning of a line. (Exceptions are quotation marks and parentheses, which must appear directly around the words they refer to.)
2. No more than one end mark of punctuation should be used. The doubling or tripling of periods, question marks, or exclamation points should be avoided in English.

*From Marcella Frank, *Writer's Companion* (Englewood Cliffs, N.J.: Prentice-Hall, 1983), pp. 36–44. Reprinted by permission.

The information about punctuation that follows is presented under these headings:

1. Commas in sentences with introductory, final grammatical elements
2. Commas in sentences with interrupting elements
3. Commas, semicolons in combined independent sentences
4. Commas in a series
5. Commas and quotation marks in direct speech
6. Other uses of punctuation for sentence structure (colon, semicolon, dash)
7. Unacceptable commas (including run-on sentences)
8. Unacceptable semicolons

Commas in Sentences with Introductory or Final Grammatical Elements

A comma is generally used after an introductory element, especially if this element is long or if the writer would normally pause at this point in speech. A comma after a short introductory element is optional.

> *Words:*   *Finally(,)*[1] they were able to take their trip around the world.
> *Phrases:*   *As a matter of fact,* they went on the trip sooner than they had expected.
> *Clauses:*   *Before they left,*[2] their friends gave them a big party.

There are some types of introductory phrases that require commas.

> *Hoping to see as much as possible,* they planned their itinerary carefully. [participial phrase]
> *Happy to be leaving at last,* they boarded the plane with great anticipation. [adjective phrase]
> *The weather causing no problems,* they had a comfortable flight. [absolute construction]

Final elements are less likely to be set off by commas, especially those indicating time. However, as with introductory elements, a pause in speech determines whether a comma will be used.

> *Words:*   They realized their dream *unexpectedly.*
> *Phrases:*   They realized their dream *in an unexpected manner.*
> *Clauses:*   Their wish came true *when they unexpectedly inherited some money.*

---

[1]The parentheses around a mark of punctuation indicates that the punctuation is optional.
[2]The comma is required after the short introductory element in this sentence to avoid a temporary misreading as: *Before they left their friends.*

The elements that require commas at the beginning of the sentence also require commas when they appear at the end of the sentence.

> They planned their itinerary carefully, *hoping to see as much as possible.* [participial phrase]
> They boarded the plane with great anticipation, *happy to be leaving at last.* [adjective phrase].
> They had a comfortable flight, *the weather causing no problems.* [absolute construction]

Commas in Sentences with Interrupting Elements

Since interrupting elements are regarded as parenthetic, commas are placed on *both sides* of the elements.

Adverbial Elements

> *Words:*   His father, *fortunately*, was very rich.
> *Phrases:* His father, *as a matter of fact*, was very rich.
> *Clauses:* His father, *as I've been told*, was very rich.

If a short word or phrase is felt to be closely related to the rest of the sentence, the commas may be omitted.

> Their wish *finally* came true.

Nonrestrictive Structures

An adjective structure that follows a noun may either narrow down (that is, restrict) the reference of the noun, or it may only add more information about the noun without identifying it further. *Those structures that do not identify their nouns are considered nonrestrictive and require commas.*

Note the difference in punctuation in the following sentences.

Restrictive—No Commas	Nonrestrictive—Commas on Both Sides
Land which is surrounded by water is an island. [The noun *land* is a general (class) word. It is identified by *which is surrounded by water.*]	*Manhattan*, which is surrounded by water, is an island. [The noun *Manhattan* is already identified by name, so *which is surrounded by water* does not limit its identity further.]

The same punctuation rule applies to participial phrases, which may be considered shortened forms of *who* or *which* clauses.

> *Restrictive:*   Land *surrounded by water* is an island.
> *Nonrestrictive:*   Manhattan, *surrounded by water,* is an island.

Other shortened forms of nonrestrictive *who* or *which* clauses also require commas if the nouns they refer to are already identified by name.

> The Palace, *a very expensive restaurant,* serves only the best food.
> The Palace, *famous for its fine food,* is a very expensive restaurant.

The nonrestrictive phrase can also be moved to the beginning of the sentence.

> *Surrounded by water,* Manhattan is an island.

Commas and Semicolons in Combined Independent Sentences

Comma

The boy was sick, *so* he didn't go to school.	When connectives like *so, and, but,* and *or* (coordinate conjunctions) join sentences, a comma is used. The comma may be omitted if both sentences are short.

Semicolon

The boy was sick; he didn't go to school.	No connective joins the sentences. Sometimes two sentences are written as one because the writer feels there is a relationship between them. In this case they are joined by a semicolon.
The boy was sick; *therefore*(,) he didn't go to school.	Adverbials like *therefore, however, otherwise, moreover* (conjunctive adverbs) can connect the sentences. These

adverbials may take other positions in the second part of the sentence: The boy was sick; he *therefore* didn't go to school. Note that *the semicolon remains in the position where the period might have been written.*

Commas in a Series (with *and, or*)

Items in a series of three or more are separated by commas.

> The advertising company is preparing a television program that can appeal to men, women(,) or children.
> In a democracy, people have the right to speak freely, to assemble without government interference(,) and to worship in the religion of their choice.

The comma before *and* or *or* is optional. If *and* or *or* is omitted, the comma must be used.

> The Constitution guarantees freedom of speech, assembly, religion.

Commas and Quotation Marks in Direct Speech

Quotation marks are used around the words of direct speech, and commas separate these words from phrases like *he said, they asked.*

> Someone in the audience shouted, "That's a crazy idea."
> She asked her husband, "Why can't we move to a better neighborhood?"

Note the following:

- The comma after *shouted* and *husband.*
- The position of the quotation marks—both the opening and closing quotes are near the top of the letters.
- The position of the final period and the question mark—these are *inside* the closing quotation marks.
- The use of a capital letter for the first word of the direct speech.

Phrases like *he said,* and *they asked* are also set off with commas when they appear in the middle or at the end of the quoted speech.

> "Why," she asked, "can't we move to a better neighborhood?"
> "That's a crazy idea," someone in the audience shouted.

Other Uses of Punctuation for Sentence Structure

Colon

The colon is a formal mark of punctuation that anticipates or explains what follows.

> The following countries make up the major part of Great Britain: England, Wales, Scotland.
>
> In a democracy, the civil rights of the individual are protected: the law guarantees freedom of speech, freedom of assembly, and freedom of religion. (In less formal usage, a semicolon can appear in such a sentence instead of the colon.)

Semicolon

The chief use of the semicolon is to permit two independent sentences to be joined into one. The semicolon replaces the period that separates the sentences. To make sentences easier to read, the writer should avoid combining long sentences with a semicolon or using more than one semicolon in a sentence.

1.   Another use of the semicolon is to mark a sharper break than a comma would.

A semicolon separates fairly long items in a list.

> I have two main objectives in going to the university: (1) to prepare for a professional career; (2) to increase my knowledge about the world and the people in it.
>
> The 1970 Census gives the following figures for the three largest metropolitan areas in the United States: New York, 11,575,740; Los Angeles, 7,032,075; Chicago, 6,978,947. (Note that the semicolon is especially necessary if there are already commas with the items on the list.)

2.   A semicolon replaces a comma before a coordinate conjunction (especially *and* or *but*) that joins two sentences if each part of the sentence is long or already has commas within it.

> They have already visited New York, Boston, and Washington in the East; and, as far as we know, the next cities on their itinerary are in the Midwest.

Dash

The dash marks a sharp interruption in the structure of a sentence.

> In some parts of the world—this is hard to believe—many people live to be well over a hundred years.

In informal writing the dash often becomes an "all-purpose" mark of punctuation that replaces the comma, the semicolon, or the colon. However, the dash should be used sparingly in formal writing.

Unacceptable Commas

A comma should not be used before *and* or *or* connecting *two* words or phrases.

> *Unacceptable:*   He likes to eat a little bread, and cheese before he goes to bed. [Two nouns—bread, cheese—are joined by *and.*]
>
> The democratic way of life offers people freedom of speech, and gives them the opportunity to make full use of their abilities. [Two verbs—offers, gives—are joined by *and.*]

However, the comma is acceptable if *and* or *or* joins two independent sentences (clauses).

A comma should not be placed between the subject-verb-complement center of the sentence.

Between a Subject and a Predicate

> *Unacceptable:*   The fact that there are a few exceptions, does not disprove his theory.
>
> The democratic way of life, provides freedom of speech and freedom of the press.

Such an unnecessary comma often appears at the end of a restrictive adjective clause, which should not be punctuated with commas at all.

> *Unacceptable:*   People who love their freedom, are willing to fight for it.

Between a Verb and Its Complement

The most common fault here is to place a comma between the verb and the word that introduces a noun-clause object.

> *Unacceptable:*   Everyone in the room said, that he was guilty.
>
> I don't know, why he did it.

An interrupting adverbial element that has a comma on one side should have a comma on the other side as well.

> *Unacceptable:*   Astrology as everyone knows, deals with the influence of the heavenly bodies on human lives. [This sentence requires another comma before *as*.]
>
> They in fact, help each other. [Since commas around this short adverbial expression are optional, the sentence can be corrected by placing another comma before *in* or omitting the comma after *fact*.]

Run-on Sentences

A comma should not be used between two sentences that have been joined into one with either no connecting word or with an adverbial such as *therefore, however, for example, in other words.*

> *Run-on sentences:*   The people in my country are friendly and honest, a visitor doesn't have to be afraid of anything.
>
> I will have to read more in college, consequently I will improve my reading skill.

Sometimes even the comma is omitted in a combined sentence.

> *Run-on sentences:*   Manhattan is an unusual island it's close enough to the East Coast to be connected by several bridges.
>
> The verbs in Portuguese have endings therefore we do not need to write down the personal pronouns.

Run-on sentences can be corrected by placing a semicolon or a period where the two sentences come together.

A comma should not be put after a conjunction.

1. After a coordinate conjunction (*and, but, or, nor, for*):

> *Unacceptable:*   But, the reason I am studying at the university is that I want to understand the world and my society.

2. After a subordinate conjunction (especially *because, although*):

> *Unacceptable:*   I do not believe in astrology although, I find it very interesting.

Unacceptable Semicolons

Most unacceptable semicolons cut off a part of a sentence instead of joining two sentences into one. Such faults can be corrected by *changing the semicolon to a comma.*

The following are examples of the most common types of final elements that are cut off with semicolons instead of commas.

> His secretary has worked overtime for several days; hoping to finish all the work she had to do.
>
> The transit workers in the city went on strike; the result being that many people could not get to their places of employment.
>
> Some people get most of their news from the newspapers; while (*or* whereas) others get their information mainly from television.
>
> I want an education that will broaden my outlook on life; an education that will help me face the world in a more mature way.
>
> Television has had a profound influence on American society; both beneficial and detrimental.
>
> Women, like most men, have desires for complete lives; which usually means having loving families and satisfaction in their careers. [In this sentence, if the indefinite *which* is replaced by *this*, a word that is not grammatically dependent on what precedes it, the semicolon may be retained.]

Sometimes the same final elements that are cut off unacceptably with semicolons are separated even more sharply from their sentences with periods. The final part that has been cut off and placed in another sentence is usually labeled a *fragment*. Other types of misuse of the semicolon are these.

Using a semicolon instead of a colon to anticipate a list.

> *Unacceptable:* Nowadays there are plenty of professional schools; business, engineering, medical schools.
> *Correction:* [Use a colon after *professional schools*.]

Using a semicolon instead of a comma or no punctuation after an expression like *for example* or *such as*.

> *Unacceptable:* For the reasons I have already given, such as; the woman's career, the need for self-fulfillment, I believe the woman should have the right to make her own choice.
> *Correction:* [Remove the semicolon after *such as*.]

Spelling Rules *

Spelling Rules for *ie* and *ei* Words

A. Use *ie* when the letters have the sound of *ee* (as in *eat*).

*From Marcella Frank, *Writer's Companion* (Englewood Cliffs, N.J.: Prentice-Hall, 1983), pp. 50–52. Reprinted by permission.

achievement, piece, chief, belief

Exceptions: 1. after *c*, use *ei*: receive, deceit
2. seize, (n)either, leisure, weird

B.   Use *ei* when the letters have other sounds than *ee*.

weight, height, foreign, their

Exception: friend

Spelling Rules for Adding Final Elements

A.   Adding *-es* rather than *-s*.
1.   Add *-es* to nouns and verbs ending in sibilant sounds—*s, z, ch, sh, x*.
glasses, buzzes, teaches, dishes, mixes

2.   Add *-es* to nouns and verbs ending in *y* preceded by a consonant; the *y* changes to *i*.

babies, carries

But: enjoys, monkeys (*y* is preceded by a vowel)

3.   Add *-es* to some nouns ending in *o*.

heroes, potatoes

Other nouns ending in *o* may take either *-s* or *-es*.

cargoes or cargos, volcanoes or volcanos.

Check the dictionary if you are not sure whether *-s* or *-es* is required with such nouns.

B.   Doubling final consonants before added syllables beginning with vowels.
Double the consonant if: the word ends in one consonant preceded by one vowel, and the stress is on the syllable where the doubling might take place.

One-syllable word:	plán + ed	= plánned
	hót + er	= hótter
Two-syllable words:	omít + ing	= omítting
	occúr + ence	= occúrrence
	but: prefér + ence	= préference (the stress shifts to the first syllable)

C.   Dropping or keeping silent *e* before added syllables.
  1.   Drop the *e* before a vowel.

  advertise + ing = advertising
  arrive + al = arrival
  noise + y = noisy (for this rule, the adjective ending *y* is treated as a
          vowel)

  Exception: When adjective suffixes beginning with *a, o, u* are added to
  words ending in *ce* or *ge*, the *e* is kept in order to prevent a change in
  pronunciation.

  noticeable, changeable

  2.   Keep the *e* before a consonant.

  advertise + ment = advertisement
  care + ful = careful
  entire + ly = entirely

  Exceptions: In a few nouns ending in *-ment*, the *e* is kept in British
  English.

  judgement, abridgement

  The *e* is dropped before *th*.

  width, ninth, fifth

  In words ending in *-ple, -ble,* or *-tle*, the *le* is dropped before *ly*.

  simply, possibly, subtly

D.   Changing final *y* to *i* before added syllables.
  1.   Change *y* to *i* before a vowel.

  mystery + ous = mysterious
  marry + age = marriage
  easy + er = easier

  2.   Change *y* to *i* before a consonant.

  happy + ness = happiness
  glory + fy = glorify
  beauty + ful = beautiful
  easy + ly = easily

Spelling Changes in Prefixes before Certain Letters

AD = *to, at, toward*

ac + c	accelerate, accidental, accommodate, accumulate, accustom
ac + q	acquaint, acquiesce, acquire, acquisition, acquittal
af + f	affectation, affidavit, affiliate, affluence, affront
ag + g	aggrandize, aggregate, aggressor
al + l	allegiance, allergy, alleviate, allocate, ally
an + n	annex, annihilate, annulment, announcement
ap + p	appreciate, approximate, apparatus, appendix, applause
ar + r	arraign, arrangement, arrest, arrival, arrogant, arrears
as + s	assignment, assimilate, assistance, association, assumption
at + t	attainment, attempt, attorney, attendant, attraction

COM or CON = *with, together;* also an intensifier (from Latin *cum*) (usually con, except before *m, p, b, r, l*)

com + m	commemorate, commercial, committee, commodity, communicate
com + p	compatible, compensate, competition, complicate, component
com + b	combat, combination, combustible
cor + r	correlate, correction, correspond, corrosion, corrupt
col + l	collaborate, collapse, collateral, collective, collision

DIS = *away, apart, deprive of, cause to be the opposite of*

dif + f	difference, difficulty, diffidence, diffuse

IN = *in, not;* also an intensifier

im + p	impartial, impetuous, impoverish, impractical, improvise
ir + r	irrational, irregular, irrelevant, irresistible, irrigate
il + l	illegal, illegible, illiterate, illuminate, illustration
im + m	immature, immigrant, immobile, immortal, immunity
im + b	imbalance, imbecile, imbibe, imbue

OB = *toward, for, about, before*

oc + c	occasion, occident, occult, occupation, occurrence
op + p	opponent, opportunity, opposite, oppression, opprobrium
of + f	offensive, offer, official

SUB = *under, below*

suc + c	successful, succinct, succumb, succor (help), successive
suf + f	suffer, suffice, sufficient, suffocate, suffrage
sug + g	suggestion, suggestive
sum + m	summarize, summit, summon
sup + p	supplement, suppliant, supplier, support, suppose, suppress

APPENDIX C

Checklists for Composition

Revision and Editing Checklist

I. **Checking the final outline and the composition for organization of ideas**
   A. *Unity*
      1. Are all the main points controlled by one central idea—the thesis?
      2. Does the thesis sentence in the outline express this central idea clearly?
      3. Are the main points stated clearly and simply in the final outline so that the reader can see how they are supporting the thesis? (Your outline should be similar to a table of contents in a book. It should avoid words like *body* or *argument*.
   B. *Order*
      1. Are all the main points and their subpoints in the best order?
      2. Is one main point finished before another point is taken up?
   C. *Logic*
      1. Do all the subpoints belong logically under their main points?
      2. Are all the points mutually exclusive so that they don't cut across each other?

3. Can some main points become subpoints under a larger heading?
4. Are there any contradictory statements?
5. Are there any digressions not related to the point under discussion?
6. Is the final outline written in the conventional form that reflects the logic of the composition?
   a. There should be an alternation between numbers and letters. Example:
   I.   First main point
      A. First subpoint
         1. First sub-subpoint
         2.
      B.
   II.
   b. The points should be stated in grammatically consistent form (all full sentences or all phrases) and in parallel form (all noun phrases, all verb phrases, or all adjective phrases).

II. **Checking the paragraphs for the development of ideas**
   A. *Introductory paragraph*
      1. Does the paragraph consider the subject from a broader perspective?
      2. Does the paragraph catch the attention of the reader (through a question that will be answered, an argument that will be refuted, a quotation, an anecdote)?
      3. Does the paragraph give an indication of the central idea (the thesis) of the composition?
      4. Does the paragraph suggest how this central idea will be developed in the composition?
   B. *Paragraphs in the body of the composition* (supporting the thesis)
      1. *Opening sentences of paragraphs*
         a. Does each opening sentence make a smooth transition from the preceding point to the one it introduces? Is the transition exact and concise? (Sometimes just one word is enough.)
         b. Does each opening sentence indicate, or lead to, the main point of the paragraph?
      2. *Supporting details in the paragraphs*
         Is the support:
         a. Sufficient to convince the reader?
         b. Significant rather than trivial?
         c. Authoritative and up to date?
         d. Relevant to the point being discussed?
         e. Clearly related to the preceding subpoint in the paragraph?
      3. *Concluding paragraph*
         a. Does the concluding paragraph open up from the narrow focus of the composition to a broader perspective (with a hope, an